In the Cities
of the South

In the Cities of the South

Scenes from a Developing World

JEREMY SEABROOK

VERSO

London • New York

First published by Verso 1996
© Jeremy Seabrook 1996
All rights reserved

The right of Jeremy Seabrook to be identified as the author
of this work has been asserted by him in accordance with
the Copyright, Designs and Patents Act 1988

Verso

UK: 6 Meard Street, London W1V 3HR
USA: 180 Varick Street, New York NY 10014–4606

Verso is the imprint of New Left Books

ISBN 1–85984–986–5
ISBN 1–85984–081–7 (pbk)

British Library Cataloguing in Publication Data
A catalogue record for this book is available from the British Library

Library of Congress Cataloging-in-Publication Data
Seabrook, Jeremy, 1939–
    In the cities of the South : scenes from a developing world / Jeremy
Seabrook.
        p.   cm.
    Includes bibliographical references and index.
    ISBN 1–85984–986–5 (hardback). — ISBN 1–85984–081–7 (pbk.)
    1. Cities and towns—Developing countries. 2. Urbanization—
Developing countries. 3. Developing countries—Social conditions.
I. Title.
HT149.5.S4   1996
307.76′09172′4—dc20   95-46223
                                                              CIP

Typeset by M Rules
Printed in Great Britain by Biddles Ltd, Guildford and King's Lynn

Contents

Acknowledgements

This book has been made by more people than I can acknowledge here, many of whom are named in the text. I am indebted to John Turner, and to the contribution of his inspiring work on self-build communities in the cities of the South. I have learned much from David Satterthwaite at the International Institute for Environment and Development in London. I am grateful to Somsuk Boonyabancha at the Urban Poor Foundation in Bangkok, the staff of the Duang Prateep Foundation in Bangkok, the Centre for the Study of Developing Societies in New Delhi, Ms Rakaowin of the Peace and Justice Commission in Bangkok, Preecha and Virasak and all at the Foundation for Rural Youth in Bangkok, the Centre for Urban Studies at Dhaka University, Gurbir Singh, P. Sebastian, Anna Kurian of Nivara Hakk in Bombay, Winin Pereira, Subhash Sule at the Centre for Holistic Studies in Bombay, Andreas Harsono in Jakarta, Johan Effendi in Jakarta, Syed Shamsul Haq in Dhaka, Munize Manzur in Dhaka, Bhav Korde and Raju Korde of the Rashtriya Ekta Samiti in Bombay, friends at the Eddie Guazon Foundation in Manila, Mohamed Idris of the Consumers Association of Penang, Subba, Uma, Meena and all other friends in Malaysia, Chandra Muzzaffar of Just World Trust, Shravan Maishe and Gurubai Koli in Bombay. I am equally grateful to many friends who live in the cities, especially to David Cavalier in Bangkok, the Pereira family in Bombay, Bharat and Madhu Dogra in New Delhi, Titos Quibuyen and Greg del Pilar in Manila, Jagat Singh Negi and his family in Uttar Pradesh, India, Dr Chaiwat Sathe-Anand in Bangkok.

I acknowledge the support of Steve Platt at *New Statesman* and Malcolm Imrie at Verso, the continuing and constructive dialogue with Trevor Blackwell, and, especially, the lasting affection and tolerance of Derek Hooper.

But above all, this book is dedicated to the millions of voiceless poor of the cities of the South, that majority of the people whose testimony remains unheard in a gaudy and raucous global market-place; particularly to the energy and fortitude of Lovely and Popi in Dhaka, the courage and resilience of Hira and Mirim in Jakarta, the endurance of Narong in Bangkok.

Jeremy Seabrook
London
December 1995

Introduction

For many years I have wanted to write about Third World cities; or rather, about those people in them to whom I am bound by affection and friendship. This book is inspired and animated by the memory of my own origins, my past and childhood in the industrial Midlands of Britain.

For these cities of the South are haunted places, occupied by the ghosts of our own urban past, which has sunk into forgetfulness in recent years. My grandmother remembered what is the common experience of migrants today – she recalled becoming urban. She used to tell how they packed up their belongings on the carrier's cart, and moved into the town, because it had become too difficult for my grandfather to walk the 12 miles three times a week to sell the shoes he had made at home. In the town, they were destined to discover new forms of poverty which they could scarcely have imagined, even in lives of landless labour in an impoverished countryside. My grandfather drank – like so many men, both in Victorian Britain and in the contemporary Third World working class; his fingers became less adept, and he could no longer cut the leather into uppers with his clicking-knife. He went into a factory and worked with machines, which he loathed, and which led him to despise himself for the loss of his own skills. The money he gave my grandmother for her surviving eleven children was never enough. She spoke of putting them to bed in the afternoon, with sacking at the windows to blot out the sun, so that they should believe it was night and sleep, forgetting, she hoped, that they had not eaten.

She remembered, too, the pooling of resources, both human and material, of kinship and neighbourhood; the consolations of the crowded street at times of death, sickness and suffering – strategies for survival that were inventive and sometimes heroic, which so many of us in the West have now carelessly cast off, but which are faithfully replicated in the cities of the South today. And they sustain hope and consolation in the same cruel, inhospitable environments.

I grew up at the time when the manufacturing towns and cities were falling into ruin; the hammers swung at the red-brick walls of the street where we had lived, releasing the sour smell of newly turned earth where the narrow houses had been, the rubble of living places recently declared 'unfit for human habitation'; even then, this phrase always seemed to me a retrospective slur on the humanity of those who had lived there from no choice of their own but had, for the most part, striven to lead decent, good lives.

I lived for a time in Birmingham, when it was a daily public spectacle to see the wholesale demolitions of chocolate-brown painted tenements, squalid paved courtyards with a growth of moss on damp yards that had seen no sunlight for a hundred years. What followed was also ambiguous: the removal of the people to the peripheral estates and high-rise towers where the old people, wisps of humanity carried out of their former homes on stretchers, knew they would not last long; and indeed, they often died soon after. The networks of kinship began to unravel, the sense of neighbourhood collapsed with the old physical structures; this coincided with the decomposition of function – the labour that had called these places into existence.

When I see the industrial and urban landscapes in Bangkok or Calcutta or Manila now, I do not feel I am in a foreign country. The people who wander through an altered decor, a different urban landscape in an unfamiliar climate, are none the less living through the same exile, experiencing the same dislocations, taking where they can the same consolations. They have known the breaking of rootedness, the traumatic reshaping of their lives and sensibility in the form required by industrial labour.

Their estrangement from the countryside was ours too, now so long ago, it seems. To visit these other urban landscapes is to revisit our past, even though the symbols of another age, the cars, the skyscrapers, the towers of marble and glass, under other skies, may blur our vision; their difference from the red-brick terraces under the cold northern drizzle is only superficial.

The comparison between our half-remembered experiences in Britain and contemporary developments in South Asia is haunting, because of the ways in which they are the same, and ways in which they are different. Almost any individual in Bangkok or Bombay can tell an epic story of social discontinuity, change and forced adaptation to an alien environment. E.P. Thompson, in *The Making of the English Working Class,* says that whatever small monetary gains people may have made in moving from the countryside to the manufacturing towns in the early industrial period, they nevertheless felt the change as brutal and disruptive. This is why monetary measures of poverty in the urban setting are always an incomplete measure of the subjective sense of upheaval and disturbance, inadequate accounts of the lives of the uprooted.

It is impossible to know now how remote the experience of young men and women arriving at the bus stations, the railway termini of Hualamphong in Bangkok, Bombay Central, or Kamalpur in Dhaka, must be from the apprehension and sorrow of those people who, one morning in the 1820s, piled up their belongings and walked into a town where they found a damp cellar room to rent, and work in a mill among the stinking discoloured canals and smoky skies of Bolton or Wigan. It is different, in that the people who entered the industrial slums were the first in history ever to have done so; for them, industrial society was as unknown a country as the cultures of India or Malaya which their betters, in the same era, were learning to explore and exploit. The young people pouring into cities now, however, come with preconceived ideas: the images of industrial life are so widely diffused that no one can remain in ignorance of the city. And yet, it is the same, in that the images that reach the rural poor are of affluence and luxury; the reality of the room shared with strangers in the factory compound, the semi-captivity in workshop, sex bar or construction site, is as foreign to them, and as inimical to their country sensibility, as the streets of Manchester once were to their early inhabitants. I remember vividly the complaint of one young man in Bangkok who could not find work, who repeated bitterly, 'I am a farmer, I am a farmer. What am I to do here?'

Today's rural poor are migrating into a far more intensive money culture than that encountered by the early industrial pioneers trekking into the cities of Britain. A friend in Bangkok observed that in the villages, where rice represented wealth, people were always ready to share any surplus with their neighbours. Many people who come to the city quickly discover that money is now wealth; but they cannot understand why it is not given to those who do not have as readily as rice was distributed; they have not yet learned that money has its own rhythms and seasons, its own different and mysterious harvests.

Whatever the differences and the similarities, the broad experience remains similar. And it is in this spirit, of kinship and love, of witness of continuity and a common destiny of the same flesh and blood, that I offer these stories and scenes of endurance, suffering, hope and sadness of the people in the cities of South Asia.

1

Myths of the Megacities

I

Our reactions to the growing urban centres in the Third World are complex and often confused. United Nations population projections for the cities in the early eighties gave alarmist estimates for the turn of the century, forecasting that by then Bombay would have 18 million people, São Paulo 20 million or more. These predictions were subsequently revised downwards. But they were symptomatic of a deeply felt fear of the city, a constant anxiety that it threatens to run out of control. 'Population' is a metaphor for uncontainability, the inadequacy of civic services, the breakdown of law and order. The terms in which the cities are discussed – urban 'explosion', 'catastrophe' – tend to assimilate them to natural disasters; they are problems crying out first for relief, and then for solutions.

Our reactions echo attitudes in the Britain of the early industrial era to the growth of Manchester, Birmingham and London. These were perceived as sites of unspeakable squalor and poverty and, hence, of disaffection, unnatural concentrations of the dangerous and perishing classes, noxious and insalubrious in every way. The horror the manufacturing districts inspired in Victorian England is repeated in much conventional writing about their Third World counterparts today. What is worse, such ideas often inform the attitudes and policies of governments, officials and the privileged; and as they seek to remodel their cities in what they perceive to be the image of the Western city – urbane, sophisticated, efficient – they are rarely tender to the fate of the urban poor.

Against this, an alternative view has grown, which sees the cities as places of enhanced opportunity for millions of people, refuges from a stifling, restrictive rural life that is no longer capable of providing a traditional sustenance. It is fashionable now – and fashionability does not invalidate the response – to applaud the courage and endurance of people in the slums, to admire and wonder at their capacity for adapting, for building their own shelters, for creating a life for themselves, for finding a livelihood somewhere in the city economy. Extraordinary stories, testimonies, come out of the cities, some of which, I hope, are reflected in this book.

Many activists and nongovernmental organizations (NGOs) who work in the cities can point to their achievements – work with pavement dwellers in Bombay, slum communities in Karachi or Bangkok, community improvement projects in Jakarta and Mexico City, which have transformed the lives of hundreds of thousands of people. The cities are not sites of hopelessness and despair. Some communities are remarkable for their high degree of organization, and the poor are swift to exploit any opportunity to make a living in the urban economy.

But with the recent enthusiasm for the value of civil society, people's self-help and community effort, there is a risk that the cities come to be seen as the opposite of the sombre and sulphurous places evoked by those for whom they are an eyesore to be removed, an embarrassment to be concealed, and a threat to social peace. The fear that the cities would become hotbeds of revolution has faded; people have been exploited for generations in most city slums without significant revolt. They learn to insert themselves into the existing structures. This has given rise to the reassuring idea that there is no real problem. The rich can go about their business, unperturbed that the city poor threaten their well-being, *might* threaten it, at least, politically; whether those substitutes for social hope – crime and robbery, the individual redressing of social evils (so widespread in the West, but as yet relatively rare in South Asia) – are a more unsettling prospect in the long run, it is difficult to say.

Whatever their advantages and consolations, for the most part the slums inflict impaired achievement, ill-health, want and acute discomfort on the majority of their inhabitants. Cairncross, Hardoy and Satterthwaite (in *The Poor Die Young*) estimate that at least 600 million urban residents in the Third World live in life-threatening homes and neighbourhoods. Many more have no security, run the risk that their homes will be cleared, burned or demolished by those who have prior claim to land constantly rising in value. Only rarely is security of tenure won; then, people can indeed be left to build communities, to get on with improvements and constructive endeavour. 'Public housing almost always fails to deliver,' says David Satterthwaite, the editor of *Urbanisation and Environment*. 'If people were given the money, the houses would get built. Bureaucratic, wrong-headed allocation of goods and services never advantages the poor.'

Given the now universal economic regime governing the value of land, the idea of giving money to the poor rather than to construction companies is unlikely to gain general popularity. Furthermore, the prestige that capital cities are supposed to embody, together with official versions of the national interest, developmentalism, the need for infrastructure, the imperatives of real estate, all contribute to render the position of the poor difficult, insecure and threatened.

David Satterthwaite has been one of the foremost proponents of a more balanced view of cities.

> The apocalyptic view of the growth of cities in the South misses the point. The catastrophe of the cities is how people are screwed, exploited and manipulated in them. Good governance can reduce the costs of being poor – control pollution, provide for basic needs, make sure that occupation exposures are minimized, ensure that children do not work twenty hours a day. If there is competent government articulated to residents' groups, this reduces the catastrophe. What is not needed is ecobabble about the unviability of cities, about them growing out of control and being agents of destruction.
>
> The cities neglect social demand which is not reflected in the purchasing power of the people who have these demands. In many cities, social demand is not met, or is met inadequately, because bureaucratic structures cannot respond.
>
> The traditional image of the city as the site of depravity and violence was a reaction against the industrial revolution. The idea that nature has been sullied by man is deep within the critique of industrialism, and has been revived by the green movement of the present day. The city became the pictorial image of all that was wrong with industrialism, because in it the best and worst of human life is concentrated. In villages, infant mortality may be higher than in squatter settlements, but villages do not present the same threatening aspect, therefore they are felt to be more benign.
>
> (personal communication)

Against this, Winin Pereira, of the Centre for Holistic Studies in Bombay, has this to say in his *Cities: Engines of Unsustainable Development*:

> Extractable surpluses from the countryside have always been the basis for city development, generally by means of physical domination.
>
> When people recognise that they live in a closed ecosystem, they are extremely careful to use resources sustainably. It is only when cities and industrial society offer illusions that we can escape restraints on resources that we lurch into reckless disregard for the basis on which we must all survive.
>
> Those who see the city as the source of 'civilised values' are always

opting for 'civilisation' over social justice. The city depends on surplus from the countryside, which means lower rewards for rural labour than for city labour, although the former is scarcely less arduous and requires no less keen an intelligence. We may question the nature of 'civilised values' that always exclude social justice. Cities cannot produce their own food supply or any of the raw materials they consume in great quantities. Bombay absorbs the topsoil of the surrounding countryside in the form of bricks, limestone that destroys watersheds. Wood is drawn from as far away as the Himalayas, or even Malaysia. Sand for construction – 4000–5000 tons every day – destroys valuable agricultural land. Water is diverted to artificial lakes up to 100 kilometres away. The food and other agricultural production from the rural areas is an export of soil fertility, since the 'wastes' do not return to the villages. Rural grass and oil-cakes feed the cows and buffaloes of Bombay and huge quantities of dung pollute rather than fertilise. It is believed that the city can go on indefinitely mining and gutting the hinterland. This belief has been given a powerful new impetus by the industrialising of agriculture. While people in urban areas usually have better access to formal health care, they are also more exposed to diseases manufactured in the cities. Industrial and vehicular emissions produce cancers, mutations and birth defects. High population densities cause contagious diseases to spread easily.

There is no point in sentimentalizing the cities, any more than there is in romanticizing the countryside. One of the most dramatic recent examples of urban malignancy occurred, not in one of the major conurbations, but in the western Indian boom city of Surat. Surat is one of the fastest-growing cities in Asia; economic prosperity, which in orthodox economic theory is supposed to be the guarantor of growing well-being, has led instead to a rapid deterioration in the quality of life. This, in turn, was partly responsible in the autumn of 1994 for the outbreak of plague, which quarantined India and spread panic among the eager proponents of accelerating liberalization.

But what could be more liberal than the externalizing of the shit and ordure of Surat, where diamonds are polished and power looms dominate the unorganized sector, where extraordinary private wealth is created, with no commensurate public services? In 1984 Surat had a population of around 925,000; that was an increase on 1974 of 471,000; by 1991, the population was over 1.5 million – a 64 per cent increase in seven years. Surat, core of the 'golden corridor' of industrialization of Gujarat in western India, turned out to be the locus where scourges of primal terror made their vibrant reappearance through the hi-tech facades of modern industry.

Surat is a centre of the manufacture of *jari*, the most delicate embroidery using mainly silver threads, with an annual turnover of 500 million rupees ($US15 million). It produces 80 per cent of the output. For the manufacture of real *jari*, silver ingots are melted at high temperature, moulded into bars, then melted and drawn into finer and finer wires, until the silver is as thin as a human hair and ready for embroidery work. This is then electroplated in gold solution to make gold thread. Work conditions are appalling and a major health hazard, with a dozen or more artisans cramped in small rooms with machines and chemicals including potassium cyanide, which is used in electroplating. A number of workers die each year through inhaling fumes.

Surat has become a maze of excessively crowded, legal and illegal houses and production units, with no civic amenities. 30 per cent of the people of Surat live in slums, in three hundred slum pockets, engaged in small enterprises such as weaving and diamond polishing; 40 per cent of households depend on the self-employed informal sector, characterized by low and fluctuating income. The vast majority of the slums have no drainage system; conditions deteriorate during the rains, and the lower-lying slums become uninhabitable. In the monsoon, water supplies are readily contaminated; jaundice, typhoid and gastroenteritis spread. Latrines are often unusable, and 80 per cent of slum dwellers defecate in the open; 90 per cent are single-room dwellings; workers sleep in shifts in some of them (the same was said of the Irish in the slums of Liverpool, where the turnover of sleepers in the same bed was so great that the beds were never cold). Malaria and tuberculosis caused 20 per cent of the deaths in the past two years. In Indian cities, the proportion of slum dwellers is now about 55 per cent in Bombay, 38 per cent in Kanpur and Calcutta, 30 per cent in Ahmedabad, 36 per cent in Madras, 20 per cent in Bangalore.

In response to the panic over plague in 1994, the social commentator Rajni Kothari said,

We need something as serious as plague to bring home to us the callous disregard we have shown in providing minimum conditions of citizen survival. There has been a continuous neglect of and disregard for the poor and peripheral strata, areas and communities. It is a curious kind of elitism that has allowed so much misery and human suffering to pile up in one city and region after another. But second, there has been a neglect by the governing classes of the larger interest (which includes its own) as a national collectivity arising out of the pursuit of prosperity and 'development' that is proving destabilizing to the basic balance and survival of the social order.

It is emerging that we are a nation of skewed priorities, trying to become a highly industrialized economy and a great power, claiming to have one of the world's largest scientific and technological capabilities, yet one in which a majority of people are living in substandard conditions, physically, medically and in respect of basic nutrition, sanitation and cleanliness. We are producing a high-rise, five-star culture which seems to be in perfect harmony with ever more deteriorating conditions of latrines and other waste disposal. More and more of our cities are reeling under heavier and heavier weight of what I would call the refuse of progress. The net result is the outbreak of a whole variety of epidemics – malaria is back, cholera is on the increase, gastro-enteritis, conjunctivitis – the incidence of blindness and other disabilities is growing, we are having more weak and physically debilitated children, a breakdown of a generation of citizens that is supposed to carry the burden of future India.

(*Times of India*, November 1994)

For every story of community achievement, there are as many others of rule by slum lords, drug networks, gangs and guns. What is more, the poor are on the receiving end of all the structural adjustment programmes currently being carried out by Third World governments worldwide, with their familiar prescriptions of cuts in government social spending on those things that the poorest depend on – education, health, nutrition. The consequence is that their already precarious foothold on the city economy is even further jeopardized.

We must not confuse the conditions in which the majority of people in the city live with their response to those conditions, sometimes highly individualistic, sometimes collective. Their ingenuity in surviving, their tenacity and their endurance provide stories of individual or community courage that inspire others and recreate hope in places that have been written off by civic and government authorities.

David Satterthwaite responds to the argument that city overcrowding creates social pathology:

The most problematic features of cities relate to the incapacity of society to throw up the necessary management to cope with them. It is not the speed of city growth that is the problem, but the slowness of society to deal with it. There is nothing inherently wrong or damaging with intense concentrations of people. Chelsea in London is one of the highest-density urban concentrations in the world, yet it is a desirable and coveted environment. You could fit the entire urban population of the world into the area covered by Senegal at the density of Chelsea.

(personal communication)

II

The fateful point at which more than half the world's population becomes urban is proving to be a strangely elusive one. Will it occur during the next ten years, or has it already happened? What is urban? Have the intensive industrialization of agriculture and the spread of mass-produced artefacts into the countryside, the penetration of the hinterland by television, rendered the frontier between urban and rural almost meaningless? And has the greening of cities, and the growth of suburbs, led to new forms of settlement that undermine earlier classifications?

Whatever the truth, there remains a world of difference between, say, a village in Rajasthan in India, or in Isan in Thailand, and the slums of Bombay and the congestion of Bangkok. In Dhaka, on the other hand, Nazrul Islam speaks of the ruralization of the city, because of the habits and customs that millions of rural migrants have brought to the metropolitan area.

Nowhere is the ambiguity between town and country better illustrated than in India. Although India remains 70 per cent – or is it 80 per cent? – rural, it now has the largest urban population in the world.

Raipur, in the very centre of India, is quite unlike the Western idea of a city. Of course, it has its government and official buildings, its commercial centre; but the self-build settlements on the periphery seem to have grown organically out of the red earth itself, and look as if they will dissolve into it once more in the next monsoon. Concrete buildings discolour swiftly, attacked by mildew in the rain; everything is weathered by the fierce heat of the sun; and brick buildings soon give way to less permanent structures, shaded by rows of *khair* or tamarind trees, in which flocks of egrets perch like silver fruit, blanching the boughs beneath them with their snow-coloured shit.

Urbanization in India is not the one-way traffic it became in Britain in the early industrial period. Even in Bombay, most slum dwellers have a home place, with which they rarely sever all connections. The Indian village was traditionally self-reliant, and despite the degradation of many villages a self-sufficient division of labour within them is still discernible, where potters and cart makers, rope makers, weavers and oil pressers work alongside workers in the fields. Over centuries, villages learned to supply basic needs. Occasionally, the nonagricultural functions grew, and then the village expanded – sometimes temporarily – achieving the status of a town.

Bhattacharya, writing of modest-scale urbanization in *Urban Development in India*, says:

> Since the change that takes place is mostly confined to its functional character, it has no measurable impact upon the society as a whole. A

greater section of the working population becomes engaged in non-agricultural functions, a string of shops appears along the principal thoroughfare; movement of vehicular traffic becomes more conspicuous; ill-built structures of all shapes and sizes, jostling for space and housing public and private organisations, add to the crowded atmosphere of the roadside areas. The land use along the two fronts of the one or two main roads is of extremely mixed character, creating confusion and utter disorder. Beyond the thin belts of congestion, high pitch of activity at once melts into the languid placidity of rural life.

Craftspeople migrated to the city to help build the cultural and economic base of urban life; but this was often a temporary arrangement. A version of this still occurs, when construction workers for the city are recruited in remote villages.

However, this ancient pattern of easy passage between town and country is different from the present-day invasion of the rural spaces by the market economy; a different kind of fluidity is being set up, in which the resilience of rural life is stretched to the limit.

Major conurbations like Raipur and Nagpur are penetrated by their rural origins and hinterland. In Raipur, the tangle of traffic is a material symbol of the agelessness of the urban settlement: the women headloaders carrying their swaying burden of fodder, the ox carts creaking imperturbably, do not acknowledge the urgency of the buses, cars and trucks; cycle rickshaws and bicycles jostle with motor scooters bearing whole families, women sidesaddle holding tiny babies with kohl-blackened eyes, and little girls in a froth of lace clutch their father's waist; the Ambassador cars garlanded with marigolds and tinsel for a wedding, trucks painted with flowers and spewing out their poisonous clouds of pollutants, the hooting Marutis, must find a passage through the pedestrians, who remain certain of their anterior right to walk along tracks that have been walked for centuries.

In any case, the world is littered with the remains of cities that have fallen into ruin, by conquest, natural calamity, loss of function, or exhaustion of the resource base that sustained them.

The abandoned city of Fatehpur Sikri near Agra in northern India is a place of melancholy grandeur. Built by the Emperor Akbar in the late sixteenth century in thanks, it is said, to Shaikh Salim Chisti who foretold the birth of his son, Jehangir, the city was deserted only sixteen years later. No one knows quite why, but with a strangely contemporary resonance, it is said that the water supply was insufficient.

It is an evocative, eerie place. A vast courtyard is enclosed by high, crenellated walls of red sandstone. Parrots flocking on the wall look like a growth of vivid green leaves. The fretted marble tombstones in the mosque are dazzling in the afternoon sun; the roofs of the *cha-tris* – lookout towers at the corners of the courtyard – are covered with lichen, while purple and orange bougainvillaea has invaded the crumbling buildings beyond the city walls. Dust and grit swirl in the courtyard, polishing the stone until it is as smooth as glass. On the screens surrounding the tomb of Shaikh Salim, childless women have left knotted ribbons.

In the shadow of the deserted city, visited now only by tourists, a culture of begging and servility has grown. Children living in the impoverished village at the foot of the walled city have acquired the accomplishment of saying to visitors 'No mother, no father' and of asking for money in all the principal European languages and Japanese. Around the monument, vendors of novelties, trinkets and mementoes cluster. The degraded village below is a curious metaphor for India: the ruins of a civilization inhabited by its own estranged descendants.

Fatehpur Sikri is 40 kilometres from Agra, site of the Taj Mahal. Expensive follies like Fatehpur Sikri are not merely historical relics; their equivalents dominate the Third World city today. The Mughal Sheraton Hotel is a contemporary equivalent: it too is an enclosed fortress, a defensive structure, a place of sequestered, mass-produced, aristocratic privilege. And within its walls are repeated some of the excesses of the Mughal emperors, and the celebration of triumphal invasions. Only this time the invaders who must be preserved from any upsetting contacts with the people who live here are tourists; and their sojourn in the present-day palace is even shorter than that of Akbar at Fatehpur Sikri.

In the service of tourism, people have come to Agra and its surroundings from all over India: the boy from Bengal sharing a single room with three others for the privilege of earning 500 rupees a month ($US18), so that he may send something home to his mother; stonemasons, whose ancestors built the Red Fort, chipping away at slabs of red sandstone in a work of skilled and loving restoration for 60 rupees a day ($US2); the security guard at the Jewel House, living in an Agra slum where four men share a bed and four others sleep beneath it; the cycle rickshaw men from Bihar, Orissa and Uttar Pradesh fighting for the work of driving tourists to the luxury of five-star hotels – tourists who, even though paying $US200 a night, will haggle over the 10 rupees (30 cents) the drivers ask.

If the tourists are important enough, they will find a welcome spelt out in jasmine and red rose petals on the floor of the hotel lobby; garlanded with marigolds, they will be escorted to the Mughal Chambers.

For their benefit, a fantasy is being enacted, of a piece with Akbar's games of hide-and-seek in his palace with women from the harem, the use of slaves as pieces on a giant outdoor chessboard. The visitors are decked out in velvet waistcoats, caps with glittering tinsel jewels, *kurta* and *kamiz*, diaphanous gold-bordered robes, before proceeding to their banquets of 'secret recipes from the Emperor's kitchen' or 'the appropriate complement to Jehangir's table'.

An astrologer is available on the premises, doubtless to justify the good fortune the stars have vouchsafed these tourists. They may choose to compare their experience here with 'honoured guests who have shared our joy' (as the Welcomgroup describes it), pictures of whom are mounted in glass cases: Peter O'Toole, the Crown Prince of Thailand, Helmut Kohl and his wife, the Director of British-American Tobacco, Elizabeth Taylor, and of course the ubiquitous Sultan of Brunei.

The hotel lobby flashes and explodes with people taking photographs of each other in their exotic wear. Here, memories are being staged, as befits a day when the tourists have seen the glory of the Taj, monument to the wife of Shah Jehan, Mumtaz Mahal, who died giving birth to the couple's fourteenth child. The tourists have seen the Red Fort where Shah Jehan was imprisoned by his grandson; he could look out from his marble jail across the Yamuna River and see the reflection of the Taj in the diamonds with which his cell was embellished.

And yet, those who must at all costs be preserved from the derelict culture beyond of dependence, poverty and dust are also, in their way, mendicants: avid for new experience, fresh sensation. Such a division of labour has been conjured up to service fantasies! On the road between Fatehpur and Agra, dancing bears on chains rear up to dance each time a tourist bus or Ambassador car approaches. If you have become too jaded to travel by car, you can go by elephant or camel. But those who perform that labour are compelled by the histrionics of servitude, which obliges their tired faces to light up at the approach of each wealthy stranger, as though every such encounter were the culminating experience of a lifetime. It is not for their masters to follow them back to the huts and hovels where they keep the letters from home and the pictures of children they have scarcely seen; to glimpse the exhaustion of overtime worked to pay a father's medical expenses, or to sustain a sibling through school; to accompany them on the journey of 2,000 kilometres in flight from casteism, communalism, so that they can send home vital and precarious remittances that are the only thing that stand between many villages in India and utter destitution.

This, then, is the contemporary city, and in it the relationship between rich and poor is made plain. The only difference is that when the plague threatens, as in 1994, the rich can withdraw; but for those who serve them there is no going back; whatever horrors the city reserves for them, they cannot return to degraded lands, mortgaged farms and ruined forests.

2

Urbanization: the Making of a
Transnational Working Class

Malaysia

The story of Fatimah is the story of millions of people worldwide, marginalized, submerged by a 'development' that has passed them by, caught up in the process of becoming urban without even moving. People have been engulfed by urbanization without migrating, their lives overturned, even while remaining on the spot where they were born.

Fatimah married a fisherman in what was the coastal village of Batu Uban on the island of Penang in Malaysia. Theirs was a traditional Malay *kampong* or village, on government land, close to the shore.

During the past twenty-five years, Penang has become increasingly urbanized, and Georgetown, the old colonial capital, has come to occupy more and more space. A major destination for tourists with a growing number of beach resorts, Penang is also the site of free trade zones, industrial development, and, especially, high-rise condominiums, both for wealthy Malaysians and for expatriates from the pollution of Taipeh, from the overcrowding of Tokyo and from the uncertainties of the future of Hong Kong. Its villages have been destroyed, its rice fields smothered, its hillsides plundered, for timber as well as stone for construction.

As Penang developed, the waters around the island, which provided a livelihood to several thousand fishing families, became more polluted. The catch of the fishermen of Batu Uban decreased. They had to buy outboard motors for their traditional craft, they had to go further out to sea. The position of the village was made worse by the construction of a road which cut off the *kampong* where Fatimah and her husband lived from the shore.

Fatimah's husband was older than she. He could not keep up with the longer hours of work required to catch enough fish to provide a sufficient income. He became sick, self-critical and insecure. Eventually, the cost of petrol for the boat exceeded the value of the depleted daily catch. In the end, he became mentally unstable and incapable of working. At first, Fatimah tried to supplement the family income by baking cakes at home and sending her oldest boy to sell them in the *kampong*. Many other women were doing the same, and she was lucky to make a few cents a day. Later, she took over as bread-winner of the family, working at Woodard Textiles, a highly mechanized Japanese company in the free trade zone. In Malay culture it was emphatically the duty of the man to provide, and Fatimah's work only further diminished her husband's weakened status. Industrialization has led many women to question the form of decision making in traditional society, to considerable advantage; but Fatimah's husband felt undermined and excluded.

He was a gentle, soft-spoken man, but became more and more disoriented. He wandered around Penang and Butterworth, the industrial town on the mainland. He was devoted to his children, but could do nothing to provide for them. He was a fisherman and could not adapt to work in a factory – most of which was work for women anyway.

He returned to his own village, where he died. People die of grief and loss every day: not only grief for loved individuals, but grief for broken cultures, ways of life that house the spirit and have fallen into ruin. He was buried there in 1979. Fatimah was left with four children, all boys. Azahari, the eldest, eleven, Yahaya, nine, Osman, seven, and Zainon, a baby of a few months. The house in the *kampong* was run-down and dilapidated. Whenever it rained, the roof leaked; the walls were repaired with planks from an old fishing boat. Fatimah was earning 200 ringgit a month (about $US80).

She worked shifts, and could not control her boys. She was constantly being summoned by the headmaster to talk about their behaviour at school. No one was there to help her, or to understand the anger of children who lose a loved parent; they see it as a desertion, and punish their mother for the loss that is hers also.

In this way, Fatimah's family became casualties of the transformation of Penang. It was the destruction not only of the livelihood of people who had always lived symbiotically with the sea, but also of the psyche and spirit of the fishing people. It was no coincidence that, at the same time, work for women was appearing in the new factories of the free trade zone, which ensured material survival.

But only just. Fatimah went to the state social welfare department. Its officials were sympathetic, but could offer only 20 ringgit a month ($US8). She was advised to apply for a Federal Welfare Scheme, which offered 80 ringgit – utterly inadequate for a woman with four children. Someone from the social welfare department visited her home to assess her means. She was told to sell a cupboard which she and her husband had bought at the time of their marriage: the ghost of the

Poor Law still haunts the former colonies of Britain. Fatimah would receive nothing at all if she continued to work in a factory.

She was urged to send the two older boys to an orphanage, where they would be given schooling. Although ashamed that she could not look after them, Fatimah agreed. She received little help from her own family. Her mother urged her to marry again, but she was unwilling because, she argued, what kind of a man will take a woman with four children?

Azahari and Yahaya stayed at the orphanage for two years. They were unhappy, and whenever she visited they begged to be taken home again. Finally, she agreed, and the staff of the orphanage were only too glad to let them go. Azahari had been absconding from school, and both were said to be disobedient and troublesome. They were, she was told, spoiling the atmosphere of the place.

They came home. Fatimah was still working shifts, and she could not supervise them adequately. They truanted from school, became friendly with older boys who influenced them. Fatimah was never sure, when she was working nights, whether the boys were at home. Sometimes they did not return, but slept at the house of their friends.

Yahaya was eighteen when he was arrested with a group of a dozen young people, smoking *ganja*. Some were also processing and distributing the drug. Yahaya was sentenced to a prison term of twelve years, and twelve lashes of the cane. Four of the others were discharged, the rest received prison sentences. Later, his sentence was commuted to eight years. He is now due for release in September 1996.

Fatimah was recently rehoused – to a new house, in one of two back-to-back rows of concrete houses on the edge of a reclamation area close to the former shoreline of Batu Uban. In fact, she is only a few hundred metres from where she lived with her husband, but the landscape has been transformed. The several acres of reclaimed area have moved the shore away from the village towards a neighbouring island, which is going to be developed as a tourist resort. Behind the row houses, scarcely 15 metres away, a seventeen-storey block of low-cost flats is under construction. Behind that are two even taller towers, luxury apartments overlooking the sea and the new bridge that connects Penang to the mainland. Whenever Fatimah looks out of her front door, she is confronted by a wall of stone. This intensifies the heat of the sun as it beats down on the urban wasteland that has replaced the fishing village.

You can still reach her house from the old road, Jalan Masjid, which branches off from the main highway to the airport, a leafy lane, shaded by plantain, dourien and palms. To reach the house from the shore side, you have to climb down a concrete embankment and cross a polluted stream of black stagnant water, which marks what used to be the boundary of the sea.

This house is, however, Fatimah says, the best she has ever lived in. The problems here are those of people moving into new housing in any urban area: the cost of maintenance, of paying for amenities like water and electricity, the necessity of buying new furniture that will live up to the standards of the new property, loss of the air and space of the old *kampong* settlement, the proximity to neighbours.

Fatimah's oldest boy, Azahari, has just married. The wedding photographs are in an album on her table. He is in the army, and sends 60 ringgit a month from his salary of 400. In fact, he earns less than his mother. She is now a cleaner in a Taiwanese textile factory, for 408 ringgit a month. There are still two boys at home: Osman, restless, changes his job frequently; the youngest, Zainon, sixteen, has just started work as a packer in the factory in the same free trade zone as his mother. Zainon packs headlights and lamps, and earns 300 ringgit a month. This boy Fatimah describes as gentle, 'too gentle, really', even a little effeminate. She is afraid that people call him 'pondan', a coarse word for gay; it is another problem for her. He is devoted to her, and she to him.

It was late in the evening the first time we visited Fatimah. The doors of most houses stood open to the cooler evening air. In front of each was a small garden, a yard really, where people sit on benches, chairs, wooden bedsteads. Children play up and down the little road, on bicycles, playing football, wearing shirts declaring their allegiance to Manchester United or Liverpool: exotic localities whose teams command powerful loyalties in the youth of an unknown country.

The area around the house is noisy; the concrete wilderness magnifies not only the heat, but also sound. Fatimah's door remains closed. She is sleeping, because she is due to go on night duty at ten. She will work until seven in the morning. When she comes home, she does not sleep; the energy of work still drives her for hours afterwards.

She opens the bedroom window; purple cotton curtains flap in the breeze. She comes down, warm, welcoming. She makes crackers for us, and coffee. She wants to prepare dinner. We protest that she has to work; even so, she brings out some squares of bread and fish curry, no doubt intended for her own supper.

Fatimah is now just fifty; she has dark hair, the firm lines of the face of a woman who has survived. She smiles readily, but the sadness of her eyes remains, untouched by her cheerfulness. She sighs; she has had to be both father and mother to her boys. What an impossible task it has been. Other people now imagine that she has money because her boys are grown up; they do not know that Osman and

Zainon give her only 20 or 30 ringgit a month for their food.

Fatimah says she will not marry again, although she has had many offers. People have gossiped about her. Fragile and defensive, she now keeps herself to herself. Her life still revolves around the children, although they have now become adults. She left her job with Woodard Textiles so that with the money due from her fifteen years of service there she could pay a lawyer to defend Yahaya.

Fatimah is resentful that many people better off than she is have received more help. Some have applied for, and been given, three or four units of housing in the new low-cost block under construction. And here is another element of industrial life long familiar in the West, the decay of a sense of common destiny, its replacement by a competitive anxiety that other people are getting something for nothing, something extra, something they do not deserve.

She visits Yahaya once a fortnight in Penang jail. When he comes out, she wonders, will he be able to find work and hold a job? What efforts at rehabilitation have been made? Will he be embittered and feel so deep a sense of failure and shame that he will do wrong again? When the children were small, she had looked to their adult years as a time of peace and deliverance for herself. Instead, she says, fear and insecurity remain.

There has been no one to see her through the lonely years of watching the children, trying to protect them against a society that is being transformed, and in a direction she can do nothing to influence. She realizes she is lucky in some ways. One of Yahaya's friends was given twelve lashes in prison as a punishment. As a result of the beating, he died. She says when Yahaya was caned, he could not eat or sleep for days beforehand. For several weeks after, he could not lie on his back. The scars become infected, and medical treatment is necessary.

The government of Malaysia is proud of its developmental record, its growth of 8.7 per cent in 1994. But such statistics do not count the social costs of industrialization – not only the incalculable sorrow of the loss of livelihood of fishing communities, but also the costs of keeping people like Fatimah's son in custodial care, the cost to those individuals perceived as failures, so that a majority can measure by their suffering its own success.

The following weekend Fatimah was to visit Yahaya in prison. She asked if we would like to go with her. We promised to pick her up at nine on Saturday morning. I wondered if it might not appear odd for a foreigner to show up out of the blue. She said let's see.

We arrive at Fatimah's house well before nine. She has prepared some breakfast: coffee, curry puffs and pancakes. Zainon has taken a day from work – losing 25 ringgit to do so – so that he can come with us. A slight boy, he is wearing a traditional Malay sarong and sweeping the floor of the house with a soft grass brush. 'Don't you think he is too soft?' his mother asks, as though he is not there. He offers a picture of sweet androgynous grace as he goes about his work. We say, 'He is young. In any case, is it not better to be too soft than too hard? There are enough hard people in the world.' She says that his brother, Osman, has tried beating him up in order to make him tougher; but it doesn't seem to have worked.

Osman is sitting with some neighbours outside on an old wooden bed. He is working as a bus driver for the yellow bus company of Penang, at present on the airport run. He earns 16 ringgit a day – about 450 a month ($US180). Fatimah says he changes his job too frequently, rarely staying more than a few weeks in one place. Penang, like most of Malaysia, has plenty of work. You can walk out of work any day and find employment somewhere else immediately. It is another uncanny echo of the experience of Western Europe in the sixties when, people say, you could leave one place at lunch time and start a new job in the afternoon.

Fatimah is wearing a green *telukung*, the Islamic head covering, and a lilac, blue and gold traditional dress: her best clothes. She chides Zainon for being slow, and he changes into a pair of dark grey jeans and a pale grey T-shirt, with a logo of the Los Angeles Dodgers. He has slicked back his long straight hair with gel.

We set off through the dense Saturday morning traffic jams of Georgetown.

The jail is a colonial building of thick stone, that was reinforced for the internment of political prisoners during the freedom struggle. There is a high perimeter wall painted pale green, topped by two rusty rolls of barbed wire. At each corner there are observation towers with louvred glass windows. We pass through the metal gate at the entrance to a wooden counter, where we must deposit identity cards, and in my case my passport, and fill in a form to state which prisoner we are visiting. No one queries my presence.

We pass into a waiting room: stone floor, hard wooden benches, white and pink paint – peeling, so that the benches are surrounded by what look like flakes of spring blossom. A notice states that it is strictly forbidden to pass anything to a prisoner without permission. The walls are decorated with murals executed by past and present occupants of the prison: behind the entrance counter, scenes of forest trees and birds, and in the waiting room a fresco of Malay culture – music, dance, ritual, a dragon dance, some tribal people; murals skilfully done by prisoners whose artistic ability had remained, until their time in prison, as securely locked away as they were to be. While we wait, I talk to Fatimah and Zainon. I ask him what he will do with the money he is now earning. He says shyly the first thing he will do is buy some vitamin pills and some Kentucky Fried Chicken, because this will help him grow strong so he will not be bullied by other boys. The rest of the money he will give to his mother. It is almost unbearably poignant – the sweet sensibility shining through a colonized mentality: for a moment it is like another prison visit. Zainon has the same features as his mother, and he stays close to her throughout the morning. They provide each other with protection against the world.

The people waiting to see the prisoners are, as everywhere in the world, the poorest. The Tamils, about 10 per cent of the population of Malaysia, are overrepresented, families with children, all touchingly dressed in their finest clothes; this is a message both to the prison authorities that they are respectable people, and also to the prisoners, that they have not lost dignity or self-respect. A mother is combing the hair of a child wearing a burgundy dress with puff sleeves and white lace socks. It is as though she is dressed for a celebration; and perhaps it is, the fortnightly visit to her captive father.

We wait forty minutes. No one complains. It is the fate of the poor to be kept waiting, so that they may reflect upon their powerlessness. At last we are issued with visitors' passes, which we clip onto our lapels, and are led into an adjacent wing of the building.

There we see a long line of mosaic-topped stone benches fitted to the concrete floor, in front of a row of partitions and grilles. These are made of a narrow-mesh mosquito wire netting. Behind this is a space of about 10 centimetres, and then a thicker, diamond-mesh grille behind a series of parallel bars. Beyond, yet another grille of narrow-mesh metal. The space between the grilles is filled with dust, dead insects, straws from cartons of drink. The screen between prisoner and visitors is such that it is impossible to touch, or even to see the prisoner properly; only by moving your head vigorously can you make out the prisoner's features. The physical separation of loved ones torments the relatives as much as the wrongdoers.

Yahaya is now twenty-six, a sturdy young man with a wide smile and a gentle face, not unlike his mother. Yahaya is surprised to see so many visitors and he responds with enthusiasm, almost gaiety; he rarely has the opportunity to meet new people. For the first few minutes he is absorbed filling up the form for the little luxuries his mother is allowed to buy for him from the prison canteen shop: some cartons of chrysanthemum tea and lychee juice, a roll of toilet paper, some peanuts and dried anchovies. The bill comes to 30 ringgit, about $US12.

Yahaya tells how they sleep four to a cell, not bunk beds but in a row, which fills up all the floor space. They have to slop out using a bucket. There is no privacy. They are up at six o'clock every morning. After a shower, they eat breakfast of *roti* and coffee. The food at midday is not good, the rice is not clean. With rice they eat dried fish and vegetables; nothing after six o'clock in the evening. They are allowed to watch TV, but not the evening programmes. They sleep at ten. Prayers are said five times a day. Three afternoons a week and on Sunday mornings, they play football. Yahaya is a striker, and the sports days give him inklings of freedom. He asks his mother if she can provide him with some trainers for sport. She asks the warder if this is permitted.

For the past six years, Yahaya has been learning carpentry. The Sanyo company has set up a workshop in the prison as part of a rehabilitation programme, and the young man makes furniture and window frames. More recently he has been doing some electrical repair work, which he prefers. He has learned a little English, mainly by watching TV.

Yahaya says above all he regrets the loss of his youth in prison. Yes, he says, I did smoke *ganja*, but I did not process or deal in it. He bitterly regrets his involvement now, and no longer smokes even cigarettes. Whether he required so long and demoralizing an experience in prison to learn the folly of what he did he does not say. He wonders whether he will be accepted when he comes out. Will he get a job, or will he be a social outcast?

Yahaya was a confused and unhappy adolescent. Now he has matured, and remains unembittered by his experience, although he maintains a great injustice was done. His mother observes that today he is very talkative. People in prison often feel they have been locked away and forgotten. Normally, says Fatimah, he responds only to her questions; he has little to tell, because prison routine is predictable and monotonous. Zainon barely exchanges a word with his brother.

In the silences, it is difficult to keep the sadness at bay; the inaccessibility of the prisoner, the blurred and faltering smile behind the grille, the warders pacing up and down behind them – all create an unnatural atmosphere for human encounters. Yahaya is wearing white shorts and a white prison vest with a blue collar, his prison number embroidered on the pocket. Some of the warders, he says, are good, considerate; others are sadistic.

Penang jail, like all prisons in the growing cities, is filled not so much with wicked people as with the poor, the disadvantaged and the unfortunate. Their role is complex, and their plight is as much an object lesson to those outside as a punishment for their wrongdoing.

After three-quarters of an hour our time is up. We say goodbye to Yahaya. We have cheered him a little: our visit is an event in the three thousand days of his sentence in this colonial jail with its colonial traditions. Leaving him, it is hard to hold back the tears.

I am going to the airport. Fatimah and Zainon will come for the ride. We drive past the industrial estate where they work, the Zon Perdagangan Bebas. All are prisoners, in their way, the workers in the industrial barracks, the 'criminals' in the jails, even the soldiers in the army. The people in industrial society exist to serve the institutions of industrial society – the factories, prisons, mental asylums – and, it seems, the people of Penang have been reshaped for that purpose. They are a people uprooted, although they have remained in the same place.

The draconian social legislation of Malaysia helps to contain some of the consequences of industrialization, at least for the time being. What the Malaysian prime minister Dr Mahathir Mohamed refers to as 'Asian values' seems to mean a repressive and punitive response to those who do not, or cannot, conform to the imperatives of accelerating industrialization. This in turn means following the Western developmental model while trying to suppress the social consequences of that development in Malaysia. At the same time, Mahathir is always harping on the levels of social dislocation and breakdown, the moral disintegration of the West. But these very same things are already beginning to appear in Malaysia. In fact, to us from Europe, Malaysia creates a ghostly sense of visiting our own recent past. It is rather like the fifties and sixties in Britain when a new-found affluence swept everyone along in a state of trancelike euphoria. People believed that social improvement was written into the structures of economic growth, that it could all go on for ever, that the key to universal happiness had been found and that nothing would ever arrest it. Yet even then, there were clear signs of the disaffection of youth, the beginnings of the increase in crime, drug taking, alcohol abuse, family breakdown – those very things that have since become the scourge of Western society and at the heart of the creation of its newly discovered 'underclass'. It is difficult to see how Malaysia – or, indeed, any of the other Asian economic miracle societies – will avoid the same fate. For a while, an alliance of frozen Victorian colonial morality and Islamic rhetoric, allied to an orgiastic consumerism, may appear to keep in check evils and wrongs that nevertheless continue to work away beneath the carefully cultivated surfaces, and which must be concealed from an admiring world in order that the true costs of development, Malaysia-style, may be confined to the untold story of people like Fatimah and her family.

3

Migrants to the City

Bangkok

'*In the village, if we are hungry, we eat. In the city, we eat whether we are hungry or not.*' – industrial worker aged twenty, Bangkok

In the centre of the commercial and tourist area of Bangkok, in a small *soi* or side street, an unobtrusive three-storey building houses a reception centre for new migrants to Bangkok. Here, young people who have just arrived can find free lodging for up to a week while they look for work. This provides them some protection from exploitative employment, or from being tempted into the sex industry.

Hospitality House, as it is known, does not provide work. Conditions are very frugal, not calculated to encourage people to linger. Father Daniel Boyd, who has lived in Bangkok for twenty years, keeps a record of who comes and why; he has gained considerable insight into the nature of rural–urban migration, its causes and consequences.

In 1993, the centre received almost 2,000 migrants, 85 per cent of them male. Almost half came from northeastern Thailand, mainly Isan, about one-quarter from the north, and 20 per cent from central Thailand. The peak age was twenty – more than 10 per cent – with lesser peaks at seventeen, and in the late twenties. More than two-thirds stayed between one and five days, and the great majority found work. Of these, 50 per cent became construction workers, almost one-quarter carpenters and masons. Eleven per cent were employed in restaurants and hotels, half as many in factories and as security guards.

Father Boyd says that people always give positive reasons for coming to the city; they must do this, because to do otherwise suggests that they are not in control of their lives. They say they come because of opportunities for employment, higher pay than is available in the rural areas, the chance for education, 'curiosity about life in Bangkok', the demand for labour in industry. The reality is that the force of these is easily outweighed by the negative factors: poverty, lack of land to

cultivate crops, low wages; the increase of population in the countryside; natural disasters, floods and droughts; deforestation; the need to
market crops at low prices because all growers bring their harvest to
market at the same time; seasonal migration to supplement declining
farm income. It is only later that these deeper reasons emerge.

As well as experiencing enormous internal upheavals generated by
development (and the Bangkok region now generates 56 per cent of
the wealth of the country), Thailand has also been the destination of
thousands of refugees from neighbouring countries: Laos, Cambodia,
Vietnam, Burma. Bangkok is vast, full of places to hide, and opportunities for work. Much of the small-scale construction work is
undertaken by 'illegals'. In the room in the modest-rent block where
I was staying in Charoenkrung, one morning the whole building was
suddenly swarming with police. At dawn, around 5.30, they sealed all
the exits and hammered on every door, demanding to see papers,
passports. In the building, there were a number of Sri Lankans,
Indians, as well as Thais and Chinese. I was the only European. Such
raids occur daily.

Father Boyd says, 'We deal with people who are so unfamiliar with
the city that they may work all month and get no money, without real-
izing this is wrong. A Burmese illegal, why should anyone pay him?
To whom will he complain? There are many people in this position
in Bangkok. This project exists to address the question of exploitation. On the domestic and on the international level, on a large
scale, Thai women are bought and sold. Go to any recruiting agency
for entertainers; the Mama San of a brothel in Tokyo buys a girl for
200,000 baht, which she has to pay back. When three-quarters of the
money is repaid, she will then be sold on to someone else. It is
bondage. We have set up an operation to receive women coming
home. If they are found to be HIV-positive, they will be forcibly repa-
triated, and then they may have no option but to re-enter the sex
industry here.

'On the domestic level, at least one million people migrate in and
out of the rice belt once or twice a year. Men and women come to
Bangkok to look for a wage-earning job. They are unskilled, unso-
phisticated. Thai people grow up with a feeling of the debt they owe
their parents. Men can earn merit for them by becoming monks, or by
achieving a high-wage job. For Thai women, there is no institutionalized religious life, so prostitution is one of the channels they can use
to expunge the debt to their parents.

'Everyone in Isan knows people who have gone to Bangkok. They
hear stories of the city, and they think if they go there, they know
what to expect. But they don't. They can't even begin to imagine

what it means to cease being a peasant and to become an industrial worker.'

So what happens to people as they are transformed by industrial life?

In the fish canning factory where Buonma worked for three years, management spiked the drinking water with amphetamines. This worked wonders for productivity, but didn't help Buonma: she was pregnant during her last year there, and she believes that her daughter's facial deformity is one of the lasting consequences of that particular efficiency drive.

Konpatin, people who migrate, those who leave home, are a vital part of the Thai success story; it is a strange success in some ways, for the human costs do not enter at all into the economic calculus.

Many of them are little more than children, and their lives speak of a profound violence that is not denied by the smiling exterior the people of this truly terrible city extend to visitors, customers and clients; there are the women who take a job, any job, working on a construction site for a wage that may not even be paid, young people who live as virtual captives in industrial units on the far periphery of the city, women in garment factories who have never seen the Royal Palace or the Victory Monument. Industry has become as mobile as the hands it commands, shifting to where the supply of fresh and unspoilt labour (that is, labour that remains innocent, both of its rights and of the power of solidarity) can be constantly replenished. In this respect, industrialization in the South is very different from early industrialization in Britain, whose rise, consolidation and decay occurred over six generations. By contrast, the garment industry in Dhaka did not exist ten years ago; if cheaper labour can be found elsewhere, it may not exist ten years from now.

On the southern edge of Bangkok, with its areas of waist-high *kok* grass, its vestigial orchards of mango and papaya, the roads cut through a desolate landscape to sites newly colonized by industry: loops of power cables hang between concrete pillars and pallid street lighting; drifts of grey dust pile up on the margin of the highway, canals are polluted a vibrant purple or rust colour by the industrial units. These units also provide accommodation for the workers, whose washing – faded jeans and coloured shirts – dances in the wind outside. Here, the owners of industry tell the raw migrant youth not 'You work for me,' but 'I feed you,' reinforcing an industrial servitude into which the migrants' needy families have compelled them.

Some of the industrial units are open to view, but others remain shielded behind a grey metal lattice over closed doors, on the other side of which children are working for as little as 20–30 baht a day

($US1), one-fifth of the minimum wage, which few here can earn.

The minimum 125 baht per day is paid only by the multinationals, like the Reebok factory, which employs 3,000 young people. The facade of Reebok stands, demure as a colonial bungalow, in a garden of coconut palms. To the multinationals $5 a day is nothing; but it makes them the most sought-after employers to the young women in their lime-coloured tunics embroidered with the company logo, who blink as they emerge into the hot sunshine at the end of their eight-hour shift. Even so, the three-day holiday for the Chinese New Year will have to be paid for: they must work eight successive Sundays of overtime.

In the small units, most workers earn between 50 and 90 baht a day. Pink plastic shoe lasts spill out onto the street like amputated limbs. Packaging from Sanyo and Toshiba products leaves strips of brightly coloured cut-offs like the residue of some carnival celebration; streams of poisonous lilac effluent form pools on the stagnant canal, where some water lilies still open their spiky white crowns to the searing sun.

The young people here are the raw material of Thailand's economic growth, the human fertilizer that produces such an abundant harvest in an industrial monoculture of money.

They do not come willingly to the city. They did not leave the mango orchards, the vegetable gardens, the rice fields, the smallholdings with their pigs, ducks and chickens, because they were attracted to Bangkok, least of all to this joyless suburb. Aree Chua-Um, a sensitive young woman of eighteen, says that the noise and confusion of Bangkok destroy the mind just as labour destroys the body. We have come, she says, because we have no choice, because the places where we grew up have been ruined. Spoiled by drought, deforestation, industrialized agriculture – by the same obsession with productivity that damaged the daughter of Buonma.

More than 5 per cent of the total land of Thailand has now been turned over to rubber plantations; the large-scale expansion of industrial shrimp farming for export destroyed nearly half the country's coastal mangrove forests between 1985 and 1990. By 1988, 15 million hectares of Thailand – nearly half the entire land area – had been allotted to private logging concessions, and 3.2 million hectares of forests and farmland had been converted to export crop production. Thailand's forest cover has declined from 53 per cent of its area in 1961 to 28 per cent in the late eighties; erosion, floods and drought are the result. A ban was placed on all logging in 1989, although it still occurs illegally, and Cambodia is now being rapidly deforested by the same loggers who ravaged Thailand.

One result of this is that the rural poor must feed the city with their children. The small farmers, in any case, are cheated by middlemen, dealers and officials; which is why so many have almost come to believe that the production of food, far from being the most useful and valuable work of humanity, is actually an ignoble, inferior occupation, from which they want their children to escape.

The myth that most people migrate for the bright lights of the city could have been conceived only by those so denatured by generations of industrial life that bright lights appear to them more attractive than the luminosity of loved flesh and blood. The testimony of the young migrants to the bleak suburb of Bangbon tells another story.

Mongkhon comes from Isan in the northeast of Thailand. He came because his family of eight faced a declining yield from their land. He was placed by an agency in a sex hotel, cleaning the toilets for 600 baht a month ($US24). Later, he worked in a metal factory, and then in a unit making air conditioners for cars. Now he is employed by the Foundation for Rural Youth (FRY), an organization devoted to the protection of young people in the city. He goes home once a year. He says that whenever he takes the bus back to the city, he finds himself anxiously checking his bag because he feels as though he has left something behind. Mongkhon says the forced adaptation of country people to the values of the city is a form of violence, but is not recognized because it is associated with money, getting richer. Mongkhon writes poetry. He reads to me in Thai, in a voice vibrant with feeling, some lines about his home, evoking the sense of expectancy just before the rains: the aridity of the land, dried and cracked by the hot breath of the sun, a landscape drained of colour, the dusty buffaloes dreaming of something green as they chew dry straw in the broken earth.

Aree Chua-Um came to Bangkok because her family is in debt, having borrowed money when the rain failed. Last year, the drought was complete, and the yield virtually nothing. 'Otherwise', she says, with the candour of her 18 years, 'why would I come here to carry cement on a construction site, or polish stone floor tiles for 80 baht a day? I had to leave my studies to come to the city.' People think they come to the city for money, but actually, the city robs them, traps them into jobs with no skills, no future, for the sake of immediate earnings that must be sent home to the family.

Anusak is an artist, who consoles himself with painting pale watercolours of his village: a smudge of colour calls up the water, the buffaloes, the tamarind trees. The sixth of seven children, he came to Bangkok five years ago. He worked serving in a restaurant, then silk screen printing, selling leather and plastic bags which he made himself out of scrap. His mother and father separated, and he cannot stay alone in the village: were he to do so, people would think there is something wrong with him – no one stays in the village without land to cultivate. Anusak says, 'Young people are cheated by the city. They must alter their mind and their character. They must change from the rhythm of the crops which come regularly if you prepare the earth, to the rhythm of money. In the village, if we have enough we are content, but this is ruined in the city; so people learn what it is to want. In Isan now, there are villages where only grandparents and babies are left – all the able-bodied young people have come to Bangkok to work.'

What Anusak said about money was reinforced by Duang, a teacher from Ubon. He said, 'In the rural areas, rice is wealth. Rice is replenished naturally each year, and varies only with the weather. In the city, money is wealth. Many young people become confused between the two forms of wealth. If I have more rice than I need for my family, I will give it to my neighbours. The young people who have been brought up in this tradition then wonder why those with an excess of money do not give to others for their survival. They do not understand the function of money, the significance of accumulation.'

A British transsexual who owns a gay club in Bangkok says of the boys who work for her, 'A fortune passes through the hands of some of them, those who are very attractive and in demand. But they have no idea of saving it. They spend whatever they have and then come and ask me for a loan. They live for the moment, they do not think about tomorrow.' Here is a cultural misunderstanding of the young migrants, who are shaped by a subsistence sensibility that has not fully learned the harsh lessons of city acquisitiveness. When they ask for money and it is refused, they are puzzled, and sometimes indignant; but when they do have it, they rush to share it with their friends.

Buonma came to Bangkok for the first time fifteen years ago. She says she ran away from poverty, but poverty was too attached to her and would not let her go. Her family are from Pisanutlok in the North. They had land, but Buonma sold it when her husband was jailed for stealing. She then made a living producing charcoal, but the trees in that part of the country were fast disappearing; that livelihood, too, soon ceased.

Buonma came with her older daughter to the city and found work on a construction site near the airport. The wage was 50 baht a day. She lived on the site for four months. Food was provided. When the building was finished, the company said it had no money left, and the workers were laid off without the pay they were owed. All were country people, new to industrial society. How could we fight? she asks; we knew nothing. We had eaten their food and lived in their barracks, we thought we were lucky not to have to pay them anything for living there.

She came to Bangbon in south Bangkok, where many factory units were under construction. She worked in a manufacturing plant where panels for industrialized building were made. She earned 50 baht a day, and her husband, freed from prison, joined her. They worked together for a short time, but he found a new wife and disappeared again. Buonma went back to the village and rented a small piece of land to grow food for herself and her daughter. But there was drought; the land produced nothing but debt. She returned to Bangbon to the same factory. The owner employed her as housekeeper at 80 baht a day. She stayed there until her husband, disillusioned with his new wife, came back to her.

She spent three years in the fish canning factory, where she earned 120 baht a night for the drug-induced energy of her labour. In the morning, exhausted, she could not understand why she was unable to sleep. She lost weight. At the factory she fell in love with another man and became pregnant. Buonma remained tired and thin. After the birth of her daughter, she worked as housekeeper, this time at the headquarters of the Thai Farmers' Bank, at 140 baht a day, the first time she had ever been employed at above the minimum wage. But this was still not enough to live on: in all her previous employment, some form of shelter had come with the job. There was simply not enough money to rent a room and to provide enough to eat.

Buonma is now housekeeper for the Migrant Youth Centre in Bangbon. At forty-two she is frail, her face grave but exuding the inner strength that has enabled her to survive. She calls Bangkok 'a city of lies'. Here you are promised everything, but if you don't fight you will not survive.

She has one older brother whom she has not seen for ten years. They lost each other when they went their ways, separated by migration in search of a livelihood far from home. She went back to the village two years ago to register the birth of her daughter and to get herself an identity card. There is no one, she says, left there.

The Migrant Youth Centre serves as both refuge and advice centre. There is a dormitory for young women, and the building is a focus for those who need help and guidance in the strange new environment of the city. It is in an area of new industrial units about 20 kilometres from downtown Bangkok. From the roof of the building, among the new white-painted buildings and construction yards, you can see the coconut palms and mango trees of one stubborn gardener who will not sell his land to developers, a man who, perversely, prefers land to money.

The centre occupies three units of a long industrial building. Upstairs, the dormitories are home to fifty young women. Neat bedrolls, small metal lockers, racks on which hang blouses, dresses, jeans and towels, the dormitories contain all the vulnerable intimate belongings of people who live without privacy. But here, at least, the women are secure, safe from the treacherous promises of easy money in the sex industry. Many of those at present living here are working in the nearby Reebok factory. Ubon Noibat, aged twenty, comes from Burilam, one of the most drought-prone regions of the country. Ubon is lucky; she has found a job at the minimum wage and a secure place to live. A placid, pleasant young woman, she says, 'Bangkok teaches you about modern life.' Actually, she has never been outside Bangbon. Her parents once visited her, but they hated the city. At home, they have 15 rai of land, growing rice and *monsanpalang*, which is used as cattlefood. Ubon says she would not like to work on the land. 'It is too hot.' Reebok is hot too, not air-conditioned, 'a different kind of hot'. Ubon exemplifies the tractable sensibility of Thai workers which make them so attractive to the roving transnationals, always on the lookout for docile labour that will not cause trouble.

Virasak has been working for four years with the Foundation for Rural Youth. 'The change from rural to city life is very drastic and confusing for young people. Although many of them are familiar with images of city life from television and film and so on, the reality is still traumatic for them. There are many accidents at work, not only because of the long hours they have to labour, but also because they are not accustomed to the life of the machine. They do not always realize that you have to respect it in a way that is different from the respect you give to farm animals. For instance, you can hit a buffalo on the rump with a stick and it may respond; the machine will just cut your hand off.

'There are no trade unions here. Factories leave places where unions are formed, and open up where they can recruit unskilled young rural labour who have never even heard of trade unions. Many of the units here subcontract: they get raw materials or components to which they add value and then return them to the parent factory. People can be controlled more easily if they have limited power over the production process, or intervene in it only in an insignificant way.

'Child labour is common too, because many parents depend upon the same employer. Other children are recruited in the village by agents; they can be paid very low wages, together with food and dormitory living. There is no security of employment, no protective wear against dangerous chemicals, fumes and machinery. And even those multinationals which make it a matter of principle to pay the minimum wage often take on young people for a four-month probationary period at a lower rate than the minimum. At the end of that time, instead of transferring them to the regular staff, the multinationals renew the four-month period. A state of permanent insecurity suits employers, because this makes people manageable.

'The young are trapped. They cannot acquire skills but must take a job for the sake not only of their own immediate survival, but also of that of their family in the village. They have no thought for the future, their rights, their education, their potential. The costs of all this are borne not by the economic system, but by the young people themselves. They have no understanding of the economic and social order in which they live. They are peasants, transplanted from the land to the city: urban technopeasants.

'Migrant youth', says Virasak, 'do not know how to survive in the city system. This is why they are so easy to exploit. They live for the day, spend all they earn. There is no government policy addressing these issues. The government claims it wants to keep people in the villages, to stop them coming to Bangkok. But economic policy is in direct contradiction to that: competitive production means cheap labour, and that means more and more recruits for the urban labour market. There is no effort to help the young people when they come to the city. It is not surprising if many of them finish up in the sex industry, the bars and clubs; that certainly appears more glamorous than a fifteen-hour day in a factory. They are left to fend for themselves, alone, against the power and strength of industry, the exploiters.

'Of course, the young people don't always see it like that. To them, the city represents freedom. They can change sexual partners frequently, because they are far from their families in the village, where such things would not happen. They rush into sexual relations which they often mistake for love. They use stimulants, amphetamines, *yama*, so that they can perform better at work after a late night spent playing cards or snooker; often they gamble away their money. Many do not eat properly, taking only junk food; some even become malnourished. On the whole, they are obedient, do not complain at injustice, because they do not recognize injustice for what it is. If they do complain, they are told they can look for work elsewhere; there are always plenty of new people ready to replace them.

'We try to spread news in the villages of the reality of life in Bangkok, via migrants who have already come. In the villages of Isan, we are working with the people in an endeavour to make life more tolerable there, but we are going against the flow of a whole social and economic system. Here, in the city, we seek out young people who have some vision, who realize that life can be better, so that they can influence their peers. Then we will be able to say to government and all the official agencies, "This is our vision, this is what the young people want."

'Many people in Thailand are working with child labour, street children, youngsters in the sex industry. We are working directly with the causes, at the point where village life, farming, food production come to appear worthless, impoverishing and burdensome, against a city that beckons as a place of excitement, glamour and wealth.'

The Cycle Rickshaw Drivers of Dhaka

Unfamiliarity with the city economy compels migrants into the lowest-paid, most menial, and sometimes degrading labour; survival now depends not upon harvest or crop yield, but on income. Characteristically, the migrants find work in construction, the public service, transport, hotels, as unskilled labour in factories, especially in the garment, plastics and metal industries, in domestic labour, and in prostitution.

A major service sector in most cities is transport – not merely buses and taxis; in cities like Calcutta, Dhaka, Nagpur, Ho Chi Minh and, to a lesser extent, Jakarta and Manila, this means some form of cycle-driven transport: rickshaws, pedalos, cyclos. The drivers usually hire these from the owners by the day, and this provides a basic income.

Nobody knows exactly how many men earn a living by pedalling the colourful cycle rickshaws of Dhaka. There are around 100,000 official licences, but many more cycle rickshaws are unlicensed, with or without the connivance of the police. Some estimates say there are 250,000.

Whatever the true figure, the vehicles are one of the most conspicuous features of Dhaka, even though they have now been banned from the main thoroughfare that leads from the airport to the commercial centre of the city. For some years there has been talk of phasing out the cycle rickshaws, or banishing them to more peripheral areas, as has occurred to some extent in Delhi. But no one can imagine an alternative livelihood.

The cycle rickshaws are three-wheelers, with a broad back axle, a long chain linking the back wheels to the pedals, and a plastic seat for the passengers. There is a folding hood on a flimsy metal frame which is raised as a protection against rain or sun. The vehicles are painted in brilliant colours, covered with flowers, birds, trees, animals. The back panel between the wheels either depicts some idealized scene from an imagined foreign city – a version of Tower Bridge, the Eiffel Tower, the Statue of Liberty – against bright skies, or shows scenes from Bengali films: lurid greenish-faced villains and plump terrorized heroines. Occasionally, there are paintings of placid mountain lakes, cherry blossom and idyllic village landscapes.

On the handlebars of the rickshaw, there is a spray of plastic flowers, some pennants streaming in the wind; altogether, they present an image of perpetual carnival, which life in Dhaka certainly is not. If the owners of the rickshaws, as well as the manufacturers, the painters, the repairers, the providers of garage space are also included, the cycle rickshaws are the second largest provider of employment in the city, second only to the million-or-so employed by the garments industry.

Some migrants who start work as rickshaw drivers move on to other labour, in factories, on construction sites. Those who do not, rapidly find their energies used up; after a few years, they are unable to work more than one day in two. They pay the owner 22 taka for half a day (50 cents), 40 taka for the whole day. Rush hours offer the spectacle of thousands of rickshaws in an apparently inextricable tangle of colour, metal and sweating humanity, moving like a single compound entity through the streets, a kind of mobile work of art. At the traffic lights, if they stray over the line, the police beat them back with batons. Occasionally, dramatic jams occur at intersections, where one mass of vehicles gets caught up in another. Motorized vehicles – now increasing significantly – keep to the outside lane, but this is frequently blocked by the rickshaw drivers, so that everything is compelled to travel at a pace determined by the rickshaws. The rickshaw drivers regard the road as their own. If an impatient motorist strikes one of the rickshaws, he is likely to be dragged out of his car and beaten.

I met one group of drivers who are living in a small slum, Mohanpur, at Shaymoli in the north of the city. Mohanpur is a small settlement of about twenty houses on a thin platform of land, on the edge of a half-dried-out pond, where coarse *kochari* leaves grow out of the stagnant mud. One row of houses is built against the compound of a big *pakka* (stone and concrete) dwelling; those opposite are on the edge of the pond, constructed on thick bamboo stilts driven deep into the muddy water, which lies about a metre below the wooden floor of the hut. This whole settlement is typical of many small slums in Dhaka, occupying corners and edges of land, built entirely of woven bamboo on a bamboo frame. The weaving of these bamboo panels is a traditional craft, and though flimsy the structures are far less repellent than those made of industrial waste materials like the plastic, polythene and metal huts of Bombay. Most of the houses in Mohanpur have beaten earth floors, but those suspended over the water are made of wood. Houses are raised on platforms of dry earth; roofs are corrugated metal. The structures form a narrow street, where the cooking fires of the previous night leave a residue of grey ash in the traditional stoves. These too are made of hardened earth; the wind scatters the ash in small dust storms.

This illegal settlement is on private land. The owner is a woman who charges 500 taka a month from each 'tenant'. This supplies her with a monthly income of about 10,000 taka – about $US250. The interiors of the huts are very simple: one or two contain a cupboard with a glass front protecting a few china cups and plates, but for the most part metal cooking vessels and plates are stacked on rough wooden shelves. Some families have a big wooden bed which fills half the space and is covered with a bamboo mat; others have a rattan bedroll which in the daytime is stacked in a corner. There is no electricity. Kerosene lamps stand on the shelves. In some huts there are brightly painted Koranic verses, a calendar, sometimes advertising Pepsi, Canon or Sanyo. Containers holding remnants of food hang from a nail, out of reach of rats or cockroaches. There is a tubewell, but in the dry season the water is depleted and rust-coloured.

At the end of the 'street' that forms the slum, there is one lavatory: a bamboo frame, covered with a layer of hessian for privacy. A trickle of filth courses down towards the water's edge. In the huts nearest to the latrine, the stench is constant and overwhelming. In a shallow scooped-out pool of dirty water, a woman is washing clothes. It seems the polluted water can only make them dirtier; but she creates a white lather with coarse soap, rinses them again and again, and beats them violently against a stone. Laid out in the sun, incredibly, they smell fresh and sweet when they are next worn. Living here is a constant war against dirt, insufficiency and want. The people are vastly resourceful, stoical and hopeful, even though everything in their existence suggests a changeless poverty. Hope is perhaps the greatest resource of the poor; certainly it is an infinitely exploitable commodity. The rickshaw drivers, for example, do not believe that their fragile and threatened livelihood could be destroyed by the appearance on the city streets of more and more motorized traffic, and this in spite of the declaration by the mayor of Dhaka that he wanted to see the rickshaw factory closed. They say that since more and more people are coming to Dhaka every day, more rickshaws will be needed. Optimism, often against the evidence, offers them a powerful form of protection, a magic invisible cloak. A more material form of protection occurs in the invisible sheltering net they have constructed around the community. No one has ever gone hungry here, they say. If someone is sick and cannot work, we will provide for the family until he is recovered. This, they say, is why the poor are not the problem in the cities: their instinctive concern for each other stretches inadequate resources to the limit. They are a threat to the rich – not a threat that they will rise up and dispossess them, but a constant irritant; for the privileged, with their waste of wealth, see the wasted bodies of the rickshaw workers as an eyesore, and consider their livelihood an affront to a modern city, this poor living place a polluting presence, fit only to be swept away.

The land on both sides of this narrow piece of ground is now a site of house construction: on one side, the concrete floor and reinforcing rods rise out of the foundations; on the other, the second floor is being completed. The rickshaw drivers know it is only a question of time before the owner sells her land for 'development' and they are evicted. They say, 'We will go elsewhere.' Since their daily food comes only as a result of their daily labour, they will not worry about future disasters, however predictable these may be.

The pond covers several acres. The marshy land of its floor is being cultivated. Enclosing embankments have been built up here and there to contain a square of water, where vivid green spikes of newly transplanted rice pierce the surface. Some women are weeding a patch of vegetables, ankles captive in the mud, reflections in the water, so that their perpetual bowing forms a closed circle of body and image. At the far edge of the stretch of water is a five-storey factory. At some time, the area has been used as a garbage dump; the compacted rubbish has formed two islands about 3 metres above the lake bottom, on each a grove of plantains has become established, green-fringed blades shielding three or four huts. The islands can be reached by walking along the embankments now. In the monsoon, a boat is needed; a shallow vessel of warping wood is tied up in the mud. As you climb the slope to the top of the island, you can see the remains of garbage, plastic bags still flapping out of the earth, indestructible tethered ghosts.

A group of rickshaw drivers from Mohanpur came to a nearby school, where we sat in a circle and talked about their working lives. Abu Sattar from Chittagong has been driving for eight years, Abul Hossein from Barisal for nine years, Bacchu from Comilla eight years. Al-Islam from Faridpur is a veteran of fifteen years. Faijuddin from Manikgunj has been working for two years, and Mohamed Khalil, who came from Karachi thirty years ago, has been a driver since he arrived in Dhaka.

They all still rent from the owners: none has ever saved the capital to buy his own cycle rickshaw. For 40 taka a day, they have the vehicle from 6 a.m till 10 p.m. At one o'clock they return home for lunch and rest, and at three they start again. At the time of our conversation it was Ramzan. None of them was fasting, because their labour depends upon immediate energy and a continuous intake of fluid; this exempts them from the duty of forgoing food and drink between sunrise and sunset. On the day we met they were not working: it is impossible to sustain the level of physical activity demanded by their job for two days without a day to recuperate in between. The average profit per day is about 100 taka, that is, given the non-working days, 50 taka a day, or a little over one US dollar.

All came to Dhaka because they were landless. Mohamed Khalil came originally to settle in what was then East Pakistan, but the land he had bought was taken by river erosion; not all migration is caused by human-made injustice. Abul has just enough land in Barisal for a house, but nothing for crops. Abu neither owned land, nor could he get anything but casual seasonal work. He came to Dhaka to look for a job; before driving a rickshaw, he used to work at the ticket counter of Dhaka zoo. After four years, his contract was not renewed, so he had no choice but to take up this, the last resort of the unemployed. Indeed, renting the rickshaw, the salvation of the poorest, finally becomes a trap, a treadmill of pedalling which uses them up.

Mohamed Khalil says that over the years the work has become harder and more dangerous because of the increasing traffic. You have to learn to be not aggressive, but confident; to make clear signals, not to hesitate; to keep your hand perpetually on the brakes. As the vehicles stop at traffic lights, they jolt the one ahead, and this sets up a series of minor collisions which reverberate along the chain of semi-stationary rickshaws. Abu learned to drive within four days of coming to Dhaka; he knew how to ride a cycle, so this work was no problem for him. Bacchu had no instruction at all – he simply rented the rickshaw and took it onto the streets. Al-Islam pushed a handcart before he became a driver; a *push-gadi* is harder work because you might have a load of bricks or bamboo scaffolding, which is heavy; you must walk in the road and avoid crashing into any other vehicle. Faijuddin was an agricultural labourer before he came to Dhaka.

We are joined by two other residents from the small colony: Mohamed Jalal, for many years a rickshaw driver but now driving a 'baby taxi' (a motorized three-wheeler), and Ashraf Ali, who is a bus helper. All the men have their families here in Dhaka, although originally, they came alone. They prefer Dhaka to the village. Why? Hope, possibilities not open to them in the country, a hope that is inscribed in the busy, mobile, changing imagery of the city. They do not think of themselves as city people; most go home at least once a year. All say it is too exhausting to drive more than fifteen days in a month. There are drivers who work every day, but they wear themselves out within a few years.

At the busiest times of day, the Dhaka traffic leaves a kind of after-fog, a haze of smoke and eye-stinging fumes, air that scrapes the

throat and fills the lungs with particles of grit and dust. The rickshaw
workers suffer from breathlessness, chest pains, lung infections, tuberculosis; they readily become dehydrated during long journeys. They
may cover 60 kilometres or more during the course of a day. There is
also a risk of traffic accidents. Bacchu has had three, one a collision
with a coaster – one of the incredibly battered, low-roofed buses that
tear like enraged animals through the streets. The second time, he
was forced onto the side of the bridge by a car, and the vehicle fell
into the water below. The third time he smashed into a Tempo, one of
the small, jeeplike taxis whose drivers are also notoriously reckless. If
there is a serious accident and the vehicle is damaged, the owners
usually pay for repairs; but if it is a minor problem, like a broken
chain or buckled wheel, the drivers themselves pay: it is in their interests to get the problem attended to immediately, in order to minimize
loss of earnings. The owners do not pay for damage to the drivers, says
Bacchu. Mohamed Khalil also once collided with a coaster; the rickshaw was wrecked but he was unhurt. Abul Hossein was struck by a
baby taxi as it turned in front of him; he was tipped out of the rickshaw but suffered only cuts and bruising. Mohamed Jalal was a
rickshaw driver for twenty-three years before he got his auto rickshaw;
he had more accidents than he can remember.

At the end of their day's labour, they come back to Mohanpur to
face the problems the women must deal with all the time: shortage of
water, lack of fuelwood, the expense of buying kerosene. To have
running water installed would cost 'more than 1,000 taka', they say,
quoting a sum possession of which would be wildly improbable; no
one can afford it.

None of the rickshaw drivers wants their children to do the same
work. They want them to go to school so they can have a better life,
and learn 'better manners', as Bacchu touchingly said; this means,
among other things, to shed their rough country ways, to be able to
deal more competently with the alien environment of the city. The
rickshaw workers do not feel highly valued. Sometimes the passengers
do not pay the agreed fare – which is always determined orally
beforehand, and which the men see as a contract; sometimes, the
passenger will give only 2 or 3 taka, even for a long ride, and there is
nothing the drivers can do about it. In any case, the price is absurdly
low – 5 taka for up to 2 kilometres. They are disregarded by those who
take for granted the service they offer; they are simply street furniture,
in the service of other people's mobility. Sometimes a whole party will
pile into the vehicle, which at best can accommodate two, without
even a glance at the stringy body of the driver. When the local *mastans*
(slum lords who control the bustees, or slums, often hired by political

bosses) get into the rickshaw, they do not expect to pay. If the driver asks them for money, he will be beaten up. The *mastans* used to control the drivers and extort money from them. This has now ceased, at least for the workers in Mohanpur. The Ward Commissioner was helpful, and by sticking together the drivers were able to refuse payment to *goondas* and slum lords.

They say their relationship with the police has also improved. If they are seen by the police not to obey the traffic signals, they will be given nothing more than a slap or a blow with a stick, and fined only 2 or 3 taka.

All have small families, most with two or three children. Faijuddin has a son who works in a garment factory. They see the prospect of factory work as an improvement for their children. The wives of Mohamed Khalil, Faijuddin and Abu also work in garment factories.

It costs 60 taka a day ($US1.50) to provide basic sustenance: rice, vegetable and *dal*, and fish once or twice a week. Since this absorbs the whole daily income of most workers, it is essential that someone else in the family also works. Their modest dream is to become owners of the vehicles they drive, which would provide them with 40 taka more: enough, they say, to be lifted out of poverty. A new rickshaw costs 7,500 taka; and there is no source of credit for people whose only security lies in the preservation of their strength and energy for the next day. In any case, it costs between 3,000 and 4,000 taka to register as an owner. The drivers pay their own licence, 80 taka, renewable annually. Whenever there is a government crackdown on illegal drivers, they rush to renew the licence. Otherwise, they do not bother. The licence serves as identity card, and does give them a certain security. The majority of drivers do not bother with a licence.

It is difficult to organize into a co-operative in order to become owners, because people move in and out of the job frequently; some return seasonally to work on their small piece of land, others fall sick or are evicted from where they live.

Some make small savings. Bacchu is with a savings group, and is proud that he can save 15 taka a week (about 40 US cents). Mohamed Khalil, because his wife is a factory operator, is able to save 300 taka a month. If they are sick, the rickshaw owners lend them money, often at zero interest. Many owners were once pullers of rented rickshaws, so they remember with compassion. It is the big owners, those with fleets of 60 or 70 vehicles, who are heartless.

In 1994, the agitation by the opposition Awami League against the ruling Bangladesh National Party (BNP) led to a series of hartals and closedowns in Dhaka. In all, some forty days were interrupted by political strikes. If a driver takes out his vehicle on days when the city is shut down, he risks being attacked by militants who may damage or destroy the vehicle. If the owner insists that the worker take out the vehicle on a hartal day, then he must bear the cost of any damage; if the worker takes it because he does not want to lose money, he will be held responsible for whatever may happen.

Mohamed Khalil says the hartal is a weapon to kill poor people, another means of destroying their livelihood. The drivers have no interest in any of the political parties, whose quarrels they observe with a resentful eye. 'All say what they are doing is for the sake of the poor, yet this cannot be, because the greatest need of the poor is to be allowed to get on with earning a living.' The workers say they do not care when the elections come, or even whether they come at all. 'Nothing will change for us', they say.

The rickshaw drivers reflect on the difference between poverty in the village and poverty in the city. There *is* a difference, they acknowledge. Village life is better, but if you don't have enough to eat, there is no remedy. In the city, you can find some labour, some form of income, and if you can't you can beg or even steal. Even the poorest in the village do not steal. To some extent, the poor try to re-create the social relationships of the village; and there are little oases – as here in Mohanpur – of mutual help and protection. The bonds, strengthened by their recognition of a shared predicament, are sometimes strained in the cruel, competitive environment of the city; but they do not break.

4

Bombay in the Nineties

Just as London lost about three-quarters of a million jobs in manufacturing and ancillary sectors in the seventies and eighties, replaced, to some degree, by jobs in the financial and service sectors, Bombay must expect to see a displacement of many of the five or six million traditionally employed in the industrial and self-employed sector. 'This is the pattern we foresee for the city,' said Larry d'Souza, secretary of the Bombay Chamber of Commerce and Industry late in 1994. 'We don't need to kick anyone out – market forces will automatically do that.' Unfortunately for those whose eyes are fixed on Western cities – and London is scarcely a model of either social peace, or equity or employment opportunities – Bombay cannot expect so ready a filtering of population out of the capital. The experience of India is of enormous, increased migration into the cities; and even if Bombay does not remain a major destination for the rural outflow, it continues to attract thousands each year who simply have nowhere else to go. The proponents of corporate-led projects, those who speak of turning Bombay into another Singapore, believe that the market mechanism will be the most effective answer to the problems of Bombay.

To the cheerful supporters of liberalization, market forces appear to be a species of impersonal bailiffs who will more or less painlessly evict the five or six million poor in Bombay. Alas, they will have to be assisted by real flesh and blood, a military operation far greater in scale even than Mrs Gandhi's relocation of the Bombay poor during the Emergency of the mid-1970s. Not everybody recognizes the wisdom of appointing market forces as the arbiters of their lives.

Early in 1995, the new government of Maharashtra, a coalition of the communalist Hindu Bharitaya Janata Party (BJP) and the even more extreme Shiv Sena, came up with a remarkable new policy: lands occupied by slum dwellers are to be given to builders. They must use a proportion of that land to re-house the slum dwellers in high-rise buildings. The rest of the land can be used for speculative construction for sale. Some 4,000,000 slum dwellers would benefit from this scheme.

The slums would be abolished and Bombay would become a high-rise modern city undisfigured by the sprawling shanties and makeshift shelters of the poor.

This declaration did wonders for the BJP and Shiv Sena in an election year. Few have paused to ponder where the building materials will come from, or how a collapsing infrastructure can provide the necessary water, sewage systems, garbage collections for the 800,000 apartments. Many are sceptical of the change of heart by a government which, hitherto, has continued the programme of demolitions and destruction of the settlements of the urban poor.

A slum of about three hundred dwellings in Bandra East; about fifteen hundred people live here – the daily increment of Bombay's population. The settlement consists of tents, fragile shelters of hessian, polythene and rags, held together by bamboo poles. The people have not built stronger shelters because these are likely to be broken by municipal workers and police, as has occurred regularly every few weeks. In the late evening, women of the camp are preparing the evening meal. Candles or cooking fires glow through the canvas walls, and enlarged shadows of the people are projected onto the flimsy material. Some people have not even bothered to rebuild since the most recent demolition. They sleep on bundles of clothing in open spaces, among the ashes of yesterday's fire and the pools of turbid waste water. The people come from all over India – not only from Maharashtra, whence some fled the earthquake two years ago, but from Tamil Nadu, Bihar, Orissa, and even Nepal. If their rough shelters look like a refugee camp, this is precisely what it is. They have been overtaken by disasters, most of which are human-created and are the consequences of development.

Kisan Mehta, chair of the Save Bombay Committee, says that the whole thrust of economic development cannot be separated from the growth of the cities. 'We cannot restrict our campaigns to Bombay alone – we must support those which are part of a wider process. The degradation of the Himalayas through deforestation is also part of a development that has its repercussions on Bombay. Only by looking at the dynamic relationship between the rural districts and the cities can you understand what is happening; you cannot just take narrow sectoral specialisms. A municipal plan was published for Bombay in 1977. We came up with an alternative Citizens' Plan. The Save Bombay Committee was asked to submit a synopsis of the municipal plan, because no one could understand it. Bombay has a population density of 17,676 people per square kilometre. In London, the figure is around 1,200.

'Under the 1976 Urban Ceiling Act, 2,951 hectares were identified as vacant. These were owned by 1,351 people, average 2½ hectares each.

Yet 1,400 hectares were owned by 51 people, 300 hectares each. Instead of this land being used for slum rehabilitation, corruption and money meant that it was released hectare by hectare at the sweet will of the owners; and then only for housing schemes that will benefit the rich.

'If the 3,000 hectares of land had been released to slum co-operatives, 300 dwellings per hectare, there could have been 900,000 dwellings – enough to accommodate the five million staying in slums. But it has not happened.

'There is no argument in favour of Bombay as a Western enclave in India. There is no need for so much wealth and so many facilities to be concentrated here, and then for the benefit only of a minority.'

Forty per cent of the formal-sector jobs in Bombay are concentrated within a two-mile radius of Flora Fountain around the Fort. There are 144 jobs for every 100 residents in the Fort area. This creates enormous congestion. The suburban railway system has reached breaking point. Late in 1994, exasperated by delays and by an overcrowding that is impossible to describe, commuters set fire to and destroyed a number of trains on the Western Railway. In the trains, bodies are pressed so tightly together that there are even stories of people having sexual intercourse in the trains unperceived by those standing next to them.

Pressure on the urban space marginalizes the original inhabitants of Bombay, the inhabitants of the ancient fishing villages, who find themselves squeezed both by pollution of their fishing grounds in the Arabian Sea and by appropriation of the foreshore for road and housing construction.

Late in 1994, fishing communities mounted a protest against the granting of licences for deep-sea fishing to Indian companies and their foreign collaborators. Over 170 licences had been issued by the end of 1994, covering 800 deep-sea vessels; some were issued to trawlers and boats exceeding the maximum size, potentially displacing 750,000 fishing people. The licences were 100 per cent export-oriented; this would deprive a further 30 million people of fish. The total world catch of fish is falling – in 1990 it was 97.5 million tonnes, in 1993 it was down to 86.6 million tonnes. The Bombay authorities are planning sea routes through the city suburbs – these will disrupt the work of the fishing communities on the shoreline, at Nariman Point, Bandra and Versova.

Every day, 550 million gallons of drinking water must be brought to Bombay from a distance of over 100 miles. Meanwhile in November 1994 the Civic Executive Health Officer denied that Bombay is a centre for malaria, tuberculosis, polio, hepatitis, gastroenteritis and now AIDS. Insisting that 'civic services are working optimally', he said, 'But most of our efforts get neutralized, sometimes even defeated, by the huge concentrations of slums, mostly unauthorized, which have abysmal hygienic conditions and are the ideal breeding ground for disease.'

He also said that the urban poor are there to service industries that are dangerous to life. A Supreme Court lawyer, M.C. Mehta, warned in December 1994 that Bombay is sitting on a live volcano because of the danger from the chemical industries in the city. Hospitals in the city are not able to cater to the thousands who could be affected by major gas leakages. There are virtually no exit routes from the city, so the people are captive. In the past ten years, there have been at least eight chemicals-related disasters:

1985:   chlorine gas leak in Thane, 1 killed, 129 injured
1985:   benzylchloride gas leakage, 95 injured
1985:   chlorine gas leak in Chembur, 1 killed, 149 injured
1985:   chlorine gas leak in Thane, 141 affected
1988:   refinery blaze at Chembur, 35 killed
1990:   gas leak at Nagothane, 32 killed
1991:   accident while liquid natural gas was being transported on the Bombay–Ahmedabad highway, 100 killed
1993:   gas leak at Kalyan, 9 killed, 123 injured.

In December 1994, it was reported that the Mahim and Malad creeks are too polluted to support any aquatic life during low tide, with the dissolved oxygen levels far below the stipulated standards. The Bombay Environmental Action Group pointed out that the government has relaxed stringent environmental regulations in the name of liberalization. Dr Vijay Joshi, a scientist at the National Environmental Engineering Research Institute, also declared that the two marine outfalls for the city's proposed sewerage project would be inadequate to deal with the 2,000 million litres of waste generated in Bombay by the year 2005.

A report in January 1995 prepared in co-operation with the World Bank, nongovernmental organizations (NGOs) and government, and which studied the Bombay metropolitan region from 1992 to 1994, presented a story of pollution, inadequate landfills, hazardous industrial wastes, and rampant diseases. Sewage in the city is not treated before discharge into the Arabian Sea at any of the three Corporation areas. All sewers overflowed into coastal waters adjoining Bombay, which made them unfit for recreational use throughout the year. Hundreds of septic tanks overflow into the ground, causing flies and mosquitoes to breed. Two million people live with no toilet facility. Drinking water supplies have to be delivered by tankers to supplement piped water. Over 5.5 million people live in slums where enteric and respiratory disorders are common and gastroenteritis, tuberculosis, malaria and filaria are 'rampant'. Each day, despite the work of recycling, Bombay produces 5,000 tons of garbage.

The poor in the cities are suffering disproportionately from the effects of liberalization, the economic adjustment programme. Certainly three and a half years of 'reforms' have been cruellest for the poor, in that the prices of *roti, kapada, makaan* – bread, clothing and housing – have risen dramatically, with double-digit inflation for much of the time. This has been the worst time for the poor since Independence. Prices of foodgrains rose between June 1991 and December 1994 by 58.2, per cent, pulses by 59.5 per cent, sugar by 56.6 per cent, textiles by 42.5 per cent, wood products by 169.4 per cent, chemicals by 51 per cent, drugs and medicines by 41.9 per cent, electricity by 63.4 per cent.

Prices of goods in the Public Distribution System (PDS) increased by 85 per cent between December 1991 and October 1994, which resulted in decreased provisioning in the ration shops. This has been widely interpreted by supporters of liberalization as a result of people buying in the open market instead. The evidence from the poor people of Bombay is that they cannot afford to buy even in the PDS, and in any case the quality of produce in the PDS is adulterated (see page 72). The price index increase between December 1993 and December 1994 was between 10.5 and 11 per cent, producing an annual compound inflation rate during the first four years of the decade of 10.3 per cent, compared with 7 per cent in the first half of the eighties and 7.4 per cent in the second half of the eighties.

In 1939, the basic wage required to sustain life was 30 rupees a month. By that reckoning, in 1994, the minimum should be Rs1,951. Nowhere in India is this reached. Delhi comes closest with Rs1,420; Tamil Nadu has Rs1,000, while the average in West Bengal is Rs750.

Further effects of structural adjustment on the urban poor are not merely anecdotal. The National Malaria Eradication Programme petitioned the government to raise by 50 per cent the budget to combat malaria. This year's Rs1,100 million is a decrease on last year. More money is needed because of the growing immunity of mosquitoes to DDT. The number of deaths from cerebral malaria has grown: the parasite *plasmodium falciparus* is resisting anti-malaria drugs, according to the WHO, and the vector *anopheles stephensi* has grown resistant to usual pesticides. The panic over plague led to malaria programmes being put on hold.

The export of marine products from India was Rs8,930 million in 1990–91; it was Rs25,030 million in 1993–94. To earn foreign exchange to service its $US90 billion debt, India is exporting increasing quantities of foodstuffs. Agricultural exports are expected to rise from Rs80,000 million in 1993 to between Rs200,000 and 300,000 million by the year 2000. Food processing is now the third-largest area of inward investment into the country (after power and fuel). The Indian government is to set up exclusive industrial estates for food processing to provide the necessary infrastructural support. Food processing industries need to be segregated from the pollution created by other industries (*Times of India*, 18 January 1995). In 1993–94 Japan consumed 47 per cent of India's marine exports. The export of foodstuffs from a country in which several hundred million people are undernourished is a strange way of 'evolving modern and suitable instruments for change, for eliminating poverty and for coming closer to the modern world', in the words of the Union Finance Minister, Manmohan Singh.

Over 94 million job seekers will need employment in the next five years. The labour force is projected to increase by 35 million during 1992–97 and 36 million during 1997–2002.

The total number of vehicles in India in 1992 was 23 million; over 63 per cent of them were two-wheelers, 14 per cent cars, 7 per cent trucks. The total length of roads increased from 400,000 kilometres in 1951 to over 2 million kilometres in 1991. An appalling 60,000 people are killed on India's roads each year; the country has a similar number of vehicles to the United Kingdom (where about 3,500 die on the roads each year), but significantly fewer cars.

A study published late in 1994 shows that planners are indifferent to the urban poor. Inadequate budget allocations, bad municipal administration, a widening gap between the demand for and supply of services and infrastructure have damaged the physical environment and the quality of life. The rapid rise in urban population has made things worse. India's urban population of 79 million in 1961 increased to 220 million in 1992, and will be 315–25 million at the beginning of the next century. Of the central budget allocation in 1993–94, only 1 per cent of total outlay was for urban development. The increase in urban poverty easily overshadows the role of cities as engines of economic growth. The contribution of the urban sector to GDP increased from 29 per cent in 1950–51 to 47 per cent in 1980–81.

But there are limits to what can be done to improve civic services in isolation from conditions of life in the hinterland. It is cheaper to spend on rural development and to undertake activities that would make it possible for people to stay in the villages rather than add to the number of slum dwellers.

According to the World Resources Institute in Washington, the last twenty years have done little for poverty abatement in India but have contributed significantly to environmental degradation. In the three highly industrialized states of Maharashtra (of which Bombay is the capital), Gujarat and Tamil Nadu, per capita incomes are above the national average, yet deaths in urban areas from respiratory and waterborne diseases are disproportionately high. In 1988 these three states with 20.6 per cent of India's population, had 40 per cent of fatalities from waterborne diseases and 48 per cent of deaths from respiratory diseases, defying the logic that higher per capita income leads to better health standards. Industrial concerns dumped hundreds of thousands of tons of hazardous wastes on fallow or public lands without any proper safeguards, thus allowing toxic substances to make their way into the air or water.

In the presence of all this, the politicians and officials speak another language. The former Sheriff of Bombay had a vision for the city of tree-lined boulevards, fountains and playgrounds. 'There will be no slums. The streets will be clean with wide pavements unencumbered by hawkers. People will stroll through pedestrian plazas. The night will be brilliant with majestic buildings and fountains.'

The history of Bombay is, and continues to be, a colonial history. Most of what is now Greater Bombay was fertile fields a hundred years ago. The British would acquire a particular region for a derisory sum paid to the owners who had no right to contest the acquisition. The colonial authorities would destroy all buildings, efface all farms, and fell forests, fill up low-lying areas, mark a few roads, and then sell the area back at high prices to the local people as 'developed land'. In addition, they would then levy nonagricultural taxes (higher than the agricultural taxes). The people ousted were never adequately compensated for their lost livelihood – they were the nineteenth-century equivalent of the tribals displaced today for dams and power projects. Many of those ousted were forced to become clerks in the British colonial government service.

Today, about 60 kilometres north of Bombay, the Vasai region is being turned into a dormitory town. This was a purely agricultural area, with very fertile soil, and water available only 5 metres below ground level. Bananas and vegetables were profitably grown in large quantities by farmers owning only a fraction of an acre of land.

Now it is an area of extensive apartments. Much of the groundwater has been drained just for construction work, lowering the water table, drying up many surface wells and causing severe losses to farmers. Worse, salt water is seeping in from the nearby sea, turning the remaining farmland saline. The demand for flats is so great that crime syndicates have taken control of much construction work. They force farmers to sell their land at low prices, and beat them up if they won't. Some who refused to sell, or who threatened to expose the mafia, were killed. Alternatively, a reluctant farmer is dealt with by the purchase of all the plots surrounding his or her plot: the farmer is then denied access to the land. The new flat dwellers are also victims of the system. The buildings are constructed haphazardly, without proper roads or an adequate water supply, and with no sanitation, and no means of garbage disposal. In most places, there is no public transport.

It is a double colonialism: rural lands are colonized by the city, in the interests of what remains a colonial economic system, so that wealth is drained from the periphery to the centre; and while Bombay is a major concentration of wealth in India, it is also a conduit for the export of the country's wealth to the rest of the world, on terms that certainly do not favour the Indian people.

Dharavi I

Early in 1995, the Indian Urban Institute issued a report stating that the housing crisis in the country is worsening. About 165 million people in the urban areas are living in slums or dilapidated housing. In Bombay, it is reported, 68 per cent of the people are now living in such conditions – far more than is admitted by most official estimates.

A breathless advertisement for Star Plus TV in March 1995, trailing a programme, affirms: 'Bombay is a very happening city. Bombay is at the heart of movies, fashion and satellite TV; it has a pace, a pulse all its own. This is what we'll show you on Nikki Tonight.'

Mike Douglass, of the University of Hawaii, says, 'There are few urban issues that are not embedded in questions of land ownership and tenure. All societies have rules that govern the use of land, but the treatment of land as a commodity that can be bought and sold for a market price is historically a recent phenomenon in Asia; in most instances, less than a century has passed since land registration was required by governments and real estate markets emerged.' The story of Dharavi in Bombay illustrates the effect upon large numbers of people who thought they were occupying 'worthless' or 'free' land, in part reclaimed by themselves from the marshes of the island city.

Dharavi is a city within a city, dark heart of a gaudy Bombay: another place, one that is home to half a million people – or is it closer to three-quarters? It remains curiously unknown, for all the clichés it evokes: 'the largest slum in Asia', 'a blot on the landscape of India's richest city', 'a refuge for anti-social elements'. It is surprising how many well-to-do Bombay people, who take for granted travel to Delhi, London or Vancouver, have never been to Dharavi.

This unfamiliarity with the forbidden city of Dharavi is understandable. For one thing, there is no public transport in Dharavi.

Buses merely skirt the periphery. Auto rickshaws cannot go there, because, anomalously, Dharavi is part of central Bombay, where three-wheelers are banned.

Only one main road traverses the slum, the miscalled '90-foot Road', which has been reduced to less than half that for most of its length. Some of the side alleys and lanes are so narrow that not even a bicycle can pass. Whole neighbourhoods consist of tenement build-ings, two or three storeys high with rusty iron stairways to the upper part, where a single room is rented by a whole family, sometimes twelve or more people; it is a kind of tropical version of the industrial dwellings of Victorian London's East End.

But Dharavi is a keeper of more sombre secrets than the revulsion it inspires in the rich, a revulsion, moreover, that is in direct proportion to the role it serves in the creation of the wealth of Bombay. In this place of shadowless, treeless sunlight, uncollected garbage, stagnant pools of foul water, where the only nonhuman creatures are the shining black crows and long grey rats, some of the most beautiful, valuable and useful articles in India are made. From Dharavi come delicate ceramics and pottery, exquisite embroidery and *zari* work, sophisticated leather goods, high-fashion garments, finely wrought metalwork, delicate jew-ellery settings, wood carvings and furniture that will find its way into the richest houses, both in India and abroad. One of the best-kept secrets enfolded within Dharavi is that many of the people who actually make and create these thing are among the poorest. It is only to be expected that the image projected of Dharavi should be one in which the people are perceived as idle, worthless; for this is a prerequisite for the justifi-cation of the levels of exploitation and injustice to be found there.

But extraordinary though it is, the production of such articles is not the real wonder of Dharavi. The true marvel is the ability of the poor to reclaim and to reuse almost any item of consumption that has been dis-carded: used-up papers and rags, metals, glass, plastic, cardboard, to save and to conserve, to keep and to mend. In this sense, Dharavi is a model of recycling. Only the spectacle of children burrowing through heaps of fetid garbage, the women, arms stained with filth, cuts festering where they have injured themselves on pieces of glass and jagged tin, infants who can scarcely walk hunting for an old bottle or a few stinking plastic bags to place on the rusty metal scales of one of the hundreds of dealers in precious junk for the sake of 25 paise, speak of the depths of destitu-tion to which many have been brought. It is only people who are not recyclable; and this illuminates the most cruel secret of all: that here human beings are expendable. The energy, health and well-being of the people do not count in the ugly calculus of profit and loss that domi-nates not merely Dharavi, but Bombay and the world beyond.

In this, Dharavi is united in its 'invisibility' with so many other places in the world, equally 'unknown', not only to the powerful, but also to each other. The poor of Tangerang in Jakarta, of Jurain in Dhaka, of Nova Iguacu in Rio, of Tondo in Manila, do not yet know that they are all part of that most poisonous by-product of industry, a global wastage of humanity.

Of course in Dharavi there are also many who have grown rich, and who have chosen to remain there, whether out of sentiment or in order to supervise more closely the creation of their wealth. Some who thirty or forty years ago came with nothing to this place of refugees can now boast fortunes that would permit them to live in the citadels of Malabar Hill, if they chose to do so.

It is almost impossible to evoke the charmless, functional chaos of the unique urban landscape created by this mysterious, compelling subcity.

The area was originally Mahim Creek, an inlet from the Arabian Sea, which came up as far as Kurla in north Bombay. In its clear and plentiful waters, traditional fishing communities caught shrimps, crabs, mud-skippers, and, in the deeper water, bombils. With the construction of bridges over the creek, the laying of the sewage and water pipes supplying Bombay, the inlet became silted up and stagnated; later industrial pollution has contributed further hazards. Fishing became impossible in the creek, and the fishing people were squeezed closer and closer to the foreshore in Bandra. Many who could no longer make a livelihood from the waters turned to making liquor, the fate of many dispossessed communities all over India.

With the expansion of Bombay, Bandra in the north, with its population of Portuguese-speaking 'East Indians', and Sion in the south became middle-class communities; the marshy, mangrove lands between were left to poor migrants to the city, Untouchables, those now called Scheduled Castes, and poor Muslims; these still comprise the vast majority of the population of Dharavi.

The land that is now Dharavi was slowly filled in with waste, or *kachera*, largely by the people who lived there. Ultimately the land level rose until it was above the usual flood level. What began as small, wretched huts were extended and reconstructed; but because they were always densely packed together, the only direction in which they could expand was upwards.

Today Dharavi presents a startling picture. You can wander into the slum at almost any point and find rambling buildings of corrugated metal, 20 metres high in places, rusted by many monsoons: vast sheds, for the treatment of hides and tanning. Some of these are open on all four sides, supported by pillars; this has the effect of dispersing the stench throughout whole neighbourhoods. Here the skins arrive, newly torn from the carcasses of animals, still with fragments of flesh adhering to them. In the tanning sheds, workers are employed to remove the remains of the meat, an overwhelmingly nauseating occupation. Men in rubber aprons with sharp knives are engaged on an endless labour of scraping and cleaning the raw skins; the smell clings to them wherever they go. After this the hides are steeped in acid and preservative before the tanning process. These repelling worksites, covering several acres, are the starting point for the production of leather goods that will find their way, through a complex chain of middlemen and salespeople, into the shops and boutiques of Bombay, the Gulf and the United States; by that time, they will be only faintly redolent of their animal origin, and cleansed of any shreds of exploitation that might adhere to the fabric.

Or the mutton tallow processing plants: a hangar of jagged metal, worn into an almost lacelike lattice of rust. On the threshold a pile of animal bones, like the remains of some terrible plague pit. These will be passed on to a glue-making enterprise nearby. Around this factory hungry dogs roam, some of them almost devoid of fur, snarling at the inaccessible food. Inside, men crouch around an open fire on which a metal vat of animal fat is simmering in a greasy blue cloud of smoke.

But then, passing between two buildings, you find an open space where somebody has planted a few green blades of plantain and some palm saplings. Here some of the houses have been renewed, with concrete walls painted a cool blue, tiled floors and fans stirring the humid air, comfortable chairs, a TV, colour-washed kitchens with shining steel and polished brass utensils. A little further on, where the road broadens, hotels and restaurants have appeared, with marble steps, facades of ceramic tiles, and names spelt out in silver metal Marathi characters. Inside, the wooden benches are cushioned by plastic-covered foam. The sides of the road, however, remain piled high with uncollected garbage which overflows a yellow metal skip, around which outsize blue-black crows wheel and dip; a litter of coconut shells, pineapple tops, rotten fruit, faded garlands of marigolds, frayed stalks of sugar cane from which the juice has been squeezed.

There is always something to astonish in Dharavi. One surprising thing is the number of people working with and on behalf of the voiceless poor. This has become all the more necessary recently because the Bombay authorities now see only the value of the land which the people of Dharavi occupy, rather than the worth of the people themselves. This has been aggravated by the coming to power in Maharashtra of the BJP, the Bharatiya Janata Party, and its Bombay ally the Shiv Sena, with its obsession with illegals, especially Bangladeshis, and its increasingly articulated belief that Muslims have to prove themselves citizens of

India or get out. This makes the work of integration and harmony more difficult than it has ever been, even after the riots of 1992.

A new commercial centre is being created as an extension of the overcrowded downtown area around Dalal Street, what is called the Bandra–Kurla Complex, to the north of Dharavi. Raju Korde, a social activist who was born and lives in Dharavi, says, 'They are trying to make a mini Hong Kong here.' The implications for Dharavi of such a plan are plain. 'Land in Bombay is already among the most expensive in the world, rivalled only by Tokyo and New York. Because it is built on islands, some of them reclaimed from the Arabian Sea, the pressure is enormous. Since the authorities cannot see the people of Dharavi because they are dazzled by the value of the land, they will have few scruples in trying to remove them.'

But six hundred thousand people are not so easily removed. Indeed the fragile social peace that exists there now is almost entirely due, not to the establishment of law and order by government, police or the military, in the wake of the anti-Muslim riots that followed the demolition of the mosque at Ayodhya in December 1992, but to the efforts of groups like the Rashtriya Ekta Samiti, the National Integration Committee, in Dharavi itself. Although Bombay Municipal Corporation has frequently demolished 'unauthorized' slums, with the help of police and officials, it is one thing to break one hundred huts on a small piece of land but quite another to tackle the scale of displacement that would be required if the land on which Dharavi stands were to be 'reclaimed' not this time from the creek – the people have done that already – but from its present lawful occupants.

'This is why', says Bhav Korde (no relation to Raju), also an activist of the Rashtriya Ekta Samiti, 'they have to develop more sophisticated strategies for dislodging the people. This is no new thing. The free flats for slum dwellers is only the latest.'

One of the most ingenious schemes devised with this objective was the so-called Prime Minister's Grand Project, conceived by Rajiv Gandhi in 1989. This was to have replaced much of the slum housing of Dharavi with multistorey apartment blocks. The people who lived in the *jopris* (huts) were promised that they would be given the first option to buy the flats that were to be constructed on the site of their then houses. Because in many families three or four people were working, many were able to pay the 5,000 rupees down-payment (about $US160) which would guarantee them a place in the new buildings.

And some of them have indeed been rehoused. But the story they tell reveals a reality far from the promises made by the government when the people consented to the destruction of homes they had built themselves. The flats have now been completed. The number of apartments constructed is far short of the original plan – only around 100 or so. The living space in each is 180 square feet, including a bathroom and kitchen area: effectively, a single room. Many of the huts that were demolished occupied 200 square feet or more, and with the addition of an upper storey, their actual space was far more extensive. What happened here with the Prime Minister's Project only illustrates (yet again) what is well known: that the reason the urban poor live in self-build huts is that they cannot afford the price of industrialized housing.

Nijma is living with her four children in a flat on the third floor. The building is constructed around a small, oppressive courtyard. The waste-water drain is already choked with debris and garbage. The staircases have been made of inferior concrete and already, barely one year after completion, they are chipped and cracked.

Nijma's flat is cramped. She has erected a thin partition to separate the kitchen from the main room, the larger part of which is occupied by a large wooden bed. She says, 'The government came and asked us if we would like to own a flat in a tenement. It sounded good. We paid our 5,000 rupees. In the hut where we were staying, we had been paying 20 rupees a month to Bombay Municipal Corporation. Now we are paying 500 a month. We were told the cost of the apartment would be 37,000 rupees. We had to move to a transit camp in Kurla for eighteen months. We didn't mind because we thought we would at last be secure. We stayed there four years. Then the Municipal Corporation came and said the cost of construction was much higher than they had planned and the real cost was 67,000 rupees.

'In the *jopri*, as well as the 20 rupees rent we paid for electricity and water, which came to 40 rupees [$US1.30] a month. Now we have also been asked for a 275 rupees a month assessment tax for the room, as well as the interest charges on the cost of construction. Then there is still water, electricity and maintenance. Only they maintain nothing.'

Nijma's husband is working in Saudi Arabia, and the money he remits has enabled her, so far, to keep up the payments. 'He is working there as a tailor, and sends home enough money. The unfortunate thing is, he cannot afford to come home because he would never earn so much here. Poor people are always cheated. He had to pay 40,000 rupees to an agent for a visa. Sometimes they give a visa for a tailor, then when you arrive in Saudi Arabia you find it is a driver they want, so you have to come home.'

Despite her income from the Gulf, Nijma has just received a notice to quit because of arrears. 'I won't leave. We have already paid 35,000 rupees in costs and interest, which is what they told us would be the total cost. We were cheated by the Housing Development Authority.'

Now in her early thirties, Nijma was born in Dharavi. Her parents came here from Lucknow in Uttar Pradesh. Her father was a *zari* worker, producing beautifully crafted embroidery by hand, borders for sarees. He came to Bombay because the market was here. Nijma's brothers do the same work. It is a skill they observe and absorb as small children. 'Our fingers know the work,' they say poignantly. 'For one saree they will get only 50 rupees, but that same saree will sell in the stores for 2,000 or 3,000 rupees. They have no capital, so they are trapped into working for other people who never pay them the value of their labour.'

Many occupants of the flats have actually rented out their property for commercial purposes. Some flats on the ground floor are now garment-making enterprises: ten or fifteen people are bent over sewing machines – that ubiquitous emblematic image of contemporary South Asia. The owners have gone back to live in the slum. 'This is how the poor are removed. They are promised housing which they cannot afford, so they will vacate it and go somewhere else. It looks more humane than simply evicting them, but it comes to the same thing in the end. The Prime Minister's Grand Project never really came to any-thing. People who need the apartments cannot afford to live in them. Most are daily wage earners, and most of their income goes on food.'

Adjacent to the new block, a man is making shoes on the threshold of his small hut. He manufactures the whole article, gumming and stitching it on his last. These are men's fashion shoes, pointed, with an ornamental metal cap at the toe. The wholesaler brings him the raw material. The shoemaker gets Rs8 (25 US cents) for each shoe, and makes a dozen pairs in two days, earning Rs96 a day ($US3). He works from early morning until the light fades. The shoes are sold in the mar-ket for Rs200–250 a pair. The main profit is taken by those who control the materials and by those who promote and market the finished goods. He says, 'The closer you come to the person who does the hardest, most skilled and the longest hours of work, the less he gets.'

Dharavi is a major centre for garment manufacture. Most of the workshops are small-scale enterprises, with between ten and twenty-five workers. Some sell in the domestic market, some for export. Conditions are overcrowded, hot and dusty, and unlike most of the garments indus-try in Asia the factories employ more men than women. In one unit, cream-coloured shirts with thin blue stripes are being made. On the concrete floor just inside the cement building, three young women work. They are trimming and cutting threads and sewing buttons on the finished shirts. They earn Rs650 a month (80 US cents a day). A seven-teen-year-old says she is working to help increase the family income; her companion is twelve; although her father works on the railways, he is a drinker and her income is essential for the family's survival.

The master cutter of the material for the shirts is a young man, perhaps in his mid-twenties. His is the most skilled work, and he commands Rs3,000 a month ($US100). A steep metal ladder in one corner of the room leads to an upper storey. This is a low, cramped room, where ten or twelve men sit at sewing machines, each doing piecework. Here the activity is intense and without pause: the machines whirr as the men pass collars, cuffs, hems, beneath the darting needle. Those working on hems and cuffs get Rs1.75 for each shirt, the collar-makers Rs2.60, the makers of the body of the shirt Rs3.50, the sleeve-makers Rs2. The total labour for each shirt is less than Rs15, excluding the labour of the cutter. The men earn on average Rs80 a day, for about twelve hours' work.

In a far smaller tin shed, five or six Muslim boys are doing embroidery work, decorating the borders of sarees of orange, lilac, and green material. The area to be embroidered is held taut over a small wooden hoop around which their fingers move like dark birds, swooping first above and then beneath the wooden frame, as the design of peacock, or lotus or abstract pattern of thread and coloured sequins and beads appears, as though conjured out of their darting fingers. The families of these young men – aged between about thirteen and seventeen – come from Uttar Pradesh. Each earns between Rs70 and Rs75 a day.

Abdul Hamid owns a small factory where garments are made for export: these are traditionally designed loose pants and pyjama tops of rayon crepe de Chine, sheer and cool, mainly for markets in the Gulf, the United States, Germany and Japan. Abdul himself is a job worker, has no export licence, and subcontracts to the exporter. Here, the cloth is cut, stitched and pressed, before being returned to the parent company. Even the threads and buttons are supplied by the exporter. Abdul's profit margin is very narrow; at times he is scarcely better off than his workers.

When I visited the factory, in October 1994, the volume of work had decreased dramatically because of the scare about the plague in India. Orders had been cancelled from the Gulf, while the United States had banned the import of the garments for a different reason: they had been declared a fire hazard, although, says Abdul Hamid, there has been no known case of anyone suffering any injury from the effects of any such garment catching fire.

The subcontracting process is of great advantage to the exporters, who buy the cloth and material in response to the orders they get: if they had to find the space to make the goods themselves, it would cost millions of rupees in rent. The exporters have no responsibility for the workers, they are not concerned about the rate of pay, conditions of work, accidents; they have no worry about bonuses, medical care or provident funds. The existence of established small-scale factories, often paying low rents or none because the buildings belong to the employers, makes for ferocious competition. And the presence in Dharavi of thousands of workers depresses wages to the level of the barest subsistence. All the workers in Abdul Hamid's unit come from his own village. He collects young men whenever he returns to his home, and brings them to the factory building. If they have work in the village, it is as daily wage labourers for a mere Rs20 a day (66 US cents). Here, they earn up to Rs60 a day. 'When a boy comes here to learn the work, he must pay for six months or one year 400 or 500 rupees. Then, when he knows the work, he can earn between 40 and 60 rupees a day.'

When business is good, there are twenty to twenty-five young men working here. With the impact on business of the plague, there are now only a dozen. 'What is this plague?' asks Abdul Hamid. 'Plague is there, all over the world. Only when it happens in India is it news.' Abdul Hamid comes from near Lucknow, and started business in Dharavi thirteen years ago. His profit is around Rs10,000 a month, well below a middle-class salary in Bombay. This is why the workers are from his village: there is no sense that they are being exploited by him. Quite the reverse: they are thankful that he supplies them with the means to send some money home to their families.

The workshop here is also upstairs, a long crowded room suffocatingly hot beneath a metal roof. The sewing machines are close together, with only benches between them, and no support for the worker's back. Here, up to twenty young men must live, work and sleep. Some sleep on the benches, others on the sewing-machine tables themselves. They work between twelve and fourteen hours a day, which earns them about Rs80 a day (a little under $US3). On Sundays they are free, but they are not paid. Sometimes they go to see a Hindi movie, or to the sea; sometimes they simply sleep. They are cheerful in spite of the living conditions, the offcuts of rayon on the floor, the cotton dust everywhere, the oppressive proximity. No, they say, we do not have quarrels or fights, we are all brothers. *Kya karna?* Zamal Uddin is the youngest at twenty. His family are proud of him because he has come to the city and can send money home. This, for poor country people, represents success beyond anything they have ever anticipated.

Meals are provided for the men by Abdul Rehman, who comes from Bihar. He rents a room from a neighbouring hut and has turned it into a kind of canteen, where every day he prepares rice, *dal*, vegetables and chappatis for between fifty and sixty workers in the neighbourhood. Mealtimes are usually 1 p.m. and 9, the latter sometimes coinciding with the end of the day's work. On a slow-burning *chulha*, or stove, Abdul Rehman has big metal tubs, which he will deliver to the workplaces at lunch time. Each worker pays Rs100 for two meals a day for a week. Because he can buy in large quantities in the market, Abdul Rehman is able to make a reasonable living and to send money home to his wife and children in Bihar.

One of the most touching workplaces is another small factory unit, where leather pouches are being made, 'for other people's money', as one of the young workers says. Here about fifteen young men work, live, sleep, bathe, eat in a single room. All are from Bihar; the youngest is a boy of twelve, the oldest perhaps in his mid-twenties. The skilled workers earn up to Rs1,700 a month, the boys under training Rs900 ($US60 and $US30). The leather pouches are partly stitched by machine, partly made by hand and glued, and the zips and buckles are added by hand. The workers earn Rs55 for each one. These will sell for Rs100–125 in the local market, for Rs250 in more fashionable districts like Bandra, and up to Rs700 in the boutiques in the Taj or Oberoi hotels.

The workshop has no windows, and although the door stands open and the air is kept moving by a plastic ceiling fan, it is pervaded by the feral smell of leather and faintly rancid masculinity. It is without ornament. The paint is flaking from the brick walls. At one end of the shop there is a waist-high wall, behind which a brass tap and waste-water hole in the concrete provide the bathing facilities. From nails driven into the wall hangs the clothing of the young men: some shirts, a change of trousers. Their suitcases, battered tin and plastic, stand on a shelf above the place where they work, evocative of home, the last contact with the loving hands of women – mothers, wives, sisters, whom they see only once a year. It is a horrible, claustrophobic place of confinement, where their youth is imprisoned and all their need for tenderness and relaxation is denied. Yet they smile, a smile of acceptance and thankfulness that they are not like the boys who must sleep on the footpath at the mercy of police and gangs, and not like the exhausted starvelings of the Bihar countryside, their underemployed and hungry brothers.

'All India is in Dharavi,' says Raju Korde. And indeed the local communities do indeed reconstitute a disorganized map of India: a Tamil community with its own school and small Tamil restaurants selling *uttapam* and *dhosas*, an area of Muslims from Uttar Pradesh with their embroidery shops, a group of people from Kerala, workshops and factories consisting entirely of people from Bihar, shops where the signs are only in Oriya or Gujarati, a Telugu-speaking enclave, a colony of Thor leather workers and, of course, many communities of Maharashtrans, often living together according to their place of origin – Ratnagiri, Vidarbha, Nasik.

One of the most conspicuous communities is in Kumbarwadi: potters, originally from Saurashtra in Gujarat, whose pots, jugs, oil lamps, dishes and urns are displayed along the 90-foot Road. As it is close to Divali, business is brisk, particularly for the little earthen oil lamps which are lighted outside people's homes; that means particularly in poorer households, because the better-off have deserted the traditional lamps for multicoloured electric lights.

Behind the displays of pottery are the small, narrow shops of the *kumbars,* above them the living quarters. Many have been here for three generations, and some are now very prosperous. But passing through the buildings with their stores of raw materials – still mainly clay brought in trucks from Saurashtra – the scene is transformed. Here are the traditional *bhattis,* or kilns, structures two metres high, where the pots are fired These are packed with slow-burning fuel, from which a constant stream of acrid, choking smoke swirls – yet another image reminiscent of the early industrial period in Britain, this time from around the Staffordshire potteries. The buildings where the finished articles, as well as the clay, are stored, are ragged tin structures blackened by dust and soot from the kilns. Men, women and children carry fresh loads of fuel from the godowns to the kilns. Inside, the potters are shaping the articles by hand in the traditional manner. The smoke stings the eyes and damages the lungs of the people, darkening the sky and altering the sunlight. Few true potters live beyond the age of forty-five.

Nathalal Chauhan is a member of a particularly successful *kumbar* family. His grandfather came here about seventy years ago. At that time, he says, this piece of land was still jungle. There were no buildings, and you could see Bandra station on one side, and the marshy waters of the creek were still open.

Until about ten years ago, the potters were not particularly prosperous. The principal articles they made, apart from seasonal Divali lanterns, were drinking water containers: the characteristic earthen pots, and the more sophisticated jars, to the base of which taps are added. Since Nathalal and his brother have come into the business, they have seen the demand for a much wider range of pots and ornaments. They now design and create their own. He shows a catalogue of objects and artefacts designed by his brother: vessels into the neck of which are worked the forms and faces of animals, gods and humans; multicoloured glazed containers for flowers, sweets, fruit; *objets d'art,* many of which have been exhibited all over the world. 'Previously', he says, 'the middlemen never allowed the skilled people to enter the market. They simply bought the goods at prices they fixed among themselves, and the potters had no access to any other outlet. Now we have changed that. We have been well educated and trained in potteries. I studied at the Bangalore Centre for Traditional Crafts. My brother's designs have been shown in Japan at the world fair. Much of what we make now goes for export, to the Gulf and to the USA. We use a mixture of materials now; some silica and china clay is added to the original Saurashtra clay.'

Nathalal has also modified the traditional *bhatti*, which stands at the back of his house, so that it is less polluting. He uses wood as fuel but the walls of the *bhatti* are of iron sheets, and the doors are lined with mineral wool, which can heat to 2,000°C without igniting. This contains the smoke within the *bhatti*. Inside the shed where the potters are working, a middle-aged man is deftly applying clay to the shape that emerges beneath his touch. He is being watched by a young boy of about six. 'The children need no training. They know it from instinct and observation. There is no need for formal instruction. They go to school, of course, but when they are ready they will start to make Divali lanterns or water vessels.'

The *kumbars* all suffer from respiratory disorders, and accept their reduced life expectancy. 'If we stop doing this, what else will we do?' The use of chimneys helps to disperse the smoke, but few can afford the modified *bhattis* of Nathalal. All kinds of fuel are used: cotton, plastic waste, old clothes, coconut shells, much of which aggravates the damaging effect of the smoke.

Dharavi II

Mike Douglass, writing in *Environment and Urbanization* (October 1992), argues that governments have for the most part failed to reverse the deterioration in the urban environment of cities in the Third World.

> More than just remaining unaccountable to the poor, governments also work to deny the legitimacy of political associations emerging from civil society, and are thus actively involved in the disempowerment of the poor and in attempts to undermine political community outside of the state.

The usual response to this by academics and observers is to advocate 'participation', 'empowerment', 'autonomy', 'devolution of control'. This, however, runs counter to the dynamic of economic imperatives become global – growing centralization, and integration into the world market – and counter to the effects of reduced government spending, that is, the reduction of government intervention on behalf of the poor.

If the problems created by urbanization are not going to be resolved by governments, particularly when these are the willing agents of an unjust global system, is it possible they can be dealt with at community level, by the poorest and most dispossessed? Certainly the people have a clear view of the issues. Douglass states that 'the question to be addressed is not how to slow down the migration of the poor to the city but how to integrate them into urban life in a more equitable manner.' The point is that it was inequity that dispossessed them of their rural security in the first place; the system that drove them to the city is unlikely to be more merciful in accommodating them there. And it isn't.

Certainly the government does little enough for the people of Dharavi. No college serves the slum, and only primary schooling is publicly provided. When I was there, on most days the government health post was unattended. Bhav Korde says, 'Government workers are secure, so they see no reason why they should perform the labour they are paid for. The only question they ask is, "You retire when?" There is no check on the quality of their work, or their competence. The health post is empty; do you think this is because there is no sickness in Dharavi? Dharavi suffers most of almost anything you can think of. The government employees' unions are strong, you cannot remove a lazy or negligent worker. Think of those children working twelve hours a day in the leather and garment factories, and the absentee workers here, and ask if government is going to set about achieving social justice.'

Much popular organization is linked to and supported by networks of professionals, nongovernmental organizations and social activists outside the slums. Some even come as exploiters and are so profoundly affected by their experience that they become committed to those from whose misery they intended to make their living.

Dr Khan established his surgery in Dharavi seven years ago. He provides free medical services to those who cannot pay. A homeopathic practitioner now studying law so that he will be able to help people gain redress against negligent and exploitative doctors, he came here as a private doctor, like so many others. 'But there was one incident that made a strong impression. I had been here two years. A young girl of twelve came and said her father had tried to rape her. He was a drunkard – after drinking he always tried to abuse her. She was crying, asking me for help. What to do? At that time, I was young: if I helped a twelve-year-old, people might think anything. I hesitated. I asked people in the community to find a boy close to her age to marry her. Since the father had attacked her, she was sleeping outside. Street boys were coming to torment her, trying to rape her also. I let her sleep on the roof of the dispensary. After one month, a boy was found, a mechanic in a garage, and he offered to marry her.

'This made me see that private practice had no meaning. I began to see the damage done by addiction: when a father cannot recognize his own daughter under the influence of alcohol, there can be no limit to the crimes others might commit in a similar state. This is how we came to start the detoxification centre for alcoholics; we also give counselling. Once people are detoxified, we give homeopathic medicine which directly affects the mind. Many addicts, to drugs and alcohol, are thrown out of the family. So we called family meetings, and explained to them that after treatment the individual requires all the moral, mental, physical and emotional support he or she can get.'

Dharavi is completely without planning. There is no sewerage, there is negligible public lighting, no garbage collections. The crime rate is high, the dropout rate from school after the age of twelve is 80 per cent; and many of the private schools are of little educational value. Many children work, if their parents are strict; if not, they fall prey to petty crime, hanging around the video parlours, paying Rs2 to see movies, a good time-pass. They are unchecked, they start stealing, and eventually become talented criminals. In Dharavi every *gali* (lane) has a *dada* (protector). A boy gets hired by him, recognizes him as boss, and then younger boys look up to him because he has a bigger criminal record. The boys get a reputation: this shopkeeper was beaten and robbed by this young man, and that becomes his reference in the underworld; he is admired. He gets promoted, and is known as a *supari* – a hired killer, who will be paid Rs20,000 or Rs30,000 to get rid of someone. A *supari*, in the old days, was the betel nut that was offered when a deal was concluded, an innocent deal. It is used now in a quite different context.

The present Deputy Commissioner of Police in Dharavi is committed to the eradication of crime. Since the riots of January 1993, a Mohalla Committee has been formed, a peace committee of both Hindus and Muslims, which works with the police. Dharavi is divided into four police beats, each of which has eleven peace committee members, whose job is to help maintain social peace, and to deal with civil issues, to prevent them from becoming police matters: quarrels between and within families, communal disputes that threaten to escalate. Previously, if a husband and wife brought their quarrel to the police, the police would take money from them, wasting their time while more important crimes went unchecked.

The Rashtriya Ekta Samiti recognizes the interlocking factors of deprivation that compel people into a cycle of poverty, exclusion and hopelessness. There is no point in tackling one or two symptoms – child labour, say, or illiteracy – while these remain part of a deeper structural violence. For this reason, the activists are working on many fronts simultaneously.

In many neighbourhoods, women have formed groups against liquor, which remains one of the most debilitating and destructive forces in slum communities. They can call on women who will demonstrate outside liquor dens and drinking houses. They will protest that the community needs schools and hospitals rather than liquor shops. Amina Bie Shamim Khan, one of the leaders of the Women's Anti-Liquor Movement in Dharavi, says: 'We ask the liquor shop owners not to ruin the lives of our children. Then if the shop does not close down, we will close it, and if it is an unauthorized shop we will take the owner to the police and make a complaint.

'Some drinking parlours are legal, some illegal. With the legal ones, the strategy is different. We take a memo to the Chief Minister. According to a new law recently enacted in Maharashtra, if 50 per cent of the women in an area are against a legal liquor shop, and will sign a petition, that shop too can be closed down. We want no liquor shops here, authorized or unauthorized.'

The liquor comes mainly from outside Dharavi, from Kurla and beyond, where there are many places to hide the stills. Two years ago, I went to a slum occupied mainly by leprosy patients, many of them rejected by their families. The only work open to them was the distilling and distribution of *daru*, illicit liquor. No doubt some of this finds its way into Dharavi: victims create more victims; the most despised can make a living only by exploiting other poor people.

Amina estimates that three-quarters of the men drink. Her husband does not, and encourages her campaign. 'Women and men are equal,' she says, 'but when we protest, we feel that we are more courageous. Because of addiction, whether alcohol or brown sugar (a heroin derivative), the ultimate sufferers are the women and children, so we have to be stronger. Women do not drink as men do. For men, drink is a way out of the misery of their lives. Women have none. If a husband is no good, the women will go and work to provide rice and *dal* for their children. Some women even give money to the husband for his drink.'

Amina, born in Dharavi, says that people think that is a stigma, but there are many good people here ready to fight against liquor, poverty and exploitation. Amina's husband is a building contractor. He gathers workers and takes contracts; he is responsible for paying the labourers. Amina did not join the Nashabandi (movement against drink) for selfish or even personal reasons. She saw the lives of many of her neighbours ruined by alcohol, and did not question that it was her duty to do something about it.

Kanni, a sad-faced young woman now living apart from her husband, did suffer from drink. 'He used to drink all the time, and never gave me money. He brought other men to the house, and they demanded money from me.' When Kanni gave birth, it was to a girl. Her husband said, 'That is not my child, that is someone else's.' Kanni left him to stay with her mother. She cannot reason with him when he is drunk. Her daughter is now five, her brother works in a shop making spectacle frames, her father is dead. 'When he was alive, he protected us from my husband's rage. Now my brother has to fight for us. We struggle with all our strength and courage, because we have suffered directly through alcohol. We feel great joy after we have closed down a liquor shop. We have also totally finished a bar and cabaret, the Karishma Bar. We demonstrated outside until they were forced to close it.' Kanni herself is unemployed, seeking work as either a domestic or a garment worker. Until two months ago, she was working in a dressmaking unit, but it closed. Small workshops open for a brief period, subcontractors make money and go. It is not stable, permanent employment; the work as flimsy as many of the garments, items of briefly fashionable wear called into existence by distant markets, whose changing whims will just as quickly finish them.

Mariam Rashid co-ordinates the network of groups that together form the Rashtriya Ekta Samiti. She confirms the overwhelming complaint of Dharavi people that civic amenities, inadequate in all of Bombay, are virtually nonexistent here. 'Everything provided is for the name's sake only. Nothing works properly. There are government-built latrines now in ruins. They were supplied with water and electricity, but this has now stopped because government accused the community of not maintaining them properly. Life gets harder for people as everything ceases to function – roads, drainage, waste water, gutters, toilets – no government money is spent on these things. But the government says, "We have provided you with this, so if it doesn't work, it is your fault." But provided means only on paper. People see only a blank when they look at Dharavi. It is a dark patch in Bombay, a stigma and a nuisance. We appealed for a bus service. The authority said there are bus services, which run on time. On paper, three buses come through Dharavi, but they do not come.

'We are replacing municipal toilets with the help of a company called Sulabh International. We formed nine societies, which have come together to arrange toilet provision through a private project. People are so desperate that they are ready to pay a small sum for the facility. Earlier, people used to carry away the filth and night soil on their heads. Mahatma Gandhi said this was degrading and should stop; out of that work came Sulabh. The toilets are easy to construct and maintain. Central and state governments give a subsidy, Sulabh do the construction. They have worked all over India, and in the cities if people make a small contribution they feel involved in keeping them clean. It took a long time to persuade the people it is worth 10 rupees a month [33 US cents] per family. Nine groups, 3,600 families, have agreed to take part.'

Raju Korde disagrees with private provision of toilets. 'The problem with Dharavi is that there is no government infrastructure. Privatization looks like an improvement, but it is an improvement on nothing. For a time, people will say, "Oh, this is much better." But then Sulabh, a private company, can put up its prices as it chooses. There is no substitute for universal public provision. Because this has not worked in India, does not mean the principle is bad or false.'

Mariam Rashid too has been involved in the anti-liquor movement. Following the riots in Bombay provoked by the destruction of the mosque at Ayodhya, further quarrels and disturbances broke out, mainly as a result of drink. 'It is difficult to get women to go against their husbands. We started with a group of forty. We targeted the Karishma Bar, where there was dancing and prostitution as well as liquor, and that was closed. We went to houses selling liquor, and found in many cases women were doing the selling. Because their husbands were not working, or to pay for their children's education, they were doing this business. We could not tell them to abandon their only means of livelihood. But some have now found alternative forms of employment, even if it is only cutting threads at 10 paise a piece.'

It is impossible to exaggerate the hardships of women. Ramina is a domestic worker in an apartment in Sion. Her first job is to bring water for the use of her husband and five children. The water comes only in the early hours (the municipal water supply is erratic), so she must be up before five. By seven the children must be up and ready for school. She makes breakfast for her husband, who works in a cycle repair shop, makes tiffin for him and the children. Ramina works in two houses, cleaning vessels, and washing floors, two hours daily in each. From each she earns Rs140 a month (less than $US5). She comes home, cleans and washes, makes and mends clothes for the family, and goes to the market to get food for the evening meal.

Many other women work at home, sewing beads on sarees, making *bidis, rakhi, bindis, papad, agarbatti.* Some collect garbage, wash old plastic in acid, which destroys their hands. Others work in soap factories or dyeing clothes. Homeworkers are often helped by their children. Many women are anaemic, children suffer a deficiency of Vitamin D, lack folic acid which is essential for building the body. Children eat only chappatis in the morning, *dal* and rice at night, small amounts of protein. Some children have never tasted fruit, not even bananas, which are the cheapest. 'There is a government nutrition programme,' says Mariam. 'They used to provide bread with vitamins and protein added, but it was often very bad, adulterated with *kachera* [dirt] and all kinds of things. We once found a cockroach in some bread, and we took out a *morcha* [a demonstration] to protest. The children will not eat it. Now they give cereals, *channa* and green peas. But corruption is there, between the supplier and the purchaser who works for the nutrition programme; the percentage of corruption is reflected in the quality of the food. Sometimes, of one kilo of *channa*, you must throw away half of it, because it is inedible. We are now feeding 500 children through our own scheme, with the Society for Human and Environmental Development, SHED.

'People live crowded together, but neighbourhood is our survival. If anything happens to someone, a hundred people will come running. We want a better environment, but we do not want to be placed in apartment blocks.' Crowded public spaces in the slums are to some extent a safeguard against abuse and violence. 'If I have a fight with someone in the morning, and in the evening he is ill, I will go to him. If Dharavi is to be reconstructed, it should be on the *chawl* system [single- or two-storey row houses], not apartment blocks. Here, abused and neglected children are taken in, the poor offer food to the hungry. If a rape happens, the news will come out. In apartment blocks, people close their doors and no one knows what happens behind them.'

We visit Raju Korde's house, a neat, well-maintained place in the heart of Dharavi. It has a tiled floor, fan and TV; there is an upper storey, so that the total space is over 400 square feet, more than twice the size of the apartments in the Prime Minister's Grand Project, which, says Raju, ate up crores of rupees to so little effect. Raju lives with his parents. They have taken in a young boy from Tamil Nadu. This child, Kannan, was brought from Madras by his grandfather two years ago when he was ten. He was placed in a 'hotel' – a small tea-and-snack shop – where he was employed and given lodging. He broke something, was thrown out, and had nowhere to stay. He was begging on the road for several days before Raju found him and brought him to his house. Now Kannan works: he takes Rs100-worth of material for snacks – *chikki* with *gur* (peanuts baked with molasses) and potato snacks. He fills little plastic bags with the food, seals the packets, and takes them to sell on Sion station. He can make Rs50–100 every day. Since the worry about the plague, he has sold less. Because business is slack, he has begun to buy books and sell these instead. He must give 10 per cent of what he earns to the police; if he doesn't, they will confiscate his goods. He used to send money home, but he no longer does so. His *chacha* (grandfather) who brought him here disappeared; since then, he has had no contact with his family. They are landless labourers. Raju says that if Kannan is always smiling, 'this is because he has nowhere to shed his tears'. He adds, 'We have found seventy boys since then, but we do not yet have a place for them to stay. That is our next effort.'

*

Chamrabazar is an industrial area of Dharavi with many long-established businesses; people who have been here thirty years or more. One of these is Ali Ahmed, who came in 1968 and whose work-shop repairs and restores metal oil drums and containers for chemicals. In Dharavi all material things are mended and reused, recycled, turned to some other use.

'When I came here,' Ali Ahmed says, 'from this spot you could see Bandra and Kurla stations, King's Circle and Matunga. You could even see the airport. No one owned the land, no one wanted it. We were farmers in Uttar Pradesh, but we came to Bombay because it was a growing port and many new factories were coming up. Male mem-bers of the family came first, and when they found they could earn their bread and butter, they settled and called their families. Most people had land, but they thought they would have a better life here. When I first came I broke stones for the road, but I soon saw the chance to repair drums used for oil and chemicals.'

Ali Ahmed is an active member of the Rashtriya Ekta Samiti. We sit in his small office; metal chairs around a big table with a plastic mar-ble top; a clock, some calendars on the peeling walls. In the godown behind, men are hammering and flattening metal, welding and beat-ing drums into shape. Ali Ahmed says, 'The administration and the elected representatives of the Bombay Municipal Corporation do not function properly, and that is why Dharavi remains dirty, undisciplined and unplanned. If planning had followed government instructions, there would have been land for gardens, hospitals, schools. If the municipal corporation cannot do it, we shall do it ourselves. We made our houses, we can make our city; Dharavi should be made by Dharavians only. Because of negligence by all sections of the adminis-tration, people have not been given sufficient opportunities.

'There is plenty of work in Dharavi. Nowhere do you see anyone sit-ting and looking at the sky. If the energy of the people is properly channelled, there need be no one without work. The elected repre-sentatives eat money that is given by government for a slum project. They put forward a scheme, get the money, and then divert it to their own purposes. Corruption is there in the administration, to the extent that if the government sanctions a loan of Rs10,000 to a poor man to start some small enterprise, he will have to bribe the authorities with Rs2,000 to get it. After getting the Rs8,000, he will have to pay for a licence, for water facilities, for electricity and other factors necessary for running a business. It will be impossible for him to start.

'I have been here many years, but I have no licence because I refuse to pay bribes. I have to pay the court often, because they charge me with having no licence. I say Why should I pay a bribe to get what is lawfully mine? This is the story of many Dharavians. So I pay a fine of Rsl,000 every month. I have a good business. Once a year, fifteen to twenty days, I go back to my village. I employ twenty, twenty-five people here. Business has gone down since the riots. I am a secular man, and have always worked for communal harmony. At the time of the riots, in January 1993, although I was sick, I moved on the roads to help create peace. Hindus and Muslims in Dharavi have more to unite than to divide them.

'Much remains to be done here. If someone is dying, or very ill, you cannot get any public vehicle to help them, there is no means of transportation. You must either walk, or get a private vehicle. This area is designated part of Bombay city, even though Dharavi gets none of the amenities you associate with the city. With no college here, how can the citizens of Bombay be expected to participate, to understand the issues that affect their lives? On plots reserved for schools, encroachments have taken place, new private buildings have come up. The elected representatives have sold plots privately to desperate people who come to the city. During the riots some of our representatives were actively supporting the antisocial elements and communalists. And now we have government by communalists.'

A frail, elderly man, Abul Baqqa, joins us. His business has been here since 1962, part of which is the manufacture of suture and surgical thread materials. His output has been used in operations in hospitals all over the world. He is one of the first victims of the new GATT agreement, now incorporated into the World Trade Organization (WTO). His surgical threads have now been banned on the grounds that the conditions in which they are produced do not meet the rigorous standards of hygiene required.

What makes this even more unjust is the fact that almost next door to his factory, and also in Dharavi, is a unit belonging to the multinational Johnson & Johnson, making an identical product. Of course the Johnson & Johnson factory is in a cream-painted building surrounded by ashoka trees and barbed wire, while Abul Baqqa's factory is an ordinary, though scrupulously clean, concrete building. 'Since the plague, foreign countries have refused to take our goods. The European countries say that according to the GATT, a 50 per cent improvement must be made as far as hygiene is concerned. They say when Dharavi is clean and hygienic, then only will they take material from here. But Johnson & Johnson is in the same area. Maybe the people in Europe and Japan do not know where their material is made.'

Before the GATT agreement, all Abul Baqqa's output from his Ideal Threading Company was exported. No issue of hygiene or of unsatisfactory standards was ever raised. This, he believes, is a non-tariff barrier, which the West uses freely but will not permit the South to use. 'When they want to sell us their cigarettes,' he points out, 'we may not object that this is injurious to our people's health – that is a barrier to free trade. The real purpose of the GATT and WTO can be seen here. It is to strengthen the monopoly of the transnational companies. Many businesses like mine will suffer, in food, medicine and pharmaceuticals especially.

'We have made representations to the ministry. Twice visits have been made from the central ministry, who say they have set important landmarks for export products. If we fulfil certain norms, we'll get an export registration number and we'll be allowed further trading for exports. But then, even if the Indian government gives us clearance, other governments in Europe or Japan may not accept.'

On the day we visited, an item in the *Times of India* quoted the Union Minister of State for Small-Scale, Agro and Rural Industries as saying that small and tiny industries would not be affected by the liberalization policy of the government. Mr Baqqa is incensed by the double standards employed, both by government and the Western powers. He says it is like the return of the East India Company, yet this time GATT and the WTO have been agreed to by the sovereign government of India itself. 'When the East India Company came they folded hands with our rulers and said, "We shall come for trading only," and soon they had taken over our whole country. Now we are folding hands with their heirs, who are saying the same thing, that they only want to trade with us.

'Because of this our livelihood is suffering. I had sixty or sixty-five workers here. Now I am still paying their salary, but there is no work for them. Johnson & Johnson have control of the local market in India, so what chance do we have, even in our own country? During the riots, business went down; after the bomb blasts we suffered also, because some of our workers ran away; even the plague has hurt us. But it is GATT and the WTO that are bringing us to ruin.'

We visit the factory building; at the top of a steep flight of polished stone steps a container in a shallow stone trench disinfects the feet of all who enter the unit. Inside are the supervisor and two women workers. The metal benches at which the thread is made are clean, but quite empty. There is no activity at all. 'Indigenous industry is being extinguished. And for what? To further the interests of transnational monopolies.'

The Rashtriya Ekta Samiti was formed at the time of the riots in December 1992 and January 1993. Its work is based on an understanding that the poor have more to unite than to divide them along caste and communal lines. To carry this idea further, its members have initiated a number of campaigns to enhance the sense of solidarity among the poorest people, those who always suffer most, whether from riots, sickness, plague, oppression or corruption.

'Many people must take loans, especially when their work is disrupted or they become unemployed. Moneylenders in Dharavi charge ten to fifteen per cent interest per month,' says Bhav Korde, 'and that is compounded. People have a photo pass, which is the only evidence they have that the hut where they stay is theirs. If the moneylender gives a loan of say a thousand rupees, he will take the photo pass as security. After two or three years, with the interest compounded, the owner of the hut will never be in a position to repay, so the moneylender takes the house instead.

'After the chaos of the riots, people came together from different secularist organizations in Dharavi and discovered that the real problems went deeper. During that period, much household labour, home-based workers, cottage industries, could not pursue their labour. Many people fled, Muslims to stay with Muslims, Hindus with Hindus. For rehabilitation, we asked for help, and we received six *lakhs* of rupees [600,000 rupees – about $US18,000] in donations from people who came forward. We promised that the people to whom we made loans would return the money in instalments in due course, although the donors never asked for interest. So far, sixty to seventy thousand rupees have been repaid. We have offered this money back to those who gave, but they have said, "Keep it and use it as you think best for the improvement of people's lives." With this, we have started a co-operative bank. We approached the government authorities, and sanction was given, so we can give loans at a rate of eighteen per cent per annum. This will help small businesses, hawkers and women vendors. They need money on a daily basis. At present, they are taking loans from lenders of 250 rupees a month, 25 rupees a day interest, so that at the end of twenty-five days, they have to repay 625 rupees in interest. They do it, and somehow they survive, but there is no facility for them to get money from any government agency or established bank. We are starting according to the principles of the Grameen Bank [a mainly rural credit bank whose repayment rates on loans to poor farmers and artisans is spectacularly high] in Bangladesh.

'The next thing was the question of the ration card, to which all people are entitled. We found people paying five hundred to one thousand rupees just to get the card, for which they should give only five. The Public Distribution System began in 1966, after drought and famine in India. It was designed to provide subsidized necessities to the people. It used to supply a certain quantity per person of wheat, rice, *dal, bajra, maida* [wheat flour], tea powder, janata cloth, oil, kerosene, all at a price which even the poorest were supposed to be able to afford. Now over the years, that has been eroded, and now only rice, wheat, sugar, oil and kerosene are provided.

'Under the government's liberalization policy, it has been prompted by the World Bank and IMF to cut spending, including food subsidies. So the government itself is now undermining the PDS. Rice is now Rs7.90 a kilo on the ration card and Rs8 in the open market. People, instead of standing in line for the sake of 10 paise, are now buying in the market. The government then says this is proof that the people do not want the PDS, so it can be stopped.

'The government says, "We have given a higher price to the farmer, and this is why the price has increased, to pay higher wages to the landless labourer." This is not true. Who is selling rice to the government? Not the small farmers, but the big rich farmers.

'Sugar is Rs9.05 on the ration card, Rs16 in the market. Each person is allowed 450 grams. Now tea, with sugar and bread, is the poor person's breakfast. 450 grams is not enough. Often you cannot collect it because it has been sold off to private traders. For six weeks there was no sugar in the PDS. The price rose to Rs16 a kilogram. Sugar was lying in the port of Bombay to drive up the price.

'All welfare schemes are now being cut; education grants have been reduced, which excludes children of poor families. Private schools in Dharavi are charging Rs200 a month. Mothers will sell their *mangal sutra,* their wedding jewellery, to pay for education for their children. Twenty years ago it was possible for poor kids to get into engineering or medical schools through subsidies. Now that is stopped. There was a scheme for children of Scheduled Castes to get into college after matriculation. Now they have to get a 60 per cent pass mark to qualify. The SC children do not stand a chance – most are working, they cannot achieve so high. And if they do get it, the amount is so low – only Rs100 a year. Poor children must walk five or six kilometres to schools, they must work in fields or factories after school, how can they get such marks? Eighty per cent of the people in Dharavi are SCs or Muslims. Because Mahim and Sion were upper-caste areas, the SCs came here: *thors* who process leather, *mahars* who do tanning, *chamars* who make leather goods.

'The people have made Dharavi. They brought mud and sand and stones and filled up the marsh, raised it above flood level. They built their houses. After thirty years, this place has been made by the work of the poor, not by government. Our government now wants to create a second Hong Kong. They say Dharavi is the biggest, dirtiest slum, it must now shift to make way for this new Hong Kong. In Dharavi now, a hut costs one lakh. The government has promised to pay even more, and to give us nice houses outside Bombay. That is a big challenge to people whose livelihood is here. What good is one or two lakh? It will soon be eaten up if they are moved away and have no alternative employment. People get a sum of money, think they are rich. After two years they are poor again, and go back to stay in a hut. The Prime Minister's Grand Project is the best example of what will happen.'

Rangalal is a painter of portraits, signs, advertisements. He lives in a hut on the edge of the slum, less than 10 metres from where the Western Railway commuter trains thunder past, day and night. He has been one of the principal activists in obtaining ration cards for the people. We sit with him in a little clearing behind his hut. There, three metal towers carry high-tension wires. These wires are only about 14 feet from the ground, scarcely higher than some of the roofs. A red danger sign bearing a skull and crossbones emblem warns the people. Recently a boy standing on a roof accidentally touched the high-tension cables with a stick. He and two companions were killed. 'If we go for compensation, we file against the Bombay Electricity Supply & Transport Company. Tata, who supply electricity to BEST, had stated in writing that if there were any accident, they would accept no responsibility. BEST gives electricity to the people on the understanding that if there is any accident, they also accept no responsibility. After the death of the three boys, BEST threatened to disconnect the supply if anyone went to court. So there is no compensation for the death of three children. The height of the houses should be ten to eleven feet. Some have now gone to sixteen feet or more, and too close to the high-tension wires. They are allowed to do so by paying a bribe of 5,000 rupees to the Bombay Municipal Corporation.'

Rangalal says, 'The ration card struggle was important because a ration card is proof that you stay here. This gives people some security. That and a photo pass. People think that if the area is redeveloped and they are evicted, at least they have proof of residence here, and therefore they may get alternative accommodation if demolition takes place. That is why people had deemed it worthwhile to run after officials and pay even five or eight hundred rupees to get the card. It is a kind of insurance.

'That is a separate issue from food entitlement, but we are working on that also. The ration shop gets grains from the central godown. The godown gives a sample in a gunny bag, rice or wheat. The sample is sealed. The ration shop owner keeps this small sample for display, and this is the quality he is supposed to provide for the people. But what he actually gives is adulterated. We found women who were domestic workers in a neighbouring rich housing colony; they were given the ration card supply by their employers and it was high-quality rice, quite different from anything we were getting in Dharavi. We asked, "If it is available there, why is it not available here?" We found that government is giving the same material, but the worst quality comes here because they take out some of the rice and replace it with *kachera* and stones. The government says there may be 10 grams waste per kilo. We found 100 grams, 200: stones and glass. Naturally women will go and buy in the market. That is how the PDS is undermined.'

Rangalal's house has a small trellis with a creeper to screen it from the trains and the glare of the afternoon sun. Inside, it is hot. Keeping it clean against the dust from the trains is a full-time job.

There are brass and steel vessels in the kitchen, bedrolls and covers, folding tin chairs in the living area. He has painted the brick walls and corrugated metal partition white, with a pink and green frieze.

'We have begun to fight against corruption. Now the officials who were browbeating the people are asking for transfers out of Dharavi. Officials pay money to their superiors to be marked present, and then they do not come to their duties. See, now it is Divali the corporation is paying bonuses, so no one is here. They are sitting in queue, playing cards, as well as drawing their salary of at least three thousand rupees.'

From his painting Rangalal earns Rs50–100. He is a talented man; he paints holy pictures and portraits as well as commercial signs. 'His ability is not properly used,' says Bhav Korde, 'like that of most people in Dharavi. It is the society that loses, it is the nation that suffers through this terrible neglect of humanity in Dharavi and the slums.'

We cross the railway line by the bridge. Two or three people die each month on the railway line here. In the whole of Bombay seven hundred die on the railways each year. Beneath us we can see a dark grey muddy pool, a kind of ditch, right on the edge of the railway line. This expanse of water is bounded by heaps of garbage and kept from spilling onto the railway by some rough concrete steps; the water is thick, viscous: so polluted it seems almost solid. This is the waste water from the houses of the rich colony on the other side of the railway. In the filthy water, women are standing waist-high, washing clothes. They beat the garments with great energy against the stone steps, which have been worn smooth by countless beatings. The slap of the clothes on the stone, the turbid wavelets made by the women as they move, while all around them, small children bathe among the decaying vegetable matter, rusty metal, old boxes, ancient shoes, plastic bags and shit – the scene is cruelly reminiscent of women at a village river bank, an ugly caricature, since the only water available is that discarded by privilege.

Bhav Korde stands in the middle of the railway bridge. He points to the women labouring in the filth below, 'This is India,' he says, and then, indicating the apartments of Sion, with their screen of palms and trees, 'And this is also India.'

5

People of the City I

The Exile, Bangkok

I met Henry on the way to Bangkok, where he goes at least twice a year to see what he calls his 'Thai wife'. What he didn't say in the beginning was that he also has an English wife, who stays at home in their little house in south London. For the past five years Henry has regularly spent six or eight weeks a year in Bangkok in pursuit of his mildly polygamous life.

Henry is in his mid-sixties, corpulent, with grey-white hair and pale-blue eyes. He wears smart cream-coloured trousers, a blue shirt and casual white shoes. This is, as it were, the uniform of infidelity, for he dresses far more conservatively at home. He worked for over twenty years in southeast London as an engineer with a multinational company that made machinery for cigarette manufacture. He was made redundant ten years ago when the company shifted its operations, significantly, to the Third World; Henry has made the same journey in its wake, even though in pursuit of different satisfactions. In many ways Henry exemplifies the relationship between the Western working class and its equivalent in the South.

In 1983 he received a severance gratuity, which pays for his twice-yearly trips to Thailand. 'They were good employers,' he says. 'They used to provide a turkey at Christmas for every employee, and Havana cigars.' Whether this act of charity is now extended to the employees in its present location may be doubted.

Henry's wife – his English wife – is not keen on vacations and does not care to accompany him to Thailand. She doesn't like leaving home, and she knows nothing of the existence of the Thai wife. 'I'm not taking anything away from my wife,' he says. 'When I married her I gave up a lot of things for her sake. I had to sacrifice my love of opera and ballet, because she couldn't stand the music. For thirty years I behaved myself. Even now I wouldn't fool around on my own doorstep. I suppose I'm still puritanical at heart. But I've made sure that if I die my wife will be all right; the bank balance is sound. While my daughter was young and I was working, I never looked at another woman. I kept on the straight and narrow until I was sixty, and surely that's long enough for anybody.

'The first time I went to Thailand, it was just for a holiday. My daughter had been, and she suggested it. I met Pia in a bar. She was wiping the glasses at the back of the bar. She was thirty-six then, and considered to be an old lady: too old to satisfy the punters who come to Thailand for the young girls. Their working life is finished by the age of thirty. So in a way I rescued her. And now she looks after me. She can't do enough for me. That's the way Thai women are. They feel good if they have someone to look after. Put it like this: when you go into the bathroom in the morning, you find the toothpaste already squeezed onto the brush waiting for you. I call that caring. The women in Thailand have something that Western women don't have.

'It's taken years off me, meeting Pia. I've some money in my account which my wife doesn't know about. I feel I've earned it, and now I deserve a bit of life. Of course, when I go home I feel a pang of conscience – I might decorate a room or dig the garden.

'My wife doesn't like me going off on my own. But she doesn't know how to enjoy herself. She has her own friends. They go to the shops, visit the supermarket, hunt for bargains. If they come back with some cardigan or hat they got a bit cheap, you'd think it was a trophy of war. That's their life, and they're welcome to it. But for me there has to be something more, or what's the point? To have lived and died, done nothing, gone nowhere: that isn't a life, it's an existence.

'I need to get away. There was an old couple near where we live. Darby and Joan everybody called them. One day the woman met my wife in the street. She told her she hated the sight of him. Why don't you leave him? she said. "Oh I couldn't leave him. I could murder him, but I couldn't leave him."

'It's wrong to live in one another's pockets. Put it like this. I'd never leave my wife, but if anything happened to her I'd come and live in Thailand tomorrow. In Thailand you meet a lot of ex-pats, people who've packed up and left. There's a cop I know from Brooklyn; he's been shot three times on duty. He came to Thailand because it's peaceful. It's safe. You can walk the streets without fear of being mugged. There was one fellow from Liverpool I knew, his wife had left him. He came to Thailand to spend his last few years. As a matter of fact he died there. His Thai wife looked after him till the end.

'Britain has lost a lot. I wouldn't want to be young in our country now. We've seen our best years. Where we live, there's too many blacks. It's like living in a foreign country. You're always looking over your shoulder to see who's following you, who's going to threaten you, pull a knife, rob you of what you've got. The wife would like to move. You feel you're under siege. They deal in drugs just a couple of doors away. It's not Britain any more. But it's the same everywhere. We gave all these countries their freedom, and what have they done with it? They've all gone to rack and ruin since we left.

'I share my Thai lady with a German. He takes his son with him to visit her, he's quite open about it. I could never do that. He's separated from his wife. He sent for Pia to go to Germany. She went for six months. She said, "If I like it, I'll marry you." But it didn't work out, so she came home. I've met him, I've shaken hands with him.

'Pia was married, an arranged marriage. She was nineteen, he was twenty-eight. He was very brutal to her sexually, and that was when she left him to go to Pattaya to make a career in the bars. Thai women like older men. Youngsters are too selfish. Older men know how to treat them decently. I put two thousand pounds in her account. She has a smallholding in her village, pigs and chickens, and spends most of her time there. I write when I'm coming to Bangkok, and she'll be in the bar, waiting.

'Once, when I arrived, she wasn't there. I went to the bar, and her friend said she would send a telegram. In the meantime I had to have someone to take care of me. I went to the bar and said, "Would anyone like to take care of me for a couple of days until Pia gets here?" A 22-year-old offered herself. She was very nice, but when she asked me if I wanted to make love to her I couldn't. It would be like my own granddaughter. When Pia arrived at the hotel they rang from reception, because they knew I was upstairs with Dim. They said, "Shall we keep her down here?" I said, "No, let her come up. It's no secret." She didn't like it. But by God, next time she was there, ready and waiting. Two big tears rolled down her cheeks. She said, "If you do that again, you will not see my love any more."

'They know how to show affection. They're not afraid to. Taking care of you. I realize I'm lucky. I've had a good life. There's no justice in the world, I know that. Going to Thailand, I don't call it a holiday. I call it investing in memories for the future.'

The Poet, Dhaka

Syed Shamsal Haq for some years worked for the BBC World Service. His two children are grown up and remain in Britain; he himself is too deeply rooted in Bengal to stay away for long.

'All people tell stories about themselves, both to outsiders and to each other. For most Bengalis it is axiomatic that we are all village people. Even the inhabitants of Dhaka and Calcutta insist they are essentially rural, and many of their responses to the city are in reality the reactions of simple country people. We look upon the car in the same way we look upon our bullock cart. This is why we drive so dangerously. After all, we had no part in the invention of the car. If it stalls, we kick it in the same way we might kick a bullock. A Westerner might also kick his car if it breaks down, but the Westerner will do it in rage at the mechanical breakdown; we will do it as though it were a living creature.

'The decorations on the cycle rickshaws and auto rickshaws are the same as those that once adorned the horse-drawn landau; the pennants and floral paintings, the country scenes, are replicas of paintings that would have ornamented the silks and fabrics of the landau.

'This is how cultural continuity exists alongside technological change. You cannot see modernization as simply usurping tradition. There is a more subtle interplay between them, whereby cultural traits survive, adapt themselves even to what appear radical displacements.

'Even our emotional responses are nonurban. If a friend tells me that he has placed his mother in an old people's home, I will be shocked, even though in the middle class now the nuclear family is more often the norm. But our response is carried over from the extended village family. When we are introduced to people we call them *Bhai* (Brother), or Auntie or Uncle; we want to integrate everyone into a kinship system that actually, for many people, has perished.

'People come to Dhaka not only because they cannot find a livelihood or have no land, although of course those are also reasons for coming. There is another important factor, and that is insecurity in the village, in the sense that robbers and bullies can get away with injustice against the poor, steal their land, make life hell. To be a nobody is to be a somebody in the city. The city gives a kind of respect to people. In the centre of Dhaka you cannot behave badly to a rickshaw puller; whereas only thirty or forty kilometres outside the city, you can slap him, beat him, not pay the fare, and you can get away with it.

'The first question people always ask you in Dhaka is, Where do you come from? To establish where your roots are is the most basic thing. In the West the most usual question is, What do you do? Your function is more important than your origins. These apparently insignificant differences are deeply indicative of cultural characteristics, and they illuminate ways in which Dhaka is, and is not, a city. People here will not even ask your name; after where you come from, they will ask, Do you have a family? Is your father living or dead? Do you have children? Only much later will you be asked what you do. Then they will ask how much you earn, a question considered indiscreet in the West, where people's money and their relationship with it have become very secret. When I take my leave of someone, only then he or she may ask, And what is your name?

'We are living in a time of great disillusionment. Many intellectuals do not believe the country has a future. Just as a former generation looked to Britain, many young people want to go to the USA or Australia.

'Why has it become like this? In 1971, after the liberation, we dreamed of "Golden Bengal", that is an expression of Tagore, from the national anthem, "I love you, O my golden Bengal." That was very much current in 1970–71. The poet Das also wrote songs on the beauty of the natural landscape, the flora and fauna of Bengal. The air was full of myths of the soil, *ruposhi* Bangla, beautiful Bengal. The educated middle class believed in a golden Bengal and imagined that by liberating the country from Pakistan we would be walking straight into this Bengal, rather than creating it. When people fought the war, they were fighting for what they imagined was there, only the door was barred by the Pakistanis. We were naïve.

'People knew they were living under a colonial power, and had to throw them out. They wanted inspiration to help get rid of the oppressors. The common people suffered; their houses were burned, women were raped, they had to hang on to something. After such horrors, we thought tomorrow must be easy. After the war and the liberation, after the euphoria, we found to our shock that we were inheriting a devastated, ugly Bengal, of inequality and poverty. The people who had thrown off the colonial masters assumed their place – in business, administration, government. Industrialists were as bad as or worse than the Pakistanis. They took on the mantle of a controlling power. What the middle class were actually doing was making way for the rule of *goondas* and plunderers. We were duped. I accept responsibility for my part in this. We failed in our duty. We should have been able to foresee, to tell the people, but we didn't realize. We were carried away on a wave of emotion when we should have looked critically at what was happening. I'm shocked at myself now. Yet at the time we needed a myth, we needed the belief in ourselves to get rid of the occupying power. History is not changed by emotional outbursts.

'So we were left with shattered dreams: intellectual, political and economic ruin. Now nobody believes in Golden Bengal. Politicians, government take stopgap measures to deal with each emergency or problem. There is no vision, no programme, no long-term plan, no idea of how we create a decent, humane society, let alone a golden one.

'Politics are governed by negative responses. During the Raj, India was divided between Hindus and Muslims. The Muslim League had a

majority only in Bengal. The Muslims were very poor, they did the tilling, the weaving, they were the poorest class. The educated and
affluent were the Hindus; therefore people came to the conclusion
that we had been exploited by the Hindus. We should of course have
realized that the poor are exploited by the rich, the lower classes by
the upper, the illiterate by the literate. But for political reasons it
became Muslims exploited by Hindus. We didn't say we don't like
exploitation, we said we don't like Hindus. Hence the Muslim League
majority in Bengal. We voted for a party that led directly to the division of India; and that was how we became part of Pakistan. We, the
articulate middle class, soon realized that the British colonists had
been replaced by colonists of our own colour and religion.

'The majority do not really believe in the country. Even the rickshaw *wala* on the street would rather go to the Gulf. Many students
want to go out. They see the half-educated, or the downright ignorant, do better than they ever can.

'Of course nationalist sentiment is there. It is a defensiveness
against foreigners. Since we don't believe in our nation, we talk of
nationalism in flowery terms, but that should not be confused with
commitment. It is a kind of poetic fiction, a debased version of
Golden Bengal for a generation that has experienced a Bengal that is
anything but golden.

'I worked for the BBC World Service from 1972 until 1979. I came
back to Bangladesh because this, after all, is where I belong. It is what
nourishes me. In the UK, I studied two hundred years of British colonial domination of Bengal; what I came back to was a shambles of a
country.

'When I go to my village now, people say, "He is not one of us."
They feel I should go there, stay there. Even within this country I have
a sense of exile. If I live in London, people say, "He left us." If I live
here in Dhaka, people from my village in the north who also live
here will say, "Will you do this for me, that for me, will you expose this
or that injustice?" If I go to live in the north, people from my village
will say, "He was born here, our landscape and our people are in his
fiction, yet he doesn't come here to live."

'I don't feel I have a duty to return; it is a question of my existence,
my identity. You don't ask to be born. You grow up and you realize
you're a member of a given society, a certain culture. You try to fit
yourself into that. The acquisition of a cultural identity is more important for me than anything else. You can only express that identity in
that culture.'

I met Syed in the Dhaka Club, an oasis of calm in a frantic city, a
colonial relic with several acres of lawns, tennis courts, reading rooms.

We ate breakfast in a cavernous room, a vast stone chamber with a ceremonial stone laid by Sir Lancelot Hare in 1911. The area had been known as the Shahbhag, but had become neglected and overgrown. The British rehabilitated it in the late nineteenth century, and created a racecourse on what is now the park, where they made a lake which they called the Serpentine.

As we sat in splendid solitude on comfortable leather chairs in the great dining room, an official approached Syed. Placing his hand before his ear, he conducted a theatrical whispered conversation. Later Syed told me he had said that if guests come into the club, shirts with full-length sleeves are essential. I had been wearing a T-shirt, which is considered incorrect dress. I felt I too had become, in a very minor way, a victim of an archaic and defunct colonialism.

But only for an instant. Immediately afterwards my status was restored and I became once more a member of the reconstituted Raj. I was suffering from a subcutaneous skin infection, and a patch of menacing violet was spreading from my foot to my ankle. Syed took me to the nearby hospital, whose medical director was a friend of his wife. The hospital specializes in diabetes, but uses this as a mechanism to trace many other diseases. The medical director has a daughter who lives in Gants Hill, east of London. The doctor who saw me had also studied in London. To reach his consulting room we passed through a throng of people, some on crutches, some with bandaged and wounded limbs. It did not feel good to pass through a crowd in far worse shape than I was, and to gain admittance to the doctor's consulting room. But neither did I offer to wait my turn. Inside were a poor man whose tongue was covered with sores, and another whose neck was distended and misshapen.

The doctor diagnosed cellulitis and gave me a prescription. I asked him how much, and he said it was complimentary. I felt I had stolen something from this poor, sad, beautiful country; but that, too, is in keeping with its long history of domination and plunder.

The Child, Bombay

Maneka was born on a strip of waste ground that separates the *koli* (fishing) community from the soaring blocks of apartments in south Bombay; the place where her family settled was one of the last remaining enclaves of poor people in that part of the city. The huts were mostly of wood and bleached palm leaves, roofs of polythene, held down by stones and old tyres so they should not blow away in the fierce monsoon winds.

When Maneka's parents came to Bombay from their native Solapur, they envied the fishing people their livelihood; but Maneka saw the waters of the Arabian Sea turn to poisonous colours of cobalt and sulphur with the effluents that poured into them. She watched the fishing people become poorer, coming back sometimes with strangely diseased sea creatures in their nets.

The only work for Maneka's mother was as a domestic. Her father pulled a cart, drawing loads of building materials on the long rectangular vehicle, running between the shafts he held in his hands.

Maneka's mother worked for a Parsee family in Colaba. She washed and cleaned the house each morning. After that, she worked in a second house. From each, she earned Rs250 a month. She had discovered on the night of her wedding that her husband was a drinker. He neglected the family, and even himself, and soon became too weak for manual labour. Maneka had one brother, Munnu, three years younger than herself. There was a school in the slum run by Catholic nuns whom the children called 'Auntie'. Maneka enjoyed sitting in the hut the nuns rented for classes. She loved to chalk the letters of the Marathi alphabet, and the metal globe that the teacher sent spinning with one movement of her finger.

When she was twelve Maneka left school. For some months her mother had been losing weight, and she could not do her work properly without her daughter's help. Just going up the four flights of stairs to where her elderly Parsee employer lived left her breathless. She would place one trembling hand on the peeling blue-washed wall to steady herself before ringing the bell. Maneka began to go with her; while her mother cleaned and dusted indoors, the child went to the market for fish, milk, vegetables. She was fascinated by the Parsee woman, the melancholy eyes in a face the colour of wax.

Life became more oppressive at home. In the evenings Maneka took over the housework from her mother, who lay on the bedroll in the corner, her eyes closed. Her daughter made a fire, cooked rice and dal, and occasionally a few vegetables she had withheld from the employer. When her father came in he was always unsteady and smelled of daru. His wife turned her face to the wall and pretended to sleep.

In the Parsee colony Maneka's mother met a woman who worked as a live-in servant. She had a son of twenty-two, and her husband was employed as a maintenance worker on the building. Maneka's mother looked enviously at the one room and kitchen in which the woman lived with her husband and son. She knew she had not long to live, and she thought if she could leave her daughter with a roof over her head this would be her most valuable gift. The place where they were squatting offered no security. All around, more big buildings were coming up, more glass and stone office blocks guarded by uniformed men with rifles.

By this time the monthly income was earned solely by the labour of Maneka, now fourteen. Some days her mother didn't get up at all, but remained in the hut, coughing in the smoke from the cooking fire, sweating under the thin cotton blanket. To see her daughter married before she died became her obsession. A room in a building. A dowry for which her daughter would thank her for the rest of her life.

One morning, while the people were away at their work, the demolition workers from the municipality came. The men were on construction sites or the docks; the women were domestic workers or in the wholesale fish market. Many older children also worked: in hotels, on stalls, selling cigarette lighters or garlands.

The demolition workers came with police in big blue vans with wire windows. The police stood leaning on their lathis, bulging stomachs hanging over their khaki belts. The workers simply advanced upon the front line of huts, shouted a warning to those inside to come out, and set about the destruction with bars and picks. The belongings of the people were thrown outside the compound. The houses came apart quite easily. The building materials were piled onto the back of waiting trucks. Some of the police poked around in the pathetic piles of possessions and helped themselves to some cooking vessels, a clock, a radio, a little money that fell out of a bedroll.

The only people at home at that time were those too old to work, a girl who was deaf and dumb, the boy who had lost his legs in a railway accident, some children left behind to look after the babies. They could do nothing. By the time they had run to fetch their parents, the work of destruction was finished. Maneka's mother struggled out of the hut. She begged the workers not to destroy their home. One of them looked at her with compassion and said, What can we do. We too are poor people. Into her hand he pressed a 50-rupee note.

Maneka's mother sat huddled under her quilt at the roadside, shivering in spite of the sun and the warm sea wind. She watched as the house she had constructed with her own hands was torn down. All around, the air was thick with the dust that had gathered in the folds of the polythene, and the beaten earth of the slum. Within less than an hour the piece of land that had been a dense maze of tiny narrow streets, where almost a thousand people had lived, was empty. Nothing was left but a few old shoes, some splinters of wood, fragments of broken glass. Some of the men who had been called away from their place of work tried physically to prevent the destruction, but they were arrested and thrown into the back of police vans.

That night, dejected but resolute, the people set up temporary shelters made of bamboo sticks, palm leaves and jute sacks on the edge of the road outside the compound which, by this time, had been cordoned off with barbed wire. The wind of cars and trucks passing by fanned the scarlet embers of cooking fires, made the canvas flap and the dry palm branches rustle.

For Maneka's mother it became more urgent than ever that her daughter should marry. The woman with whom she had worked was not averse to the idea of Maneka as a daughter-in-law. Maneka was submissive and hard-working. Someone in the slum had warned Maneka's mother against Shantibhai. She was said to be cruel and calculating. Maneka's mother could not listen, and heard only jealousy in the warning.

Maneka did not want to marry. She dreamed of returning to school, although for the moment she had to continue working, while her mother grew weaker every day. Shantibhai said her son had eyes for no one but Maneka, with her small hands, slight figure and corn-coloured skin.

One hot June morning, just before the monsoon, while the coppery clouds gathered and the city simmered in a metallic heat, Maneka's mother died on the pavement among the fumes and noise of the traffic. She was carried by her husband and some neighbours to the pyres at Charni Road. Maneka and Munnu walked behind the sad procession, the shrunken body wrapped in cerements and covered with petals of roses and marigolds.

Maneka insisted she was too young to marry. Shantibhai called the *panchayat* (the local community committee) together and the *panchayat*, all men, deemed in favour of the boy's family. Shantibhai made a virtue of accepting a girl with no dowry.

The people who had been cleared were considered an eyesore as they squatted on the edge of the road in front of big buildings where important people, businessmen and tourists, came and went each day, to whom their ragged presence might cause offence. After some months, and a campaign supported by some human rights lawyers and even film stars like Shabana Azmi, they were relocated on a piece of ground 30 kilometres away, a rough rocky piece of land without work, without amenity. Maneka's father and Munnu moved to the remote settlement. 'See how lucky you are', Shantibhai said to her daughter-in-law. 'These people will have to travel in the train to their work, while you can reach it in two or three minutes. You can clean at another house now that you do not have responsibility for your father and brother.'

The room at the top of the Parsee colony was hot and crowded. The stone seemed to absorb all the heat of the sun by day and return it at night. Maneka could not sleep. But when the monsoon came she watched the long steel rods of rain in the road below, and she thanked her mother for providing her with a secure place to live.

Maneka now worked in three houses. She gave all the money she earned to her mother-in-law. But even with the extra work the income seemed insufficient. She was made to feel guilty that she had brought no dowry, and shame that her father was a drunkard and her mother a tuberculosis patient. What kind of marriage gift is that to bring to honest, hard-working people? Shantibhai asked bitterly. Not only that. Maneka was aware that she inspired hostility, if not revulsion, in Suresh, her husband. She could not understand it; she made herself as compliant and pleasant as she could. At the same time she was obscurely aware that her father-in-law had been looking at her with a strange compelling light in his eye.

After three months she was pregnant. Suresh immediately denied that the child was his. Maneka understood that he was accusing her of having allowed his father to usurp his place in the bed.

She could not bear to sleep in the enclosed space of the room. She slept on the landing outside. She continued to work, but now the money was paid directly to Shantibhai by her employers, She had nothing of her own. Her husband would not listen to her. Only the father-in-law remained silent; and no word of blame was directed at him.

One evening when Maneka was four months pregnant, she went from her place of work and took a train from Churchgate to Santa Cruz. She had no money for the fare, and dreaded that she would be arrested by the railway police. She walked from the station, crossed the main highway, and followed the dusty winding road with the new buildings on either side until she came to the site where the people from Colaba had been relocated. Her father had another wife, who nevertheless welcomed Maneka. Munnu was working for a timber merchant near Film City.

Now Maneka travelled with the rest of the people, back to south Bombay. The journey took almost two hours each way. She rose in the steely dawn to get water from the crowded public tap, then took a bus ride to the station and travelled the 40 minutes to Churchgate; then she had the long walk to work. One day, as she was coming out of her place of work she was met by her father-in-law and two *goondas*, who seized her and tried to take her forcibly back with them. Her cries aroused other servants in the houses and they rescued her, beating off the kidnappers with sticks.

Maneka decided she would have the child aborted. The women's compartments of the railway carriages were full of advertisements offering termination of pregnancy for 90 rupees. She told Suresh of her intention. He flew into a rage and hit her. She returned to her father's house and decided that she would keep the child after all, bring it up by herself.

The baby was born in the spring of 1993, a girl. Maneka was transformed by the child. She says she will make sure her daughter never has to work as she has done. Her daughter will go to school, get an education, escape the cycle of work and want.

Maneka herself is tormented by a dry persistent cough. She is very thin. Some days, at work, she is very tired. The baby remains for the moment with her father's second wife, a kindly, compassionate woman.

Maneka gets up at five in the morning and can be seen joining the shadowy figures waiting at the bus stop in the thin dry dust of the colourless mornings, on their way to Bombay Central and Colaba to labour as peons, servants, menials, vendors; the queue is a frieze of servitude, all of them are bearers of silent stories of survival. Maneka says her cough comes from the foul air of the Bombay traffic. It is nothing. When she has provided her baby with everything she needs, then she will save some money for medicine. She is sixteen.

6

Labour in the Cities

Jakarta

I

People come to the city above all for the sake of livelihood, to labour, in an effort to make good the felt deficiencies in the rural areas, the decay of self-reliance, the ruined subsistence. Many migrants discover at the end of their journey that industrial life is an ambiguous and often treacherous liberator. But they learn other lessons too. Even the poorest communities create informal networks and bondings to defend themselves. In Jakarta workers in the formal and informal sectors, slum dwellers, if they are to create a decent life for themselves, must do so in some of the most hostile conditions, against some of the most repressive social forces on earth; their triumphs, however partial and temporary, are the more inspiring for that.

The imposition of the market economy on a highly militarized society such as that of Indonesia is likely to make even the most ardent defenders of the no-alternative school recoil. The official state ideology – 'panchasila', Suharto's version of harmony, democracy and truth – blended with an opportunistic and selective appeal to Islamic values, especially when it is a question of social discipline and control, provides little space for workers or poor people to organize independently. A regime born of the massacres of scores of thousands of 'communists' thirty years ago when, as surviving witnesses recall, the rivers of Java literally ran red with blood, is bound to be haunted by ghosts. These the government sees everywhere, especially in any attempt to defend the rights of labour, in unauthorized versions of reality by independent writers, journalists or the electronic media, and in the asking of awkward questions by students, whose function now is to insert themselves quietly into the existing order.

Civil society here is occupied territory. On the forty-ninth anniversary of independence, even the poorest slum communities are decorated with ceremonial arches depicting the glorious struggle against the Dutch: images of soldiers with guns among the flowers and celebratory lights, guns that have long been turned upon the people in whose name independence was won.

Nor does the government disdain to apply colonial laws dating from the Dutch occupation when it suits them, such as the prohibition upon meetings of more than five people without permission, the obligation upon any society, institution or NGO to seek acceptance by the state before it can operate.

This recourse to the instruments of colonialism is not surprising, since the government is implementing a colonial economic policy. This colonialism has little territory to occupy, plunder and lay under contributions; and this is why the annexation and occupation of East Timor is such a sensitive issue: it reveals too clearly the true nature of the regime and the continuity with its own colonial antecedents. Apart from such overt piratical excursions, this colonialism has no resources to exploit save those of its own hinterland; it has no populations to subdue and compel into its service but its own people, whose rights it has violated, and continues to violate, with a vigour worthy of its avowedly colonial predecessors.

All this occurs now, of course, under the banner of 'development', that promise of liberation now offered to the former fiefdoms of imperial powers – by those same powers – to replace all the subverted attempts to create socialism, social justice or a more equitable order. 'Development', here, is a code word for new forms of enslavement.

'Development' gains eager assent from one significant section of Indonesian society, those who are its immediate beneficiaries, the new high-consuming middle class. This middle class is, however, unlikely to rise up as its counterparts did in the Philippines in 1986, or in Thailand in 1992, because in Indonesia the members of the middle class are largely pensioners of government, dependants upon the apparatus of military organization and control.

Indonesia shares, though in a more florid way, many of the characteristics of other South Asian authoritarian societies. Military organization pervades even the lowest level of village and neighbourhood government. The economy remains highly regulated and its rewards are directed solely to those who support the existing holders of power and privilege. The suppression of workers' movements makes Jakarta, Medan and Surabaya havens for subcontractors to the multinationals.

One of the most powerful effects of a 'single global market' has been the separation of producers from consumers. The buyers and shoppers in the malls and gallerias of the world – including those at the heart of Jakarta itself – are thereby safeguarded from any knowledge of the real cost of the commodities their money procures for them. If people in the West even glance at the label on the fashionwear they buy, they may note in passing that it was made in Thailand, Indonesia or Bangladesh, and they may even wonder that such products travel vast distances; they are less likely to enquire what percentage of the price they pay actually reached the women who created the article, the purchase of which is legitimated by 'our' money and the power this bestows on us: the bottom line for busy consumers. One young woman I met working in a garment factory in Jakarta suggested every item should have a 'price of pain' printed on it, so that people would know how many tears and how much sweat are stitched into every article.

To reflect upon the nature of global power relations in something so banal as buying a simple blouse or skirt would seem to most people an obscure, irrelevant consideration. Yet to do this is vital to an understanding of how the 'real world', so sternly invoked by economists, is structured, and how its rewards are won and distributed.

Jakarta is perhaps more than other cities in South Asia symbolic in this respect. The atrocious working and living places of Bekasi and Tangerang are well away from the central commercial area of the city, the industrial barracks concealed from the eyes of curious outsiders by military guards. One Sunday in Bekasi, I found the industrial areas closed by black-and-yellow-striped barriers, the security normally set up for enclaves of extreme wealth. Here, it seems, the same protection must be provided to conceal a brutal and coercive poverty.

Government-controlled neighbourhood officials, as well as a wider, informal network of informers and spies, help to keep labour in order. In the constantly recurring episodes from our industrial past which the cities of the South evoke, Jakarta is reminiscent of the close of the eighteenth century, the fear of the French Revolution, which saw government spies penetrate all popular and dissenting movements. Ostensibly set up to safeguard Indonesia against communist insurrection, it is impossible to say what dark functions the remaining apparatus of security now serves, if not to assuage the haunted conscience of the ruling power.

In Bekasi, the already misty skies of Jakarta turn to a sulphurous yellow-grey. The processing of chemicals, the tanning of leather, the treatment of metals, cast a perpetual gloom above the overheated factories and slums, darken the stagnant rivers, or suddenly illuminate them with gashes of silver and crimson when dyes or waste are discharged. Here we can see why even the descriptive powers of Dickens and Mrs Gaskell faltered when confronted by Coketown or Milton, dissolving into impotent superlatives: 'indescribable filth', 'utmost squalor', 'unspeakable poverty'. Those same landscapes can be found in Jakarta as in most of the cities of South Asia.

In Indonesia only the government-sponsored trade union, the

SPSI, is permitted in the presence of these assaults upon humanity. The minimum wage (September 1994) is 3,800 rupiah per day ($US1.80), scarcely enough to feed a single person, let alone a whole family. And even this basic minimum, which a significant minority of employers none the less manage to evade, is officially recognized to answer no more than 80 per cent of *kabutuhan* – the most basic needs. What is more, the formula for gauging those needs was laid down in 1957 and has not changed despite the rapid industrialization of the past three decades. The standard set at that time remains: rice, clothing of the lowest quality. It did not allow for electricity, but only for the price of kerosene. Bedding meant a coarse length of mangrove matting, protein meant salted fish, and footwear meant sandals cut from worn-out rubber tyres.

Norms that evolved forty years ago have been applied without modification by the Ministry of Manpower, and make no allowance for transport – a considerable burden to those who must go by bus or jeep to their place of work. There is nothing for education or recreation. Independent observers, including workers at the Legal Aid Foundation, estimate that the real cost of minimum needs in Jakarta must be close to 10,000 rupiah per day ($US5). In Indonesia, labour costs account for only 8–11 per cent of total production in textiles and manufacture. In Thailand, by contrast, wages now comprise 28–30 per cent of total costs.

Many major transnationals have a presence here. Their illuminated logos hum and wink, staining the night sky with gassy colour. Their office headquarters are cream-washed stone buildings, with a portico, beds of scarlet canna lilies and rows of feathery casuarinas. Conditions and pay for their core workers are exemplary. But the real work is done through chains of subcontractors, most of them equally strangers to the needs of the people of Indonesia, often owned by Singaporean, Hong Kong, Taiwanese or South Korean interests. Some of these impose disciplines and humiliations upon their workpeople which would have shocked the Gradgrinds of Victorian England.

Hira and Mirim work in a garments factory which, until recently, was a subcontractor to Levi-Strauss, the Californian jeans company which prides itself on its vigilant oversight of the conditions in which its overseas workers labour. This factory, Duta Busana, is owned by a Singapore company. A few months ago, says Hira, there was an accident in the factory. The word is a euphemism.

All women workers in Indonesia are, by law, entitled to one day's leave during their menstrual cycle. When the women at Duta Busana put the law to the test, and asked for the right, management could not refuse; but they set the condition that each employee remove her

underwear and offer it for inspection to representatives of management as proof that she was indeed entitled to the day's leave.

The two young women contacted a newspaper, and the story was
published. Levi-Strauss discontinued the contract with the company.
Hira insists that this event, shocking as it was, was only one relatively
minor problem among the daily injuries inflicted upon women workers. 'We are regularly insulted, as a matter of course. When the boss
gets angry, he calls the women dogs, pigs, sluts, all of which we have to
endure patiently, without reacting.' The salary of 3,800 rupiah per day
does not include a food allowance – many factories provide enough
for at least one modest meal, of rice and *bakso* (meatballs) – in the
interests of workers' energy efficiency, if not charity. Previously the
company provided 250 rupiah (12.5 US cents), but when the minimum wage was raised this stopped. 'The white-collar staff are treated
as though they were different human beings. Sometimes officials from
the Labour Ministry visit the factory to inspect its compliance with
labour laws, but they take bribes from management, so there is no one
the workers can complain to.'

If the workers protest, they are accused of being 'pro-communist',
still a grave charge in Indonesia. The outlawing of communism was
given a new impetus by the fall of the Soviet Union and most communist regimes in the world: to call anyone concerned with social
justice 'communist' is now an invitation to ridicule – as though social
justice is no longer an issue in the world.

'The workers know nothing of communism,' says Hira; 'most of us
were not even born at that time. But they know injustice and they recognize cruelty. Does that make people communist?'

Mirim, who is twenty-nine, says that the government reasons that
way because the cultural tradition in Java has been for all disputes and
conflicts to be settled by compromise and understanding. But if disputes are always resolved on the terms of the powerful, how can the
powerless gain justice? 'It means that we must give in on everything,
or we will be accused of subversion, of undermining the nation.

'We work officially from seven in the morning until three, but
there is often compulsory overtime, sometimes – especially if there is
an urgent order to be delivered – until nine. However tired we are, we
are not allowed to go home. We may get an extra 200 rupiah (10 US
cents).' (There is in fact a complicated formula for working out overtime rates per hour, but few of the workers are able to calculate
whether or not they are being paid their due.) 'We can report employers to the Human Rights Council, but they, too, are state officials.

'We go on foot to the factory from where we live. Inside it is very
hot. The building has a metal roof, and there is not much space for all

the workers. It is very cramped. There are over two hundred people working there, mostly women, but there is only one toilet for the whole factory. Most of the workers come from central Java. We are not migrants. We are now settled in Jakarta. We do not go home in the harvest season, as some workers do.' Mirim has been here five years, and Hira came to join her here only just over a year ago.

'Management agreed to a workers' organization, but only on condition that the labour tells outsiders that there is a good welfare policy, good wages, good conditions. The truth is that when we come home from work, we have no energy left to do anything but eat and sleep.'

Home is a single room, 2 metres by 3 metres, which the two young women share. It is part of an upper storey added to what was originally a shack in a slum area. The lower portion of the building has been strengthened by cement. There is a raised concrete step to protect the lower part of the building from flooding. In the owner's part of the building, there are plastic-covered armchairs and a sofa, a TV and glass-fronted cupboards; a bicycle is parked in the room. To reach the room where Mirim and Hira live, you pass through this room to a rough wooden staircase, uneven planks forming each step, then through a hinged trapdoor to the upper storey. There is a wooden floor, a narrow corridor, about 15 metres long, and four rooms on either side, 3 metres by 2. It is nine in the evening when we arrive. The doors of some rooms stand open; people are eating; in one room a group of men are playing cards. Some are simply talking, sharing a moment of relaxation before sleeping. On the floor of one room stands a half-consumed bottle of liquor.

Mira was sleeping; but she tells us not to go away. She is more than happy to talk. She wraps herself in a bedcover, and shakes her head vigorously to wake herself up.

The two women pay 32,000 rupiah a month for the room ($US16). With eight rooms, the landlord has no need to work. The rooms are created by rough plywood partitions about 2 metres high. Above that, they are open to the roof of the building – a frame of bamboo, a lattice of wood covered with tiles, a sheet of blue polythene stretched beneath to prevent the rain from coming in. The room is cheap, but it costs each of them four and a half days' pay per month. 'It costs three thousand to eat so that you don't feel hungry. That doesn't mean you won't suffer from protein and vitamin deficiency. We have to pay 150 rupiah for two cans of water. In the dry season it is difficult even to get that. Some days we cannot take a bath, but have to go to a friend's place.

'We come home on an ordinary day at three-thirty or four. We cannot use the toilet because there is no water. And then there are too many people around in the daytime. Sometimes we must wait until midnight before we can use the toilet.'

You can see what she means. The toilets are on the edge of the slum, beside a black, stinking canal which separates the area from the main road and a complex of new office buildings. The toilets are constructed of wooden slats which reach chest height. The men's are adjacent to those of the women, but both are in full view of passers-by; a functional privacy is established by looking away.

Mirim says that everyone in this building works in factories. Some are in a roasted peanut factory, others make snacks, crackers and biscuits, while some are garment workers.

Hira comes from a poor family. She came from central Java to Jakarta to earn so that she could continue her education. She thought she would get enough to study, and even to send something home. She has discovered that both are impossible. She feels she cannot go back to her village to see her mother because of the shame of having come to the city and failed in her ambition. 'If you leave home, you must go back as a success. You must go with gifts, you must wear city clothes, to show everyone that you have done well. You cannot go if you do not do what you set out to do, even though it may break your heart.'.

Whatever disappointments Hira and Mirim have experienced, they have certainly continued their education, only not quite in the way they might have anticipated. Both have found that there is no going back; and, even more significantly, that there is no going forward either, unless they struggle and fight here, in this place they have not chosen, under conditions they have not willed. Both are committed to the education they could not realize, to the dreams of the city that could not be fulfilled, to the duty to family that their Java pride will not permit them to abandon and, above all, to collective struggle with and for all the women who labour in Jakarta.

Hira fills notebooks with her thoughts, her passionate resentment at injustice, her determination that the children she may one day have will not labour under the same oppressive circumstances. She says wistfully, 'I had a boyfriend but I lost him, because he complained that I was not giving enough time to him. I was not serious enough. He didn't understand that I work long hours, that I am committed to my friends in the workplace. This is my life, although naturally one day I hope to be married and have children. I have one sister. My father died when I was a child; my mother lives with her relatives.'

Mirim's father used to work for the army police. He is now retired and stays at home, where her family keep chickens and rabbits on their small piece of land.

The room speaks of their pinched existence, with its shaming emptiness. There is a length of frayed fabric at the crudely made door, so that as it opens to admit some cooler air they maintain a little privacy. Two empty dishes from the evening meal of noodles and sauce remain on the floor. The floor is covered with thin, shiny plastic cloth. The bedroll is little more than a single mat covered with cheap batik material, little softer than the floor. Along the length of one wall is a string on which today's washing hangs; on another wall are some family pictures, a calendar and some Koranic verses. On a ledge formed by a piece of wood joining the plywood panels are a tin of Johnson's baby powder, a plastic bottle of shampoo, a tube of lipstick, a tablet of Lux soap, a hairbrush and comb. At the top of the plywood wall Hira has written in English, 'No gains without pains.' There is a mirror, a 'wardrobe' made of transparent plastic, with a zip, which protects their clothes from dust. A necklace of cream-coloured beads hangs from a nail, together with a watch. The nakedness of their poverty would be pathetic if it were not for the courage and passion that animate the two women.

'In the past, the government insisted that companies had one labour organization, managed and controlled by the government. Under pressure from outside, from America and Europe, the government agreed we could have our own organization. But it must be directed by management. So nothing has changed. We labour here, and our only purpose is to produce luxury goods for other people, like Levi jeans. They put Levis in shop windows in your country. If someone steals them police will beat the thief. Here, the police beat the labour that produces them.

'Since the new labour organization was set up, there has been a little improvement. If a worker is fired she will get some compensation. The right to menstruation leave is established, but if the company offers money instead, most women will take it and come to work anyway. I feel I am seen as a machine for producing, and if the machine stops, management thinks we are rebels. They do not understand human beings.

'All labour thinks as we do, but they cannot express what they feel because they are afraid, afraid of so many things: the military, management, losing their livelihood. So they co-operate. And management has no idea of what is in their hearts.

'If we struggle for improvements, the white-collar staff also benefit, but they do not recognize it. Management benefits also, because with better welfare, people work better. That is OK. But if the workers go to prison for taking part in the struggle, it is not the staff or the management who will go to prison with them.

'I know I won't have a better life. It may be that my children will. But if I marry a labouring man, then my children will have no more chance than I have had. They say that life is a wheel rotating through time; we are all on the wheel, sometimes at the top, sometimes below. I don't believe that any more, because too many people die not because of the will of God, but because of the actions of other human beings.'

It is late in the night when we take our leave of the two young women. By this time, the whole building is sleeping. Through the partitions you can hear people breathing; the sounds of the recharging of the exhausted reservoir of labour preparing to work another day.

II

Under pressure, internal and external, over its repression of the rights of labour, the Indonesian government agreed in 1994 to allow workers to set up independent trade unions outside the All-Indonesian Workers' Union, the SPSI, which is sponsored and controlled by government.

The largest truly independent union is the SBSI, the Union for Workers' Prosperity. It has twice been refused registration by the government, which in effect makes it an illegal organization.

Illegal, but far from ineffective, despite the fact that its chairman, Muchtar Pakpahan, was arrested and detained after riots in Medan in April 1994. At the time of the riots he was in Jakarta, nowhere near the site of the disturbances. None the less, he was put on trial for 'incitement to riot'. Following renewed pressure from, among others, the United States Trade Department, he was released in the spring of 1995.

The SBSI continues to operate from its office in a small narrow street in industrial west Jakarta. The union carefully observes all conditions laid down in the Constitution; recognizes the supremacy of *panchasila*, claims the right to freedom of association and to independent organization, as the Constitution permits.

Although constantly threatened and harassed, the SBSI has succeeded in organizing workers in many factories, in both east and west Jakarta, in Bekasi and Bogor. In February 1994 a one-hour general strike brought some 250,000 people from the garments, textiles, plastics and metal industries onto the streets. These lightning tactics are necessary because military and police power would be deployed against any more prolonged action. The strike was against the perpetual abuse and oppression of workers. By law the working day should be eight hours, but this law is routinely breached by employers who insist on compulsory overtime, sometimes almost as much again as the day's official labour. The union further estimates that unemployment and disguised unemployment in the Jakarta area is around 2 million, while 800,000 have no work or income of any kind.

In spite of this, Jakarta is not crime-ridden or violent in the way that most Western cities have become. There is crime, and it is rising. But the streets remain relatively peaceful. There are few random attacks on strangers for money. Robberies, break-ins and muggings on the scale familiar in London, Los Angeles or Paris are rare. There are good cultural and social reasons for this. The streets remain crowded, the public spaces have not been evacuated in favour of private transport. Crowds in the streets are self-policing, allow fewer opportunities for violent crime. Most people live in close neighbourhoods and community vigilance (not military and police vigilance) deters wrongdoers. Crime, in the West, has become the last resort of the despairing, those who have lost faith in the possibility of attaining social justice by political means. Crime is an individual response to the decay of social hope.

In Jakarta, despite the privations and miseries that people suffer, the loss of social hope is not one of them. The SBSI taps into deep levels of explicitly social discontent and resentment. These are never far below the surface. As a foreigner – and presumably, therefore, not a spy or informer – I found myself listening to the complaints of many people weary of corruption, injustice, the absurd ideological posturings, the oppressive militarization of neighbourhoods, the inadequate rewards for labour, the rapacity of politicians, the coercive imposition of the market economy upon the recently self-reliant – all commonly articulated resentments. At times I was reminded of the last days of the Marcos regime in the Philippines; but no middle-class eruption is about to occur. There is only popular discontent, which still lacks the leadership or self-confidence, let alone the organization, to bring about even the limited political gains of the Philippines in 1986, or Thailand in 1992.

The ruling elite itself is far from united. There are factions within the military at odds with one another over the levels of repression necessary to fulfil their aim of modernizing, taking forward the industrializing of the country. Sections of the military have at times even expressed support for the SBSI; but that cannot be relied upon as a source of protection. It has more to do with infighting among the ruling elites than with any sudden conversion to the upholding of the Constitution of Indonesia, says Rekson Silaban, one of the secretaries of the West Jakarta branch of the SBSI.

'The present rulers of Indonesia were formed during the period of Japanese occupation in the 1940s. You must remember, too, that the Dutch in Indonesia were very different from the Americans in the Philippines. The Dutch supported the feudal structure, they didn't want the people to become educated. The US in the Philippines created a strong education system, even if its objective was to colonize the people. The Dutch were very hard, brutally extractive. Indonesia is rich in resources, and this still governs the major export earnings of the country – timber, now plywood, processed here, garments and semi-finished goods.

'Most people in Jakarta were not born here. They have come from villages, and most stay in slums. The conditions for those workers directly employed by big companies and transnationals are good; but for the majority it is labour in subcontracted insecurity, on temporary contracts, and they are still paid a daily wage even after years of employment in the same factory.

'There are still more men than women in the industrial sector, but only just. It's now about 55 per cent male and 45 per cent female. Women are mainly in electronics and garments. Many workers do not know their rights; compensation for dismissal, or for accidents, will be negligible or nonexistent.

'If an employer feels he cannot pay the minimum wage, he can make a proposal to the Minister of Manpower to pay less – 3,000 or 3,500 rupiah a day – and gain exemption from the law. Local government inspectors are supposed to ensure that conditions and wages are attended to, but they can easily be bought off. It is hard to find out exactly what does happen in some factories hidden behind high walls. If women workers in Jakarta go on strike, they will be detained, abused and raped by the military and the police. Sometimes managers make sex a condition for giving them the job.

'Many workers have been educated only up to the age of twelve or thirteen. It is easy to take advantage. There is much sickness in the industrial areas – hepatitis from drinking dirty water is common. This has a bad long-term effect, makes people tired and less efficient. You would think it in the interests of employers to ensure they at least had safe drinking water, but prejudice against labour sometimes even overrides self-interest. Malnourishment and vitamin deficiency are common. Workers will eat *bakso*, 500 rupiah for one plate, noodles or spaghetti, with hot sauce, chilli, for flavouring. Some factories give subsidies for food, or give rice, but this provides a small quantity, not enough to maintain health. Children suffer because their parents do not get a living wage. If workers are unmarried, they share dormitory rooms, 3 metres by 4 metres for four or five young men or women. The electricity bulb will be about 10 watt, so they cannot even see to read. They are paid twenty-five days in the month. In bad factories, where they are earning only 3,000, that means 75,000 a month [\$US37.50].

'Some workers pay to get a job. If they know someone in the factory, they stand a better chance. Organizing for the SBSI is made more difficult by spies in the labour force. Management always finds someone they can pay to inform on their fellow workers.'

Even so, the SBSI has managed to organize in many factories. In one biscuit factory, where a wage of 3,000 rupiah was being paid, the SBSI succeeded in raising the level to the minimum of 3,800. Employers often tell workers they are being taken on for a three-month training period; during that time, they are paid 3,000 rupiah or less, even though they may be doing the same work as long-term employees. At the end of that time, the law states that they should become permanent. But the employer often dismisses them and takes on more bogus trainees.

Eduard Marpaung is the SBSI organizer for east Jakarta, where the union has a growing presence, especially in steel, plastics, garments, biscuits, food processing, chemicals, metal works and electronics. 'We organized in a factory subcontracting to Toshiba, a factory making steel reinforcement rods for construction. In that place the workers had no protective wear, only cotton gloves, no helmet, no visor; and they were heating, hammering and welding metal. Now at least they have protective wear. Some workers didn't even realize this was nec-essary. Many are new to industry and are not aware of the risks they run. In plastics factories, too, although injection moulding is done by machine, people have to paint and spray the finished articles, and the dust and chemicals are harmful. In one steel factory they dismissed six of our members to destroy our influence. Those people would then be blacklisted, so they cannot get work in the area again. Even so, in that factory we got them to make a daily payment for rice for the workers, a contribution towards house rent and transport, because some people have to travel a long way by bus.'

Overtime pay depends upon a complicated formula. Officially, it should be three-twentieths of the minimum wage times one and a half for the first hour and doubled for each hour after that (i.e. 885 rupiah for the first hour, 1,400 after that. Five hours' overtime should pay 5,441 rupiah, a little over $US2.50). Workers are often unfamiliar with this calculation, and may get just 500 rupiah an hour. It is cheaper for employers to give overtime to existing workers than to take on the unemployed; and it keeps the unemployed omnipresent, as a threat to the present workforce.

Aruna works in a private hospital, where she has tried to organize the nurses. 'Nurses in the private sector', she says, 'do much of the work that is normally performed by doctors. They give medicines and injections. Some of the things we see in the hospitals are the conse-quence of social neglect, avoidable illness, the results of bad food and dirty water. We have the strange phenomenon of low pay for health staff who deal with problems it would be cheaper to prevent;

but that is how their mind works. Hepatitis, cholera, typhoid, AIDS. There is no medical insurance to cover AIDS, therefore patients must pay. They come to us because they have been refused admission to government hospitals. Nurses have to clean the wards, clear up the mess from vomiting or incontinence. I worked for twelve years in one hospital, until I was dismissed as a troublemaker.

'Nurses are not allowed to leave this country to find work elsewhere. Nurses in government hospitals take other jobs to make enough money to live. I get 350,000 a month after nineteen years' experience. A nurse here is a kind of general labourer, performing some of the functions of doctors, others of cleaning and domestic staff. There is no limit to what we are supposed to do. When we protested, the military came to my home. Military intelligence want to keep track of everything we are doing, so we feel we are permanently under surveillance.'

Sarimin works for a construction company. He was in a garment factory but lost his job when the factory burnt down. 'Insurance payment to the owner was 6 billion rupiah. Almost 350 workers lost their jobs; but an equal number were not dismissed. Production continued but with a much reduced labour force. In fact the workers lost their jobs before the fire and they had been trying to negotiate with the company for arbitrary and unfair dismissal. According to the labour laws, something should be paid to workers who are retrenched. If more than ten workers are dismissed at a time, the levels of compensation are supposed to be determined by the Ministry of Manpower. The 6 billion rupiah which the owner of the garment factory received from the insurance did not reach the workers. Two million rupiah was distributed among 338 workers, that is about 6,000 rupiah each ($US3). There was a demonstration outside the Ministry of Manpower. The people were all picked up and taken to KODEM, the military district headquarters, where they were beaten and burned with cigarette ends.'

Fire, it seems, has become a major resource in the assault on the poor: burn factories in which there are recalcitrant workers, burn down houses that occupy valuable land wanted for shopping malls or condos; and in some places, burn individuals who will not conform. From all the cities come stories of mysterious fires that sweep through slum areas which, by coincidence, are required for 'development'. The intricacies of official procedures, drawn-out negotiations over compensation, legal niceties, can be neatly avoided by recourse to the swift, clean, purifying element of fire.

'We don't like to ask for help from other people,' says Rekson Silaban. 'But this is a matter of humanity. We must ask the US to take up our cause; we must appeal to labour unions and people's organizations in other countries to organize a boycott of Indonesian products until the people here are treated with respect and dignity.'

'This country is deeply in debt,' says Agos, a former steel worker, 'and it is the people who are repaying it. None of the people in Tangerang or Bekasi ever benefited by one rupiah from the loans from the IMF and World Bank which they are now having to pay for.' Agos was dismissed from his factory because of his efforts to organize: he was assumed to be the leader, and they thought his dismissal would destroy the SBSI. The rumour was spread that Agos had been bribed by the employer and given money to leave. This didn't work. Organization in that factory is still strong, although it has now been driven underground. He now works full time for the SBSI.

4 September 1994. Today, a Sunday, there is to be a meeting in Bekasi of SBSI workers in a plastics factory, necessarily clandestine, because illegal. The union leaders will go and speak to the workers, offer encouragement and moral support, as well as discuss tactics for deepening and strengthening the organization.

The atmosphere is tense, but there is a strong feeling of elation and excitement. By 9.30, about fifteen people have gathered at the office ready for the half-hour trip to the industrial area on the periphery. Among them are a journalist from a mass circulation Indonesia–Bahasa newspaper, a lawyer, two union activists, an employee in a garment factory, a woman leader from the plastics factory, a steel worker and a punk artist with a conspicuous Mohican hairstyle – a rare and provocative sight in Jakarta. (In fact, his paintings were confiscated by the military as 'subversive'. He never expected to see them again, but they were returned to him after three months. He was thrown out of his job as a designer with an American company.)

We make a highly conspicuous group as we stand on the main road waiting for three taxis that will drive us to the meeting. It takes some minutes before the convoy is ready to set off. Passers-by, shoppers in the local market, stop and stare. I wonder whether someone might have alerted the authorities that such a strange group has set off from the SBSI building. If they have, it is unlikely that we will be detected. The taxi drivers are aware of the urgency of the journey. We are soon on the ring road, and at the beginning of the most terrifying ride I have ever experienced. The drivers remain together, weaving in and out of the Sunday traffic. They change from lane to lane, overtaking every vehicle in front of them, gauging to a split second the opportunity to pass between the bus in front and an oncoming truck, whistling past a car, narrowly missing a danger sign, taking corners at a speed just within the limit of the car staying upright. At one point

our cab tries to overtake a bus; a stream of cars coming in the opposite direction have no intention of slowing but burn their headlights
angrily as a warning. The driver applies his brakes at the last moment,
scrapes the bus as he pulls behind it. One of the workers in the car
says, 'If we're going to die as martyrs, let's do it for a cause and not on
the highway.' Everybody laughs. It is frightening but exhilarating; like
Jakarta itself.

After twenty minutes or so we turn off the main road, and soon we
are in a new suburban area that eats into what were, until recently, rice
fields: lower middle-class, single-storey houses, the prize for success of
those in modest but regular employment, people who will pay for
the privilege of living in this desolate place by a two-hour journey to
and from work each day. Beyond this is a more neglected area, of
dusty unmade roads, houses which are a mixture of tin, wood and
concrete, a squatter settlement. We get lost a couple of times. The
taxis must slow down as the speed-breakers scrape the underside of
the vehicles. The drivers do not care, because these are cabs which
they rent from the owners at 100,000 rupiah a day.

We have taken a wrong turning. The taxis come to a halt in a small
street, creating a storm of dust. Dogs are sleeping in the traffic-free
road, chickens are foraging under the plantains, pedicab drivers are
waiting at the road intersections. (Pedicabs are cycles with seats in
front, in a red-painted metal cage, like something from a children's
amusement park. These are the only form of transport in these raw
new suburbs. The drivers earn up to 5,000 rupiah a day.)

We turn around and go back the way we came. We find the right
turning and pass through a squatter area which mimics the traditional *kampong*: houses built separately, although of poor industrial
materials – plywood and metal – but in the well-tended gardens there
are bananas, mango and papaya trees, grass and medicinal herbs,
geese and rabbits. A little further into the village there is a more substantial house. Outside are about sixty pairs of shoes: the little paved
forecourt looks like the stall of a pavement shoe vendor; the *chappals*,
sandals, are the cheapest footwear of the poor.

The people are waiting for us, everything ready for the meeting.
One thing is immediately clear: the intensity of an oppression that drives these young women and men, mostly migrants from west and
central Java, to risk everything – freedom, livelihood, even life itself –
for the sake of a single meeting in defence of their own dignity and
their sense of social justice. Uncelebrated, unknown, secret, certainly
to the personal advantage of no one present, the meeting evokes a
strange sensation: this is what it must have been like when working
men and women in Britain met, in defiance of Combination Acts and

repressive anti-labour legislation, two hundred years ago. Our own past lives on, unrecognized and unrecognizable to us, made invisible by racism and by the erasure of memory.

A majority of the people here are women. Most are young, in their late teens or early or mid-twenties. All work at the W Plastics factory. Perhaps one-third of the employees in the unit have come.

The room is L-shaped. We sit cross-legged on the floor, which is covered with rattan mats. There are glasses of herb tea, plates of cakes beside us; a big kettle of boiled drinking water is passed round. A sound system has been installed, but it whistles noisily, so it is turned off. The speakers are perfectly audible in the stillness and concentration. Nisma, a young woman in her twenties, speaks for the women workers. In this factory they make plastic furniture, boxes for TV sets, household articles, baskets, stools and containers. Basic manufacture is done by injection moulding. The finished goods must then be polished, smoothed and trimmed by hand so that there are no rough edges. Then each object is spray-painted. Workers are issued with masks, but they are expected to use the same mask for weeks or months, even a year at a time. The colour mixing and spraying are the most unhealthy occupations in the enclosed space. There is never any health check. Many women have breathing problems and respiratory infections. The salary is 3,800 rupiah a day, less for some women, with no allowance for meals.

Nisma came from central Java ten years ago. Her father is a rice farmer. Her husband drives a truck. She has her own home, a reasonable living. It is this measure of security that enables her to speak out on behalf of those who have nothing, who depend upon their daily wage for subsistence. The generosity of those who could ignore the condition of their fellow workers if they chose, but who elect to throw in their lot with the disadvantaged, is one of the most inspiring aspects of life under this repressive regime. For every individual who opts out, who keeps quiet for the sake of a 'better life', there are many others who remain to continue the fight.

We are asked to introduce ourselves to the factory workers. I say I am a visitor from Britain, representing no institution, but present in peace and solidarity. The people applaud. I feel ashamed and yet privileged to be here.

The union leaders say that Indonesia ratified the International Labour Organization (ILO) Convention Number 98 in 1956; this gives workers the right to associate in independent trade unions. After so many years the SBSI has still not been allowed to register, even though it faithfully expresses its adherence to official state ideology, is committed to nonviolent change, and the objective suggested by its name – the greater prosperity of workers – is scarcely inimical to the purposes of capitalism.

It is very hot in the room. The rotating electric fan is the only other sound as the people listen intently to voices raised, not in anger – although that is there too – but in an unshakeable resolve to resist the institutionalized injustices and cruelties in Indonesian society, the violence that leaves them no choice but to stand and fight. Roswita, a young woman in violet-coloured head covering and burgundy sarong, says she has worked in the factory since 1981. Her basic pay is 3,200 rupiah. She gets 900 for food and 600 for transport. There is no sick pay. Workers who are ill must go to a government hospital, and if they cannot get treatment there they must get permission before they are allowed to seek help at the Islamic hospital. 'One woman had salmonella from something she ate in the factory. She was given treatment by the company doctor but she got no better. The company would not give her permission to go to hospital. She became worse, and died at home. She didn't have the money to go to a private doctor. The company owns people's lives; they can dispose of us as they wish. They have the power of life and death over us. This is not labour. It is slavery.

'The factory works according to the orders it gets, which are erratic. The workload goes up and down unpredictably, so that sometimes there are long hours of compulsory overtime, and at others, less than a day's labour. Most people here are rural migrants, have come in the last ten years. We would never have left the village if there had been work there; but the cost of growing rice is not matched by what we can sell it for in the market. We must buy seeds, fertilizer, pesticides, and even though yields may rise, the price we get does not keep pace with what we must pay.'

In the still hot air, the sound of children playing comes through the open door, a TV programme from a neighbouring house; some cocks crowing. A man rides by on a bicycle with a load of plastic toys – footballs, aircraft, dolls, guns – his cargo makes it almost impossible for him to pass along the rough narrow road. Occasionally a neighbour casts a curious glance into the room. There is no need to close the door against them. Most have never heard of trade unions, and have no idea of the purpose of the meeting. And the atmosphere inside is not one to excite interest; the passion is restrained, the feeling one of mature and calm determination. There is an almost religious intensity, a quiet gravity, as the people contemplate the possible consequences of their persistence in this innocent, illegal activity.

After about an hour and a half there is a break for lunch. The owner of the house is not present. He has given it to his sister for the day; she works in the factory. They have prepared lunch for seventy or eighty people: a huge vat of fragrant rice, vegetables, curried meat, fish, slices of watermelon and pineapple. As they eat, the people relax, but they continue to talk about the conditions under which they must work. The drinking water in the factory, they say, is boiled; management do not really want the workforce incapacitated by typhoid. The roof of the factory is made of metal, so that intensifies the heat. There are fans, but they have the disadvantage of keeping the dust and particles of chemical colouring in movement.

Then they ask me questions, questions that are impossible to answer. What do the people in your country think about the condition of the workers in Indonesia? What do they think about the SBSI? If we ask them to boycott goods made in such terrible circumstances, will they listen to us? Can you tell them how we suffer?

This plastics factory is a symbolic place, for it illuminates the complexity of the new international division of labour in the global market. The raw material – in the form of foam – is imported, mainly from Canada, the United States and Korea. The labour of moulding, trimming, polishing, colouring the articles is carried out in Indonesia, and then many of the finished products are exported – principally to Korea, Taiwan and Japan. Some major transnationals get the core of their products made here: Sony, Panasonic, Johnson and Grundig have, or have had, contracts with this factory for the casing of their TV sets, videos or other household goods.

In this sense Bekasi is the unknown element in many 'household' names. Bekasi is the link, destined to remain concealed, between producers and consumers, the no-man's land where relationships between makers and buyers of goods in the malls and galleries are lost in an inferno of smoke, violence, pollution, dirt and poverty. Bekasi is the place where those in the West who refuse 'guilt trips' over their lifestyle must justify their willed unknowing; and must defend their privilege in dialogues that will never take place with these abused and humiliated young people.

Indonesia, in the name of the free market system, promotes the grossest violations of human rights, and undermines the right to subsist of those on whose labour its competitive advantage rests.

The small and medium-sized units which subcontract to the multinationals are the precise localities where the sound of the hammering, tapping, beating of metal comes from the forges where the chains are made for industrial bondage.

Bekasi, even on a Sunday, is covered by a shimmer of smoky cloud around the grey metal towers, hangars and sheds of its factories. The entrance to the industrial estates is protected by a barrier, like the border post of another country, guarded by security personnel who are the soldiery policing the frontier between producers and consumers. In the sulphur factory, where matches are made, conditions evoke the ghosts of the young women at Bryant & May in London's East End. Conditions in the metal factories, where swarf and metal get under the fingernails and discolour the skin of workers, in the tractor assembly plant, where management gives alcohol to the workers to numb their feelings, suggest rigours that would be considered intolerable in the West now, but which are regarded by the Indonesian government as indispensable for the maintenance of the system to which no alternative is either conceivable or desirable.

The logos of the transnationals shed their gaseous aurora over the night-time city: Fuji, Toshiba, Procter & Gamble, Hitachi, Taisho textiles; Fuji, whose film has rarely recorded the conditions in which its subcontracted workers labour, Toshiba, whose appliances are beyond the reach of those who make them; the textile companies whose delicate fabrics will never adorn the wasted bodies of their operatives.

After the meal, the meeting reconvenes. There are no speeches, just a heartfelt expression of solidarity between oppressed flesh and blood. The event ends with a moment of prayer; that is, a silence, in which you can feel the concentrated energy of the defenceless become tangible. At this moment their being together transcends even their brave struggle against local injustice, and interrogates a world in which the intractable injustices that beset all humanity – loss, sickness and death – are aggravated by alterable injustices inflicted by other human beings. Does humanity not suffer enough, they ask, without adding to our burden avoidable ills and unnecessary sorrows?

A few days later I went to the Legal Aid Foundation in Jakarta and spoke with Teten, a labour lawyer. He had just come from a meeting with a US delegation visiting Indonesia under the General System of Preferences (that is, the system under which a number of Indonesian goods entering the US qualify for duty-free treatment: 14 per cent of its exports to the US, worth about $US90 million). Their mission was to find out the real conditions of Indonesian labour.

'They asked if there had been any improvement since the GSP was suspended for six months in April. We said there had been no change in the government's policy towards labour. There is still no freedom to associate. The government recognizes only the SPSI. The Department of Manpower is to publish new regulations on labour disputes. In the draft, there is nothing new – it still rejects withdrawal of labour as a legitimate option for trade unions.

'The working of *panchasila* in industrial relations means that ideological control is maintained, and that workers and management must work things out together. For workers, this means it must all be done on someone else's terms. Treatment of the issue under the General System of Preferences conditions is not useful for improving labour conditions. The instrument is not effective, because many other agreements override GSP: like GATT for instance, under which the US reduced its quota of textiles from Indonesia, this also has its effect, but the government does not respond. In 1987, they also discussed stopping the GSP, so that the US could get economic concessions from Indonesia. The only thing that changed was that the export of Hollywood films to Indonesia went up, and our own domestic film production went down.

'We suggested to the GSP delegation that in order to be effective against Indonesian conditions, an independent commission should be set up, to monitor labour conditions for recommendation to GSP. Government-to-government dialogues. "This is long-term," they said; basically, they are looking for ways to legitimate GSP status.

'It opens up the whole story of North–South relations. The standard should be the same for every country in terms of the costs of production. The wages component should be constant as a percentage of the costs of production.

'Many transnationals are subcontracting here: Levi-Strauss, Nike, Reebok. A lot of the subcontractors are Korean-owned. They all tend to low wages and brutal management. Nike and Levis issue a code of conduct as to criteria for investment; but, in reality, under the tender system they always go for the lowest cost of production. At one subcontractor to Levis, the workers struck and Levis were worried by the publicity, so they stopped the contract. If they had wanted to, they could have forced their local suppliers to impose decent labour conditions. Instead they went to another company not tainted by scandal. Some subcontractors move out of Jakarta to smaller towns, where workers are even less capable of combining to improve their conditions.

'There are other instruments in the US for regulating foreign investment. The Overseas Private Investment Corporation is a government body in the US, part of the government's international trade regulatory body. If multinational companies want to base themselves outside of the US, they are supposed to do so in countries which respect human rights and the conditions of workers. So if the US government was serious, it would use some of the other instruments at its disposal.

'There is a dilemma in our asking for assistance from Europe, America, Australia. There has been some improvement here because of pressure from consumers' movements in Germany and France early in 1994. The problem is with the labour market. There are so many people without a job, who will compete to take up anything. If

we ask for a boycott, this is not popular. If we show up labour conditions, we will be abused, both by government and people. A boycott by
the North would have to cover products from all countries in the
South, because companies can just move elsewhere if one country is
picked out, and find even cheaper labour. How to establish links
between North and South so that international standards can be set in
labour conditions: this goes to the heart of the relationship between
North and South.

'Things have changed in the past ten years, now that there is mass
unemployment in the North again. People there have the same problems with the multinationals, people of one country are played off
against those of another. Yet there are no new theories to deal with
the changing reality; that there is no alternative seems to have paral-
ysed everybody by its self-evident truth.

'The government has no vision. And there is no significant resistance, apart from labour. The middle class is controlled by
government, as are most of the NGOs, and all political parties. In
some places religious leaders make a stand against industrialization.
But religion, on the whole, becomes a safe haven from reality. We are
living in an unnatural, irrational society. Religious leaders occasionally
make a call to stop TV in the evening.

'Westernization is very strong. It is hard for religious leaders to
resist, even in the villages. You cannot harness the social discontent to
a religious revival. This is a waiting time, when no great change can
occur. Discussion groups with young people have been established,
student groups in universities. That will spread out, and they will start
other groups. That is how the longer-term regeneration can be
accomplished. For a decade now, people have been talking of the
beginning of the end. But still it goes on.

'I could not envisage an Iranian-style revolution here, under the
rule of the mullahs. Here there are no charismatic leaders, and it is not
the tradition here. Ours is a pluralistic Islam. The government uses
Islam simply as a political tool against the West. This makes it a double
assault on Islam. We must develop a cultural Islam, human, natural,
inclusive, with links to other faiths. We must work for all humanity.
There is a Department of Religious Affairs which talks of "religious
development". What is this? To establish mosques is not really a religious achievement, it is material. There are no spiritual indicators in
our country, only material indicators. We have a Department of
Education and Culture which has nothing to do either with education
or with culture; so we are starting from a very low base.

'The government promises cheap labour to foreign investors. One
of the tenets of *panchasila* is social justice, which has been preached

since 1945. The reality is so much at odds with the public pro-
nouncements. And then, the fear of Communism is preached until
today. The information system of this country is a monologue, top-
down only. But it has its effect. People think politics is dangerous, and
they want to stay away from it.'

In August 1994, the Minister of Manpower expressed his intention
of exporting more surplus Indonesian labour. His government's ambition is to achieve 2.5 million migrants from Indonesia by the turn of
the century. This migration, it foresees, will produce $US10 billion in
remittances from Malaysia, Singapore, Brunei and the Gulf. Labour is
seen as another export commodity, like timber or tropical fruits. The
uprooting and scattering of human beings is perceived only in terms
of 'remittances'. The extreme reductionism of the economic calculus
is at its most stark here. The costs of labour exported like this cannot
be counted: the breaking of families, the ruin of village culture, the
undermining of social stability, not to mention the spread of AIDS,
when men alone with no outlet for their isolation and exile take such
consolations as they can. AIDS is then brought back as a poisonous
gift to wives and girlfriends, which places all the washing machines,
videos and pieces of jewellery they bring as trophies of their economic 'success' in a quite different context.

The Garment Sweatshops of Bangkok

Huaykhwang. The small garment-making row houses are mostly in
three-storey buildings in this crowded part of east-central Bangkok, off
the main roads and between polluted canals. The seamstresses, 80 per
cent of them young women, nearly all unmarried, live in dormitories
on the top floor, with a washroom and small kitchen; the owner and
her or his family live on the middle floor; the ground floor is the
workshop or factory.

The workroom is open to the street during working hours, and
presents a scene of more or less peaceable domestic activity: women
sewing at machines, ironing, trimming threads. Vendors come and go
providing snacks, drinks, small comforts to keep people – and their
labour – going. It all looks easy, comfortable, accessible; there is little
sign of the intensity of exploitation – sometimes self-exploitation – on
which the workshops depend. Everything here is transparent and visible in a way that astonishes after the tension and secrecy of Jakarta.

The characteristic shop consists of two rows of sewing machines –
Singer or Juki – along each wall of the long rectangular interior. In
the centre are a row of trestle tables, metal or wood, for cutting and

ironing. There is a round metal stool at each machine. On the concrete floor lie cut-offs and fragments of material which must be constantly swept up; there is white strip lighting on the wall above the machines. The walls, which the young women face, were originally colour-washed, usually blue, but now peeling and, in any case, covered with posters of Thai pop singers and movie stars, or an occasional picture of Alpine mountains, lakes and trees in blossom – a gesture, perhaps to the elsewhere from which the young women come, or the place to which they would like to escape.

Work starts at between seven and eight in the morning. There is a break for lunch at 11.00 and for dinner at 5.00, both of which are provided by the shop owner. Breakfast is not provided. The working day ends late; anything between nine and midnight.

The owners, who are subcontractors, generally keep control of pattern cutting, which increases their power over the seamstresses. Most of the owners were themselves originally machinists; some do learn, and a few acquire the funds to start their own shop.

One of the most obvious things in Bangkok is the absence of conflict between the owners and their workers. There is nothing of the concealment of Jakarta, or the defensiveness of Dhaka here. Neither side appears to see the relationship as exploitative, even though the employers are clearly far better off than those who work for them. They may have sold their land or taken a loan to open the shop. Their profit margins are usually small, and they too work long hours. Many bring workers from their own village, often their own kinsfolk or neighbours. The real point of exploitation is the interaction between the middlemen and the shop owners.

One subcontractor employing fourteen seamstresses says she gets 18 baht for a long-sleeved shirt from the middleman in the market at Pratunam; the worker gets 7 baht, 5 baht for a short-sleeved shirt. Yet although the owner gets 11–13 baht profit on each piece, she must provide food, shelter, transport to fetch the material and to return the finished articles, electricity, medicine if the workers are sick. And they do look after the workers. Whatever they lack in free time, leisure and pay, the workers feel secure. Many come from Isan in the northeast of Thailand, and there is a strong sense of regional solidarity and kinship. In any case, the middlemen will get up to ten times as much as the factory owner – 180 baht for the shirt the subcontractor delivers. This is another force that unites the owners with the workers. Essentially the owners are seen as providing work and shelter. The middleman has no responsibility for workers or the conditions or rates of pay under which they labour; they merely send the materials and receive delivery of the product within a fixed time. The subcontractor has to keep the cloth and finished pieces at the convenience of the middlemen. Often, the subcontractor must wait for money in payment of work done. She has no bargaining power with the middlemen.

In Bangkok the people must bear intolerable curtailment of their freedom in the service of free markets. In 1978 it became government policy to promote textiles as the major export commodity from Thailand. Textiles remain the major export, although they now represent a declining proportion. The row houses produce also for the domestic market. Wages have risen far above those in Dhaka and Jakarta; it is the extraordinary capacity of Thai workers to absorb what elsewhere might be regarded as intolerable burdens of work, the nonconfrontational tradition and, perhaps above all, the levels of social cohesion, networks of kinship and regional solidarity that have maintained competitive advantage.

Sanyan has been working in a row house for four years. She is single, has three brothers and one sister at home in Isan. There, the family has 40 rai of land. Sanyan works from 8.00 until 11.00, then 12.00 to 5.00 and 6.00 until 11.00 or later, if there is an order to be finished. She is working on shirts that will be exported to Australia, ironing the material on the trestle table before she sews it, so that it is smooth. The material is green and blue check for casual shirts, thin blue or pink stripes for more formal wear. Sanyan is paid 140 baht for twenty shirts a day (almost $US6). She makes the whole garment: collars, cuffs, buttonholes, sleeves, body. In this shop there are ten women and four men. The tables in the centre of the factory are collapsible, assembled from grey metal. The floor is littered with cut-offs, small irregular pieces of striped and check material. This is not wasted; it is swept up and sold on to women who unpick the cloth and then use it as stuffing for dolls.

Sanyan works six days a week, occasionally seven. Sundays, she says, the workers rest, sleep, go to Lumpini Park for a picnic. Sanyan went home last month for four or five days. She tries to send home 2,000 or 3,000 baht every three months or so. Many workers start by sending home a significant portion of their earnings; but city life increases their own expenses and needs. Sometimes they cease sending, or send only intermittently. Sanyan wants to study further: informal education, not college. Her education finished so that she could come to Bangkok to work.

The owner of this shop is also from Isan. All the workers are from the same area, although they did not know each other before they came. Some are from the owner's village. When she needs workers, she goes home to recruit them. The women do not regard the excessive hours of work as an imposition: they are simply grateful that they can send money home to their families. The livelihood of whole families, as well as the economy of many villages, is sustained only by their remittances; it would not occur to them to protest at low pay or overwork.

In a neighbouring shop Kaew, a pale-faced young woman of twenty, who came from Isan five years ago, is working. Her family owns 30 rai of land, and she has one brother. She can make thirty shirts a day for 200 baht. She says she came to Bangkok because she doesn't like to stay at home. Sometimes the bland reasons the young women give for leaving home cover truths too terrible to be told. Kaew works from seven in the morning until midnight, with two meal breaks. She sends home 2,000 baht, 'sometimes'. She prefers Bangkok to home because here there is work and money. Although she is on a piece rate, she must fulfil a minimum number of shirts. The shirts are for export to South Africa; shiny material, grey, green, dark blue. Curiously the materials evoke the final wearers; you can see the young men in the Johannesburg townships in the shiny shirts on Saturday night, just as you could see the city Australians in their pinstripe shirts. The owner, Chusi, is perhaps in her thirties. She used to be a seamstress; she started twenty years ago. Ten years ago, with her husband, she established the shop. They had to take a loan from middlemen for materials. They started with only two machines. Now there are sixteen. Chusi also sends money to her family in Isan, who have no income at all. She employs twenty people. This row house is also long and rectangular, with wooden benches at which people stand to cut the collars and cuffs and to insert the stiff material that reinforces them. The walls are colour-washed pale blue to maximize the light; there are loops of cobwebs from strip lighting to ceiling which have caught coloured cotton dust in their fabric. Chusi herself is now getting only 12 baht per shirt. This material is not good quality. She is looking for another supplier, because she cannot negotiate a better price with the current middleman. It is now July, the time of the Buddhist Lent, and orders are low. By October the high season begins, and orders should improve.

Chusi is not reticent. She pays 6,000 baht rent per month on the three-storey building. The 'owners' do not own the properties in which they work. She buys in meals for the employees; only rice is cooked on the premises. Each sewing machine costs 10,000 baht; but if you buy them on the instalment plan, you pay twice as much.

The women here earn only 5 or 6 baht per shirt, and although they work at great speed there is an enormous amount of stitching in each one; afterwards, they have to trim the material and cut the loose threads.

They must sit for many hours in the same posture, with no back support. The air is dusty, and respiratory disorders are common. On the other hand, so long as they get the work done, they are free to come and go as they wish, for reasonable breaks; and the *soi* is often crowded with young women going to buy a drink or some snack, or to sit for a few minutes by the polluted *klong*. In some of the shops, cassettes play Thai popular music. Chusi says that whatever the problems with the row houses, this is better than the factory system.

In a neighbouring *soi* there is a row house where all the workers are from Songkhla in the south. The people here are working with different material, a traditional fabric made up to the design of the owner. Prajuab is in her late thirties and came to Bangkok eight years ago. She is still single. She sits at a Juki sewing machine, in a position looking out onto the street. She completes twenty pieces a day, and gets 5 baht a piece – a loose blouse with blue and white splashes. All the people here are from the same place. Prajuab's parents have 12 rai of land, where they grow rice. She prefers to be in Bangkok because she can send money home; but if the same work existed in Songkhla, they all agree they would go home tomorrow. Prajuab has six brothers and sisters, three of them here; she then reveals that the owner of the shop is her older brother. They get the material directly from Bobe market, but they make their own designs. These have to be approved by the middlemen. The owner gets 9 baht per piece, and pays the workers 5 baht. The middlemen provide everything: cloth, buttons, even thread. The middlemen sell each blouse for 70 baht a piece.

Wisuphon is the male owner of a shop that is busy with an order for denim skirts, an export order to Poland: the skirts of coarse denim, with gold thread and floral designs on the rear pocket, evoke the broad Polish women who will wear them. A Thai girl holds up a single skirt and giggles: she says it would be big enough for three Thai women to wear. Wisuphon came to Bangkok in 1976 and opened his workshop ten years ago. He came as a trainee to a tailor, and worked cleaning and packaging. It took him a long time even to become a seamster. He lives on the premises with his wife and two children. With time, he says, he developed a gift for design. When he first started, he rented a small room with two machines, Now he employs fifteen people. A friend of his arrives with some beachwear: sunhats, tops and T-shirts with a design of a setting sun and 'Thailand' in black lettering. He says business is good, even though this is the low season.

Wisuphon says trade depends on the quality of each workshop. They have to maintain a reputation. If the quality is high, there is nearly always plenty of orders. All the workers in Wisuphon's shop are from Isan, some are his relatives. He too says that many villages could not survive without money sent from Bangkok. It is another ironic reversal that causes people to see Bangkok as succouring the countryside, when in fact the opposite is true: the villages feed the city with their produce, their labour and their people.

Making the denim skirts is hard work. The material is thick and not pliable. The women work dexterously; the spool of gold thread on the spindle on top of the machine quickly unwinds. The women reinforce the waist with an extra length of denim, sew the seams and pockets, and then apply the denim patch, with its red and green bird of paradise, onto the pockets. They get 20 baht for each piece, and make at least ten per day, more if they work longer hours. The skirts are sold by the middlemen for 100 baht, but by the time they reach the shops in Poland this may have increased six- or seven-fold.

The women start work at 8.00 a.m. but may work until midnight. Rampai comes from the same village as Wisuphon, and is related to him. She has been here eleven years. She makes at least ten skirts a day, and sends home 1,000 baht a month. She makes the whole garment from pieces that have been supplied by the cutter. All the seamstresses must do two or three years' training. The patterns for the various garments are cut in cardboard, hanging on pegs in the wall. The middlemen trust Wisuphon to produce good designs; when he creates a new one, he submits it to them for approval. The middlemen ask the client, and if the response is positive, he places an order. Wisuphon has just won a domestic order for soft pale denim short skirts, very different from the Polish export order.

Wisuphon has no worries for the moment, but the business is fiercely competitive. With Bangladesh, Indonesia, India and many other countries in the region competing for similar business, nothing is guaranteed in the long term.

Not all workers are as unaware of their exploitation as the young women of Huaykhwang; or perhaps it is simply that the young women do not articulate it. I met Narong one Saturday evening in Lumpini Park in the centre of Bangkok: a slight young man of twenty-six in white T-shirt and dark blue jeans. At first I thought he was another hustler: there are plenty of those at dusk in the park. He was in an unusually cheerful mood, because today he had taken a day off work. Normally he has only Sunday free, and he spends most of the day sleeping to catch up on the week's deficit of rest. He works in Din Daeng, machining in a garment factory. He works from 8 a.m. until midnight. There is a break at noon for lunch and at six for dinner, both provided by the employer. He does not live on the premises, but is at the workplace for sixteen hours a day; during the 90 minutes' break he does not leave the factory. He shares a room – a clean, though frugal cell – with a friend from Ubon, a town close to his home village. He earns 165 baht a day ($US7.50), that is 10 baht an hour, or 40 US cents.

It is a familiar story. He has been in Bangkok since he was seventeen, and he sends 1,800 baht to his parents every month. They have 16 rai of land, and six children younger than Narong. He pays 670 baht a month for the shared room, which leaves him 1,500 a month ($US60) to live on: that is, for one meal a day, and food on Sunday, clothing, laundry, travel and luxuries – whatever they may be, he says. The park is the only place that costs him nothing. What do you do here? I asked. Just sit. I looked at him: a long narrow face, irregular teeth, short hair. Not a hustler. He, like many others, wanted to practise his English, because he thought that might help his job prospects. I said, you can't learn English in one day.

I took him for a meal in a restaurant of the Salt and Pepper chain. He chose the cheapest item on the menu. After, he asked for an ice cream, plain vanilla. I ordered the most fancy ice cream for myself, and then gave it to him. He was touched. He said, 'My life is work and sleep. On Sundays I sleep till five or six in the afternoon. Then I wash my clothes. You do not know what a luxury sleep is until you cannot get enough. When I wake up, I go out to eat something on the street. Sometimes I meet my friends, we drink some Thai whisky, but we must not be late, because of work on Monday morning. No one knows how hard our life is. If I had spent all my youth in a prison, it could not have been more wasted. Now I'm no longer young. I cannot think of marrying, because I have no money.'

Narong said his only other pleasure is *chak wo*, flying a kite, which means wanking, so called because of the hand-jerking movement of effective kite flying. Most days, he says, bitterly, I am too tired even for that. Once, he says, I met a girl on the street and took her back to my room. That is the only time I have ever been with a woman. Whenever I fly a kite, I have to use a book of porn, because my mood is too tired to imagine anything else.

It is just before the festival of Songkhran, the water festival. Narong will have ten days off work, but he has no money to go home. I give him the fare. I don't expect to see him again. Standing in the street he presses his nose against my cheek, a Thai kiss, and then disappears into the Sunday-night crowds on Silom Road.

Ms Rakaowin of the Justice and Peace Commission has been working with the women in the garments industry for five years, and has learned much about the complexity of the situation the women face.

'We thought from the beginning that exploitation must be bad, therefore our very first interventions were mistaken. They live like family, in fact they are often related to the owners. The problem is with the wholesaler in Pratunam and the other markets. We thought, this is slave labour, but we soon discovered that most regarded it as a privilege to come to work in Bangkok. It is not like certain capitalists who recruit children and young people from the bus terminals and railway stations, and then put them in closed houses as virtual captives.

'The row houses are mostly people from the northeast. They live close together, and exist in a fiercely competitive market, and they are very vulnerable to anything that affects world trade. During the Gulf crisis trade was seriously reduced; but people stayed together and helped one another. They replicate that northern rural community even in the city. It is almost as though they were not in Bangkok at all.

'This gave us the idea that the work should be decentralized, taken to the villages. Garments could be made there, and that would prevent the need for young women to migrate on this scale. But the cost of transport, the lack of quality control and discipline made the difference between just making a profit and losing money.

'It remains essentially a patron–client relationship. They feel they are one family. It is harder to reach the migrants from the south, from Songkhla. They are more closed, although they stay together in the same way that the northerners do. The needs and problems are the same. We are trying to bring them together, so that they can collectively ask for assistance from the government.

'The entrepreneur has to take care of all the workers, meals, accommodation; they deduct 200 baht a month for water, health care, electricity. If they are sick, the employer must send them to the clinic. The workers have come straight from the village; they live together, eat together, and when they marry they rent a separate room. When they have children they keep them here for the first two or three months, then send them back home. In front of the sewing machines you often see a photograph of a little child. We have told the Municipal Authority that a child care centre is vital, so they don't have to send the children to the grandparents in the village.

'They dream of going back, but only a few return to do dressmaking in the village. After a few years, their children have grown up in the care of grandparents, and the parents sometimes feel the years have cheated them of the enjoyment of their children's childhood.

'The municipality has little information on the five to ten thousand enterprises in this sector. It is covered by no legislation. The number of workers fluctuates – some may employ twenty-five in the high season, but they go back home for harvesting and cultivating, and during the Buddhist Lent for three months work drops. The people make merit, rural people don't have weddings, dresses, so orders go down.

It is hard to regulate; the owners cannot say how many machines or workers there are – it may be five or ten or twelve, it varies. But they contribute a lot to the Thai economy, they give a chance for the poor of Bangkok to survive. They can live cheaply, northeastern food, 5 baht chicken wings, 7 baht *somtam*, papaya salad, 3 baht sticky rice. There is no need to increase wages. This is why it is cheaper to produce here than in Singapore, Malaysia. They may get only 100 baht a day, but they have meals and security of shelter. The men mostly go to construction sites.

'We are investigating the health consequences of piecework, twelve to fourteen hours a day, the effects of dust and poor posture, leakage of electricity. We do not criticize. We call the employers and put the problem before them. The authorities cannot enforce better conditions, both because they know it is a variable income, and because it is also a declining business. The European market is closing for garments – imports from Indonesia and China are cheaper. This is going to present serious problems in the next five years. That is why we plan with the Municipal Authority to give other skills to the workers, otherwise they will be lost.

'The government does not bother at any level. The bureaucracy has no information, no details of the industry, the conditions the likely development and its implications for the poor seamstresses. Migrants don't have the right to vote – they are not resident in Bangkok. Migrants are seen as a burden rather than the resource they are. You cannot stop migration, but what you can do is give it dignity and find space for it in industrial society. The workshops are better than factories. Here they are more free, they can move around, listen to music, buy things to eat and drink without being scolded. It is more human. If they must come to Bangkok, they should be supported, given skills, upgraded.

'Some of the owners have sold their land in the village to open a shop house, or have taken all their parents' savings. It costs them thirty to fifty thousand to open a shop. They too are living on the edge of survival. It is more complicated than it appears to anyone who simply looks at the circumstances of labour without understanding the context in which all this is taking place.'

The Garment Workers of Dhaka

The export of garments now earns 56 per cent of the foreign exchange of Bangladesh. The industry consists basically of the making up of garments from cloth and designs imported from Taiwan, Hong

Kong and Korea, for export to many parts of the world, including the European Union, North America, Japan and the Gulf. The industry is catering to a mass market, and the products are made cheap by extremely low labour costs, which are often less than 5 per cent of the total production cost.

The industry, which scarcely existed twenty years ago, has drawn into the labour market an estimated 1,200,000 mainly young people, 80 per cent of them women, of whom more than 600,000 live and work in Dhaka. This has led to significant shifts in social values and traditions. It has contributed to growing freedoms for many young women, and at the same time has called forth a reaction on the part of fundamentalists, who consider the weakening of (external) controls over factory workers a disaster.

I visited a number of garment factories, met many workers and went with them to the slum areas where they live.

The factories

Many of the garment factories in Dhaka compare favourably with their counterparts in Jakarta, Bombay and Bangkok; this is not because of any tenderness towards the workers, but because for the most part the buildings are fairly new, and were originally designed for commercial purposes. Many are not, therefore, the squalid sweat-shops of popular imagination. They are often on the second or third floor of stone buildings, and there is usually plenty of light and air. But because they were not intended as factories they are very cramped, sometimes with two or three hundred workers in what was to have been a single open-plan office. Rows of workers sit at Juki or Brother sewing machines, helpers on the floor stitch, trim and cut threads. The work is monotonous and intensive, and often results in damage to the spine, particularly in those who started work as children.

Following the threat of the Harkin Bill in the US Congress in 1993, about two-thirds of the children working in the industry were dismissed. Nevertheless, there were children, in all the factories I visited subsequently. The US Congress exhibited little concern for children working in far more dangerous and degrading occupations; which prompts the suspicion in Bangladesh that the USA is more interested in protecting its own garments industry than in the rights of children in a distant country.

Mifkif Garments is making denim shirts and shorts, mainly for export to the USA. The factory is on the second floor of a concrete building. A square-mesh grille controls access to the workshop which, when we arrived, was locked. Since a factory fire in 1992 in which twenty-five workers died in a locked factory, the locking of factory premises has remained a sensitive issue in Dhaka. In this case, the key was at least on the premises.

In none of the factories was the owner present. We depended upon the sympathy and good will of managers and supervisors, most of whom had started out as shopfloor workers. Two hundred people are working on a floor space of about 4,000 square metres. There are open-mesh windows through which the air circulates freely. There are sixty-eight machines in the room, mostly Brother sewing machines, but some are also for making buttonholes. Many helpers work on the floor, which is covered with thin plastic cloth. These are mainly children and young school-leavers, earning 400–500 taka a month ($US10–12). They are learning the trade, and can expect in due course to become operators with a salary of 800–900 taka ($US20–25).

Workers were so crowded that some helpers were actually working under the cutting table. There are about twenty different operations here, including the making of collars, cuffs, buttonholes, sleeves, as well as the shaping of the main body piece. Most operatives remain with the same job. Nearly all are migrants to Dhaka, frequently from Barisal, Mymensingh, Faridpur. Many young women live together in a shared rented room in a slum community. Some of the landlords own a large number of houses, fifty or more, from each of which they can command a rent of about 500 taka a month from three young women.

Ahmed Garments is quite different. In the central district of Dhaka, it is a cramped ground-floor building in a compound where other industrial units are operating. Next door is a factory making cardboard containers for Clean-O-Dent toothpaste; most of the workers are children.

At the far end of the long narrow factory of Ahmed Garments there was only one small, barred window. The atmosphere was stifling, even in February. Some 125 workers were densely packed in three long columns of sewing machines. The garments, made with Japanese machinery, were destined for the USA. A number of children were working here, the youngest about eleven. These were trimming, using outsize scissors to shape the rough edges after the garments had been stitched. Some boys were ironing the shape of the shirt collar, using a crescent-shaped piece of metal to ensure that the shape was standardized.

This factory was working with flannel material imported from Pakistan: red-and-black and green-and-blue check, to make padded jackets for the North American winter. Garments from here were also destined for Russia and the European Union. Quilting for the jackets came from Korea.

The workers are the daughters of small farmers or landless families. They tell a similar story: they have come to Dhaka to earn money to send home. Many discover that their living expenses in the city make this all but impossible. Even so, by dint of great frugality, most manage to remit something. When two or three young women live together, they pool their resources and send home 200–300 taka a month.

Although Friday is the Muslim holiday, it is usually given up to compulsory overtime, especially when there are urgent orders to be completed. When the buyer gives a letter of credit, the time for completion is usually fixed at 90 or 120 days, so there are constant deadlines to be met. With Bangladesh now offering the cheapest labour in Asia, there appears to be unlimited scope for the extension and growth of the industry.

The workers do not know that they are in competition with their sisters in Indonesia, Thailand and India: all they see is an opportunity to improve the living conditions of their family.

The atmosphere in Ahmed Garments is hot and dusty; the cotton waste and fluff from the material are kept in perpetual movement by the fans, and constitute a health hazard.

The Silver Garments factory is also in the central district, near Topkhana Road, an inconspicuous building not at all like a factory. It is only at 7.30 in the morning and late in the evening that it becomes clear that Dhaka is overwhelmingly a city of women factory workers; at those times the streets are full of young women, *chappals* creating a cloud of dust on the margins of the road. The wonder is that they emerge each new day from some of the most frightful living places imaginable, clean, radiant in brilliant colours. This is achieved by rising at 4.30 or 5.00 to wash and use the shared latrine, wash their clothes and oil their hair. Even the most simple daily tasks are accomplished only with great effort in Dhaka, and the dignity, pride and endurance of these young women is one of the marvels of the city.

Silver Garments employs five hundred workers. Conditions are crowded, but there is air. The factory was decorated with gold and crimson streamers in preparation for a festival. They are working on a consignment of shirts for the Walmart chain of superstores in the USA. Those working on this order must produce at least 500 complete pieces a day: their hourly production achievement is chalked up on a blackboard in front of the rows of women whose heads are bowed before their sewing machines; power is provided by a treadle, while their fingers deftly move the seams beneath the fast-moving needle that punctures and stitches the garment at speeds to deceive the eye, while the cotton on the bobbin spins, a cylinder of red or blue.

The material has been imported from Hong Kong and Korea. Silver Garments is a relatively good employer: twelve days annual holiday with pay, and wages and overtime paid regularly. In some factories wages are paid up to three months in arrears, and sometimes overtime remains unpaid. The production manager at Silver Garments was once a worker, and he has persuaded the owner that it is in his interests to take some responsibility for the workers and their lives. He assures us this is an exception in Dhaka; many employers regard their workers as dispensable, instantly replaceable; it is of no concern to them when, how or why they come and go.

It is Ramzan. Nearly all the workers observe the sunrise-to-sunset fast. During this month, work finishes early in most factories, so that the workers can buy the *iftar* foods: snacks of puffed rice, *channa* and *bhajis*, which are on sale at the roadside after six in the evening. Some factories require them to return to work afterwards. At Silver Garments, the bonus for the festival of Eid will be an extra 50 per cent on the month's salary. Other factories give 20 per cent, some nothing at all. The National Garment Workers' Federation held a torchlight procession one evening to protest at the denial of Eid bonus to many workers in the industry.

In 1993 the Bangladesh government declared that labour costs and other raw material inputs should ensure that the value added to garments in Bangladesh reaches at least 30 per cent. But because of the unavailability of local raw materials or semi-finished goods – even buttons and zip fasteners have to be sourced abroad – the rate rarely rises above 25 per cent. At present Dhaka is part of a global putting-out system, and the workers are among the most exploited in the world. 'What is needed', says Amirul Haq Amir, general secretary of the Garment Workers' Union, 'is the construction of an indigenous textile industry. There is no sign that this is happening.'

The principal health hazards are eye problems, respiratory diseases, accidents, insufficient light, shoulder and back pains from sitting too long in the same posture. The hours of labour are by law eight per day, with two hours' overtime, not compulsory. The reality is very different. Many workers do twelve or fourteen hours, without the opportunity to refuse. If they won't do it, they will be 'terminated'.

There is much movement between factories. Workers come and go, find some slight advantage here, a better position there. For the first year the rate of pay is usually 400–500 taka; then 700 for the second year, and 900–1,000 taka for a machine operator.

Before the emergence of the garment industry, the only work for young girls in Dhaka was in domestic service. To some extent children have taken the place of young women as domestic servants, but the complaint of the middle class is that servants will not stay and have become too demanding; it is reminiscent of Victorian England, where mistresses complained bitterly that maidservants were asking for snuff and tea as part of their conditions of employment.

Girls whose parents can no longer afford to keep them in school study only up to Class 8 or 9 (age thirteen or fourteen); and many of them come to Dhaka to work in the factories. They come as raw, fresh labour, with no experience of industry. They know little of their rights, and do not realize that 400 taka – a large sum to those unused to money – will not provide them with a decent living. Many are trapped. They cannot send money home yet cannot return either, because they no longer have a place in the rural economy. Factory work provides discipline, which certainly prepares them for the kind of married life most can expect. Many marry cycle rickshaw drivers. Their husbands are happy for them to continue work after marriage – so long as they also do the domestic work as well: cooking, looking after the children, fetching water and fuel.

The lives of the workers are a continuing battle against inadequate nourishment, poor shelter, ill health, unsafe drinking water, transport problems, insufficient rest. Even so, most say that living in Dhaka is better than the village. This we explored more thoroughly in the discussions with the workers themselves.

The next factory visit we made was under very unhappy circumstances. On 11 February 1995, at M/S Proster Garments, a joint Hong Kong and Bangladeshi venture in the industrial suburb of Mirpur, panic over an outbreak of fire caused five deaths as 1,200 workers tried to flee the building. There had been a minor fire a few days before, but at that time there was no one in the building because it was the moment for breaking the daily Ramzan fast. A few days later, a transformer exploded. There was minimal damage, but rumour spread that the building was on fire. Four young women were trampled to death, while another leapt from the roof of the four-storey building. Many women were injured in the stampede and taken to hospital.

As we asked directions to the site of the accident, all the local people we met said the same thing: 'Do not believe the official figures of casualties. At least a hundred have been killed.' This was an exaggeration; but rumours always flourish in the absence of reliable information, and the true dimensions of industrial accidents are often concealed by the authorities to minimize their impact. It is not unknown for hospitals to dispose of the dead, with the connivance of the police, so that only grieving relatives are left knowing that their loved ones have perished.

We could not go inside the brick building because there was a heavy police presence. Representatives of management were there to explain that it was simply an unfortunate accident. If the workers had not panicked, death and injury would have been avoided.

On a piece of ground opposite the factory were the sad red earth mounds of five newly dug graves of young women. The community is tense and uneasy. The factory will remain closed for three days as a mark of respect to the dead; the workers laid off will not expect to be paid for the period of mourning. This factory makes baseball caps, the headgear worn – often back to front – by young people all over the world. These are for the Hong Kong and US markets.

The garment workers

The office of the National Garment Workers' Federation is just off Topkhana Road, close to the Press Club in the centre of Dhaka. It is a small one-roomed building, with a concrete floor, a table, some benches, a filing cabinet. There are about fifteen workers present. Some have come specifically to talk to me, but others have come to the union for more pressing reasons. One middle-aged woman is there because her grandson, a garment worker, has been murdered. The workers in the slum stay and move round together in groups. A gang of youths controlled by the *mastaan,* or slum lord, had been harassing the workers. The boy was at home one evening when a friend called to take him to a restaurant. On the road the rival gang set upon the garment workers, and in the fray the woman's grandson was killed. This is one of the extra-industrial hazards of life in the slums, many of which are controlled by *goondas* with connections in political parties or the police. The union will contact some journalists sympathetic to labour struggles in order to publicize the case. This is not enough for the stricken woman. She wants justice. Justice, says one of the other workers, is a commodity which only the rich can afford.

Later, I spoke to some of the young women workers about their lives.

Rehana is eighteen. She comes from Khulna, and has been in Dhaka seven months. She works at Mifkif Garments as a quality inspector, earning 1,100 taka a month ($US28). Able young people can soon rise to supervisor or quality inspector. Rehana studied to higher secondary level. Her family owns 13 bighas of land (5 acres). She came to Dhaka 'because I knew there was work here. At home there is nothing for young women to do.' Rehana has five brothers and four sisters. She came alone to the city and was frightened when she first arrived, overwhelmed. Now she is used to it. She is surprised how little money she can send home. She shares a room with two other young women, and each pays 333 taka a month. The room is in a slum. Rehana prefers life in the village, but knows her future is here. She wants to work with the union. She says that many factory owners do not pay their workers punctually, or cheat them of their wages. These things are illegal but they occur daily, and the only way the workers can get justice is by organizing.

Rehana is working thirteen hours a day, the nine statutory hours (including the one-hour meal break) and four hours' overtime. She and her friends prepare their meal at home and bring food each day to the factory. They cook again when they reach home at around nine at night. They work seven days a week, and rarely see the place where they live by daylight. The food they can afford is not good. It costs 550–600 taka a month for food. They rarely eat fruit apart from bananas, which are 2 taka each. There is no Eid bonus in the factory. The Eid festival is the only guaranteed holiday of the year. It will last three days.

Lila Begum is also eighteen, but she has already been in Dhaka for five years. She also came 'for a job', when she was thirteen, from her native Faridpur. Her first job was with Blue Band Garments, where she earned 30 taka a month ($US8) as a helper. Her parents are poor, with 4 bighas of land (less than 2 acres). She has two brothers and four sisters. During her time in Dhaka she has worked in three factories. She left the first one for higher wages. She was sick at the second and applied for leave because she had jaundice. Leave was denied her and she was terminated.

Lila is now working for Mifkif, for a monthly wage of 1,350 taka, which includes payment for compulsory overtime. If hours of overtime are exceptionally long, she might get an extra 30 or 40 taka. She works twelve or thirteen hours a day, seven days a week. Sometimes she falls sick because of the excessive workload, and says money cannot compensate for the mental stress.

Lila's husband is a private tutor; that is, he is one of the tens of thousands of educated unemployed in Dhaka who seek a living by teaching others the useless knowledge they have acquired. He earns less than his wife. He was also in a garment factory, but felt he was working beneath his dignity and capacity. Lila pays 600 taka a month for a one-roomed house in a slum. They spend between 500 and 600 taka a month on food: rice for breakfast, rice and vegetable in the evening; meat two or three times a month. Lila says she is better off materially in the city, but her earlier life was psychologically better because she was supported emotionally by her family. In Dhaka she misses the space and open fields of Faridpur.

Lila exemplifies the common experience of many who have lived in the city for some years. First of all there is the shock of arriving in the city, bewilderment and revulsion at the pace of life, the indifference of people. When the young women have found work, made friends, their attitude changes and they say they prefer Dhaka to the village; their sensibility has rapidly been altered, so that they fit the faster rhythm of the metropolis; and this makes it exciting. The tempo of village life then seems dull. They have become accustomed to the variety of stimuli the city provides.

There is another aspect of this reconciliation to city life. The destiny of migrants is usually not to go back. They do not see the journey to the city as easily reversible (although some certainly will go home). Going to the city is seen as success by the family, and the move is a kind of commitment. They feel compelled to like the place where they must now make their life, and to show they are successful.

After a few years in the city, a more balanced judgement can be made, particularly when women marry and continue to work. It is then they realize the importance of the absent supports of family, the loneliness and drudgery of a domestic labour without end as well as long hours in the factory. Lila's reflections have a characteristic resonance, although most young women may not articulate them.

Hosniyara is sixteen. She came from Shariadpur with her mother to join her father, who was working with a shipping company in Dhaka. The family has only the small piece of ground on which their house stands. The landless make up a significant portion of migrants. Some 60 per cent of the people of Bangladesh have less than 3 bighas of cultivable land. Hosniyara says she likes Dhaka because her family is here: three sisters and two brothers; one brother remains in the village.

Hosniyara works at Mifkif. Before that she worked in a factory a long way from where she lives. One day she arrived late and was dismissed. She is now earning 1,200 taka as an operator. At Eid there will be three days' leave, although the festival lasts five or seven days. Two members of her family are working. They live in a single room at Jatrabari, about 4 kilometres from the factory. She travels to work by bus, and gives all the money she earns to her father. He then gives her a small amount to spend each month. She has many friends at work, but finds it exhausting. She works long days – twelve or thirteen hours, with compulsory overtime, seven days a week.

Shafia is twenty-one. She came to Dhaka from Khulna when she was fifteen to live with her older sister, who was married. She started work three years ago. The family has about 5 bighas of land (2 acres), where they grow rice and vegetables. She likes Dhaka and had already visited the city several times before she came here, so it was less of a shock to her than to some young women.

Shafia works at Ahmed Garments earning 2,500 taka ($US60) as a supervisor. This is a relatively high wage, but she insists it is still not enough for the better life she believed Dhaka would provide. The conditions at Ahmed Garments are bad, the air hot and foul. Shafia is sharing a room with her friend Rehana and another young woman, and paying one-third of the 1,000 taka per month rent. The three girls protect and look after each other, and in this lies one of the answers to why they prefer Dhaka. Bonds of friendship, affection and sisterhood grow, a subpolitical solidarity where the young women see themselves in the sorrows and misfortunes of each other and are always ready to help with accommodation, money, consolation, even when they themselves are living on the most frugal income.

Shafia lives 3 kilometres from the factory. She walks to work because this saves bus fares (60 taka a month, $US50). Work is usually thirteen hours a day, seven days a week. She is angry at what she calls 'authority', meaning the owners, who, she says, take advantage of the young women workers. When she is at home with her friends in the evening, they talk about factory conditions and how these can be improved, how the lives of poor people can be made better. All union activity has to be carried on secretly or those involved will be terminated.

Shafia says when she was with her family she had less freedom, because she had no money to spend. Now, although most of her income goes on living, she does not have to send anything home. Her father gives tuition, her elder brother is a teacher. Shafia says women are beginning to demand more freedom. Twenty years ago it would have been shocking for three young women to come to Dhaka to share a rented room; now it is taken for granted.

Shafia gets up at five to five-thirty in the morning to prepare for work and get breakfast. They eat *moori,* puffed rice, with onion, *dal* and raisins and rice. They share resources to live more cheaply.

The presence of so many (slightly more) independent young women in Dhaka has other economic effects. For one thing, the cosmetics industry also benefits: small luxuries like fancy soap, Johnson's baby powder, soft drinks and biscuits offer the promise of an enhanced life, although for many even these small consolations remain out of reach.

Shamsun Nahan is vice-president of the National Garment Workers' Federation. An older woman, deeply committed to the young women she helps to organize, she is a powerful presence.

Shamsun came to Dhaka in 1982 and got her first factory job in 1985. At that time, the workers had great difficulty in securing the wages due to them. The authority tried to grab the money it owed. This led to a protest by the women workers. In consequence, the factory closed down, without paying the three months' outstanding wages to the workers. They continued their protest and were finally paid, but the factory remained closed. A month later it opened under a new name elsewhere. This is common practice in dealing with labour 'problems'.

Shamsun works in the Arrow garment factory, earning 2,000 taka as an operator ($US50). She works a thirteen-hour day, with a one-hour lunch break, seven days a week. Overtime is paid, but is calculated at a rate of 80 per cent of the normal hourly wage. The union is trying to have this figure raised to 120 per cent, as is the norm in the better factories. When the workers first tried to get this improvement, authority threatened them and said that if they persisted, their jobs would be lost.

Arrow is better than many, she says. But if any worker is absent, even on a Friday, the Muslim holy day, she will be fined, losing not one but two days' pay. This is contrary to Islam, says Shamsun, and is also inhuman. The workers have demanded the right to one day's rest in the week, but management say they will be ruined if they give concessions, because all the other factory owners will take advantage.

Shamsun and her husband feel they can never go back to Faridpur. Their life is destined to be in the city. It is here that they, like thousands of others, must fail or succeed, must fight or perish. This is creating a new consciousness, that there is no way out of industrial society. They organize secretly. When the workers become strong enough in a particular factory, they can then make an open protest: when solidarity is more or less total, they can be effective. This happened for the first time in South Garments. Shamsun had helped organize all the workers. Authority came to hear of it and dismissed her verbally. All the workers ceased work and stayed away. The owners asked them to return to finish an order. The factory closed down soon afterwards.

Shamsun has a highly developed awareness of what is happening within the country, but she remains close to the workers, and represents their feelings. She says no one knows what the future of Bangladesh will be; the only thing everyone knows is that presidents, prime ministers, dictators come and go, and none of this improves the lives of the people. The leadership of the country does not represent the interests of the poor workers, whether in the formal or the informal sector. This was confirmed by nearly all the workers I spoke to, the cycle rickshaw drivers, vendors, rag pickers, garment workers. The quarrels between Zia Khaleda and Hasina (respectively the Prime Minister of the Bangladeshi National Party and leader of the Awami League opposition party) are seen as disputes among the powerful, and however these may be resolved, nothing will change for the people.

Shamsun is twenty-six years old.

Nina has been in Dhaka only twelve days. She is fourteen, and very shy. She is delighted with the city. She is staying with Rehana and Shafia. She came from Barisal, leaving two sisters and a brother there. She has been taken in as a guest by the three young women sharing the house, who will look after her until she is sufficiently independent to make her own arrangements. She is at Ahmed Garments working as a helper for 500 taka a month.

Shilpi is also little more than a child, but has been in Dhaka since she was small. Her mother is dead and her father made a second marriage. She lives with her aunt near her place of work, Ononto Garments in Elephant Road. She earns 450 taka as a helper. She likes Dhaka because here there is TV and cinema, which do not exist in the village. She says, 'TV brings America in our homes, so we don't need to go there.'

The workers of New Delta

A group of workers has come to the union office from New Delta Garments. There are six women – Shathi, Lovely, Zahura, Shillvie, Popi, Rabeya – and two men – Roton and Babul. They need help over irregularities in payment of wages and overtime. Seven months of wages, including the current one, have not yet been paid. Authority keeps promising to pay, but continuously defers the date. If the workers strike, management hires thugs and *goondas* to beat them. Roton had come to the office earlier in the day to inform the union that he had been attacked by the company's hired musclemen. In fact it probably costs them more to pay hitmen than to pay the workers their due. Roton is the only male worker in the sewing department. He persistently raised the question of the unpaid wages. Roton says there is a club nearby where the Bangladeshi National Party (BNP) organizes the hooligans. A group of armed men threatened to shoot him. They abused him verbally, and threatened to cut the tendons of those who continue to protest.

The workers at New Delta are paid between 800 and 1,000 taka a month. Roton gets more because he is a supervisor. The factory is making shirting and pants, subcontracting to a major exporter, goods for Canada, the USA and Europe. Lovely says she wants people in those countries to buy the garments they make, but they should know how the workers are treated, how they have not been paid, how they must work overtime for nothing. If management closes the factory for a day for their own reasons – to avoid a politically organized hartal – the workers lose a day's pay and are fined as well. This is not because the workers support the hartal – quite the reverse. It is the owners who belong to the political parties, some BNP, some Awami League, some Jatiya. Lovely sees no point in the workers supporting any political party. We earn foreign exchange for Bangladesh, says Roton, yet we are excluded from politics. We exist on the margins of the economy which is essential for the survival of our country.

Lovely has been at New Delta for two months. Before that she worked at Dolphin Garments. She left because they did not pay over-time; she has eleven months of overtime outstanding there. After she left, Dolphin management said they had no record she ever worked there.

'In our legal system', says Amirul, 'workers can go for legal action, but often they have no papers, only an attendance card. The time-keeper signs this every day, and at the end of the month the card is deposited with the timekeepers and they are issued with a new one. Whoever heard of anyone going to court without papers? We have no records. Authority simply takes a photograph of the workers they recruit and keeps the application document; if there is a dispute, they can destroy all evidence that the worker was ever there.'

This is why they have come to the federation. Shafia said that she too had outstanding dues of three months, but after the federation organized in the factory the money was paid. This is what must be done at New Delta. It is a small workforce, seventy or so.

Popi and Lovely offer to take me to the place where they and many other factory workers live. The settlement is about 3 kilometres from the union office, and then a walk of about 1 kilometre along the rail-way line.

We get into a baby taxi (a three-wheeler) and race through the streets of the city among the choking dust and fumes of homegoing traffic. The vehicle strikes against a cycle rickshaw, buckling the wheel. The angry cyclist shouts, and a small crowd gathers. The three-wheeler moves on, honking furiously to remove pedestrians from the road. The street market is busy: vendors of pyramids of oranges, papayas, bananas, black grapes from India, sellers of vegetables, *iftari*, dried fruits, all encroach onto the road, so that driving is at its most hazardous at this time of day.

The vehicle stops when it reaches rough terrain, a kind of termi-nus, with a jangle of cycle rickshaws and three-wheelers This marks the limit of the definable road. Beyond is a wall of darkness; nothing is visible. Lovely and Popi take me by the hand to guide me through what is one of the most densely packed slums in Dhaka. The only light is a flicker of candle flame through the hessian walls of a hut, the greenish flare of a kerosene lamp beside a vendor selling *brinjals*, flour or *dal.* The earth is very uneven, and the huts are so close together it is almost impossible for people to pass one another. In front of some houses are piles of metal rods or scrap which the owners collect for a living; the jagged metal of rooftops grazes my cheeks. Popi and Lovely know every inch of the road. This is Mirhajbag. They are stopped by a neighbour sitting outside and preparing vegetables by candlelight. She asks us inside. There is a tin chair, a couple of plastic stools; some clothes on bamboo poles, cooking vessels, a traditional village stove on the threshold. No ornament, no concession to frivolity or relaxation: an austere resting place for labour.

Sitara Begum, however, is a smiling, welcoming woman, perhaps in her late thirties. She works in a garment factory for 700 taka a month, and came from Barisal when her husband died. They had no land. Her son Noorislam has been working for seven years and now gets 1,400 taka a month. He is eighteen. Sitara Begum's eleven-year-old daughter Kurshida is a helper for 400 taka a month. They pay no rent for the hut, which they constructed themselves on government land. Sitara Begum says it takes 100 taka a day to feed the five people in the family. Her youngest boy, a child of ten, has yet to be claimed by factory life.

We pass on, climbing a rough slope, so that we are now walking on the elevated embankment of the railway track. The moon provides the brightest light: on both sides of the track the huddled outlines of hutments are visible, some of them semicircular, flexible bamboo draped with polythene; it is a camp rather than a settlement, a transit stop for people displaced from country to city. The huts are all on low ground; when it rains the embankment is weakened and the floodwater simply cascades into them. Here and there is a brighter light: the fluorescent strip of a pharmacy, where antibiotics, painkillers and remedies for jaundice and dysentery absorb so much painfully earned money.

Popi and Lovely are very attentive. They take my hand. The people laugh to see these two young women leading a foreigner through the darkness. Popi's hut is in a small turning at the base of the railway line; small streets go off at all angles, crooked because the huts have been built irregularly.

Popi's mother is a vegetable vendor. There are also two brothers. Her father married another woman and left. They have been here for three years, paying 500 taka a month to a private owner. The landlord owns sixty-four slum properties. Popi is working at Lizen Garments, where she earns 1,300 taka a month. She has been there seven months. Popi is only fifteen. The family came from Vikrampur, not far from Dhaka. Popi says Dhaka is better because here they can see their life improving daily. A neighbour calls to see who has come. Shanaz Begum, also a garment worker, earns 1,200 a month, while her husband Hiron brings home 1,600 as a press operator in a plastics factory.

Popi's mother is still at work, although it is now after nine. She will not return until all the people coming from work have been provided with vegetables for the evening meal. As we cross the railway line, a blinding searchlight suddenly illuminates the scene, and we have to jump quickly out of the way of an oncoming train to Chittagong. The cone of light shines on the huts, crouching like frightened beasts, long shadows of people are thrown forward onto the rough earth, flying night creatures dance in the shifting beam. The train whistles past, setting up a tornado of dust. Popi says that many children are injured and some killed each year on the railway track. The houses are less than 2 metres from the trains.

Lovely's house is just off the turning from the railway line. She and her family have been here two months. They moved house because this is cheaper than the place where they were living – 500 taka against 700 a month. Lovely has one sister, Liju, aged eight, and a brother, Monir, who is working in the Dolphin factory as a helper for 500 taka a month. He is thirteen and works from 7.00 a.m. until 9.00 p.m. There is a one-hour lunch break, and he works seven days a week, although on Fridays they finish at 3.00 p.m.

Lovely's grandmother is living with the family. Few people here have survived to be old. Although apparently an old woman, she is probably not much over sixty. She remembers when Pakistan became independent from Britain 'long ago'. She cannot say that their life has improved; they have lived through so much strife, unhappiness and suffering. She came from Barisal because her son, Lovely's father, died.

Lovely's house, like all the others here, contains few possessions. There is a large wooden bed with a blue cover, which fills half the room. There are some plastic water containers, some drinking vessels, cooking utensils, clothing on bamboo poles. There is electricity, however; a thin light that flickers, around which the mosquitoes weave their invisible skeins of movement. Dhaka is known as the city of mosquitoes, says Lovely. One of the first 'luxuries' people buy is a mosquito net, especially for babies. In some houses a blue nylon net covers the enormous beds, a room within a room, like a cage. Five people live here. Lovely's mother earns 1,000 taka a month as an operator at Dolphin. There are only two latrines here for fifteen families – about 120 people. There is a tubewell, but people must stand in line to fetch water in the early morning. Lovely's family buy gas for cooking, so they do not have to buy firewood in the market. Sometimes people use scraps of leather and plastic for cooking, and they suffer from inhaling fumes. Popi and Lovely get up at 5.00 a.m. to get ready for work. It is a long business; the astonishing thing is their exuberance and resilience at the end of such a long day. Please, said Lovely, tell the people in your country how we live.

They come with me to the main road at the other end of the slum, where some baby taxis are waiting. They stand and wave until I am out of sight, saying to be sure to see them again next time I come to Bangladesh. They are fifteen and sixteen. I am moved by their energy, commitment and maturity. Lovely and Popi. If anyone will change the living conditions and wretchedness of the people of Bangladesh, it will be these young women and the thousands like them who pour forth from the slums of Dhaka each morning to labour on garments that we unthinkingly buy, and into which the youth and energy and beauty of Popi and Lovely are sewn fast.

7

People of the City II

The Intellectual, Jakarta

Dr Habib Chirzin lives in central Jakarta, just off Jalan Proklamasi, an area of the city settled long ago. The streets are narrow and twisting, but the houses are substantial. The people who live here think of themselves as the true natives of Jakarta. These are the people who built the city, who came here before the great expansion of the past twenty years. If this land were to be threatened by 'development', as has happened with many other central districts, they would not give in without a struggle, says Dr Chirzin. This is a suburb of small traders, vendors, many of whom have seen their children join the professional classes. They have a sense of rootedness and of achievement.

Dr Chirzin is a critic of development from within the Islamic tradition; his is a generous and inclusive Islam, not the caricature preferred and promoted by the West.

'According to some Muslim leaders, one of the greatest dangers to our culture comes from consumerism and hedonism, which are rooted in the obsessions of capitalism. Therefore, even at public meetings, these things are openly aired as concerns of Muslim society. The assault of consumerism comes in many forms; we say "assault" because consumerism is not people-oriented, it does not target basic needs, it involves a radical falsification of human priorities.

'Our Islamic critique is that this process is designed not to sustain the earth and life, but to sustain lifestyles of privilege. These issues are long and deeply discussed in Muslim gatherings, even in neighbourhoods and mosques. Judgements are made on whether these new lifestyles are good or bad, how powerful they may be, and how they invade the most intimate spaces of life even before you realize it.

'Religion has the role of criticism, but also of liberation. Where are we going and why? Religion alone can provide the strength for resistance and liberation, and this is what shows people the way.

'Government claims that we can have all the economic goods of

131

development with none of the social costs, because we are an Islamic society, and our values will protect us from the worst excesses of the West. But values must be a living force in people's lives, they are not a talisman to protect you. Consumer capitalism comes as a package – you cannot have these kinds of goods without the social disintegration that goes with them.

'Since the seventies we have been looking for an alternative. In the new context of the end of the Cold War and globalization, we must also globalize civil society in resistance to it. We now see Vietnam going the same way: the country that defeated the military might of the USA now humbly begs its economic might to flood in and overwhelm it. It is a cultural and structural violence against the people. Everywhere governments must control popular movements and workers' organizations in order to "stabilize" the country, that is, to make it safe for foreign investment.

'If we accept an even more coercive version of this ideology in Indonesia, this comes perhaps from the Javanese idea of *Mataram*, the power of the kingdom, an inherited, oppressive tradition that re-emerges in new forms. The domination of other cultures by capitalism is nearly always rooted in indigenous forms of oppression. There are few societies that do not have authoritarian and unjust practices and antecedents which ruling castes and elites can invoke to pave the way for new forms of dominance. We are no exception. We are, however, different from the Philippines, for example, which had been more totally colonized at a much earlier period, had been culturally transformed and Christianized.

'The concern of the Dutch here was solely economic exploitation. It was different from the British, Spanish and French, however important this was also in their colonial policies. Although the Dutch were here three hundred and fifty years, they never colonized the whole archipelago. They used divide-and-rule techniques, negotiating with local elites and rulers while they dominated them. They used indigenous aristocrats to oppress the people, and the buffer of Eastern foreigners – the Chinese – to control the economy, without direct intervention.

'Indonesia was also deeply marked by a small but powerful group of officers created and trained by the Japanese between 1942 and 1944, as were Burma and Thailand; the New Defenders, they were called. This layer is now still an influential force. Those who came immediately after are different, they have a less intensely military mentality.

'The doctrine of the dual function of the army in Indonesia must be understood: the military function, and also the socio-political function. They will maintain and defend this because of the privileges they enjoy; what they say, of course, is that this has brought stability to the country. So to some extent the civilians also believe that they owe their security to the military, and the people fear the loss of that stability. The military are welcome in all neighbourhoods; they are close to the neighbourhood communities. The military are also from the people. They are still seen as liberators. The way the people are organized within the military framework of values begins in the primary schools, with the inculcation of *panchasila*. Community leaders are trained in the values of *panchasila* – some do a hundred hours, others forty, others twenty, so there are varying degrees of penetration. There are thirty-six points of *panchasila* which community leaders are supposed to understand and memorize. The purpose of the ideology is to domesticate and reduce the people to obedience.

'It has some roots in Javanese culture. The ways of our ancestors were the ways of harmony and conciliation; even though harmony and conciliation on the terms of the powerful may seem, at a deeper level, a profound contradiction. But it does mean that the informing spirit behind *panchasila* is not alien, but has its roots here. For that reason it is both more powerful and pervasive.

'Even the vast spillage of blood in the sixties did not mark the end of resistance. In 1974 there were riots in Jakarta against the new Japanese invasion via its multinational companies, Mitsubishi, Toyota and the rest. After that, there was much repression of people's power, especially of the students. The universities became more regulated. Student councils were supervised, there were bans on magazines and newspapers. There was more militarization. This was intensified after 1978, when more student riots occurred.

'There is no space for the marginalized, there is no room for self-reliance. Rapid urbanization also raises new questions and new anxieties – even here, in this part of Jakarta, which has always been the centre of popular movements. Close to here there is a small mosque that was recently rehabilitated: this mosque was the centre of operations of urban guerrillas during the independence struggle. The people here are known for their high courage. They will stand up even to government ministers. They feel they own Jakarta. In other areas, they sweep away the urban poor, with little or no compensation, in the name of development. But here, they hesitate.

'Indonesia entered the world market in the 1970s. The tradition of self-reliance was fully overthrown. Even in the sixties we didn't know what developmentalism was: the word then was revolution. Sukarno at that time said "To hell with aid", self-reliance was his aim. We even withdrew from the UN in 1963. We spoke then of the unity of the newly decolonized countries "emerging forces" against the old colonial powers. Now it is "world community", which means that everything is determined by the rich countries.

'This is why I believe Islam is our best hope now; as a profound, peaceful, liberating force. Islam is a middle path; *salaam* means peace. Of course capitalism must manipulate the feelings of its people against Islam because, to some extent, it stands in the way of its further growth and expansion.

'Since 1978 Islam has been articulating alternative economics, culture, education. *Alternative* is a key word, even alternative research for social transformation. The government did not want popular organizations and movements, so we started organizing people in regional networks, popularizing people's culture. Since 1979 we have had a programme of popular theatre, a self-sustaining cultural activity designed to raise the self-esteem and enhance the identity of the people, to understand our own potential, without looking to the Western lifestyle. Our own values, our own traditional medicine and technology are more suited to our environment and culture. Our understanding of planting rice, our own seeds, must be reclaimed from domination by the transnational seed companies: we have our own seed bank in central Java. In 1976 we started our organization, SEARICE, because the land problem was directly related to the development process. Our understanding of land is different from the capitalist understanding of land as a commodity; for us, it is a community resource. We saw how the Green Revolution destroyed self-reliance. Farmers know that chemical inputs, the purchase of hybrid seeds with their pesticides and insecticides, destroy both land and livelihood. They must sell to the government, to our national stock. If you grew certain seeds in the seventies and eighties, they would send the military to destroy your crop. In the eighties the farmers used to talk of the "green pest", meaning the military. Those of us resisting at that time felt very alone; in such an atmosphere, to be radical is to be part of a small and threatened minority, is to be labelled subversive, no matter how peaceable your activities.

'Now we feel increasingly that we are part of a worldwide movement of rejection of developmentalism, of a crazy industrialization that manages to avoid addressing basic needs; we feel part of a movement for modest self-reliance where possible and appropriate, of true interdependence where this is proper; and that does not mean the subordination of a majority of humankind to the whim of a global elite.'

The leaders of the 'world community' look uneasily upon their allies in Indonesia because the rulers of Indonesia illuminate too clearly the coercive nature of the developmental processes, which can be both more effectively and less obtrusively achieved through economic, rather than military forces. In such circumstances there are no dictators, no conspicuous military elites to become a focus for popular resentment. This is the lesson of the dictatorships of the 1970s and of their overthrow and the fanfare of the 'return to democracy' in the 1980s. The dictators existed to pave the way for the more subtle dictatorship of the world market. When the purpose of the Marcoses and Pinochets and Galtieris and Zias had been served, they could be abandoned to their fate, and democracy restored. By that time, the alternatives of self-reliance had been buried and laid to rest. Then 'freedom' could be declared once more. Indonesia continues practices that have outlived their usefulness, and that now embarrass those who less than two decades ago, in the crusade against a moribund creed of communism, were happy to underwrite such excesses all over the world.

The Industrialist, Dhaka

Munize Manzur is director of the Apex Leather Group in Dhaka, a branch of Manzur Industries. She is at the head of a vibrant and dynamic company which makes leather garments solely for export, now with an annual turnover of more than $US5 million. In 1994, the company exported more than 49,500 pieces to Italy, Germany and Switzerland, just short of its target of 50,000.

This is the only leather garments factory in Bangladesh, and one of the few involved in the entire production of garments, from leather tanning and dressing to making and exporting the garments.

Munize Manzur is an energetic young woman; educated at Bryn Mawr in the USA, she chose to return to Dhaka because she wanted to make a positive contribution to her country. She admits that to be a woman industrialist is in Bangladesh an uncommon phenomenon. 'When people come and visit me from various government departments, they do not even ask for bribes, because they simply do not know how to deal with me. They all used to call me "Sir" in the beginning. I didn't mind, because for them, who do not know English, the word was not gender-specific, but simply a mark of my status. But I'm quite pleased that some of the younger ones now call me "Madam". My criterion for starting business was to help with the development of Bangladesh; also to be a role model for women and girls of the next generation. Men go into business, women go into teaching and traditional female roles. There is nothing wrong with that; it's only when you can see nothing else that it becomes limiting for women. I decided I was successful not because of the volume of business, but when a man I met in business said that after meeting me he no longer feels bad about having three daughters and no son. He will be more than happy to see his daughters carry on the work he has been doing.

'When I was in the USA, I was fascinated by the discussions on feminism, but I have found the discussions on political correctness bizarre. I had nothing to contribute to such debates. For people in the West, being a woman is decontextualized. When I told them, Yes I am a feminist, but I am also a Muslim and a Bengali, they seemed offended. It was as though they resented the persistence of any other characteristics than gender; as if these were quaint survivals from the past. Of course the women at Bryn Mawr were quite sophisticated, but they were still appallingly ignorant of anything beyond their own frontiers. In the end I stopped explaining the differences between India, Pakistan and Bangladesh.

'I don't think Taslima Nasreen has helped the position of women in our country. There are far more people working in a quieter and more effective way. She has been used by the West as an anti-Islam symbol. I spent four years in the USA; you meet a great deal of anti-Islamic feeling: terrorism and Islam have almost become synonyms.

'We started in collaboration with an Italian agent for technical advice and marketing, and we still rely on European designers because the fashion shifts subtly and swiftly so you need someone there who is *au fait* with the market. Our collaborator found the buyers initially in Italy and Switzerland; we met our German contacts through the Hong Kong leather fair.

'We target Europe because they will pay the price if they can depend on quality and delivery. The US wants cheap products – a large quantity at a lower price – and India and Pakistan can provide them with jackets at $45. Our leather is expensive, we have to source trims, zippers, liners and snap buttons from abroad: Korea, Hong Kong, Taiwan. The middle market is our range. We get $75–80 from the wholesaler, and these then sell for $500–600 in Europe. Of course Italy was the centre of designer leather fashion, but they have been transferring technology abroad to less developed countries because of labour costs, to Turkey and Asia.

'India and Pakistan produce generic goods, we are designer-oriented. Slight modifications in fashion make a great difference to us: cowhide or goatskin, an antique, stonewashed look or fully finished. We buy the raw hides in Bangladesh; one-third of production comes at Qurbani, after Eid, when a goat or cow is sacrificed. Approximately 70 per cent is cowhide, 30 per cent goat. Now in February is the low season, we produce only three garments per hour; but this will double in the summer season from April. It is now Ramzan, so we finish at 3.30

in the afternoon, because people are weaker with fasting. At Eid workers go to villages, so we have a ten-day closedown then. We don't use pigskin because you cannot ask Muslims to work with such material.

'All our leather is locally produced, that is 60 per cent of the cost; imported trims account for 8 per cent, overheads and the rest 28 per cent, labour is 4 per cent of the cost, that is, salary and overtime in the peak season. The Europeans cannot compete with this.

'If you don't have a tannery, you cannot start a leather garment factory. My father has his own tannery. The leather industry is not very clean, the machinery is expensive. We never give out the formula for our tanning process. There are 350 people in the factory. It is a medium-sized enterprise. It requires more skill than the garments sector, although all our workers had been in garments before. We have to initiate an extra training programme for them to work in leather. You have to be more careful; with fabric you can get away with a slightly crooked seam, in leather you cannot. They are allowed just one centimetre. Some leave to go to Malaysia, where leather is also picking up.

'In spite of all the political strife and hartals, Bangladesh has a 5 per cent growth rate; I am helping to bring in foreign exchange, and creating positive publicity for my country which has not seen a great deal that is positive about it in the world press. During the recent political strikes we didn't close. Most of the workers live in the area, so they came anyway.

'We are finding that more women are coming back to Bangladesh after studying outside. I think at Bryn Mawr I learned the value of independence and I gained self-confidence; I am who I am, a mixture of East and West. When I first started, everybody was watching to see if I was serious, if I'd make a success of it. I call myself a good Muslim. I am a religious person; I pray and fast and get strength from my faith. Many mullahs also believe that women should be working, if they maintain a sense of decorum. I'm tough inside; but women are.

'The garments industry has brought so many women into the labour force, women with earning power. They look around and become more aware. They learn that they are not just born to bear children and cook, but can have other functions too. Of course, there are 106 males for every 100 females in Bangladesh; there has been glaring differential treatment between boys and girls, so you can see we have a long way to go.'

I went with Munize to her factory. It is in Dhanmondi, in a spacious three-storey U-shaped building; although it is situated in an area of small tanneries, where working conditions are generally poor, the Apex tannery is as clean as such a place can be. The skins are sorted and cleaned in an open hangar; men sit and scrape the remains of flesh and hair from the skins before these are treated in vats of brine. The skins are then sorted, weighed and labelled for quality. They are then steeped in wet-blue, which dyes them all a pale blue colour. The workers have plenty of room, and the air can circulate in the sheds – the contrast with the tanneries in Dharavi in Bombay could not be more dramatic. When Munize's father bought the tannery, it was bankrupt, and only one-quarter its present size.

The dyeing is an Italian technique using Paletto machines; the skins are carried on a stringlike conveyor belt, behind protective glass so that the dye does not escape. Outside the factory, the waste water runs brownish red with dye; this, like all the foul water, goes back to the river, the river being the reason why this became a site for tanning. The dyes are imported chemical dyes. There is a machine that embosses a crocodile pattern onto some skins. After processing, the hides have to be dried for two or three days before going into the factory.

The pattern section contains the cardboard and metal shapes of garments; patterns come from abroad because of rapid changes in fashion. When the designers send a pattern sample, the factory makes a counter-sample and sends it to the buyers for approval. There are a number of machines – mostly Italian – which give the leather differ-ent finishes: matt, gloss, antique, stonewash. The goatskins must be in one piece; you cannot stitch two skins together to make a garment. Munize has installed her own generator in the factory, because fre-quent power failures interrupt production. She has her own bonded warehouse for trims, zips, studs, linings and buttons. The thread is supplied locally. She would welcome competition because if there were other leather factories, supporting industries would come up, which would permit her to source the ancillary materials from within Bangladesh. Some of the linings come from Italy; there are some local cotton linings, and some nylon from Korea.

The heaps of waste leather will be sold to small makers of leather products – purses, key rings and footballs, which are made of patches of leather.

Work in the cutting department requires great skill, so that as little as possible of each skin is wasted. All the cutters were trained in the fac-tory. It is a well-paid job, and most are men, although cutting is now being done by some women. They cut at plywood tables topped with plastic. In India and Turkey they use a knife to cut on glass-topped tables, but here they trace the shape around a stainless steel pattern, and cut with big scissors, fleece on the handles to prevent blisters.

Twenty-six pieces must be cut out to make up each garment. The component pieces are tied in bundles ready for sewing; locally produced gauze is used as interlining to stop stretching, and two women glue the gauze onto the back of each component. The edges of each sleeve and collar have to be shaved so that the stitching can be straighter and easier. The sewing machines are Italian.

The workers sit in rows, in five lines. The component pieces are put in plastic baskets, a different colour for each line, so that every garment can be traced back to the team if there is any problem. If the baskets mount up at any part of the process, you can tell which operative is not working as fast as she or he should. The production-line helpers join the pieces together. Where the joins occur, the leather is hammered on a block so that there are no uneven bumps. As the baskets move down the line, so the garment becomes more complete: the sleeves, collars, pockets and pocket flaps, epaulettes, etcetera, are added to the basic body shape. There is a machine at the end for punching buttonholes. There are seventeen operations, and most of the stitching is done by women. As the garment becomes more complete, it also becomes more unwieldy.

The workers change jobs frequently; they are all equally skilled, and the changes give them variety in their work.

Checking for defects must be rigorous in these exported garments. We saw one arm–shoulder seam that was out by over two centimetres. It was set aside to be done again. Even those with minute defects must be redone, especially if a buyer is taking only a limited number – ten or twenty. You cannot cut corners in designer brands. The various styles of jacket all have names: Rocky, Scott, Elvis. The finished product is inspected, folded and packed in polythene. It costs $US6 to send each garment by air, $US2 by sea. In the peak season they go by sea, unless the buyer is prepared to pay the air freight cost. It takes a month by sea; there is always danger of fungal growth, so the garment is treated with a drying agent.

On display in Munize's office is the President's Trophy for Exports, awarded in 1987–88 and 1989–90. 'In the developed world, tanneries are closing because of pollution. Even here there is an effort being made to shift the tanneries from Dhanmondi, which is primarily a residential area. The people complain of the smell, and of the waste that goes into the river after the skins are washed, and after the dyeing.

'I started from scratch. I interviewed all the workers myself. Apart from the dirty processes it is very labour-oriented. People do come and go, and sometimes I feel sad that their loyalties are not stronger, but if higher wages are on offer they will go. The workers are on 900 a month, which is a good average for the industry. They know they'll get overtime, they know there is a medical and welfare programme, which does not exist in most garment factories. If you lose people in the peak season you have a problem, because it takes time to train new ones. But I feel it is a major achievement, and I'm proud of what I have done, and I am pleased to confound all the stereotypes of Bangladesh and of Muslim women, without in any way being disloyal either to my country or my religion.'

The Migrant Worker, Bangkok

I became attached to Pong during the two months I knew him. A young man of twenty-five, father from Laos, mother from the north of Thailand, he was working as a bell captain in a serviced apartment block, of a kind many foreign business personnel now use instead of hotels.

I met him one hot evening on the steps of the Rama IV monument. His English is fluent, learned simply from contact with the people he serves. He is a curious mixture: conventional Thai values and deep personal unhappiness. At first he was not inclined to speak about himself. When I asked him about his family he turned away. Something attracted me to him, and although he showed no real interest in pursuing our acquaintance something made him reluctant to leave on the first evening. This set the tone for our friendship. Several times I thought I would never see him again, but he always telephoned afterwards to say he was sorry and wanted to meet me.

We fell into an extremely un-Thai pattern of arguing whenever we met. He said he wanted money because he was a poor boy and I was a rich *farang*. I said Are you a money-boy then? No. How could you think such a thing? He had given up his studies because of pressure of work. His mother had lost the sight of one eye and he was still paying off the loan he had taken to pay the hospital bills. He was earning 4,000 baht a month (about $US135), which is reasonable. He shared a room for 1,200 baht with a friend working in the same apartments. He was sending 2,000 baht a month to his mother.

I told him I was not rich but working in Bangkok. He said You have more money than I do, which was true. I even tried – vainly – to tell him that I too had come from a poor family, that they had also been ordinary factory workers. It was clear he could see no connection between the experience of a foreigner in Bangkok and the life of his own family in a wooden hut on a small piece of land in the little town of Sanamchaiyaket.

Later he talked, but never in response to questions. At the hint of any inquisitiveness he would fall silent, but in his own time he wanted to speak. He told me his father hated him, and that he was placed in a *wat* (temple) at the age of eight. He stayed there until he was nearly twenty, when he left to come to Bangkok for the first time. His mother visited him at the temple, but he never once went home in those years, and had not seen his father. It may be that his father did not believe that Pong was his son.

His father was killed in a road accident in 1993, and for the first time Pong went home. He slept on a mat on the floor of the house, close to his mother. It was the first time he had felt wanted in twelve years. In the *wat* he was sent to school, he studied, his immediate needs were answered, but not his need for affection, for guidance.

He had never been loved. He felt his mother had been given an ultimatum by the father and had chosen her husband over her son. He knew neither how to give nor how to accept affection. He quarrelled with all his friends. He got good jobs, but left them because he would fight with the manager, the boss, anyone in authority. Because his English is excellent, it was always Pong who was sent to placate the foreigner who complained. Sometimes he had to stand and listen to their abuse. You must be fucking stupid, why are you Thais so goddam lazy, why can't you understand a simple order. He said 'I'm sorry sir' or 'I'll do my best to put it right.' He said that if *farangs* hate Thailand so much, why do they come here.

There was a deep sadness in him. Sometimes when he telephoned his voice, which was very beautiful, betrayed an inner desolation that moved me and made me want to see him. Yet it was impossible to remain friends with him. Some days he would look the other way, respond in monosyllables. On other occasions he would come to my room and sit absorbed in frightful TV films like *Predator Two*, dubbed into Thai. Then he would say You forget me, forget my name. If I see you again, do not speak to me.

One day, early in our friendship, he tore up the address he had given me and the phone number I had given him, and threw them dramatically into a rubbish can on the street. Later he called. I said I thought you had torn up the number. He said, 'I remembered it.'

There was a strange ambiguity about his sexuality. For a long time we did not discuss it. He scarcely touched me, just a brief formal handshake when we met. He always sat at a distance. On the bus he always sat apart. In the restaurant I joked that perhaps he would prefer another table. He said You do not understand Thais. They think bad things. I said You mean they will think I am a *farang* and I am paying you to be my boyfriend. He said You talk too much.

One day, the night-watchman in the rooms where I was staying, an Indian, said to me in Hindi '*Apka larka aya hai*', Your boy has come. When I told Pong this he became very angry. He went to the astonished Indian and made it clear that he was not my boy, but my friend.

He was often very tiring to be with. I would feel drained and exhausted by his emotional silences, his sulky resentments, which were not really directed at me, I understood that, but were aimed at the absent humanity of his deprived childhood. Several times I said to him I thought it would be better if we did not meet again. He said yes, but then a few hours later he would phone and say I want to see you. And I was very drawn to him. I always said yes. Once or twice when we had mutually agreed to call it a day, we both went instinctively to the place where we had met, and found each other again.

After the first day he never asked me for anything. At festivals I would give him something to send to his mother. One day he arrived with an expensive attaché case and a gold watch. A Japanese who had checked out of the apartment had left them. He had been on night duty. There was no one from management there so he had taken charge of them. Inside there was a pack of credit cards, some business documents. He repeatedly called the hotel to see if the man had reported the missing items. At 1.00 a.m. he went by taxi to return them to their owner. Next day he was very excited. As a reward the man had given him the gold watch. He said it is worth a lot of money. I can sell it and send money to my mother. It turned out to be worth 300 baht – 12 dollars. I gave him 20 dollars to send home.

Some time later when I met him he was troubled and unsmiling. He said I have a problem. I assumed this was a prelude to a request for money. But I had misjudged him, and not for the first time. He spoke hesitantly. He said I do not know what I am, if I like men or women. I cannot do sex. I thought he was referring to impotence. In fact, it turned out, he had a very tight foreskin which would not release the head of the penis, so that sex was impossibly painful for him. This secret, together with his feeling of exclusion and having been unloved, had only deepened his sense of inferiority, had fed his defensive aggressiveness.

I felt very close to him and was very touched. I said to him You know that isn't really a problem. It can easily be set right. A small operation, it will take only a few days, and you'll be fine. He said How can I spend money on such things. I offered to pay for the operation. I will come to the hospital with you. No, he said, I shy: he frequently pretended his English was inadequate when he was embarrassed. He clearly regretted having spoken, and would not discuss the matter further.

A few days after that he came and said he had given up his room, abandoned his job. He was going home to his province. He would stay with his mother and work in the Wella shampoo factory there for 80 baht a day. I mocked him and said he wouldn't have much chance to practise his English there. If he stayed in hotel work he would certainly rise to management level; he was skilled and presentable. He needed the city, would be bored and lonely at home. He said I am bored and lonely here. You do not understand Thai people. My mother needs me. She is old. She cannot see. Tomorrow I am leaving on the early bus. I just came to say goodbye.

OK, I said nonchalantly. Maybe I'll see you tomorrow. I'm going home tomorrow. He had been saying that ever since I met him. I thought it was another threat, a test to see if I really cared for him. Perhaps he wanted me to beg him to stay. I smiled. He said Sleep well, and shut the door. I never saw him again.

The Refugee, Bangkok

I met Tin Shwe at the Centre for Migrants in Bangkok. A Mon, he had fled his native Burma six years ago. He had been staying at the centre since the police raided the apartment where he was living. He was there temporarily with his wife and baby of a few months.

'There are about 3 million Mon people in Burma. We were a separate kingdom until the eighteenth century, when we were overrun and annexed by Burma. The Mon have been conducting an armed insurrection against the SLORC [State Law and Order Reconciliation Council], which although less well known than the Karens has met with equal brutality and repression.'

Tin Shwe is an articulate and passionate defender of the rights of his people to self-determination. 'The problem with Thailand is that it does not recognize the Mon people as refugees. There was an uprising six years ago and I got through the border to escape the repression.' He came to Bangkok and worked illegally. There is always employment – at very low wages – for illegals, who are caught in permanent bondage by their status. Tin Shwe was living in a one-room apartment in Bangkok's Chinatown. One day the Thai police came. He was not at home. They told his wife to clear out the same day. The landlord can be fined if he rents rooms to foreigners with no documents. The child of three months is also an illegal immigrant; he came through the forbidden channel of Tin Shwe's wife's body. The baby was born on the construction site where Tin Shwe and his wife were working at the time.

To get a job Tin Shwe had borrowed an identity card from a Thai workmate. After two weeks it became clear to the construction site manager that he could not speak Thai. He was allowed to work illegally because the Mon are known to be reliable workers. Tin Shwe worked for two years on construction sites – not the big projects, the shopping malls and condos, but in the peripheral areas where a Thai worker will be paid 150 baht a day ($US6). 'We were paid 100 baht. They blackmail us with our illegal status. On one site I had an accident and my finger was smashed. The hospital doctor said he will have to cut the finger off. I said, "No, without my finger I cannot write or work. Please don't cut it off." They X-rayed it and found that the bone was intact so they said, "We can mend it, if you pay 4,000 baht [$US160]."'

Tin Shwe's wife is also a Mon. They met on a construction site. The baby was born in April, when the temperature reached 45–50°C inside the shelter. 'We could bear it but the baby could not, so we left. Work on the site was from 5.30 in the morning to 7.30 at night, with no holiday. If you wanted to leave the building site you had to ask for permission. If you fail to work on any day, for whatever reason, you have to pay for the living quarters; if you work you don't pay. You pay 20 baht for electricity and water. Small companies welcome illegal labour because it makes them competitive.'

The Mon struggle started as a student protest, but now it has become a struggle for independence. Mon was the earliest language in Burma but the authorities tried to suppress it. Early in 1994 SLORC soldiers burned some villages near the Thai border claiming that they harboured guerrillas. Some 5,000 refugees fled to Thailand. They were not welcome there because Thailand wants to 'engage constructively' with Burma and wants the Mon to reconcile themselves to Burmese rule.

Tin Shwe says, 'The Mon people are farmers. I cannot contact my family. They agree with what I am doing, they support the struggle, but cannot say so. The Mon people are now being used as forced labour in Burma to construct a railway for a joint Thai–Burma oil pipeline. This is a new version of the Burma Railway, only this time the government is the occupying power.

'Many Mon people who came to Thailand did so to escape slave labour. The Thai government says, "You have no permit, you can only stay in the border area." We are not officially recognized. The UNHCR [United Nations High Commission for Refugees] says we should go back, they will recognize us only if we go into the Thai camps at Songhkla Buri. But we will not. The Thai authorities gave an assurance that those who went to the camps would be safe; then they were forced back to Burma, where our villages were burned. We cannot trust the Thai government so we will not go into camps; the UNHCR will not recognize us unless we have an official Thai number.'

Tin Shwe has an application form to enter Australia, but since he has no official number he has no chance of being admitted. Two days after our conversation a demonstration was held by Mon and other Burmese refugees outside the UNHCR office in Bangkok against the forcible repatriation of refugees. The Commissioner listened favourably. But the Thai government insisted they return and blocked all access to the camp, so all those in it were forced back to Burma. Tin Shwe says, 'We are trapped; we cannot go back and we have no right to be anywhere else. My child was born as an illegal; what kind of future can she expect?'

8

Ho Chi Minh City: Back to Saigon

I

Vietnam is a country in transition, but in transition it seems increasingly to its own past, to subordination, poverty and impotence.

Ho Chi Minh City is the centre of the transformation; Saigon, which fell twenty years ago, is now reverting to its former identity. But the twenty years it has spent in quarantine against development, thanks to the US-led embargo against the country, have left it strangely untouched. It remains on a more human scale than others of the principal cities of South Asia, less frenzied, with an elegant core. All of this is rapidly being remedied now that Vietnam has accepted the dominant wisdom of the world. But tantalizingly, it hints at other possibilities, a less driven development path, but one that has now been closed by the unspoken admission by Vietnam that its liberation struggle was a tragic error.

The centre of the city is a monument to the French colonial period: soaring trees shade boulevards reminiscent of Paris, restored public buildings and red-roofed white villas create an effect of archaic provincial charm. This is overlaid by the architecture of the liberation period – the Soviet-influenced monumentalism of the Palace of Reunification, and the hotels demolished after 1975 and rebuilt for Soviet experts, advisers and tourists. Many of these have now been prettified: the ornamental night-time lighting of the Rex Hotel suggests different contours from the stark angularity of its daytime appearance.

Most recently the real-estate boom of the past five years, the construction of accommodation to receive an army of tourists – far more effective an invasion than any military expeditionary force – shows the lineaments of a future city more like Bangkok than Saigon. Great gaps have appeared in the fabric of the downtown area, where malls and condominiums and white marble-and-glass palaces with names like Ocean Towers are transforming the skyline.

But these are merely symbols of a deeper transformation, the

146

'restructuring' of the economy of Vietnam, its 'integration' into the world economy, a restructuring that is not merely the erasure of economic disaster but the dismantling of the social achievements of the socialist interregnum.

Tourism has conjured forth a culture of mendicancy: disabled people, women and children offer some trifling object for sale to conserve some pretence of economic activity – a dumb woman with a box of chewing gum, a child with a rag and a tin of boot polish, the vendors of war toys made from cans of Coke, Sprite and Orangina. The streets are populated by stunted and deformed children (the aftermath of the pouring onto Vietnam of millions of tons of defoliants and chemicals), are haunted by people with war wounds that will never heal. One man lies face down on a platform on wheels, his face supported by a rough cushion, legs contorted behind him; a tin vessel receives the contribution of conscience-stricken foreigners.

Many cyclo drivers (the cyclo is the cheapest form of transport, a sort of cycle rickshaw, in which the passenger sits in front) are also touts; they know how to serve those returning to Saigon increasingly in search of the rest and recreation for which it was celebrated in the years of US occupation. The cyclo drivers will take you to the brothels, karaoke bars and massage parlours where the girls are. Not that the girls are absent from the streets; a notable feature of Saigon is the young women on motorbikes, upright, respectable-looking, hair swept up prim as schoolmistresses, elbow-length gloves, hookers on Hondas cruising the city for customers. I kept meeting two girls, eighteen or nineteen, human merchandise being wheeled round by a cyclo driver and sitting in the metal tub of the one-seater vehicle. Each time I passed them they called out, 'You come with me.' Each time I replied, 'Tomorrow.' 'Tomorrow I die,' they said.

The culture of begging is the other side of the coin of market 'reforms', which re-form not only the economy but also the sensibility and psychic structures of a generation grown to maturity assured of health care, access to education, and a life expectancy of sixty-eight years for women, sixty-five for men; and all that in spite of the economic embargo conducted by the US and its allies since 1975. Assured no longer. All we hear now is stories of high economic growth – 7 per cent; while inflation is 18 per cent and there are now levels of malnutrition second only to those of Bangladesh.

There are also, of course, the trappings of carnival to celebrate the return of Vietnam to capitalism: vendors of carved Disney figures, coloured teddy bears and electric-blue pandas from Hong Kong, plastic guns and musical cigarette lighters, balloons and candy, Mars bars, beverages from Nestlé, soft drinks and Coke; if people go hungry it is in a world made safe once more for the luxury products of the transnationals. Across Saigon River, above the shacks of rusty tin and the greenery of plantain and water palms, painted boards bear the logos of Panasonic, Trinitron, Nike, Reebok, Raymond Weil, Sanyo, Canon, Toshiba – the claims of gold prospectors staked on the wide open spaces evacuated by socialism, virgin territory, a Klondyke, another frontier.

Here the fate of the countries of the South is made stark. People are being pressed into the service of a global wealth creation that is increasingly disarticulated from human need. The passing of communism is a tragedy not because of the death of a totalizing creed, but because its absence leaves no adequate critique of monstrous social injustice, no challenge to levels of inequality that threaten to squeeze the poorest out of existence: the right to life is now subordinate to the right to privilege.

If the only choice for the world lay between communist lies and capitalist illusion there was never any doubt which most people would choose. Lies are more instantly recognizable, and most of us will opt for illusion. But to call that illusion truth, or freedom, sets up a different order of falsehood. The paradox that the creation of wealth also requires an intensification of poverty is not one that the leaders of Vietnam care to explore. Instead, they speak of maintaining a socialist orientation within a free market economy, words which instead of revealing the contradictions are intended to spirit them away.

The Museum of War Crimes remains in Ho Chi Minh as a tourist attraction. The exhibits have become rusty: American tanks, aircraft, howitzers lie ancient and neglected. The images of the My Lai massacre remain, pictures that shocked the world, the grin on the face of a soldier who holds up the head and shoulders of a dismembered Vietnamese, the heroes with their trophies of the heads of captives – all appear grainy and indistinct now, half effaced, like memory itself. Yet the great question that frames itself in the presence of these monstrosities cannot be spoken. What was it all for? Too many people died – over 2 million Vietnamese – there was too great a burden of human sacrifice, too many people lost those they loved, too many wraiths haunt the sidewalks of Ho Chi Minh, too many deformities have resulted from all the untested chemicals that were poured onto the countryside: all these demand that the rhetoric at least be maintained. The words 'futile' and 'in vain' do not appear anywhere in the official versions of *doi moi*, renovation, which means in effect capitulation to the superior wisdom of aggressors now become mentors.

And among the people there is an extraordinary level of forgiveness. Resentment remains, but against the Chinese for their role in

Kampuchea – and for more ancient wrongs against the Vietnamese –
against the Russians for the impoverishment that followed liberation,
and for the overnight dissolution of their dogmas of emancipation,
leaving Vietnam to make its own accommodation with the world.

So much suffering has been endured since the defeat of the French
at Dien Bien Phu: the coming of the Americans to prop up the
regimes of Diem and Thieu, the 'Vietnamization' of the war, the fall
of Saigon, the revenge against collaborators, the threat of Pol Pot
and the occupation of Kampuchea, the command economy and now
its dismantling in the name of free markets, the obligation forced
upon the government to recognize the debts of the former South
Vietnam in order to gain credit from the International Monetary
Fund and World Bank. It is not surprising if most people say that all
they want now is to be left alone to get on with their lives.

If only it were so easy. But their own lives are themselves being
invaded – by growing insecurity, by unemployment, by the reduction
in health care and the erosion of free education.

Vietnam, it seems, is being retrospectively punished for having
taken on and having 'defeated' the Americans. But the reparations
are being paid by the weakest and most vulnerable; the guilt for the
war has now been assigned to those who dared to call into question a
system since become, global and to which alternatives are now
declared void.

Vietnam now is a strange hybrid; left with a socialist rhetoric that
cannot be disavowed because of the suffering with which freedom was
achieved, it is nevertheless offering the labour of its people to the
global market at a knockdown price; a bureaucracy polices the betrayal
of the people, protecting a government coerced into compliance with
the will of its late enemy. It is the worst of all worlds: an authoritarian
system diverted into the protection of free market reforms.

It is possible to argue that Vietnam now has the preconditions for
takeoff that characterized the other successful South Asian
economies – Singapore, Taiwan, South Korea – although they, of
course, had authoritarian governments of the Right rather than the
Left. It doesn't seem to matter; so long as the people can be compelled into conformity with the rigours of the market economy, what
does it matter who does the compelling? The legacy of the socialist
interlude – a puritanical work ethic, a disciplined and controlled population – serves the end admirably. Perhaps this is what a US
economist at an Asian Development Bank seminar in Manila late in
1994 had in mind when he suggested that democracy was often damaging to the economy and was essentially a luxury for 'developed'
rather than developing nations.

Back to Saigon in less than a generation. Ho Chi Minh, it seems, was only a diversion. If the city is energized now by new hopes of affluence, will these compensate the poor and excluded for the destruction of that fragile security they won at such grievous cost only two decades ago?

There are of course many who welcome the market economy; indeed, some in Saigon were never reconciled to the victory of Ho Chi Minh in the first place. Some people are finding space to improve their lives under the new economic regime.

I met Ty, a cyclo driver, a man of forty, with a weathered face, poor teeth from years of malnourishment, creases of fatigue around the eyes. He came from the Mekong Delta when he was twenty-five. He is the eldest of seven children, and his family have two hectares of land, where they grow enough rice to feed themselves. As the eldest it was his duty to come to the city to earn money to sustain the family. When he first came he rented the cyclo at 7,000 dong a day, 70 cents. He bought his vehicle, $US200, from the government and has paid off the loan. He earns between 15 and 17 dollars on a good day, 5 to 7 on a bad one. His wife works in a rice noodle shop close to her mother's house, where they live. She earns 5 dollars a day. Ty wants his three children to become professionals.

Ty speaks good English. Under the seat of his cyclo he has a much-used English grammar, as well as a Berlitz French phrasebook. His greatest regret is that he was unable to go to school. After the Russians came, he says, everything went down. They ruined the economy of Vietnam. Now things are improving once more.

Ty's earliest memories, like those of many, are of the shelling and killing of the years of war. He always wanted the US-backed government to win the war, an admission I was to hear many times in Ho Chi Minh. His family are still poor, and he sends money home each month.

I was sitting one evening on a bench in the square close to Notre Dame cathedral when I met Tam. A young man aged twenty-four like thousands of young people, he was driving his Japanese motorcycle around the city streets. He stopped close to where I was sitting and invited me to take a ride. Why? I like you. He took me to a café where I had a beer and he a coffee. He told me he is gay, but that in Ho Chi Minh there is no meeting place for gay men, no bar, no park, no club.

He works in a hairdressing salon in the tourist area; it opened only in July 1994. It is a smart establishment, black-and-white tiled floor, seats of black wood around glass-topped tables with mirrors, decorated with pink fabric. There are seven young women and two men working there. Formerly one was a cashier, one an army barber, two were in factories, another worked in an old-fashioned barber's shop.

Tam says this job is the best thing that has ever happened to him. He earns 60 dollars a month including tips. The owner is from Hong Kong, and the salon advertises 'Hong Kong styles', a phrase that evidently suggests something exciting and futuristic. On the morning I went I was the only customer; they gave me tea and biscuits, and their delight in having a foreign customer was plain. All agreed that life in Ho Chi Minh was becoming better. Before, life was drab, there was nothing to do. Now the young women can go disco dancing with their boyfriends. They welcome the coming of tourists.

Such testimony cannot be discounted, even though it is contrary to that of professionals working in the health, nutrition or education programmes.

Dr Thai Thiu Ngoc Du is a senior lecturer in the Department of Women's Studies at the Open University in Ho Chi Minh. She says government cuts in health, welfare and education are already having their effect. 'During the period of centralized bureaucracy the framework existed for a network of health care centres all over the country. Government health workers were deployed in every village, there was a dispensary, and basic medicines were universally available. But it was a limited service; only the most common medicines were free, and the remote areas were not always adequately covered. Now it is government policy to make those who can afford it pay a contribution to health costs. This should in theory enable continued subsidy to the poor. If people have enough money they can provide themselves with health care. This means there is increasing diversity in provision.' Diversity is a euphemism for inequality.

'At first, after 1975, there was much rhetoric about building socialism. The government claimed to have eradicated begging in Ho Chi Minh, which became much worse when the Americans were here. I left Vietnam in 1964 to study in France. When I returned to Saigon in 1973 I was shocked by the level of begging. The problem was dealt with by forcible restraint after 1975; and to some extent the root cause was dealt with, in that basic welfare was available. Similarly prostitution was forcibly stopped. Repression of the sex industry was severe. Most women did turn to other forms of economic activity. It may not have been so lucrative, they may have felt resentful, but prostitution was much reduced after 1975. Control was strict and there were not the rich clients. With the return of foreign tourists there is more scope for sex workers. Many women soliciting are also working – they may be in government jobs or the new service sector. Those women on Hondas are not necessarily driven by poverty, but by the desire to get more. Before 1975, the girls were there to serve the US and Vietnamese military. Prostitution is technically forbidden, but people find ingenious ways round it.

'There is now a spectacular gap between rich and poor. A tension has been set up between the social goals of government and freeing up the economy. Can free enterprise, foreign capital, tourism, coexist with adequate social care for the poor? Social security improved after 1975. There was less crime, more social cohesion, less malnutrition and avoidable sickness. These indices are rising once more.

'We may advise health workers to tell mothers which vegetables are good for nutrition, but that doesn't help mothers to buy them in the market. Malnutrition may be higher among urban families than in the rural districts because they do not have the money to purchase an adequate diet. In the countryside old habits of subsistence remain: people with a little land grow rice and vegetables, they have always caught fish and crabs in rivers and canals. But in the city money is the lifeblood; they cease to be self-provisioning. That too is a form of pauperization.

'Before 1975 there were high living standards in the urban areas; after 1975 city living standards dropped under the social policy of the subsidized system. Now they are rising again, but how far that is at the expense of the rural poor is another question.

'The period between 1975 and 1985 was an economic disaster for Vietnam. Socially it was not so. The relations between people were more human, people prized human values above money, whereas previously money had dominated our lives. That it is possible for people to have more money and to become less happy has not occurred to the zealots of reform.'

Dr Ngoc Du and many other intellectuals are asking whether the country would not be better to pursue a lower rate of economic growth and a higher level of social development and integration. 'People are told we have to sacrifice our social objectives to save our country by economic growth, to attract foreign investment we have to sacrifice our autonomy, the rights of our workers. Surely we can find another way. We think of the years of war, the thousands of families sacrificed, the millions who died. If people now forget that sacrifice and just do what they want to do it isn't fair. It isn't fair to the living and it isn't fair to those who died. Some of those who took part in the struggle have now risen quickly, got rich all of a sudden.

'Eighty per cent of the people still live in the countryside, most are still poor. Our efforts should concentrate on getting safe drinking water to the countryside, not promoting Coca-Cola. Half the people do not have safe water. We reduced child mortality to 45 per 1,000; before 1975 it was 80 per 1,000. Do we want to jeopardize that?

'The official policy now is to devolve production to the household as the basic unit, rather than to the anonymous co-operatives modelled on the Soviet system. Individuals are now motivated to provide themselves with good skills and professions, jobs that pay good wages. At the same time they know that as well as taking care of their own future they also must do something for the development of the country. To take care of our own lives may be basic, but it is never enough.'

Dr Nguyen Lan Dinh is the former head of the Child Nutrition Centre in Phu Nhuan district in north Ho Chi Minh; he is now a consultant and adviser on nutrition.

The centre is a substantial concrete structure. Previously a research centre for indigenous medicinal plants, now it is the focus for the nutrition programme of the whole city. In the five years to 1989 there was a feeding programme for mothers and babies in eighteen districts of the city, funded in part by an international aid agency. Rations – oil, milk, flour-based weaning foods – were distributed to all children in state crèches; 100 grams of food were provided daily to children aged from six months to three years. When this project ceased in 1989, it was decided that the remainder of the money and food would be used to create the Child Nutrition Centre so that the struggle against malnourishment should continue, concentrating now on families most in need.

The centre has five principal objectives: (1) to provide education in nutrition; (2) to serve as a clinic for outpatients, sixty or seventy a day on a short-term basis; (3) to train staff who work in health centres and the community; (4) to cultivate *spirolina,* an algae culture food rich in protein, minerals and vitamins; and (5) to serve as a factory producing twelve nutritional supplements for children, including a flour-based weaning food.

Dr Lan Dinh says that although the internationally financed feeding programme finished, the problems of malnutrition have not disappeared. 'Urbanization is changing everything. We encourage breast feeding but this becomes more difficult in an environment that is changing rapidly. Parents fear they are not earning enough to provide their children with nutritional sufficiency. This has obvious limitations: if the mother has no income, giving advice is scarcely an adequate response. The pressures from commercial advertising have two main effects: they undermine the mother's confidence in her capacity to provide for her children, even leading her to believe that breast milk is inferior to some factory preparations on sale in the market; this makes people strive to get money to procure nutritionally poorer products.

'UNICEF puts out a pamphlet called *Facts for Life* which sets out ten items essential for maintaining good health. These vary from breast feeding to taking precautions against AIDS. Yet at the same time we are being overwhelmed by products, commercial things that are not essential for life and health and are even harmful to them. There is no publicity for breast feeding in the mass media, but plenty for monosodium glutamate and beer. This undermines our work, for it is against its spirit and intention. And these forces are far more powerful than we are.

'Vietnam is seeing the re-emergence of malnutrition, a commerciogenic malnutrition which has nothing to do with absence of resources and everything to do with maximizing profit. People understand nothing of the products that come from industry. As they pass from producing their own food to becoming consumers in the market, they lose an understanding of the world that nourishes and sustains them. That loss is filled by information from companies wishing to sell products. We, too, in the centre, make instant foods, but ours are nutritionally balanced.

'As children discover the world, they need to hold food in their hands, break it open, see and feel what it is made of; that is the child's way of affirming herself in the world, of making contact with its material reality. Food is a necessary part of environmental discovery. Children in the countryside know about food. In the city they swiftly become estranged from the sources of their own sustenance. By the time children come to depend on ready-made industrialized food, they have lost an important insight into their surroundings; they become disempowered, impoverished.

'Everyone agrees we must limit the population of Vietnam; pressure on the land mass by 70 million people is already intolerable. Birth control has also been successful. In most urban families there are now just one or two children, with two parents, often four grandparents to look after them; that is six adults to look after a single child. When we were young we might have been number three or four in a family of six. I had maybe twenty uncles and aunts and a wider network of neighbourhood, supporting adults. We now increasingly isolate children from other age groups, so all those in the crèche are the same age, in kindergarten, primary school, secondary school and so on. This undermines social diversity, richness of experience; it is reductive, it prepares individuals for the exploitations of consumerism. They no longer have access to the variety and wealth of cross-generational experience, traditional songs, stories, celebrations.

'This is a critical time for the country; those who are motivated by human values are trying to work for society against the forces of commerce and profit. Some are now asking what the struggles of the last half-century were all for. That is perhaps the greatest tragedy of

Vietnam. Just as they did after 1975, we proclaim transformation, uplift, progress. The reality is another story.

'After 1975 certain things were much better for the most deprived and vulnerable. Before 1975 the whole country depended upon subsidies from the US. Now things are better; since the end of the war minefields have been turned into pastures, with cows grazing around a city that was once bristling with arms. Before 1975 Ho Chi Minh was an immense barracks serving the necessities of war.

'Such vast changes, it seems we have lived through different epochs in just one lifetime. Before 1965 I could travel around Saigon by taxi. After 1965 the taxis existed only for the Americans. Before 1965 middle-class families could employ country girls to work for them; after 1965 only Americans could afford servants. Then after 1975 all that changed. What we see now is a partial return to the previous period when the Americans were here. Now people who own villas or bigger apartments move out and let them to the representatives of foreign companies, because they can pay. We are seeing the beginnings of an economy where privilege pre-empts the necessities of the poor. And the new rich are often foreigners, investors, tourists.'

II

The changes in Vietnam can be read in the fabric of Ho Chi Minh City itself, but even more clearly in its hinterland, in the spaces between the metropolitan area and the far periphery. A mere 40 kilometres from Ho Chi Minh in the villages towards the southeastern seaboard, you can feel the gravitational pull of the city, see its growing influence.

I went with Dr Cong, a senior trainer of health service professionals, on a journey towards something that still resembles a traditional rural culture.

We visited a health centre serving four villages in Hiep Phuoc commune. The area has only recently been connected to Ho Chi Minh City by the construction of seven bridges over the canals and waterways, which formerly had to be crossed by ferry. This meant that the area remained more or less cut off until about five years ago.

We cross Saigon River; its rusting metal slums brood over the water, though these are neither as extensive nor as polluting as the slums in most other cities in the region. At the docks a long row of trucks is being filled with consignments of fertilizer to be taken into the countryside. Along the river, piles of wood, bamboo, sugar cane are waiting on rough jetties for the boats that will transport them out of the city. Here urban development is intensive: there are warehouses, factories making soap, nails, furniture, utensils. The streets are crowded with vehicles: human-drawn carts carrying cloth, cans, boxes, shoes, plastic goods; metal carts and cyclos; trucks, vans and buses. The buildings are densely packed, some of ancient metal and wood, others narrow new structures three or four storeys high with tinted glass, cream-painted balconies and red or blue tiles.

Within two or three kilometres, the industrial structures become more sparse and local building materials dominate. It is still fairly squalid. Motorbike and cycle repair shops create iridescent pools on the uneven ground, wasteland neither urban nor rural; pigs and fowls scavenge on the uncertain margins of the road. Wider stretches of water appear, half-dried paddy fields bordered by palms. But the water is grey and stagnant.

After we cross a second bridge – fairly rudimentary, of wooden slats – the aspect is more rural. There are a few concrete houses, pillars and tiled roofs, some even with ceramic terraces, but the structures are now mostly of bamboo and water palm. These wide, feathery palms grow in clumps from the water at the edge of the road; here the stumps from perpetual harvesting emerge from water which is less polluted than a few kilometres back, although clouded by greyish silt. The rough roads have been constructed with red earth brought from elsewhere and at odds with the grey and green of the environment. The expanses of water beside the road are criss-crossed by earthen walkways which link the scattered homesteads behind to the main road.

This area is poor, because the water is brackish from its closeness to the sea. People can grow only one crop of paddy a year during the rains. The earth is too saline for any other crop than the dense-growing water palms, and the beginning of the mangroves.

Rainwater is used for drinking. Rain is collected in big earthenware jars manufactured in Saigon. You can tell the relative wealth or poverty of a family by the number of earthenware jars it possesses: some have six or eight in a row beside their house of palm leaves, others a single one. A few better-off people have dug wells; they must dig 100 metres or more for fresh water.

Some paddy fields are enclosed to form permanent fishponds. Over these ponds people have constructed toilets: a wooden plank leads to a square bamboo frame, around which woven water palm or corrugated iron forms a square chamber. These toilets drain directly into the fishponds; this does not harm the fish, nor does it impair their fitness for consumption. Indeed, because the population here is sparse the waste is absorbed effectively and biodegrades readily. Within about 10 kilometres of the town, there is virtually no pollution.

The houses are poor but not wretched; constructed entirely of water palm, they are cool and spacious, with walls of woven palm and roof a thatch of intricately crafted leaves, all on a bamboo frame.

Throughout the countryside, appearing to float on the water, you see little islands of burial grounds; the people's beliefs are a mixture of Buddhism and ancestor worship. They bury their dead on their own land in order to remain close to those who have preceded them. Shining gravestones rise on fragments of land in the growing expanse of water. Many families keep ducks, for eggs rather than meat. The mud here is soft and it is easier to walk barefoot, for shoes are easily sucked into the quicksands.

People here now own their land. Co-operatives set up after 1975 were abandoned ten years later in the devolution of production to household level. This, in effect, meant that people became independent producers or small entrepreneurs. It does not mean that they ceased to co-operate, says Dr Cong. On the contrary, if they build a house they expect the help of neighbours in the labour, a service they will return when it is needed.

The most imposing buildings are those of the people's committees. The people's committee at the local level selects a president and vice-president. They go to the commune authority, where priorities are decided and which has responsibility for education, health and local taxation. In the rural areas, a commune consists of about 15,000 people, but in the cities a commune may contain four times as many.

The Party is now having difficulty attracting members, despite internal democratization. It has become more open, says Dr Cong. It accepts the free market, and is concentrating its efforts now on reducing the negative effects of this. A recurring question in Vietnam is how far political action can mitigate the undesirable social consequences of free markets. Dr Cong believes the analytical demarcation of the economic, the social, the political as separate zones makes it hard to distinguish the relationship between them. Indeed, their very existence as separate categories makes debate more obscure and opaque. 'If it were possible for political action to "correct" the social results of economic activity that leads to greater inequality, we should surely hear about it. The fact that little can be done once autonomous economic processes are set in train is not palatable to a government that likes to claim supreme power.'

After we have crossed seven or eight bridges we approach a significantly higher bridge, known as 'the golden gate', a wood-and-metal structure spanning the last waterway before the commune of Hiep Phuoc. People here still refer to the city as 'Saigon'. Dr Cong says they are now expected to be self-reliant, to solve their own problems, not wait for the government to do everything for them. They define their health needs and participate in answering them.

In the villages close to the last waterway – a river about 100 metres wide, which has no bridge – there is no electricity, but many houses have batteries or generators. Traces of the traditional self-sustaining economy remain. People use water buffalo for agriculture. In the dry season these are driven north to pasture, and they are brought back just before the onset of the rains in May–June.

The health centre is a concrete building with a wing at either end, a verandah and a number of specialist rooms leading from the main building; there is a hospital ward and a birth delivery room with bed and stirrups. A woman who gave birth the day before is lying in the maternity room with her son, a healthy child dressed in bonnet and woollen clothes. She is lying on a plain wooden bed. The midwife, Nguyen Thi Ngo Lieu, has been here for three years. She says that perinatal mortality is now around 60 per 1,000 for the country as a whole, but around Ho Chi Minh it is only 27.

There is a chart on the wall of the delivery room. Every pregnant woman in the commune is monitored. The colours on the chart indicate whether it is a first, second or third child. After the third, parents are discouraged from having more and are offered abortion or effective birth control. Persuasion is easier in areas where child mortality is low and higher levels of social security have been attained. It will be interesting to see whether the birth rate rises if the state social supports are done away with as a result of economic 'reforms'.

Malaria is endemic here, and there is an anti-malaria unit. Another ward with four or five beds serves in-patients, or can be used to accommodate visitors. There is a dispensary containing the commonest drugs: antibiotics, painkillers, anti-malaria drugs, drugs for dysentery and diarrhoea. This health centre receives some donations from Save the Children Australia, which is perhaps why it has remained unaffected by reductions in state health spending.

The cost of maintaining the centre is only two or three hundred US dollars a month, and that includes the salary of seven employees: two doctors, two assistant doctors, two nurses and a midwife. 'This shows how the pay of public servants has declined; when cyclo drivers can earn far more, doctors scrape a very modest living.' On the other hand all live nearby and come from the locality. Dr Cao Quang Nghia and his assistant, Dr Ngo Huu Tai, have been here twelve years. Because their family land still produces rice and fish the cost of living is lower than in the city, and the decline in salary is less disastrous.

The health problems here include respiratory infections and a chronic, if slight, malnutrition, which lowers resistance. People are susceptible to infections and changes in the wind coming off the sea. The poorest people are the landless, those who cannot afford to buy protein, fish and crabs, in the market.

The centre runs a feeding programme for 170 of the poorest children, but this now operates only two days a month, which will not prevent undernourishment. Instruction is given to parents on how to prepare food so that it is at its most nutritious; on feeding days the staff demonstrate the best preparation methods and then let the parents feed the children with rice, powdered milk, beans, milk-apples and other fruits.

The centre also operates a small-scale credit scheme to enable people to develop economically: to become small vendors or traders, to raise ducks or engage in aquaculture – fish, prawn and algae culture – to make water palm artefacts for sale, woven panels for construction or roof thatch. The poorest migrate to the city in search of work. Some go on a weekly basis, living on construction sites and returning at weekends.

Dr Ngo Huu Tai started work here in 1982 when the centre was built. There was no road in the commune then, no bridges over the water. The first car came here only in 1990; before that people had never seen a motor vehicle. Dr Tai insists that the most effective measure against ill-health is economic uplift. 'In our philosophy we do not separate development and health. Being able to eat well is the best protection against disease. There is a high literacy rate here; there is no crèche, but there is a kindergarten for children from the age of four. A majority of children finish elementary school and around two-thirds now go to secondary school. With the roads and bridges there is now out-migration, especially of the young. Some work as street vendors in Saigon, drive three-wheel Lambretta taxis, work as motorcycle taxi drivers.'

The health workers echo the government's view: because we are poor, we place our faith in economic growth. They see a rise in income of the poorest as the best remedy against malnutrition and want. I say to them, 'But economic development also brings Coca-Cola, Sprite and junk food; are you not afraid that these things, which appear to be prestige Western goods, will undermine people's concern for their children's nutrition?' 'So far,' they reply, 'we do not fear this.'

We walk around the village that is strung out along the bank of the river. This is more than 100 metres wide, a deep, placid stretch of water bordered by water palms and mangroves. The water is clean here, slightly clouded by silt so that its colour in the sunlight is milky gold. At first sight, everything appears traditional, ecologically benign, sustainable: the buildings are made of bamboo and water palm; the floors are of beaten earth; the furniture consists of plain wooden beds, bamboo mats, tables and chairs of palm and bamboo; even the cages for the ducks and cocks are fashioned from the same pliable material. At the water's edge two young women in cone-shaped hats sit in a boat with a consignment of woven palms they are bringing to market. There are stalls with bamboo trays of locally caught fish, and vegetables – aubergines, *kangkong*, tomatoes, cabbage, pumpkins, and fruit, pineapples and bananas. Fibre hammocks oscillate in the shady interiors, and babies move gently to and fro in a piece of cotton material tied between bamboo poles. The wood here is mostly eucalyptus; it is not indigenous, but the abundance of water here makes it a suitable exotic.

And yet in the villages there is much evidence of other, more invasive aspects of city life. Generators run video games, karaoke players, amplifiers and televisions. Two children of about eight, one wearing a leather cap back to front, are intent on a video game in which people are annihilated by well-aimed bursts of flame; a video is showing some Western pop star in concert; and there is a TV soap opera about upmarket people in Australia. 'TV here is unreal,' say the health workers. 'It is not part of their lives.'

There is a stall selling plastic bowls and pails in primary colours, nylon brushes (which are slowly displacing the traditional artefacts). Cigarettes, soap, biscuits, candy from the transnationals jostle less glamorous locally made sweets and snacks. Tiger beer, less potent, is replacing traditional rice wine. On the waterfront a half-submerged ladder leads to a crude wooden floatel, a rough bar with stools and tables, where people play cards and watch Star TV sing its advertisements for beauty products.

'Individuation is less here,' says Dr Cong. 'People still feel they are part of one another and of the environment.' He sees the coming of hi-tech entertainment as a novelty, not a significant determinant of the lives of the people.

The health workers appear unaware of the meaning of the iconography of 'modernization' that is invading this serene and beautiful place, and which will surely affect the sensibility and lives of the people.

Ly Nam is a boatman who carries goods to market from the outlying homesteads along the banks of the river. In his late forties, he appears older. He has a withered arm, the result of a war injury. He was with the Viet Cong. We go into his house, a lofty structure of palm and wood. Inside, some tiny yellow ducklings are foraging on the earth floor. There is a large wooden bed in one corner, and behind it the palm wall of a kitchen, where the cooking fire is kindled. Inside is a second chamber with a bed. The house is a cool dark retreat from the glare of sun on water. When we ask Ly Nam about the war, he smiles and says, 'That finished long ago. I retired from being a soldier then.'

He takes us out on the river in his traditional wooden boat, which is shallow like a punt, with a bamboo pole to help him steer if the outboard motor breaks down. The craft is not very stable. Ly Nam tries several times without success to start the motor by pulling a piece of rope that replaces the starter. At last, it creaks and spits into life, and he steers us towards the centre of the wide river.

The homesteads are sparse, in little clearings among the water palms and mangroves that grow densely on either side. The afternoon sun blazes on the water so that it shines a clouded silver, while the light on the palm leaves turns them into chattering metallic feathers. There are many boats on the water, houseboats of small traders and fishing families, boats with big red eyes painted onto the bow, designed to frighten monsters in the water.

As we move further downstream, the river becomes more shallow. Grasses and reeds rise above the calm surface. The palms are more sparse, the sky wider, the sun more insistent. Towards the estuary is a line of fishing boats, waiting for fish to flow into the nets as the tide comes in. In waterside clearings people are occupied weaving water palms. Here and there red hibiscus creates a splash of vivid colour in a landscape otherwise bleached by the sun. Dragonflies skim over the water making rainbows through their transparent wings.

It is easy to understand here why the United States could not win the war; the multiple waterways, many of them unnamed, the isolation of spits of land and islets in the delta, the dense growth of water palms, the maze of tiny embankments and scattered homesteads – all made it impossible to bomb into submission the elusive people to whom every fragment of this terrain was familiar.

This only makes more bitter and more poignant the present economic warfare against Vietnam. What could not be achieved with bombs can be done more effectively with dollars, the devaluing of the currency, indebted dependency, the wiping out of indigenous industrial production, the dismantling of the social welfare structures. It is sadly significant that the pamphlet offered to each visitor to the War Crimes Museum contains this final paragraph:

> The Americans were deeply shocked at the war in Vietnam. In consecutive years, protests were staged in different walks of life in the US as well as other parts of the globe. The Vietnamese have been grateful to the people around the world, especially to the Americans, for having helped them struggle for independence, freedom and happiness in Vietnam.

As I returned with Dr Cong to Ho Chi Minh he spoke of his pride in the health care system and of the fear that if the free market goes unchecked, that system will disintegrate. 'The government is saying it can combine the market system with social justice: it is giving industry and commerce freedom to develop but at the same time mitigating the side effects. We know that with development new forms of sickness and ill-health occur. AIDS will become a major drain on resources – drugs and prostitution will see to that. We foresee a growth in the incidence of crime. We have organized many conferences to discuss with women, youth, NGOs how to co-operate with government to defend ourselves from all that. We believe we can be more successful than other countries because here the government is still capable of mobilizing people and resources; we have not abandoned our objectives. Of course, it is easier to say than to carry out. There is no model for us to follow. There is only one economic way out, and we certainly need reform. The difference here is that we have the infrastructure in place. Other ex-socialist countries either didn't have it or allowed it to be swept away in their enthusiasm for the free market. This was the error of Russia; there, anger and bitterness remain at the way it permitted itself to throw away everything – even the good things it had built during the years of socialism.

'The experience of North Vietnam was of social organization, while South Vietnam had private enterprise. Within the same country, in living memory, we have had two systems, so both can learn from each other. We shall not become like Yugoslavia or Chechenya: we have had a hundred years of war. The last thing we want is more fighting. What we need to do now is build. We always knew neither North nor South could win the war alone. Our destiny was decided by outside forces, when Nixon met Mao. In one sense our fate has always been to some extent in the hands of others.

'Thirty years ago Vietnam had a higher standard of living than the Philippines and Thailand. We are, however, very weak. We are afraid that the transnationals will destroy our industry and the market system will bring back levels of poverty we thought we had abolished. Our friends in the Philippines say Vietnam still has the potential for a different kind of change. In the Philippines it is the rich who rule, whereas here there is still some popular control over resources. They say to us, "If you give that up, you will be lost."

'When foreign companies come they bring their own personnel who have a lot of money. They create new forms of social change. Their spending power raises prices so the poor can no longer buy certain things. The gap between rich and poor is now widening dramatically. The problem of urbanization grows, as more come from the countryside to try to make a living in the city; you can see the consequences of that on any street.

'Yet social solidarity remains strong. People help each other. The family is a major force, the clan, the group. We are one of the poorest countries in Asia, but there is no Smoky Mountain in Ho Chi Minh. There are slums, sure, along the canals, behind the big buildings, but not on the scale you see in Manila or Dhaka.

'There is no bitterness in Vietnam, no. We are human. We didn't belong to the regime that waged the war, and between peoples all over the world there is no conflict, no quarrel. Governments are not the people; that is the sad thing. In any case we have our more traditional resentments. Vietnam was under Chinese rule for a thousand years. We are more wary of China than America. North and South Vietnam, they were at war, many were killed; but now people want to forget. We must sit together and co-operate.

'We look at the West now and see all the social problems there, and it seems a funny thing to us. We do not understand it, the crime, the violence in the rich societies. I spent a year in France and there I found people are lonely, old people are not cared for by their families, people are afraid of each other. People in the West go to psychiatrists, we go to each other. We don't have counselling, psychoanalysis; we have our common humanity.

'How to marry welfare with wealth, that is our objective. Some people have so many problems they have no energy left to work; they must be looked after. Yet if equality is total, there is no innovation, no motivation for clever people. Between 1975 and 1985 everybody was reduced to the same level. Then, when the economy changes, some go ahead and then they push others down. Life has improved, but money is inadequate to provide all that people need. Coca-Cola becomes available, while the majority do not have clean drinking water. These are the distortions we see.

'1975 to 1990, I wouldn't say it was a disaster for Vietnam. We must learn the lessons from it. The US had made South Vietnam completely dependent. The period under communism was necessary because it taught us to stand on our own feet, the value of self-reliance and independence; even if they are weak, they are our own feet.'

For all the hope newly released in Ho Chi Minh, the outline of its future development is already appearing. The traffic is just beginning to be a serious problem. As yet nothing on the scale of the jams of Bangkok, or even Jakarta. The bicycle is still the dominant form of transport although increasingly, especially on Sunday nights, young people on motorbikes drive round and round the city centre, weaving a continuous garland of red tail-lights and white headlights. During the morning and evening rush hour, congestion builds up along Dien Bien Phu Road, as does the pollution. The development Ho Chi Minh is destined to follow is precisely that which has wounded all the other cities of South Asia. There has been no attempt to construct an adequate mass transit system, and there is insufficient infrastructure to cope with the increase in private transport. Drainage is poor, garbage collection is unreliable. As the health system declines there will be more pressure on it, from the sicknesses of overcrowding, as well as from respiratory diseases, lung and eye infections, as dust, grit, carbon dioxide and industrial pollutants sweep through the streets.

What is happening is clear. The examples, precedents and warnings are visible all over South Asia. Yet nothing is being done to prevent the same social disasters from overtaking Ho Chi Minh that afflict other major cities. There is good reason for this. It is not simply that the social costs of wealth are not included in the accounting system; it is that yet more growth and 'development' actually arise from the social dislocations and disorders that growth and development produce. There are major beneficiaries of social disasters: the transnational drug companies, fast-food outlets for people too busy to eat properly, construction conglomerates offering illusions of escape into exurban fortresses, the builders of air-conditioned malls where people can forget briefly that they are in Saigon and be transported to anywhere in the world, anywhere but where they must stay and make their lives.

9

The Ruined Hinterland:
Kerpan, Malaysia

The apocalyptic visions of the exploding megacities have so far failed to appear; what is happening in most countries is that the rate of growth has slowed down in the major cities but has accelerated in the smaller urban centres: Surat, Bangalore, Lucknow in India, Cebu in the Philippines, Surabaya in Indonesia.

This is not the whole story. Not only is agricultural production becoming more and more an aspect of industry, but urbanization is a pervasive process, reaching out from the urban centres and sweeping whole tracts of countryside into urban, suburban, exurban development. Almost the entire island of Penang in Malaysia is now semi-urban: tourism, free trade zones, housing for expatriates, golf resorts, road and bridge construction have swept away the old villages and have imposed upon Penang the aspect of a sprawling townscape which has drowned the elegant old colonial capital of Georgetown. Add to this the migration of those squeezed out of farming, or displaced from old rubber plantations, people who have no option but to come and find a place in the free trade zones or the service sector of Penang, and it is easy to see how the lineaments of the island culture, fishing, *padi* and trading were so quickly effaced.

Kerpan, in the west Malaysian state of Kedah, is an example of the kind of forced movement that is taking place. For this is the site of a 1,000-acre tiger prawn project. Unfortunately the land given by the government to the companies involved was already occupied; it had been farmed for centuries by generations of rice farmers.

Privatization has been one of the ritual incantations of orthodox economics for two decades now. Governments worldwide have divested themselves of public assets, common resources, land, mineral deposits, waters and forests. Whole industries, too, have been passed to powerful private interests, more often than not the political allies and cronies of the ruling elites.

But the time comes when there is nothing left to give away, apart from those assets that governments insist on holding onto for reasons

of national prestige. But of course there is something else to give
away – the land occupied by small private owners. This is increasingly
being expropriated for the sake of larger corporate 'private' interests.
This is what has been happening in Kerpan; it gives a whole new twist
to the meaning of 'privatization'.

In many countries aquaculture has become a recent instant money
maker. Great profits are to be made from intensive prawn and shrimp
farming, thanks to the apparently limitless appetite of those people in
the world with the greatest purchasing power. The consequences for
coastal waters in prawn farming areas – the contamination of the land
by artificial feed and antibiotics, the vulnerability to pests that can wipe
out whole prawnfields overnight – have already been well documented.
Prawn farming is basically a smash-and-grab operation, as evidence
from Taiwan, the Philippines and parts of Thailand has shown.

The farmers of Kerpan were wary when they were invited by the
government to donate their traditional rice lands to a company that
promised high rewards from an export-oriented project, a joint venture between the state government of Kedah and a local company
incorporated into a Saudi Arabian entity, operating under the name
of Samak Aquaculture.

The state government had intended to set up a 'people's
company', Asprasi Gemilang ('Happy Aspiration' in Malay), which
would operate on behalf of the farmers whose land was to be diverted
to shrimp farming and who would become shareholders at the rate of
15,000 ringgit per relong (that is, $US6,000 per 1.5 acres). Resistance
by the owners of the rice fields has made this impossible, and for the
moment (March 1995) Samak has a 60 per cent stake while the rest is
controlled by the state government.

When the 700–800 farmers were first approached, there was no
mention of acquisition of their land; they were wooed with promises
of fabulous revenues to be won from tiger prawns. Low-level government officials toured the area asking them to sign an agreement that
they would join Asprasi Gemilang. When they asked for copies of the
document they were expected to sign, officials from the Land Office
said, 'We are helping you to sort out your inheritance.' The lands have
been held by farmers for generations; nobody ever thought of applying for papers, so secure were they in possession of their property.
Some farmers signed. Others remained suspicious and asked advice of
the Consumers' Association of Penang (CAP). The farmers learned
they had a right to see, read and understand any agreement they
were expected to sign.

No copy of the document was offered. Instead more pressure was
applied by the authorities for them to accept this particular form of

participatory development. An action committee was set up by those affected by the two-phase undertaking, construction of which was scheduled to begin in February 1995. They had been given the impression that even if they surrendered their land to the project they would still retain control over it. On further inquiry they discovered that the company would become the owners. They were repeatedly told that they would get a far higher return than from *padi*; their land was to be their capital investment in the project. It was described as a new version of popular capitalism.

Many had contractually agreed to the transaction before resistance became effective. They discovered their land had been gazetted for acquisition and could be compulsorily taken. They were outraged and horrified. They had believed that land held from time beyond memory by their families was inalienable, would remain theirs for ever.

Small subsistence farmers are naturally conservative people. Tenacious, hard-working, they distrust get-rich-quick schemes because they know that nature has its own rhythms and reasons which are not those of industry and big business. When they challenged the acquisition of their land in the courts, they found out that the state can legally take it, though it is obliged to pay compensation.

Lawyers from the Consumers' Association of Penang argued that the Integrated Tiger Prawn project did not fulfil the criteria of the clear purposes for which land may be acquired. Under the Land Acquisition Act, certain purposes are defined: public purposes, such as infrastructural development, and national development purposes, such as mining and extraction of resources. In 1991, however, an amendment was enacted whereby land may be acquired and given to a corporation or any person or persons for any economic purpose where, in the opinion of the state authority, this will bring economic benefit to the country, or to any class or group of persons in the country.

The Consumers' Association of Penang had campaigned against this amendment, circulating all parliamentarians before the 1991 election. There was much sympathy among MPs within the governing coalition, because many of them were also landowners. They were told by the government that if they did not support the amendment they would not be permitted to stand as candidates in the election.

'Under the old Act,' says Meena, a lawyer with the CAP, 'there was always an element of public purpose for which land could be taken, at the behest of and on behalf of a public authority. Never was it conceived that this could be done for a private corporation.'

This new legislation, which, in one guise or another is now finding its way onto statute books all over the Third World, is symptomatic of a new thrust in the ideology of 'development'. The changing ethos is

not indifferent but actually antagonistic to the idea of public purpose. Legitimizing the confiscation of privately owned land in the
interests of 'development' means that no small farmers will ever again
be secure against the power of transnational capital.

'The criteria set down are designed to make this transfer immune
from challenge,' says Meena. 'The amendment mentions specifically
"land which, in the opinion of the State authority" will bring economic benefit to a corporation or group or class of persons. The
subjective assessment of authority is not open to question. If the state
says it is for that purpose, then it is for that purpose. Even private
property ceases to be sacrosanct when it belongs to small people; this
is usurpation by one select group of the assets of others.'

It was in keeping with the spirit of this legislation that the Kerpan
project was conceived. It strikes at the heart of Malay custom and tradition, against a culture that has evolved over centuries. It is also at
odds with the professed concern of the government of Malaysia for
the *bumiputra* population, the native Malays, 'sons of the soil'.
Whatever gains the Malays have made in relation to the economically
dominant Chinese, these are cancelled by schemes such as this.

The Kerpan project has provoked powerful reactions among the
farmers. 'Our land', they say, 'is our culture. To be told that it is no
longer ours is unthinkable and we cannot accept it.' The government
has sought to show them that the project is in their interests and accuses
them of being stubborn because now they are earning a modest two or
three hundred ringgit from *padi* but could expect to see this multiply
many times if they become 'partners in development'. The farmers
resist the seductive message of wealth: they value security over riches,
and this places an awkward obstacle on the path of development.

'What we see', says G.S. Nijar, a lawyer with Third World Network in
Penang, 'is the logic of a development that threatens to run out of
control. In order to serve this, not only must our traditions be overthrown but the laws of the land have to be amended. Freedom is
being subordinated to wealth, a trade-off which the farmers are resisting. It is also dangerous, for we can see the rule of law being
superseded by rule *by* law, which is a very different proposition.'

That this should be occurring in Kerpan for the sake of an unsustainable fad like aquaculture makes the experience even more bitter.
Vandana Shiva, the Indian environmental activist, has said that aquaculture has been portrayed as the next gold mine, the 'blue
revolution' to follow the Green Revolution.

> First, you destroy the coastal waters, the mangroves, the diverse ecology
> of fishing grounds and littoral regions, and then you create a mono-

culture in their place. It has happened in Peru, Ecuador, Taiwan. In all those countries, many schemes have collapsed. The technical knowledge does not exist to guarantee survival of such projects. The land and coastal waters are contaminated, and cannot be restored afterwards. Tigerprawns are a hit-and-run profit-taking venture, which lasts a maximum of five years. It invades one area of the world after another, devastates the local ecology, and then moves on.

(*Third World Resurgence*)

The site of the Kerpan project shows the effect of the first phase on the existing rice fields. The land of Phase Two is as yet unaffected, and the contrast in the scene is striking.

To reach the area, you follow the course of the slow-moving river from the town of Kerpan to the estuary on the Straits of Malacca. The rough road is stony, and each passing vehicle sets up clouds of dust; but it is a tranquil landscape, mangroves rising out of the shallow coastal waters, fishing boats resting on the mudflats. Irrigation canals are bordered by scarlet flame-of-the-forest trees and the purple cones of rose of India; there are cascades of bougainvillaea: orange, lilac and cream all growing from the same stem, 'paper flowers' as they are called in Malay. The long grass is dark with blue, bell-shaped wild flowers. The rice fields lie alongside the canals, pale straw bleached by the dry-season sun. The scattered homesteads are shaded by clumps of palm, plantain and angsana trees; wooden Malay houses on stilts, the cool air circulating beneath. Adjacent to the rice fields, where sheep and cows browse, are the farmers' vegetable gardens and fruit trees: the *bayon* and *kangkong* leaf vegetables, mustard, chillis, okra, aubergines, sugar cane, tapioca, papaya, cotton, coconuts, coffee. All that is needful for self-reliance is here; along the canals ducks swim, chickens forage in the grass. An otter scrambles across a rough wooden bridge that leads to one of the houses.

The rice fields are parched and cracked now, but within a few weeks the embankments will be remade, the fields will become once more broad shallow cups ready to receive the flood of rainwater. There is another irony: in the rice lands people have always cultivated fish, but for their own and local consumption, not for a global market.

It is always poignant to see land that has been under food production for centuries suddenly diverted to other uses – for resorts, motorways, golf courses. It is a violation of the resource base of the country, a brutal act against a peaceable and rooted culture.

The mechanical cranes move across the overturned embankments of Phase One, greedily uprooting all living things. They move jerkily, human-made creatures from a futuristic Jurassic Park, metal predators pecking at the open earth with their indestructible jaws. There are notices all around the site warning trespassers that they will be prosecuted; those trespassers include the owners of this land which had been so carefully tended, and which is now being torn apart. The farmers feel the wounding of the earth as if it were a blow to their own body.

What is more, in this area there are already a number of small private shrimp and prawn farms, and the owners of these tell a story that confirms the prediction of Vandana Shiva. After a few years returns diminish, the fish die, and the land cannot revert to rice cultivation, or indeed, to any other crop. Here, say the farmers, the proponents of the Kerpan project have a living example of what not to do; but still they are going ahead, because they do not care. 'They will not have to live with the consequences. They can move on, go elsewhere. We have nowhere to go. Our lives are here.'

All over this part of Kedah the flag of the PAS is flying, the Malaysian Islamic Party. It is a measure of popular disaffection that the chief beneficiaries of such developmental aberrations will be the fundamentalists. Or perhaps one form of fundamentalism calls forth another.

We visit the house of Haji Zakaria bin Ahmad, the acknowledged leader of the farmers' movement of Kerpan. He is called Ustaz, or 'teacher', a mature, reflective man who wears the traditional Malay *kain pelekat* (male sarong) and *ketayap* (skullcap). He and his extended family together owned 60 relong of land. Half of this has now been seized for the prawn project. He says the land has been theirs 'since the beginning of time. It is more than loss of land to us, it is to be cut off from our heritage.'

The house is cool and spacious, with carved wooden chairs and sofas, yellow cotton curtains, walls painted yellow and light brown. The base of the house is concrete, but the upper part is of wood. There are Islamic texts on the wall engraved in metal, a picture of a mosque. Some glass-fronted cupboards contain china ornaments. We are offered a local variety of banana from a tree in the garden; it has a sweet and delicate texture – this banana is now scarcely obtainable in the market. Haji Zakaria says that people in Kerpan have always been self-reliant. I ask him what they buy in the market. 'What is there to buy? Salt, sugar, exotic fruits like apples, for those who want them.' Even the family's coffee and sugar are locally produced. It is a cruel fate that the people of Kerpan, who have never depended for anything upon the outside world, should now be thrust into a world market for products that they regard as superfluous.

As we speak, more and more farmers arrive, until within half an hour there are about thirty men and eight women in the room. Most of the men wear trousers and shirts, but a few of the older ones keep to the traditional dress. They are solemn but they have not been depressed by the eighteen months of struggle. The solidarity that has kept them buoyant continues to sustain them. Their sense of a grievous wrong still animates their determination to continue, even though work has now started on the demolition of their land and livelihood. In February 1995, as the work was beginning, some of the farmers lay down in the path of the bulldozers. Thirty-three were arrested and kept in jail. The others collectively looked after their children; and on the day of their release, a Friday, they prayed for deliverance from injustice.

Haji Zakaria tells that originally, when the directors of the company called a meeting of the people affected, apparently to explain the project, their language was so vague that no one understood precisely what they meant. 'When it did sink in, we still could not believe it. It is so alien to our way of thinking.' They were suspicious, and felt, as the Malay saying goes, 'that there was a prawn behind the stone', a hidden agenda. In this case the saying was literally true.

Since they have lost their land those who still have rice have shared what they have with their neighbours. For many this is the first season they have ever been unable to cultivate; the urgency of preparing and planting has gone and nothing has grown in its place, except a righteous anger.

Pauziyah is an articulate woman of thirty-six dressed in red and gold, with a scarlet *telukung*, the Islamic veil. She is carrying her three-year-old child. She says, 'We are becoming beggars in our own land. We were self-reliant, and now we are being made poor. We are unimportant.' Pauziyah is a tenant on land belonging to someone else. Pauziyah started to grow *padi* there, with the permission of the owner, after the existing tenant had ceased to cultivate. But when the company offered compensation for confiscated land, the previous tenant accepted the compensation even though he was no longer legally a tenant. Pauziyah does not wish to sell out, but has been marginalized.

The people say the future is full of darkness for them. They cannot see what will happen to their children. There will be no land to inherit. This has never happened before: past and future were always long straight roads, where the view was the same whichever way they looked. Their identity and function as farmers have been broken.

Azmi Jalil is known affectionately as the 'Mandela of Kerpan'. (It is significant that they look to the liberation struggle in South Africa as inspiration and precedent.) Azmi is a man in his forties with short, slightly silvering hair, who won his nickname by articulating the people's anger. He understands the wider developmental context in which the Kerpan project is occurring. He insists that the farmers are still demanding the return of their land, but acknowledges that this might not be possible; if this is so, the people will demand realistic compensation, that is, for present and future loss. Even so, the farmers agree that what they stand to lose cannot be expressed in terms of money – the very idea is an affront to them. But since they are being compelled to bow to forces over which they have no control, they are insisting that they should be compensated at the rate of at least 50,000 ringgit per relong ($US20,000). This would mean for Haji Zakaria 3 million ringgit (over $US1 million).

'The government says it is only a minority who are resisting,' says Azmi Jalil, 'and that most farmers are in favour of the project. Now that it appears unstoppable to many people, about 50 per cent are still opposed in Phase One, but 90 per cent in Phase Two are still against it.'

What is development? I asked. 'Whatever it is,' came the reply, 'it is not for people like us. Development means priority to outsiders, foreigners, powerful interests, because that is who the prawns are for. Development means taking from the poor and giving to the rich.'

Their feeling towards the government is now, they say, one of enmity and unforgivingness. 'They say it is a project for us, but when we evaluate it we know it is not for our benefit. When we tell them this they use force to take our land. Then when we challenge it through due process of law, they bring in the police to arrest us. The government says this is being done for the people, but which people? It is we who are paying the price of this development.'

One farmer asks, 'Why, when they value our land, is it worth 34 sen a square foot; yet when the land of powerful people is valued it turns out to be worth 50 dollars per square foot, 150 times more. Even during the Japanese occupation in the Second World War the enemy never came to destroy our rice fields; it has been left to the government of free Malaysia to do such a thing.'

Another, older man goes further. 'Even under the British our way of life was respected. We were allowed to get on with cultivating our fields. In this place we always used to pray on Fridays. On that day we stopped work. Now all that is no more. Sunday must now be our day off because this suits international business. Even our Friday prayer time has been abolished. Our rights were better respected under colonial occupation. We were told that freedom would bring democracy and justice, with the courts to resolve disputes. Instead they come to steal our land. What happened to our freedom?'

This is not political, says Ahmad Fadzil, Secretary of the Action Committee. 'This is our life. It transcends politics. People are against this kind of development because they see it bringing to the Malays the same fate that befell the Indians in the United States, and the Aboriginals of Australia.'

Of course, they say, we have tried the courts. Under the law you cannot disturb people in possession of their land, where they are farming and sitting and living. The court ruled that it was government land because the government had the right to acquire it. 'When we appealed, we were told we had no right to appeal because we were not in possession of the land.'

They have not abandoned hope of winning back their land, even after it has been turned over to Samak Aquaculture. If that fails, their solidarity and tenacity will ensure compensation at a much higher rate than that offered in the first place. Some may invest this in other small enterprises; others, especially the older ones, will use up the money simply to survive, having lost their traditional symbol of survival, land.

But what of the inheritors of the disturbed tradition, of the destroyed culture and continuity? Monetary compensation offers no security at all to the next generation, those who will be expected to exercise their curtailed freedoms by moving into the urban areas, seeking work in factories in free trade zones and industrial estates. Kerpan shows how more and more of the future inhabitants of the growing cities are made: by means of eviction, dispossession, expropriation – by being compelled to join the long, forced march towards the overcrowded conurbations of the South.

10

Slums and Settlements

The distinguishing feature of the Third World city is, for many, its slums. But the word 'slum' is misleading. 'Slum' is a colonial word, borrowed from the conditions of nineteenth-century British urbanization, evoking courts, tenements, streets built pell-mell by speculative jerry-builders for profit.

It is rarely like this in Asia. Although dilapidated buildings and tenements do exist, the most characteristic 'slums' are constructed by the people themselves, sometimes with the scavenged materials of industrial waste, sometimes using traditional materials, often using a mixture of the two.

Peter Lloyd, writing in *Slums of Hope* in 1979, showed how much of scholarly literature on Third World slums reflects the gut reaction of Western observers to squalor, chaos and disease, and to a fear that the urban poor are a present or future socially destabilizing force, a view that gained popular prominence from Oscar Lewis's formulation of a self-perpetuating 'culture of poverty'. Reaction against this view in more recent times has led to an equally extreme reaction – seeing the slum dwellers as the bearers of community values, solidarity and mutuality.

The contradictions in perceptions of the slums are not incompatible. Slums can be places of cruelty and violence, but equally of solidarity, tenderness and hope; we do not always distinguish between the conditions of people's lives and the response to those conditions. Certainly in cities as diverse as Dhaka, Jakarta, Manila and Bombay the slums are one of the most salient features, although increasingly the accelerating pace of 'development' and the rise in land prices mean that these are no longer necessarily the stable communities that many had become over the years. Repeated evictions have made slum settlements more volatile, less permanent, particularly in rapidly growing cities like Bangkok and Jakarta, and more recently Bombay; in cities that are slower to 'develop', such as Dhaka and Calcutta, there is greater continuity and a kind of rootedness in many poor areas, although even here evictions and forced removals are commonplace.

Without some understanding of the origins and workings of the slums, it is impossible to appreciate the life of the cities, how the migrants, the former country dwellers, live and survive in the new environment, how their children are shaped by the new urban setting, and how all this determines in turn their attitudes, hopes and strategies for survival.

Mirpur, District Six, Dhaka

The settlement covers one side of a lake in east Dhaka, a community of three hundred families, or just under two thousand people. This is *khas*, or government land, and was settled soon after liberation in 1971. The population increased dramatically in the famine year of 1974; more recently, people have found refuge here from other areas of the city, evicted as the work of 'developing' Dhaka proceeds.

The place is oddly remote, still in some ways rural, although within a few kilometres of the commercial centre of the city. The roads leading from the main highway are green, shaded by plantain, papaya and raintrees and bordered by the grass that comes up so quickly in the monsoon. The road to this part of Mirpur soon dwindles to a rough brick track. The concrete houses give way to structures of wooden and bamboo frames, with panels of woven bamboo for walls: houses raised on earthen platforms so that the rain cannot enter.

When the track reaches the lake it ceases completely. Concrete steps lead down to the unnaturally brilliant green of the water where women are bathing and washing clothes, slapping the garments vigorously on the stone steps. The colour of the water is created partly by eutrophication, and partly by a discharge of chemical dyes from a nearby textile factory.

The houses of the slum begin where the track ends. The only way to reach them is on foot, along a rocky, uneven pathway that follows the contour of the lake or *tallab*, the 'pond' as they call it here. In some of the huts the doors are open front and back, so that they appear two-dimensional; through them you can see patches of bright green water, the sleek bodies of children bathing, the debris and waste that have been trapped in the roots of water lilies at the edge of the lake.

The houses following the line of the lake do so on two parallel ledges, one close to the water, the other about a metre higher. Further room to expand is limited by the wall of a factory compound, solid brick, crowned by parallel lines of rusty barbed wire. This factory makes poles to carry wires for telephone and electricity, amenities that do not reach Mirpur Six. Even the name has a utilitarian bleakness, nothing but a number to distinguish it from hundreds of similar communities in Dhaka.

Waste water and sewage flow into the pond at several points along the shore, while garbage decays in the placid water – vegetable and fruit rind, eggshells, rags – or fails to decay – plastic bags, polystyrene, plastic shoes. On the earthen path dividing the two levels is much evidence of the commonest ailment of the slum, diarrhoea, seeping into the earth with the help of last night's rain.

Hanufa, a woman in her forties, wearing a thin red and yellow saree, tells how her family came here from Barisal in the south because their house and land were swept away by river erosion. The land had always been unstable, but in recent years whole villages have been submerged: in Bangladesh, site of so many natural disasters, human-made ones are not always distinguishable from them. Hanufa and her family lived at first under the verandahs and on the terraces of rich people's houses in return for domestic labour. As the family grew, this ceased to be tolerable. Hanufa's husband works in the only occupation open to recent migrants to Dhaka, as a cycle rickshaw driver, earning 40 or 50 taka a day. Because of the debilitating labour, he works only on alternate days. The whole income goes on food, but is still inadequate to feed their three children properly. Only one goes to school, two kilometres away. They somehow find the money to pay 20 taka for books and writing materials: education seems to them the only way out of this desolation. They have not yet learned the bitter lesson taught to many unemployed graduates, who have discovered that the economy does not necessarily accommodate those who struggle to better themselves. Here the contours of a society in transition have not yet become clear to the people; industrial society is still defining itself. Although life is hard and unyielding, a certain unfamiliarity with its deepest purposes helps to keep hope alive.

Urbanization in parts of Dhaka is quite unlike any traditional idea of the city. Whole areas remain semi-rural, and there is little high-rise building. Tracts of open land become covered with dense grass in the monsoon, lush grazing grounds for cattle. In places trees form a dense canopy above the streets. On the edge of the community here, a little boy is working as a cowherd, tending the cattle of the better-off, watching them with a stick in his hand as they browse on a piece of coarse grassland: it is an image apparently of rural calm.

If the word *slum* is inadequate to describe the cities of South Asia, it is even more inappropriate applied to communities like those of Mirpur Six. They are not even like the shanties of Manila or Bombay, which are constructed of industrial waste – tin, plywood and polythene. Most of the houses here have bamboo frames, with walls of woven bamboo and a bamboo-panelled roof. They are built on platforms of compacted red earth which is eroded by rain and must be renewed annually. The roofs are sometimes made waterproof by lengths of polythene or bags that once held industrial chemicals, and some walls are brick-built. But for the most part the buildings retain the pattern of village construction and remain an emanation of the natural world, less ecologically degrading and destructive than their equivalents in more 'developed' cities. In that sense, if the slums of Dhaka were to be abandoned they would decay naturally, return to the earth that is one of their central components.

Even so, an invasive industrialization is their reason for existence. The tension between village and city is made visible in Dhaka, and in the end it is not the village that prevails. The cooking fires may be in traditional clay *chulhas,* or stoves, in front of the huts, but the cooking fuel proves to be a mixture of waste material from plastics and garment factories, which melts into a foul-smelling liquid.

This slum is a refuge for people displaced by erosion, cyclones, floods, famine, or that more recent generator of insecurity, development. At least here they are relatively secure: the ledge of land between the factory and the poisoned lake is accessible only by the one road. It is too narrow to be required for private housing or developmental infrastructure. The unfavoured site offers protection from rising land values in the city.

Eighty per cent of men in the community are rickshaw drivers or 'van' drivers. The 'van' is a flat wooden cart, about one metre square, made of wooden slats and harnessed to a three-wheeler cycle. It is used for carrying goods from factory to market. But sometimes it conveys the sick or infirm. One hot noon in Mirpur I saw a van on which there were four people. It was an unforgettable tableau. A sick man was lying in a diagonal position on the wooden cart; he was wearing a *lunghi* of Madras check, and a dingy white vest; he was in a high fever, and the sweat was running in glistening channels down his face. A man was holding a tattered black umbrella to shield him from the sun, a third was cradling his head in his lap, a fourth was holding his hand and gently stroking his arm. The man was clearly dying, his face yellow, his eyes a narrow ellipse of white. There was something arresting in the scene and, for a moment, indefinably disturbing to a Western observer: to be dying on a busy street in the total absence of medical technology, the only consolation the overwhelming, tangible presence of loved flesh and blood.

Habib, an old man well into his sixties, depending on a simple wooden crutch to move across the rocky paths, wears a blue check *lunghi*. His torso is bare, and his heart beats visibly against his narrow ribcage; he has stringy arms and a thin tangle of beard. He used to be a rickshaw puller in Khulna, but was involved in an accident. A car knocked him from his vehicle, and as a result he lost the use of his leg. Now, he must live from the earnings of his son, who is a rag picker and makes about 15–20 taka a day (40–50 US cents). This young man is mentally sick and cannot work every day. His wife is a maidservant, earning 60 taka a month ($US150). Habib has three daughters, all of them married. One, abandoned by her husband, has returned to Habib's house with her two children.

On the embankment leading from the higher to the lower slope, there is a growth of vivid green moss. Here and there a jackfruit tree grows, while close to the water some plantains provide shade and fruit. A few medicinal herbs close to the small houses are symbols of an older economy, gestures to a village self-reliance that has been broken.

Although the organic materials of which the slum is constructed make it appear less repelling than many industrial areas in South Asia, the lack of safe water makes it one of the most dangerous places to live. A water connection from the adjacent factory provides illegal water for the houses close to the water point – and an agreeable supplementary income for the factory officials – but those far from the outlet must beg for water from people in the big houses outside the slum. The well-to-do are reluctant to give, because if they offer water to one family fifty more will come; sometimes they too ask for money for the concession.

Barek, one of the oldest and most respected members of the slum community, has been here for nineteen years. He is from Vikrampur, not far from Dhaka. His brother was a tailor and came to the city in search of a better living. Barek at that time remained with his father, who had a small shop. The father became sick. They had to sell their land and later their homestead to pay for the medicines and treatment he needed. Sickness, says Barek, drove us from modest prosperity into the depths of poverty. He says there is no difference between being poor in Vikrampur and being poor in Dhaka, only there are more opportunities for work in the city. Barek works as 'decorator' for a small catering firm. The caterer rents out chairs, at 1 taka a time, for weddings, celebrations and festivals. Barek does the labouring work for the business, delivering the food and furniture but also constructing the wooden arches and gates which will then be festooned with coloured fabric and cloth to form ceremonial entrances to the place where the function is to be held. The work is not regular, but Barek makes on average between 1,500 and 2,000 taka a month, 50–70 taka a day. He has five children. One goes to primary school, but since the school is distant his attendance is sporadic. Barek says that people in this part of the community cannot get water from the factory. They tried to make a connection illegally, across the lake.

They paid collectively with money they had saved. Someone informed on them, and the pipe was cut. The community on the other side of the lake is equally poor: you can see their huts – bamboo, some with grass thatch, their bamboo feet in the water – about 40 metres away.

The lack of clean water and the impossibility of preventing the children from bathing in the polluted lake lead to diarrhoea, stomach disorders, outbreaks of typhoid. Malaria is common, and many children are affected by Guinea worm, which lives in the intestines and feeds on blood. In the slum there are 640 children under 15: 340 girls and 300 boys. Many of the older ones work, their occupations ranging from helpers in garment factories to collectors of cow dung for fuel, and fare collectors on Tempo taxis.

Barek articulates the feelings of many people here. He believes in education for his children, but their priority must be survival. There is no choice but for the children to work, just as there is no choice for the mostly migrant workers here: at least 70 per cent are rickshaw pullers, 10 per cent van drivers and another 10 per cent cart pullers, human beasts of draught, harnessed to the bamboo shafts of long carts perhaps 8 metres long, and carrying construction materials or goods to market. There are a few masons, carpenters, baby taxi drivers, vendors, hawkers, recyclers.

As we sit beneath a jackfruit tree in a little clearing in the slum a boy of about twelve joins us. Barek tells him to step forward and explain the work he does. The boy is carrying a big shallow bamboo basket on his head, which is protected by a cloth pad. The boy, Nayon, lowers the basket and places it before us. The basket is lined with newspaper. In a rusty, round tin he has a slab of *kotkoti*, made from molasses cooked and hardened into a yellowish-coloured toffee. This he gives to children in exchange for anything they bring to him that is saleable for recycling. Today his objects of barter are pitiful: in the basket are a piece of plastic pipe, a torn plastic cup, a piece of wood, two dented tins (one that contained chemicals, the other condensed milk), some plastic bags, a few rusty nails, and a piece of old rubber inner tube from a bicycle. The quantity of toffee he gives is in proportion to the value of the objects the children hunt out for him. It provides them with a little treat, and for Nayon, the maximum earnings from selling the goods to the larger-scale recyclers is 40 taka a day. He pays 10 taka for the *kotkoti* he buys from a woman whose livelihood this is. His daily profit is 30 taka (75 US cents).

Nayon has short, shaven hair. He wears an orange-and-lemon-coloured shirt and a plain *lunghi*. His father used to work making panels of woven bamboo for the walls of slum dwellings, but now he is sick with tuberculosis. His mother earns 60 taka a month as a domestic servant, so Nayon is the principal earner in the family. He has a slight harelip, and a crooked sweet smile. He starts work at about eight in the morning and finishes in the mid-afternoon. He would like to study, but when his work is finished he must look after his father.

Nasrul is a Tempo driver. This form of taxi is a jeep, with two rows of benches facing each other so that the knees of the passengers meet. It can hold up to twelve or fourteen people. Nasrul works from early morning, taking people to work, until late in the night. He keeps only 25 taka out of every 100 he earns. The rest goes to the vehicle's owner and to pay for fuel. He can earn up to 100 taka a day, which makes him one of the relatively privileged of the community.

Many people came to Dhaka in 1971–72, after liberation, in the aftermath of the bloodshed and hatred in which Bangladesh was born. But an even greater rural exodus occurred after the famine of 1974. It is a bitter thing, said one man in Mirpur, that we fought for independence from a Pakistan that was crushing the life and taking the wealth from Bengal, and now many young men must go from Bangladesh to find work in Karachi.

An old man wearing only a Madras cotton *lunghi* says that he came from Barisal at the time of the famine, when migration to Dhaka was the only alternative to starvation. Now he is almost seventy, and no longer works. Formerly he broke bricks for 40 or 50 taka a day. Bricks are baked in the brickfields and then brought to the city for construction. Those that are faulty are broken by hand to make hardcore for construction or roads. The brickworkers are everywhere, sitting on heaps of red rubble: men, women and children squatting under black umbrellas and crouched over a stone slab where they methodically break bricks into small stones; a cloud of brick dust rises under an oppressive sun. This elaborate, labour-intensive and damaging process is a necessary part of the building industry, since there is little natural stone for construction.

The old man says he has five children. He then adds, as a kind of afterthought, that he also has three daughters. One of these invisible women nevertheless looks after him, as well as working in a garment factory. He says he had hoped his sons would take care of him, but they are married and have their own families. The extended family is stretched as societies industrialize; indeed is extended in unforeseen ways.

Golanur, who was born in Dhaka, has lived in Mirpur for four years. Her husband is a security guard. Security is another major industry in the city, one that grows with the fear of a middle class confronted by an increasing concentration of the desperately poor. Golanur says that water is the biggest problem. Each day she has to find a house with a water connection that will let her draw enough for the day's consumption. This means going further and further afield, because the patience of the householders close to the slum is exhausted. Golanur has one daughter. It costs 35–40 taka a day to feed the family. That means rice three times a day, with *dal* and vegetables. Occasionally they buy fish. There are fish in the lake, despite the pollution, but some private individual has claimed ownership of the waterbody and fishing has been forbidden. Sometimes, she says, we fish at night.

There are advantages in the slum's inaccessibility. The road that leads to it becomes waterlogged in the rain, and even the police will not come here then. The site acts as a barrier against intruders. There are no thugs or *goondas* who extort and rob. The community is united against outsiders. Occasionally criminals seeking a hideout from the police come here, but the people will not provide them with a refuge. The bustee is secure, against both demolition and invasion from outsiders; these are considerable compensations, despite the lack of amenities.

Shade is provided by trees growing close to the lake. The clearing at the centre of the slum is sheltered by two soaring jackfruit and some smaller mango trees. This year they yielded over 100 fruits, which the people shared. Nobody stole a single fruit, says Barek proudly. There is no crime in the slum; a powerful sense of shared fate holds people together in a defensive web of protection.

A young man sits on the edge of the circle, listening intently. He is about twenty-five, a mass of curly hair and wearing a bright blue shirt. His name is Mohamed Idris and he is a rickshaw puller. He spent five years in Delhi at the same work. He had suffered from asthma, and went on a pilgrimage to the shrine of a holy man in Khavaja in Rajasthan to seek a cure. He was restored to health and went to Delhi, where he earned 100 rupees a day, sometimes 150. He lived very cheaply in a slum across the Yamuna river, with the owner of the rickshaw. He could buy a meal for a few rupees. He saved most of the money he earned, and kept it with a *bhagat* (a local healer) who lived close by. After the murder of Rajiv Gandhi the police searched all the bustees looking for antisocial elements, and this *bhagat* ran away, taking the 20,000 rupees Mohamed Idris had saved during his five years in Delhi. Mohamed Idris was found to be an illegal immigrant and was interned ready for deportation: at that time the Hindu fundamentalists had whipped up fierce anti-Bangladesh feeling. He escaped from the camp, and continued for some time as a rickshaw driver, but when the mosque at Ayodhya was demolished by Hindu extremists and there were anti-Muslim riots, he decided to return to Dhaka, where his five brothers and three sisters live.

He now pulls a rickshaw for six hours a day, for which he pays the owner 22 taka. He cannot work the full day because he no longer has the strength. He says you can't stop for a single day because if you do you get pains in the legs and knees. The muscles are wasted if you use them, but they ache if you stop.

'We cannot take in enough food for our bodies to remain strong. Every day I feel my strength gets less.' He looks at me searchingly. His complexion is yellowish, a sign of debility, maybe jaundice. He says that the owner of the rickshaws earns hundreds of taka each day without doing any work. The rickshaw costs about 7,000 taka, so at 40 taka a day he has remade his capital in less than six months; everything else is profit. Mohamed Idris says that few rickshaw drivers can work more than ten or fifteen years. Some go on longer, but many suffer from respiratory disorders, muscle wastage.

The labour performed by three-quarters of the men in this community is dehumanizing, or rather is inhuman. This beautiful young man, not yet married, is already exhausted, his energies used up. He says to me, 'Can you find me another job? What hope is there for me, for the children I may have, for another generation who have nothing but their bodies to wear out prematurely?'

Idris tells me to look at the men in the shade of the trees, sleeping longer each day in the afternoon heat, unable to pedal the distances demanded by the passengers, sleeping the sleep not of idleness, as the middle classes say, but of an exhaustion close to death. He speaks with intense feeling of a depletion of energy that is in every way a scandal and a reproach to the humanity of all those who have ever spoken of a world order: for it is only disorder for the poor. The privations the rickshaw drivers suffer are so extreme that they are terminally dispossessed of all they have, even control over their own energies. Mohamed looks at me reprovingly from the fierce dark eyes discoloured by sickness and rage. At twenty-six, he is already an old man.

He follows us as we leave the slum. I press a 20-taka note into his hand, a pathetic gesture against the measureless violence he must inflict upon himself in a search for survival, that in fact has the opposite effect, as it pushes him each day closer to the edge of existence.

Klong Toey, Bangkok

Many who have fled environmental ruin and the destruction of farmlands in order to seek refuge in the city often discover that insecurity threatens them there also. The slums characteristically grow on land that is, at the time of settlement, virtually worthless, in low-lying areas, on rocky or marshy land, on waste ground, beside canals. By constructing their homes, by reclaiming land and making it habitable, the people increase its value. As the city grows and expands they find that others, with greater purchasing power, want the amenity they have created, and they are threatened with eviction.

Nowhere is this more true than of the cities that have grown fast and become rich, those where an expanding middle class wants room for its housing, business and recreation, where international companies set up headquarters and tourists come for the particular pleasures to be found there. Bangkok is perhaps the supreme example in South Asia.

In 1965, Bangkok had 2.4 million people. Twenty years later the official figure was 5.6 million, reflecting a growth rate of 3.9 per cent a year, while the population of the country as a whole was growing at a rate of 2.6 per cent per year. The population of Bangkok is now greater than 10 million.

In 1990, according to the Policy and Planning Department of Bangkok Metropolitan Authority (BMA), there were 146,677 households in 981 slum communities, with 946,839 inhabitants, 17 per cent of the city's population. This figure is an underestimate, since many illegal communities are omitted from the count and many small pockets are overlooked.

Work is the primordial reason for slum settlements. About 40 per cent of the urban poor still walk to work in Bangkok. The slum communities, founded mostly between twenty-five and forty years ago, originally rented land on which to build their homes. Houses were mainly of wood. As more people came, lots were subdivided, basements were converted to rented rooms, passageways between the dwellings became narrower. The original drainage canals became clogged with rubbish and waste, which was never cleared. This led to flooding. Mosquitoes and rats flourished. Public utilities were not provided. Most houses were not registered, and officially did not exist. People had to buy electric connections from their richer neighbours, water had to be bought or fetched from distant standpipes. People even now pay up to 7 or 8 per cent of their total income on water and electricity.

Almost half the slum population is under the age of twenty.

Klong Toey, the oldest and most extensive slum in Bangkok, grew up to serve the port. It provided the dock workers, the labourers, the whole infrastructure of the port. This to a considerable degree remains its function, although rapid containerization is changing things.

A concrete wall with rows of barbed wire divides Klong Toey from the docks with their blocks of huge multicoloured containers labelled Mitsubishi, P & O, Sanyo, Honda. In spite of the use of containers, a majority of the men in Klong Toey still work as dock labourers. The

containers have to be unloaded manually, and the merchandise trans-
ferred to trucks. This work remains labour-intensive and arduous,
even if irregular. The cargo may be anything from a consignment of
consumer goods to dangerous chemicals.

The workers are organized in groups by middlemen attached to
the shipping companies. These pay the wages – perhaps 200 baht
($US8) a day – for the unloading of a particular cargo; but then there
may be no work for several days.

Klong Toey covers a considerable area. Parts of it have been
improved by the local people over the years; other parts have been
'developed' by municipal or private authorities, including the Port
Authority of Thailand. The people themselves have always been alert
to any opportunity to enhance their living place and to augment their
income. A recent development in Bangkok has been the appearance
of several thousand young men on motorcycles which are used as
taxis, weaving in and out of the interminable traffic jams: they provide
the only means of movement in a city immobilized by cars. These
young men earn up to 300 or 400 baht a day – $US12–16. When not
working they sit, lie or sprawl over their Yamaha or Honda machines
in Klong Toey, wearing silver- or lilac-coloured coats, half-gloves of
imitation leather, ear studs, amulets and gold chains at their necks:
they are a new aristocracy of labour, their status determined not by
skill – a ride with them can be a dangerous experience – but by the
slow choking of Bangkok by cars.

Many women work at home making garlands for temples, sweet
jasmine and marigolds for home shrines and spirit houses, or to
sweeten the air in taxicabs. Others wash and repair uniforms: you see
so many uniforms in Bangkok, halfway between military and school –
for cleaning companies, security firms, factories, stores – half the
population seems to be in the livery of subordination. Some women
make paper bags or skewers of bamboo for the vendors of kebabs
and grilled meat. In Bangkok very few people prepare food at home,
and this creates thousands of small restaurants and food vendors in
every locality; here women clean vegetables, pluck with tweezers the
remaining feathers from geese whose throats have been cut, shape
pineapples into rippling slices; make banana fritters and prepare
vats of *tom-yam* or noodles.

Klong Toey is cut off from the rest of the city, bordered on one side
by the port and on the other by a raised expressway which soars some
20 metres above the railtrack leading to the port. Along the railway
line, squatters and vendors have built rough shelters and stalls. On
the other side of the railway a dusty highway crowded with trucks also
leads to the port. The expressway – a somewhat exaggerated term for

a highway that is frequently at a standstill – was to have been an answer to the chronic and immitigable congestion of this overgrown city.

The social and physical isolation of Klong Toey has not preserved it from the rise in land and property values. The Port Authority itself requires more land for containers, whilst the Bangkok Metropolitan Authority wants to sell some of the land it owns in the slum to a developer for another shopping mall (to add to the sixty or so already constructed). The BMA has proposed the sweeping away of large parts of the existing community, with the removal of the people either to the peripheral areas of the city or to new high-rise apartments on part of the Klong Toey site.

The area was first settled over fifty years ago. Over time, many people have improved their houses. Paving and drainage systems have been installed, particularly in the core area of Klong Toey, which was regularized more than twenty years ago. Even so it is still far from salubrious. There are areas of polluted wasteland, where rubbish and decaying matter pile up, while the evil-smelling *klong*, or canal, has become stagnant and gives off a mixture of nauseous gases. Its inky water seethes with bubbles that grow and burst on the surface, a fermenting movement that suggests a life entirely absent from the dead water.

Some people will be happy to be relocated at Minburi, in the northeast of the city, particularly those who have transferable skills or businesses they can carry out just as easily elsewhere. Taxi drivers and food vendors know they will be in demand. Others hope for factory jobs with regular salaries. Meanwhile community representatives have been negotiating with the Port Authority so that those who see no prospect of work elsewhere may be offered the option of a new apartment in Klong Toey.

The desire to remain here is weakened by a number of factors. Klong Toey has been the site of a number of accidents involving explosions, fires and the release of dangerous chemicals into the atmosphere. In 1991 a major explosion wrecked a considerable area of slum housing. The Port Authority constructed some new flats, into which victims of that accident are only now being moved. At the time of the accident those who were made homeless were sheltered in temporary prefabricated shacks of asbestos, wood and tin. These have already deteriorated badly and the area has become a desolate place of waste water, garbage and squalor. In rainy weather it is virtually impassable and people walk through dirty water up to knee level, carrying their shoes in one hand and an umbrella in the other.

Only those who still have papers to prove they were the owners of the slum houses destroyed by the explosion will be allowed to move to the new apartments. Some people had already sold their properties, or even simply the documents, which comes to the same thing. This means that those to whom they sold – who may be well-off – are now exercising their right to occupy the new flats even though they may have perfectly adequate accommodation elsewhere.

The temporary accommodation that the victims of the explosion had occupied will not be demolished: it is now required by the Port Authority for other slum dwellers in Klong Toey, who are being evicted for development. When I was there in August 1994 the victims of the explosion were about to be forcibly removed. Tek, a powerful woman in her thirties, was urging the people not to move. Since those who are not entitled to a new flat – all who have no legal title to the damaged houses – have nowhere to go, they have little choice but to remain where they are and wait to see what happens.

The chemical explosion of 1991 has continued to take its toll ever since. The initial casualty list was not high, but the long-term effects of the chemicals released into the atmosphere – the nature of which was never revealed – made themselves felt later. To make matters worse many of the people who had papers proving their ownership of their property lost them in the ensuing fire. Tek says, 'You do not look for papers when life is threatened, you look for your children.'

The National Housing Authority (NHA) and the Port Authority initially agreed that the former would provide plots of land for the displaced people in Klong Toey itself, at the subsidized rate of 1 baht (4 US cents) per square wah, with the Port Authority underwriting the rest of the cost. The people would, of course, construct their own houses. The Port Authority is now challenging this agreement, having learned of a secret local government plan to build a shopping complex on a large site at the centre of Klong Toey.

The NHA has built, and continues to build, flats on the edge of Klong Toey for people ousted by development or disaster (sometimes the two seem to converge), but the people would rather manage these on a community basis than have them managed by government. In any case the flats are a mere 29 square metres, quite inadequate for a family of seven, eight or even ten people. These are more like dormitory rooms than flats: boxes bursting with the people they are expected to contain. The apartments already occupied are festooned with washing looped from the windows, whilst garbage accumulates at the base of the buildings. They are eight storeys high, with long corridors where children are expected to play and which must supply the public spaces in which people – in keeping with traditional practice – expect to pass much of their social lives.

As slum families move into flats the shortage of space often causes minor quarrels to develop into public brawls or major family rupture.

Flats do violence to the way of life of the people; they are an alien idea like so much else in this constricted, polluted city; a transplant, insensitive and inappropriate to a tropical climate. In the slums people had been able to expand their houses, both vertically by adding another storey and horizontally by extending forward and back, even though this narrowed the passageways between the structures. But there is nothing they can do to modify apartments created by the construction industry. Here, as everywhere else in the city, you can see the tendency of the market economy to enclose and provide for the people in ways that undercut their own desire to make and create things for themselves. Market provision replaces self-provisioning, and when this is finally outlawed people are expected to welcome their freedom to choose in the market.

The NHA had wanted to charge 480 baht a month ($US20) in rent. The people say that 300 ($US12) is the maximum they can afford. This has now been accepted by the NHA and Port Authority, but if tenants fall three months into arrears they will be evicted. This compulsory movement into flats leads to debates that echo arguments heard in the West in the 1950s about the fate of communities, and whether these would be destroyed by high-rise developments.

The people who came to Klong Toey were displaced from rural life. They found a precarious living in the city and are now being displaced once more. This time most will go into the city periphery, a strange limbo at present neither rural nor urban.

Mongkol is now in his fifties. He came here thirty-four years ago from Ayutthaya, where his family was landless. He met his wife in Bangkok, where he worked alongside her on a construction site. After marriage he was a fisherman in the city's still-living lakes and waterways, where twenty years ago he could earn 100 baht a day. When the ponds were filled in for construction, he opened a small store. To do so, he sold a gold chain he had bought with the money from fishing. This financed the modest stock of what was, at that time, more stall than shop. It cost him 24 baht (1 dollar) to set up the stall.

Mongkol has four children. Two work for the Bangkok Metropolitan Authority, another is a photographer who takes pictures for the identity cards that all Thais are legally obliged to carry. Mongkol now has his own taxi and is paying off at the rate of 3,000 baht a month ($US120). He recognizes that relocation is a major problem, but it is not a great worry to him. Bangkok has been good to him, he has prospered. His shop on a busy corner of two concrete pathways is a busy place, stocked with snacks, biscuits, cigarettes, toys, candy, household goods, soaps, toothpaste, cosmetics, soft drinks. Mongkol will go to

Minburi, where the government compensates people by giving them enough land to build a house. He dislikes the idea of paying rent on a flat. Building a house will be costly, but at least it will be his house. The community committee of which he is a member is negotiating with the local government for compensation for the compulsory displacement. To live on the outskirts of the city will be expensive and not everyone will find work there. The people want to take construction materials from their houses here so as not to incur more expense. The government said initially that there can be no further compensation, because the land is being given to the people. The committee is also negotiating with the Port Authority to provide them with transport to bring workers back to the port area, but since the work is tied to the time of arrival of ships coming in and the journey may take up to two hours each way, such a concession is unlikely.

The area where Mongkol lives is required for the expansion of port containerization. This is progress. The country is prospering. The port is becoming more busy. He says there has been a good sense of community here. He is optimistic about the people's ability to re-create this wherever they go.

The hopefulness of Mongkol is not shared by the low-income families here, particularly those who have nothing but their muscle power to offer in their search for work.

Urah Srisawat tells a different story of slum living. She occupies a sizeable house which leads directly off a narrow concrete path; it has a rectangular front room with a more extensive room behind. The house is made of metal and wood, with a bare concrete floor and sky-blue plastic floor-covering. An electric fan whirrs gently in the afternoon heat. Urah's mother came to Bangkok from Pisanutlok. 'My mother and father ran away together because they were in love, and they came here to avoid the disapproval of their families. They were construction workers here and settled in Klong Toey because it was close to the construction site.' Urah was born here. Later her father and mother separated; or rather, her father ran away to Korat with a new woman. 'In his life he travelled far for love,' is her stern judgement.

Urah has eight brothers and sisters, all living in Klong Toey. One makes and sells rings set with artificial gems; others work in the private sector as company employees, factory workers, security guards; one sister is a maid. Urah's husband drives a Subaru, a taxi like a jeep, for eight or ten people. They have two children, a boy and a girl, but Urah has also taken in two children abandoned by their parents who disappeared to avoid debt. Had they not gone away the creditors would have hired gangsters to beat them up or destroy their home. Urah says, in mitigation of her friends' desertion of their children, 'It isn't

easy to bring up children in Klong Toey; they want money all the time.'
Money, that is, to feed the debased version of consumerism that has
penetrated even the poorest places. 'Many people get into debt for the
sake of the children.' The rate of interest on debts to private moneylenders is 3 per cent per day. To pay the debt of the children's parents
Urah gave up her own house, which the moneylenders took as repay-
ment; it is just another story of the unrecorded generosity of the poor.

She says there are many gambling dens in Klong Toey, places where
people go in the hope of making quick money. For every one who
achieves it, a hundred lose everything. When her own house was
taken Urah returned to this, her mother's house, a cluttered space
with bundles of washing in plastic baskets, a big tarnished mirror, an
old TV, clothes racks and the wooden frame of a sofa with shreds of
horsehair clinging to it.

The poor have learned to turn the system to their advantage.
Urah's mother will accept relocation in Minburi. She will be given a
parcel of land to build a house. Urah will go to the new flats, and once
installed she will sell the flat so that the family will be able to build a
decent home in Minburi. They would prefer to stay here. The local
people had tried to negotiate with the local government to have the
area upgraded, but when it became clear that there was no chance of
remaining they devised their own strategy for survival, making the
best of a situation imposed against their will.

At the border of Klong Toey the expressway flyover gradually
becomes lower and lower until it joins the main road to the port.
The traffic is reduced to a crawl for most of the day. Trucks set up a
fog of dust, grit and particles of cement. As the space beneath the flyover decreases, people who have built their houses there must live in
spaces more and more cramped, so that where the road reaches
ground level people are packed into narrow caselike structures alongside a ditch into which runs all the foul water from the slum.

The Port Authority's new Animal Quarantine Office is close to the
container terminal. Passing through a narrow alley in the compound
of this building you reach one of the most desolate areas of Klong
Toey, Area 12, as it is called, built on an expanse of land made marshy
by seawater, seasonal rains and poor drainage. Sagging wooden slats
form a narrow causeway. Some of the planks have rotted in the monsoon; underneath is a sump of indestructible industrial garbage –
plastic, polystyrene, rusty tin cans, plastic shoes and sandals, thin bags,
green, blue and red – all simmering in the grey stagnant water. Here
and there are visible a bright green efflorescence of algae, and the acid-
green shoots of some water plants. The houses are both more scattered
and more rudimentary than elsewhere in Klong Toey, with panels of

metal, asbestos, wood, hardboard. There are stalls selling cold drinks, snacks and fruit, and the sad consolations of the poor – chocolate, soap, silver bags of prawn crackers and potato chips, cigarettes, Sprite and Pepsi. Two corpulent policemen in khaki uniforms, batons at their belt, radios on their lapels, guns bulging like displaced sex organs, patrol the alleyways. The sagging boards yield beneath their tread and threaten to release them into the bath of foul water below.

Some of the huts have been abandoned, invaded by trapped flood-water, so that strips of rusty metal and decayed wood lie overrun by plantain and white water lilies.

Oan, an elderly Chinese, lives alone in a sparsely furnished hut; a fan keeps the air moving. A collection of dusty cassettes lies on a wooden shelf; there is a plastic cloth on the floor, a rice cooker, an old sewing machine, a pretty little red spirit-house lit by a small electric candle. Oan has lived a life more or less self-reliant, undisturbed for more than forty years, in one of the last inhabited houses on the pol-luted edge of the sea. He came from Bangkok's Chinatown about 8 kilometres from here; he left home because his parents disapproved of his marriage. With a chuckle he says he never gave them the chance to disapprove of his other marriages. The area was a slum when he came here, but over the years he has fortified and improved his house. Oan earned a living as a painter in the port, maintaining the containers. Now he lives alone. Of his six children one died and two work at the Duang Prateep Foundation, a charity that has done much to defend the interests of the people of Klong Toey. Two of Oan's children live with his wife. He stopped work two years ago after being struck by a car on the road to the port. This damaged his arm so that he can no longer raise it.

The site here is designated for containers. Oan has been offered relocation at Watcharapin, near Minburi, but he hopes his children will offer him a home. Two have their families in Klong Toey. There has been no offer of apartments to the people on this, the poorest site of the area. 'No one knows when we will be evicted. Some of the land is to be turned into a car park for Port Authority employees. If the people are shifted, who knows what they will do? Most work as port labour, women do washing, they clean and scrub the containers after they have been unloaded. The port has given a livelihood to the people of Klong Toey. That is why we are here. Why must we move, when the port has been built on our labour? When I came here there was nothing: no path, no electricity. We had to buy cans of fresh water. Now we have built up a community and provided an education for our children.'

And some of the children have gone on to secondary, and even university education. They have earned a passage out of Klong Toey –

leaving behind a diminishing pool of unskilled labour, the most vulnerable and least adaptable: labourers, vendors, casual employees.

Not far from Oan we met Prasert, a dignified woman in her early sixties with greying hair and smartly dressed in blue skirt and white blouse. Her house is reached by two steps and a little concrete wall, a defence against floodwater. She is sitting on the stone floor, close to a tiny baby on a mattress under a gauze-covered frame. This child we understand is her granddaughter, the child of her daughter, who died two months ago from a staphylococcus infection, necrotizing fasciitis. She died within a day of falling ill, in terrible pain. Her picture stands in front of the shrine that dominates Prasert's room. Five steps lead towards an image of the Buddha; on each step are sacrifices and offerings – flowers, a glass of crimson watermelon juice, garlands, bananas. There are pictures of Hindu gods, Krishna and Ram, amulets and animistic symbols. Prasert can speak to the spirits.

A strong, melancholy woman, she has been here for thirty years. She came from Samut Prakhan when it was a province far beyond Bangkok (now it has been swallowed up by the city). In Samut Prakhan her family's land had been destroyed by floods, and they worked as labourers on other people's fields. She came to Bangkok, and worked digging and carrying soil to trucks to reclaim land for a big condominium. Prasert was paid 18 baht per truckload of earth. 'That was thirty-three years ago. During the time I worked I had three or four children. I used to carry them to the site so I could look after them while I worked. For ten years I dug soil. I was employed by the contractors commissioned to prepare the site for construction. I lived here before the customs department built their quarantine building and before the port had spread so far. It was always waterlogged. At the time, only five or six houses were here.' When the Port Authority built the office the river was diverted and a new embankment was built. Prasert's children worked in the port. Her daughter who died recently was thirty-nine. The baby, it turns out, is her daughter's granddaughter, Prasert's great-granddaughter.

Her husband died six years ago. He spent his life digging and carrying earth until the day he died. Prasert now washes clothes in other people's houses once or twice a week: 60 baht for a basket of washing.

Prasert sold her house to raise money for medicine for her son, after he was knocked down by a car. The driver stopped and gave him 500 baht ($US20). Prasert paid everything she had to the hospital. She no longer has any proof that she is the owner of the property and she has no claim to be relocated. She pays rent to the new owner.

There are eight people in the house including two of her children and their families. A boy of about eleven, her grandson, comes in and removes the protective covering from the baby. He takes out the wet underlay and tenderly replaces it. Prasert says, 'I do not think of being relocated. Perhaps I will die before then.'

Even when slums have been authorized and people given documents proving their ownership of a house, insecurity is not necessarily finished. At times of sickness, death, or debt they sell the papers, the only thing of value they possess. Earlier this might have been less vital, because the slums were not at risk from being swept away. But with the increasing pace of 'development' more and more poor communities are being demolished. And the law is inflexible: without documents they have no chance of compensation or relocation. Some may move into the home of relatives or rent a room in someone else's property. Others are cast adrift in the city: their precarious public lives are visible under the pillars of the expressway, where their cooking fires smudge the concrete and their most intimate existence is screened from passers-by only by a few rags strung out on a length of plastic wire along the dusty highway.

I left Bangkok for a few weeks and returned in mid-September 1994. During that time a large area of slum housing at Romklau in Klong Toey had been destroyed by fire, about eight hundred houses, home to more than 4,000 people.

The site of the disaster is one of the ugliest scenes I can remember. Charred pieces of wood, blackened metal, broken house posts look like the remains of a burned forest. Only the maze of narrow concrete walkways is still intact. The remains of people's belongings lie in the mud; molten plastic – so much plastic, liquefied by the heat and congealed into new shapes by the water – broken toys, misshapen household vessels, burnt-out television sets, singed clothes and shoes, broken glass gleaming in the sunshine. I see disconnected water pipes, bedding, foam rubber, house foundations and frames. Anything that could be rescued has gone. Some children play on the smoke-stained walkways, on battered cycles and old carts. Even two weeks after the catastrophe a smell of fire lingers.

There is anger and depression in the community caused by the silence over what caused the fire. Rumours grow in the absence of clear information. Everyone agrees that more than one fire was started at the same time. The official version, that it began as the result of a domestic accident, might have been plausible if a second fire had not begun simultaneously in another part of the slum. Some say it was started by a party of young people high on drugs. Others saw petrol bombs thrown from the expressway under which this part of Romklau stands. One fire was started by an exploding gas cylinder.

Some say they saw several fires begin at the same time.

A man from the Water Authority is at the site. He surveys the sub-merged belongings and says it is a pity that when people don't want water Romklau is regularly flooded. When they needed water the fire engines could not get close enough to be effective. The disaster occurred during the rainy season. A great deal of the area is water-logged. Some streets around the slum are almost impassable as people sink up to their knees in muddy water. Relief vans and trucks are parked under the expressway; long queues of people form, waiting for emergency rations: pieces of cooked chicken in big plastic baskets and a scoop of rice. Another lorry arrives with sacks of rice. A photogra-pher from the charity that provides the food is there to capture the scenes of public gratitude.

Some of the people from the burnt-out area have taken refuge under the expressway close to the railway line. New, temporary shelters have appeared. Mud and shit mingle along the railway track, along with a trail of waste, babies' nappies, plastic bags, abandoned mattresses, the remains of meals. A train carrying chemicals, a warning mark of skull and crossbones on the black-and-rust-coloured metal wagons, passes within centimetres of the improvised shelters along the track.

Numb with shock, people are still picking desultorily through the debris in the hope of finding something they have lost, or items they can sell. Many are fatalistic about the fire. Some say that perhaps they will be offered better accommodation. Government ministers have promised generous compensation.

This land belongs to the Port Authority. We meet Bang Oen, a middle-aged woman who sells food from a cart. Her house is on the very edge of the community and is still partly intact. Only one wall was burned and the front is still more or less undamaged. She says that, although nobody is expressing it in public, the people are very angry. She repeats the story that a fire was started by an exploding cylinder of cooking gas and that at the same time bombs were thrown from the expressway.

This, she says grimly, is not the first disaster in Klong Toey. She sends for her sister, Usa, who is inside the house. She was severely injured in the chemical explosion that destroyed their home in Kolao in 1991. Her hair is shaven and she has a long scar on her scalp and forehead. After that accident, Bang Oen says, she sold her house to pay for the medical bills for her sister's treatment. The compensation came nowhere near the cost of medical attention for her sister. Since then, Usa has been unable to work.

'They have promised 20,000 baht in compensation, but so far all we have received is 3,000 to replace kitchen and cooking utensils. The Port Authority wants us to go to Minburi. We cannot go so far because we work here. Then they say they will build us flats, but flats are too small for families of nine or ten people.'

Bang Oen's husband is a taxi driver. They came here twenty years ago from Bang Sue with her parents; at that time Bang Sue was beyond the city limits but now it is well within the metropolitan area.The Port of Thailand Authority announced after the disaster that the people would be allowed to rebuild their homes on the site for one year, after which they would be relocated. What use is it, asks Bang Oen, to build a house for just twelve months? People came here to work, they have served the port. Their life is here.

Bang Oen believes that this fire, like the chemical explosion, was part of a conspiracy to remove people from the area and to relocate them 'somewhere else, out of the way'. After the chemical explosion soldiers came and destroyed what remained of the houses. When people were evicted from the explosion area it was planned that it should be rebuilt and that people from Romklau should go there. People did not want to go there because it is still a dangerous zone, and they resisted. That, says Bang Oen firmly, is why the fire occurred. Private developers want to build a shopping mall on part of the land and the Port Authority wants the rest for further containerization.

A passer-by stops and listens to Bang Oen's tirade. She says, 'Do not listen to her. She exaggerates.' But a man says with quiet bitterness, 'The people of Thailand do not like to quarrel. We avoid confrontation. We like to come to an agreement. We like to compromise. But how do you compromise with fire?'

Chakri Tonghkam is a worker with the Duang Prateep Foundation, which has supported people's organization for many years and has provided education in the area for over two generations. He says, 'A few days ago the director of the Port Authority was dismissed from his job. The people of Klong Toey protested because they know he is not corrupt. The Board of the Authority wants to remove him for that very reason, because he supports the people. He had said the people could remain for one year on the site. The authority wants to build flats for the people from yet another district of Klong Toey, whose land it urgently wants for the expansion of its container business. In this respect the fire was useful, to say the least, in clearing them from the site, whether or not the promised flats ever materialize.

'People in the burnt-out area believe different things. The community committee know the full story, but it is complex; most people do not know, and this is how rumours spread and take root. People did see petrol bombs thrown, but they would not say so publicly to journalists. The web of conspiracy comes out as a conflicting mesh of stories and half-truths.

'People will be given some compensation. They have been told they can rebuild temporarily. The anger will cool, hope will return, and a Thai compromise will be reached. The Social Welfare Ministry gave wood for reconstruction, various foundations have made donations. If people are allowed to stay for one year, they can at least negotiate to stay longer. A co-committee has been formed consisting of members of the board of the Port Authority of Thailand and the residents. In fact that is why the director was ousted: the promise he gave publicly of a one-year reprieve cannot be reversed. He is now on extended leave. He will be promoted to Assistant to the Port Authority, which means he will be deprived of power. In fact the 3,000 baht compensation per family that has been given has come from a private individual. The Port Authority has yet to make a comparable gesture.

'The people are now scattered. Some are living under the express-way. Some are in tents on tennis courts which belong to the Port Authority, and some have gone to Kolao, the site of the 1991 explosion, which has been vacant since that time.

'The Authority probably plans that the Romklau people will go to Kolao; those displaced from Kolao will move into the flats still under construction on the edge of Klong Toey. The people on the land most urgently wanted for containerization may well then be removed onto the site gutted by last month's fire.'

Whatever the full story beyond the Romklau fire, this is only one more – and far from the most serious – of a number of fires, accidents and catastrophes that have affected Klong Toey in recent years.

In May 1989 there was a chemical explosion in the port from which more than 500 people suffered after-effects. In January 1991 there was a leak of nitric acid from a tank. In March 1991 the warehouse storing chemicals at Kolao exploded, destroying 642 houses and making over 5,500 people homeless. People have been dying of mysterious illnesses ever since. An accident in August 1992 affected 300 households, while in November 1992 a fire destroyed 63 houses. In December 1993 Klong Toey temple burned down together with 460 houses. In May 1993 there was a chemical explosion in the container park. The August 1994 fire that destroyed Romklau is only the most recent. Negligence, conspiracy, indifference – whatever the cause, it always disadvantages the poorest, and clears the site to the benefit of the powerful.

Quezon City, Metro-Manila

Until recently, whenever news from slums was reported in the West it was almost invariably some horror story: a mass poisoning by adulterated alcohol in New Delhi, cholera in Mexico City, the collapse of a building in Cairo, a fire devastating a *favela* of São Paulo. Indeed, such stories still emerge frequently from cities of the Third World. But a subtle change has occurred. Lately, a number of stories and TV documentaries have celebrated the achievements of slum dwellers – those who worked to build a drainage system in Karachi, a self-help programme that brought literacy to a slum in Calcutta, an account of how women overcame drink in Madras or organized the self-employed in Ahmedabad.

This certainly goes some way to redressing the balance, but it has to be asked whether these positive profiles of the slums at the same time serve some other ideological purpose.

For by demonstrating the ability, the courage and the capacity for self-help of slum people, the way is prepared for a withdrawal of state and local government investment and support. This is in keeping with the structural adjustment programmes supervised worldwide by the World Bank and the IMF. Vietnam, Bangladesh, India and the Philippines are all implementing such programmes. All stress the abandonment of discredited state-interventionist policies, and the introduction of a neoliberalism that the West has largely discarded in its heartland (despite the rhetoric), but which lives on in its prescriptions for the economies of those poor countries that fall under the superintendence of its financial institutions. To emphasize the ability of people to do things for themselves, to become proactive in achieving levels of health care, reconstruction, organization, may create an impression that everything is really best left to the people themselves, without resources from outside. In this way the stress on the positive elements of popular mobilization can in reality serve the purpose of aggravating the position of the poor.

This has the advantage of absolving the powerful from responsibility for the sufferings of the poorest, and of drawing attention away from the magnitude of the problem of the cities. This is not to diminish the spectacular examples and achievements of the urban poor – the work of SPARC in Bombay, of the Coalition for Housing Rights in Calcutta and Bangkok, of the numberless NGOs in the Philippines, the heroism of popular movements under military threat in Indonesia. There are many truly inspiring examples of self-help; NGOs and voluntary groups, charities and religious bodies – Islamic, Christian and Buddhist – community organizations and political parties have all helped to make life tolerable for millions of poor people, rural and urban. But in terms of the macro policies, the relentless growth of cities, and the damage to peasant and farming traditions which sends developmental and environmental refugees in growing numbers to the harsh shelter of the urban centres, is little affected by these often noble and sometimes spectacular achievements. This is why it is important neither to deny the ability of the people themselves – and their daily survival is a constant tribute to human ingenuity and tenacity, to the humanizing power of women, to the capacity for altruism and self-sacrifice of the poor – nor to assume that this will rescue the cities from the multiple afflictions that abridge and cripple the lives of hundreds of millions of people.

It would be foolish to pass from one distortion – that the slums are places of crime, disease and despair – to the opposite: that they can be safely left to look after themselves.

The soaring building of the fundamentalist Iglesia ni Cristo dominates the central part of Quezon City, one of the five municipalities of Metro-Manila. A white Gothic apparition, the church seems to be floating in the clouds, a sort of materialized pie-in-the-sky for the inhabitants of the slum behind its shining façade.

The people began to organize here after demolitions in 1983. At that time there was a pitched battle between the residents and municipal demolition workers. Three people were injured when police opened fire on protesters.

Josepina, now in her fifties, was among those in the forefront of resistance. On the wall of her breezeblock house is the samurai sword with which she defied those who had come to destroy the house she had made with her own hands. Josepina is characteristic of the women of the slums, whose combative spirit and resolve to protect the only shelter they have nourish popular movements in all the insecure, menaced city communities.

Her house is poor: a battered sofa, shiny blue and white sacking to cover the walls. A tree in front of the house preserved it from the typhoons that swept away her neighbours' houses. Josepina's husband was a driver, killed in a road accident when she was eight months pregnant. After that she did washing for 3 pesos a day and later worked as a vegetable seller.

Her son Ariel is unemployed. He gives much time and energy to working with the community. Half the day he works unofficially with the illegal lottery system, *jueteng*. The rest he devotes to the poor. The other member of the household is a child abandoned by her mother and adopted by Josepina. This girl is now twelve.

Josepina still sells vegetables door to door. When her husband died she was left completely without resources, apart from those she found within herself. These proved to be considerable: the power to improvise, to build, to create work for herself, to bring up her son, to help improve the quality of the community over the years.

Rosita and Dominador live behind the main thoroughfare of the slum, in the substantial house they have made. Dominador is from Tarlac, home state of the former president of the Philippines, Corazon Aquino. His family lived on the Hacienda Luisita, the Aquino plantation. Since there is work for only six months of the year, at least one member of every family must leave; this brought him to Manila. Rosita is from Leyte, one of the most impoverished islands in the archipelago. Her family had a subsistence smallholding and a little store. She came to Manila for the same reason as her husband. They built their house on reclaimed land in 1970. Imelda Marcos saw the area in 1975 and said she wanted to 'develop' it for a lagoon, a park, and a future memorial to Marcos. It was that project that led to the demolitions.

When we settled here, says Rosita, the ground was covered with high grasses and trees. It extends over 440 hectares. Since 1980 people have come in increasing numbers, fleeing land grabbing by the rich, degradation of farmland, human rights abuses, evictions at gunpoint in the name of a banditry they call development. The site still bears traces of its country past. There are some big trees providing shade, and in the gardens people grow bananas, flowers, medicinal herbs. In 1970 Rosita paid 300 pesos per 100 square metres for the right to build, but now it is worth 60,000 pesos. Developers have their eyes on this land again. It is at the heart of Quezon City, close to the university campus, a very desirable piece of real estate.

Aquino recognized the people's organizations here when she was campaigning in 1986–87, and she promised then that if she were elected she would give the people the land they occupied. In the event she gave 180 hectares, but the precise status of the people remained unclear and they are still negotiating for leases. At the same time migrants are still coming to the area. In 1987 there were 11,000 families on this land. Now there are believed to be 45,000 (that is, almost a quarter of a million people). After the eruption of the Pinatubo volcano in 1992, much land in Tarlac and Pampangas was covered with *lahar*, the lava that spread a destructive crust across thousands of hectares of land. Many people originally from those areas already lived in this part of Quezon City, and they gave accommodation to their displaced relatives.

Others here are from Bicol, Samar, Leyte, words synonymous in the Philippines with poverty, want, and forced migration. They tell stories of militarization, takeover of their land by industry and plantations, destruction of forests, environmental ruin. They bear the costs and the wounds of a development that can be sustained only by intensifying pressure upon the poor and upon the resource base. In the city they work as drivers, carpenters, vendors, but perhaps half the people in the slum are jobless. Some of the young unemployed deal in, or use *shabu* (a heroin derivative), marijuana, cough syrup, solvents. Illegal liquor is brewed. The crime rate is high. The people say, 'You have to lock your doors at night. We try to make a decent living, but we are always under threat from gangs and drug dealers.'

Cleopatra Lucenara came to Manila when she was fourteen to look after children and to do housework. Her mother and father had separated, and of their four children Cleopatra was the only girl. She studied while she worked, and obtained a qualification in cosmetology in 1968. She worked for 35 pesos a month picking up nail clippings for the stylists in a beauty parlour. She later became a hair stylist and make-up artist, and in 1972 she was appointed personal beautician to Imelda Marcos, her responsibilities including hair-shaping, manicure and pedicure. 'Imelda was good to me. She is kind to the poor. She feels for them. Her heart is generous.' But Cleopatra's husband was jealous of her success and made her resign. 'Imelda wanted me to travel with her, to accompany her on her trips abroad, official visits and everything. But my husband didn't like that I should become exposed to rich people, so I had to give it up. Then my husband got a job working in Saudi Arabia so he has gone there, and now I work for the community.

'The demolitions in 1983 were terrible. That was when we organized to fight the destruction of our homes. Sama-Sama is the name of the organization we formed. We supported Corazon Aquino and she proclaimed that this land would be ours. The problem is that only part of the site was given to the people. Those on the rest of the land are also fighting for security of tenure. *We* are lucky, but we cannot just see them evicted. We are fighting to extend the right to the land to all the people now occupying it.'

This area is called Bulaklak Chapter. Bulaklak means 'flower', and the names of the streets are called by the names of flowers: Gumamela Everlasting, Sampagita. The people here have contributed to a self-financing drainage project and to a scheme that will mark the boundary of each individual plot of land. The drainage work is already in progress. Each house will pay 5,000 pesos over fifteen years. This is self-improvement by the people. The upgrading of self-built housing is far more effective than housing created by a building industry, which the urban poor can never afford.

The community labours under great difficulties – livelihood, security, gambling, drink, addictions, crime. The private armies of the Iglesia ni Cristo are in league with the *barangay* (local community) officials. The church extorts donations from the people. The popular organization is the only focus of resistance to unemployment, poverty, corruption, violence and the arbitrary predations of the security forces.

Denis Murphy is an American married to a Filipina, who has lived in the Philippines for twenty-five years. He is the co-ordinator of the Urban Poor Associates, which is designed specifically to limit evictions in the Philippines. He says the mayor of Quezon City has his own unofficial demolition squads, thugs and off-duty police. His own Housing Bureau does not know the extent of the evictions he authorizes. He does this on behalf of landlords, property interests and developers. Land is useless if occupied by those the government sees as squatters, but if it is cleared it is worth 3,000–4,000 pesos a square metre. When Denis Murphy first came to Manila in the mid-fifties it was a pleasant city of about 1 million people. Now the population is closer to 9 million, with officially 2.5 million squatters, although the true figure may well be nearer 4 million. More than half a million people have come from central Luzon since the eruption of Pinatubo. In any case, land in the countryside has been divided and subdivided through inheritance, degraded and exhausted, and people have nowhere else to go.

Metro-Manila consists of five separate authorities: Quezon, Pasig, Manila, Valoocan, Makati. The quality of the municipal staff is not good because they are neither highly regarded nor well-paid. Denis Murphy believes that a metro-wide agency is needed that would attract good professionals. The Philippines is now included with Burma, Bangladesh, Nepal and Vietnam as one of the most poverty-stricken countries of Asia. What is more, the Philippines is now 40 per cent urban, 60 per cent rural. Within the next decade it will be more than half urban. The urban poor will become a larger sector than the peasantry by the turn of the century, and more numerous than the industrial sector. Governments are not equal to the challenge; their shortcomings become more and more marked. Even government programmes that have been well conceived are rarely properly administered. As the urban poor become a more significant phenomenon, the tendency of most municipal authorities in South Asia has been to respond by becoming more punitive and repressive. The Philippines government says it plans to evict 200,000 families because of public works programmes.

Denis Murphy says that so long as evictions can take place without resistance, no local government and no landowner will negotiate seriously. It is only when people actively stand up to demolitions that they will be regarded as partners in the process of urban renewal. Denis Murphy regards effectiveness to resist eviction as a community's equivalent of a labour union's capacity to mount a strike: without this, both will be disregarded.

The people of the Commonwealth settlement, as indeed those of most slums, are perceived as a threat to order; this is no longer because they are going to overthrow society, or are prey to destabilizing leftist beliefs, but because their capacity for autonomy, self-reliance and independence suggests that they hold the key to a different way of doing things, that they represent the embryo of an alternative social order that is more egalitarian and solidaristic – the reverse of that ideology of extreme individualism preached by the powerful. Concentrations of poor people have a formidable ability to organize; whether this will be recognized and supported, or resisted as a threat to established institutions, is the crucial decision facing the leaders not merely of the growing municipalities, but of national governments and international agencies as well. Denis Murphy pays a modest tribute to the promulgation of the United Nations Covenant on Economic, Social and Cultural Rights of 1974 (where housing rights are clearly recognized), and the 1976 UN Conference on Human Settlements in 1976 (Habitat) when he says that in the past twenty years there may have been fewer evictions than might otherwise have occurred.

In 1993 the United Nations Committee on Economic, Social and Cultural Rights wrote to the Foreign Secretary of the Philippines asking for a response to the charge that the government of the Philippines had consistently violated the housing rights of thousands of its citizens. This was the first time that the UN had involved itself with housing rights in Asia. Denis Murphy is optimistic: this, he asserts, is symptomatic of the growing significance of the urban poor, and an increasing acknowledgement that they cannot simply be removed, evicted, demolished, bulldozed out of existence.

Relocating the Urban Poor, Bangkok

The more prosperous the cities become, the less secure are the poor, the more readily swept away. The poor of Bangkok have been made invisible, concealed behind the façades and burnished surfaces of the city. Its malls and office blocks rival anything to be seen in Houston, Frankfurt or Osaka. Over the past twenty years there have been sweeping clearances of the poor. Those who remain anywhere near the central area cling to small parcels of wasteland, or hang over the edge of stinking canals and marshland.

Many of the poor have been sent out to the periphery. The government has provided small pieces of land for people to build their houses on, but these cannot furnish a livelihood or an adequate income.

Saw Pattaya is an old settlement of urban poor. It stands close to a symmetrical new development called Royal Avenue, a crescent of white-painted apartments and shopping units. A strip of coarse grass-land separates Saw Pattaya from the new buildings; the construction company has built a brick wall 2 metres high to hide the slum. On the other side is a wire grille: the result is that the community appears half prison, half zoo.

There are about sixty families here, some five hundred people squeezed onto a strip of marshy land and living under the threat of eviction. This is railway land, bounded on the far side by the track. People's houses are within a couple of metres of the noisy locomo-tives; the fourth side which completes this claustral enclosure is coarse flowering grass of the swamp.

These are a captive people. Yet their cramped and resented pres-ence is vital to the city economy. Their labour makes life easier for others who live and work in Bangkok. Some are food vendors, women who get up at 2.00 a.m. to go to the wholesale market where they buy fresh chickens, eggs, pork, fruit. Some women have a food cart: a metal box on two wheels, perhaps with a small grill for cooking skew-ered pieces of pork or chicken. An umbrella on a bamboo stick protects the food from rain or sun. Some have a glass display case for slices of pineapple or red watermelon; a plastic container of beansprouts or green vegetables; a cylinder of chillies chopped in fish sauce, the cheap spice that gives savour to the food of the poor. Some carry food in the traditional *hai-hap*, two baskets on a bamboo pole carried across the shoulders.

The houses of Saw Pattaya have been constructed piecemeal over a long period. Some have a double storey, the upper room reached by a ladder; others are a single room with a verandah of decaying wood in front, where people sit and work. Walls and roof are metal, much of it rusting and frayed by the rain of many seasons. The windows are without glass. It is an irony that one of the most prosperous sectors in the Bangkok economy is construction; many of those who work on the immense skyscrapers and condominiums live in places like Saw Pattaya; the least well-housed contribute to the speculative hotels and malls and commercial buildings that have eclipsed the temples, mar-kets and little *sois* of the old city.

Wanidah, a woman in her mid-thirties, sits behind the counter of her small open-fronted shop. The word *shop* is too grand to describe the booth with its modest merchandise on the wooden counter and thinly stacked shelves behind: packets of cigarettes, a few loaves, bis-cuits, soap, cooking oil, soy sauce, packets of noodles. Wanidah's family lived in the west of Thailand, where they had a garden for fruit and vegetables. They sold the land to a relative and came to the city. People who used to grow food for themselves now sell food to others, not rice, fruit and vegetables but industrialized and packaged food. Wanidah bought this shop and house for 2,000 baht ($US80), an illegal transaction, because it had been constructed by the original occupant on railway land.

Wanidah has three children. Her husband is a construction worker but is not permanently employed. At present he is working on the other side of the city, where he lives in temporary barracks on the site. He is earning 200 baht a day.

To stock the shop Wanidah must borrow from a moneylender. The interest is 20 per cent a day. If she borrows 1,500 baht to buy cigarettes, oil and rice she must pay back 300 baht a day, so in order to make any profit at all she must be sure of earning more than 300 baht. Rice is sold at 12 baht a kilo.

Electricity is provided illegally, for which Wanidah pays 700 baht a month. Water formerly had to be fetched from outside, but since the community has organized – originally to resist eviction – they also collect money for water which is paid directly to the municipal supplier; for this Wanidah pays 200 baht a month.

There is no garbage collection. The waste accumulates in the muddy sump below the buildings' rickety platforms: bags, cans, junk, metal, and especially plastic, that indestructible symbol of industrial life.

I asked Wanidah what were her hopes for her three children. She would like the two boys to join the army or the police. The greatest security the poor can imagine is to become part of the agencies of the state that oppress them. She smiles; she knows this is only a dream – she will never have the money to pay for their education beyond the statutory minimum sixth grade, that is, beyond eleven.

The economic activity of the people is highly visible and public. Outside one house strings of sausages are looped on a plywood fence. These are dried, cooked and sold from a cart. On the sagging wooden fence in front of their house, two elderly sisters are preparing the skewered chicken they will sell in the neighbourhood at midday. They came here many years ago from Minburi – then a country area well out of the city, but by a cruel irony now one of the relocation areas for the urban poor. Puen, now sixty-two, came to work as a field labourer, and then as a construction worker, because her family had no land. She worked on a building site all the time she was pregnant with her first child, and then she carried him on her back while she worked. Her husband, also a building worker, died twelve years ago. He had cancer; and when he became too sick to remain on the site, he worked on the railway. Even when he was so sick he could no longer eat, he continued to work; and that is where he died.

Puen's son lives in the neighbouring house with his wife and children, but one son and a daughter remain with Puen; neither has work. 'This used to be a rice field when I came here,' says Puen, indicating the swamp. 'My first job was working on the rice farm. Next to it was forest land. The water was clean and we used it for cooking and washing. The children could bathe in it.' Now, although the children still play in it, the water is dirty and dangerous.

Puen buys chickens from the market. She cooks them on a small barbecue grill here and sells them locally. She makes about 50 baht profit each day ($US2). There is never enough money and she is constantly in debt. Her daughter, separated from her husband, has returned home with her three children. Puen borrows money, and pays back at the rate of 20 per cent per day: 100 baht on a 500-baht loan.

Puen gets up at three in the morning to go to market: at four, the roads are reasonably free of traffic. By early afternoon, her day is over; she is exhausted by labour concentrated in the early morning hours. She sleeps by seven or eight in the evening.

Puen says if eviction comes, she does not know how they will survive. Even if the Housing Authority offers a relocation site they will be unable to pay back the 1,500 baht a month for the piece of land they will be offered. In any case there is no livelihood in the relocation sites. Puen says the life of her parents was better than hers. Although they worked as labourers on other people's land, they always had enough to eat and made their own clothes. Life for them was simple; the city only makes the simple things of life more complicated and, therefore, more expensive. Luckily, her son is a security guard – the universal low-paid employment for young men, who patrol the marble commercial buildings and shopping malls in their peaked caps and braided jackets.

Puen and her sister Tongbai wear bright floral dresses; their hair is still dark, but their faces are sunken, eyes haunted by years of want and anxiety. Over the hut the flies swarm in a dark cloud of music. Ants move across the floor and up the wooden pillars in purposeful columns. Outside, ducks and geese peck at the marshy earth. Some older men sit in a group nearby examining the condition of a bronze and black fighting cock with powerful beak and yellow, scaly claws. Gaming is one of the few ways of making some extra money.

The railway authority, on whose land Puen's property stands, has said it will not pay compensation. An NGO, the Urban Development Foundation, which has been helping people to organize, advises the people to stay together and to refuse to move until compensation has been collectively negotiated. Forced displacements have been frequent in Bangkok: the army evicted the slum of Duang Pitak in 1991 in order to build an approach road to the Queen Sirikit Conference Centre, which was to accommodate a World Bank meeting.

Saw Pattaya lies in the path of the new road-and-rail rapid transit system under construction by the Hopewell company. Construction is moving close to Saw Pattaya, its progress marked in mounds of demolished buildings and turned earth. An idealized drawing of the future structure shows skyscrapers, glass and concrete buildings, cars and pedestrians using the station; but no suggestion that slums exist, or ever existed.

The people of Saw Pattaya can expect to follow the path beaten by many slum communities from central Bangkok, which have been relocated beyond Minburi, on the northeastern periphery. The authorities in Thailand, though inflexible about removing the poor, have nevertheless on the whole made efforts to resettle them, which has not always been true of their counterparts in Manila, Bombay or Jakarta.

At Minburi those relocated have been offered small pieces of land, 19 square wah – about 38 square metres – where they can build their own houses. They repay 1,200 baht a month ($US50) over ten years. Those who have managed to find work in the new area can do this readily (construction workers, for example, earn 150 baht, $US6, a day) but others must sell their plot, illegally, to those better off than themselves and return to squat in some other niche in the city, in another slum, under the bridges, along the canalside.

The area was until recently rich agricultural land, but in the course of Bangkok's dramatic increase in population in recent decades thousands of hectares of productive land have been colonized. On this site there is also middle-class housing built by the National Housing Authority; this costs 7,000 baht a month in repayments (almost $US300). New speculative building is being squeezed into the last remnants of old orchards and rice fields.

Some of the new structures speak of considerable prosperity, boasting terraces with blue-glazed balustrades, mosaic flooring, ornamental metal grilles. Other structures, shacks of wood and hardboard with metal roofs, suggest continuing poverty. Unlike the old slums, there is here a conspicuous hierarchy of status in the buildings. Some people use their house for new economic activities, as little shops selling drinks, cigarettes, canned fish, oil and bread. Others sell food from glass and metal handcarts. Some have borrowed money to build grand houses and are in debt, unable to repay.

'Resettlement' does not tell the whole story. On the limit of the National Housing Authority land there is a boundary wall; behind it is another long-established slum, on ground prone to flooding from the adjacent canal. Here the people must wade through muddy water to reach their houses, constructed of industrial waste, their tin and wood softened by rain. Garbage and offal float in the foul water that laps at the threshold of their homes, and in heavy rain spills over into their living places.

Some people have managed to create work in the new community; there are some jobs in industrial units close by. But income generation in the new locality is always the principal issue: travel costs for those who journey back to their old job become prohibitive, undermine livelihood. Environmentally people agree it is better, cleaner and safer, but economically it is often worse. They resent being removed from the source of their work – their very reason for coming to the city in the first place.

Piriya and her family were evicted by the construction of the expressway. They received compensation of 20,000 baht ($US800), which they spent mainly on building material and the stock for their new shop. The range of goods is wider than that in the slums, and includes more industrially made foods: sweets, instant noodles, biscuits, ice cream, canned goods, Coke and Seven-Up. Piriya's family originally had a fruit garden in the south of Thailand. She came to the city when she was twenty. She is happy for her children to grow up here, not in the city, where she says the young people sniff solvent and thinner, and move in bad company.

The biggest factory here is a company making car seats. This employs women at 2,000 baht a month. Others work in the noodle factory or as outworkers sewing, making up bows, shoulder pads, ornamental flowers for dresses, sewing sequins on blouses, embroidering lapels. They earn enough to live from day to day, but it is impossible to save. Piriya says of the small piece of land on which she has built her shop that it is the first she has ever owned. Next door is a mushroom house run by a co-operative set up by the Urban Development Foundation to augment income. Thirteen people have invested in it; the spores are in muslin cylinders on bamboo racks, which sprout spindly yellowish mushrooms overnight. These are picked daily and sold in the market for 22 baht a kilo. The mushroom house is wood and bamboo, very humid, with a roof of *djakh*, woven plantain leaves. It provides a little extra money for the co-operative, but is not a main livelihood.

Vimon sells fish at Bangkapi market. She buys the fish from middlemen who come to Bangkok from the sea. She can make 300 baht a day, but to do so she must get up at 2.30 a.m. Her day's work is finished by 10 or 11 in the morning. Vimon has six children and was displaced from her previous home by construction work. Here her family has been able to build and maintain a better house.

Phyao stays at home to look after her children. Her husband works as a labourer for the electricity company, earning 300 baht a day. The work of creating an urban infrastructure – electricity, water, roads, buildings, transport – ensures that a proportion of people will work locally. Phyao lived in a railway slum. Here life is better.

In their small neat house Chuan, her daughter and son are working. The tiled floor is piled high with silver sachets of soup base, chilli hot'n'spicy flavouring and oil. These must be put into a small plastic bag and sealed; ultimately they will be inserted for flavouring into packets of instant noodles. The three sit cross-legged and invite us to join them. The work is not hard, but infinitely tedious. They are paid 1 baht per kilo. The three of them earn about 60 baht a day in total: 20 kilos each. No one else in the family has work. Earlier they were living in Din Daeng, but were removed because their home was in the path of the expressway. Chuan comes from Pichit province in the north. She left for Bangkok because there was no income at home: her family had borrowed money from a neighbour to grow sugar cane, and paying back the loan required all their earnings. They sold the land and came to Bangkok. In Din Daeng there were many garment factories and plenty of work. In compensation for their home, they received 17,000 baht (about $US700), with which they were to have bought the land for their home from the National Housing Authority. So far they have paid only one instalment on the land. Their income allows them to eat but little else. The authority has threatened to take them to court, but Chuan says that whatever that may achieve, it will not produce money if they have none.

Warut, who comes from Ubon, is a slight young man of twenty-three. He is living with his sister and her family in a house at the end of a long track, an improvised street, that eats into the ragged, wasting landscape of former rice fields. The style of the house has some features of the village dwelling: a large single living area, cement and wood-tiled floor, bare cement walls, grilles with mosquito netting. There is little furniture, only a large plywood cupboard faced with green plastic marble, a tarnished mirror, and some wooden stands with a TV, a music player and some boxes of cassettes. On the floor, on the thin plastic covering, is a box of children's toys: a sword, a truck, an aeroplane, a doll, all in moulded plastic. There is a glass-fronted cupboard with some Chinese soup bowls, porcelain spoons and some cups: a dingy red plastic container for drinking water; a fan on a stand with plastic blades protected by a metal web. The kitchen is half outside: the floor is bare concrete, and there is a cooking stove with gas cylinder, two cooking rings. Food is kept in plastic containers on the wall. The rain barrel outside is overflowing in the rain, full of fallen leaves and drowned insects. There is a plastic washing-up bowl full of plastic dishes, a plastic rack for drying plates. Most containers are of latticework plastic, like launderette baskets. So much plastic.

Warut's sister Noi sits with a box of white satin material cut into crescent shapes. She sews thread through each one until the fabric bunches up to form a kind of flower; these will decorate the scalloped fringes at the base of wedding gowns. She is paid 15 baht a hundred. Some days she will do 500, others only 100, depending on the demands on her time. Her two children are eight and six.

Noi's husband repairs cars. In the front yard the shells of five or six are spread out on the concrete, with door frames, fenders, panels, engine parts, pools of rainbow-coloured oil; a harvest of metal, symbols of the city. A Toyota Corolla newly painted and refurbished has pride of place in front of the house. Noi's husband employs two ten-year-olds who are working away at the chassis with spanners and paint brushes. These boys earn 300 baht a month. At the back of the house a cockerel and some hens are half-hidden in the long grass, ducks seek shade beneath the acacia trees. It is a curious scene: in front of the house the oil, grease and metal of motor vehicles, at the back a wild semi-rural expanse of neglected countryside. Warut and Noi come from a family of rice farmers.

Sometimes when people come to the city they cannot bear to contemplate what they have left behind and seem determined to transform their living place into a totally urban environment, turning their backs on the peasant economy which they have come to resent for its incapacity to sustain them.

Here in Minburi, women on bicycles are carrying their home piecework back to the factory. Noi says she would rather be in Ubon because people are more kind and helpful there. They do not turn their back upon the misfortunes of their neighbours. Even though here there are many migrants from her home area, it is not the same. The city changes them.

In fact, it is a strange parody of village life, a life which is transplanted, like the people, into the city. The air here is clean; only dust from the unmade road blows in the wind, and the mosquitoes are a constant problem. Noi goes back home whenever she can, but her brother has only revulsion for the family farm. Warut is vain. In his corner of the room, he has a cupboard with all his new clothes, his changes of trousers and shirts, which he contemplates with great satisfaction, the tangible emblems of city success. Warut works for a transport company whose buses are hired by a private school; his work is as bus monitor, to collect the children from their homes in the early morning and see that they reach home safely at night. He must get up at 4.30 in the morning, go to the bus garage at 6.00. It takes three hours to deliver all the children to school. He returns at 3.30 in the afternoon and gets home at 6.30, earning 1,800 baht a month. He takes his work very seriously. Why, I asked him, is this better than growing rice? He looked at me incredulously. This wins him prestige and money for new clothes; he can even send a little money home. 'It must be better,' he says. 'We are paid for it.'

The area still has an improvised appearance, as though impermanent, the appearance of a frontier, conquered from the declining agricultural base. Building merchants are doing good business, people selling planks, wire, poles, corrugated metal, pipes, nails, tiles. Some trees and shrubs from the old countryside remain; bright yellow acacias have been planted in streets that remain uneven and potholed. There are concrete street lights and power-line poles, structures at varying stages of completion. Most people build their own houses: domestic construction at this level has not yet passed over to the market and professional builders. There is a vibrancy and energy in the work, the sounds of the tapping and hammering of wood and metal, people carry bundles of bamboo, loads of breezeblocks and tiles. A few houses are already complete, with glazed tiles, yellow sunflowers in a strip of earth, palms in pots; others have been invaded by the rank grass and wild maroon daisies that flourish in the rain.

Some seven thousand families will soon have been resettled here. The better life. It is not so different from the exurban estates in the West to which the poor have been banished. Easterhouse, Thamesmead, Creteil, Torre della Bella Monaca, even Nuova Iguacu in Rio, and Dindoshi in Bombay. Many of the problems are the same: the expense of travel into the city, the broken sense of community, the competitiveness in the new setting, the lack of work for the young people. It is sad that a different landscape or culture masks the sameness of the struggles and common experience of the urban poor all over the world. As the global economy becomes more integrated, it is impossible not to wonder whether we, in the West, shall see the workers of Bangkok or Manila as our rivals, taking away our jobs, or whether we shall understand the sameness of our relationship and theirs with the centres of wealth and power in the world; shall we be divided by a serviceable racism and exploited ethnocentricity, or shall we come to see a common fate in the same woundings, the identical injuries to our humanity?

11

Cities of the Rich

Increasingly the well-to-do in the cities are living in guarded enclaves, in an attempt to avoid the consequences of increasing violence, crime, overcrowding, environmental degradation.

Sometimes these enclaves take the form of high-rise apartments in compounds; or they may be villas in exclusive residential areas, the streets of which are protected by security personnel behind bullet-proof glass, streets on the other side of a black-and-yellow barrier, demarcating the frontier of wealth. All who enter this gilded captivity must give evidence of their identity and of those they wish to visit; a note is taken of their car number, or sometimes identification is required by the ill-paid guards who police the increasingly conspicuous boundary between rich and poor.

Sometimes the houses are individually fortified buildings, as in parts of Rio de Janeiro: ironwork at the windows, spikes outside, like the cages of zoo creatures, rolls of razor wire – one of the recurring images from these cities is coils of barbed wire – the paraphernalia of war zones, sometimes rusty, in parallel lines, sometimes in gleaming new coils, sometimes in a tangle like metallic hair, to keep out unauthorized persons; or glass-topped walls, fragments of broken bottles set into concrete so that the sun glints on a jagged jewellery of green, brown and crystal on top of a rampart; sometimes fish-hook spikes deter intruders; but more often it is grilles, some of which have been wrought into ornamental designs to mitigate the harshness of their function. The afternoon sun projects the parallel bars of cages onto the soft pastel shades of dainty baroque villas.

I stayed alone and briefly in an apartment in New Delhi in one of the most exclusive districts in the city. It was December. The overarching jamun trees created a curious architecture, hushed as the nave of a church, and the mists drifted through the muted streets; there was an eerie, funereal silence, with no sign of the city at all. The apartment looked out onto Lodi Gardens, the ruined Shish Gumbad, onto the red sandstone with its azure ceramic frieze, and a blaze of

English summer flowers – scarlet dahlias and pink asters – in the tepid winter sunshine. The only sound in the still morning was of the sweeper's brush as she scooped up the fallen petals of the bougainvillaea. Servants moved with muffled footsteps on cold marble. At the gate, shrouded in a thick blanket, the *chowkidar* (watchman) sat with his gun in a sentry box; so that it was like living in a military installation. The cook was a man who had served the Raj and Western embassies, a beautiful old hill man from Nainital who could bake cakes and make English custard, a man whose life of involuntary exile from his beloved Kumaon had been dedicated to consoling other kinds of involuntary exiles.

I found it a frightening experience: doors that closed within other closed doors, with bolts driven deep into the floor, failed to provide the kind of security such places are supposed to furnish. I have never slept so badly. Every sound of creaking floor, of wood contracting in the cold night air, of mouse or night creature stirring in the garden, and I was wide awake, peering through windows that had been strengthened against mosquitoes and barred to intruders.

The kind of fear psychosis that is commonplace in Western cities has taken hold also of the rich in the *beaux quartiers* of the Third World city. Regularly at social gatherings the conversation turns to the growing crime wave, even though in comparison with the West these cities are still extremely safe places. Robberies, burglaries, attacks upon people do occur, but they are still relatively rare. But the sense of being beleaguered, threatened, serves other, ideological functions. The newspapers manage to find stories of an old woman murdered by her servant, of chain-snatching gangs in the buses, of robberies in daylight, of hijacked cars, of kidnappings of children at the gates of their exclusive school, children whose ear or finger are sent through the post to support a ransom demand. Hence, in the afternoon, limousines with liveried drivers stand in line outside the leafy educational retreats of the rich so that the children may be escorted home safely to villas and flats where the servants will look after them until their busy parents return. As they grow older they will be sent abroad to study, into the anonymity of North America or Europe. And this is the beginning of a generation whose lives are increasingly articulated not to India, or Bangladesh or Thailand, but more and more to an international circuit of transnational companies and diplomacy, officialdom and politics, media stars and celebrities. They cease to be citizens of their country and become nomads belonging to, and owing allegiance to, a supraterrestrial topography of money; they become patriots of wealth, nationalists of an elusive and golden nowhere. Their shopping trips are transnational, forming a skein of flights across the world in search of identical artefacts distinguished only by the location of purchase, as though jewellery acquired in London or Rome bore some significant additional lustre, as though a frock from Paris or New York set apart its wearer from those who found the same apparel in Hong Kong or Manila. These are people possessed of strange emulous desires to differentiate themselves from their fellow countrypeople, even indeed from their colour. Their reference groups are not within their own country, their eyes are on distant, invisible horizons; their troubled relationships are the concern of the journalists of global media conglomerates; the arrangements of their divorce settlements, their golden children discovered suffering from an overdose of drugs, or trapped in an upturned foreign sports car travelling at 200 kilometres an hour, furnish sad lessons to the poor on the folly of yearning to be like them.

Beneath these is a growing segment of the middle class: those midway in corporate hierarchies, independent business people, shopkeepers, owners of small enterprises, lawyers, doctors, professionals, people who live in the growing middle-class though less exclusive enclaves, not so glamorous as the very rich, but far more numerous. They occupy condominiums, with uniformed security guards patrolling lifts, staircases and car parks; others live in estates of white, red-tiled villas in the suburbs, with balustraded patios and heavy wooden furniture, ceramic floors and chandeliers. These are the people for whose purchasing power the malls and gallerias compete. Such amenities as they enjoy are privately provided, from health insurance to transport, from education to restaurant meals.

I lived for a time in one such development in Delhi; being India, it was less sophisticated than Thailand.

A long vista of apartment blocks in compounds, a charmless landscape without infrastructure. The thoroughfares are rugged and unmade, with drifts of fine dust on the margins, which every passing vehicle stirs into an ochre fog. There are few traces of any growing things in the concrete wastes. The intermittent flicker of street-lamps, faint drooping flowers that scarcely penetrate the winter mist, throw an eerie light on the series of compounds, where security guards from Bihar maintain their twelve-hour vigils.

Spacious apartments with symmetrical rooms which cry out for the douceurs of Western consumerism; curtains and blinds to shield you from the neighbours' eyes and Delhi sun and dust; comfortable chairs and cushions, so that you can rest from your heroic bus journey from the office, with the help of a glass of imported liquor, and the latest reach-me-down entertainment from Star TV. In this place – as in thousands of similar developments in the cities of India – the traditional sensibility is being broken and re-assembled in the image of the market economy; the creation of a tawdry privilege that sets the new middle class apart from the poverty of the mass of the people.

Although there is a virtually total lack of public amenities, private enterprise has moved swiftly into the vacuum to service the needs of this new population. There may be frequent power-cuts, which fill the windows with flickering candles like some universally observed religious rite, public transport may be deficient, but there are at least five beauty parlours to choose from, and many stores which serve as outlets for Western cosmetics – Imperial Leather, Lux, shampoos, gels and after-shaves, talcum powder, even though the contents of some of these may have been adapted to match the more modest purchasing power of India; that is, their inferior quality creates a kind of consumerist apartheid. There are many conduits for the dumping of transnational pharmaceuticals, chemists and drug-stores where you can buy substances to stimulate or pacify, to calm or to awaken, to put to sleep or otherwise deaden the unbearable pain of being; many of them, moreover, banned in the West.

(Notes from Another India)

The middle class in Asia has been subjected to a considerable erasure of cultural memory, fashioned as it has been in the image of the West. And for good reason. The industrialization of Britain called forth a turbulent and unruly working class, and the salvation of this transformation was the emergence of, and concessions made to, a middle class demanding recognition of its role in industrial society, and which served as a bulwark against social breakdown. It is to a similarly exalted function that the privileged are called in the Third World now; and the cities are their appropriate place.

I spent a few evenings with some of the young men of this secondarily privileged caste in Bombay, in the 'permit rooms' of Colaba, that is the licensed drinking places: austere benches at marbled plastic-topped tables encumbered with Kingfisher beer bottles and overflowing ashtrays. You can tell social class in India by the size of the people: these are hefty and well-fed, like the heroes of Hindi movies; in poor societies to be fat, or at least plump, is a signal of status. They have just finished their BA in commerce, marketing, travel, business administration. Some expect to work in their father's business, others are desperate to find work abroad, where fabulous incomes will assure them of fast cars, sex and booze. These young men have been thoroughly acculturated to foreign values, and their presence in India is an irritant to the kind of life they consider their due. Their tastes are for

Western music, Madonna, Paul Simon, Sting; their Maruti cars and Kawasaki bikes gleam in the road outside. After they have pooled their meagre experience of sex they tell jokes, jokes that speak more eloquently of their own undermined identity than of their sense of humour, jokes that are racist, sexist, anti-Muslim. 'Why do Pakistanis keep shit in their wallets?' 'For identification.' (I had heard the same 'joke' in Britain.) 'How do you get an Iranian girl pregnant?' 'You come on her shoes and let the flies do the rest.' 'What do you have when two blacks are in a shoebox?' 'A pair of loafers.' 'Why do blacks always have sex on their minds?' 'Because they have pubic hair on their heads.' Their cultural debt to a West they have not yet visited is plain.

Empty bottles fall from the edge of the table. Waiters impassively clear up the broken glass: thin patient young men from Tamil Nadu or Kerala, whose work involves holding no opinion on these colonized Indians but simply taking their money with a smile.

The cultural contamination by the West affects not only those who enjoy a lifestyle of conspicuous consumption; there is a whole class of urban people who imitate them, those who will do anything to get out of India (or Bangladesh or Thailand), who attach themselves to foreigners, seeking sponsorship, a visa, a job, a way out. The iconography of the West has bitten deeply into the psyche of the South; one of the reasons why the former imperial powers are not resented for their colonial role is that Westerners are seen as bearers of nonspecific hopes of freedoms that most people in the cities of the South can only dream of.

Perhaps this is why there is always a cluster of people outside the five-star hotels, some begging, others offering to service the tourists, others simply hoping that the effect of wealth may rub off on them by sheer proximity. These hotels have become the object of a kind of cult, and with good reason. They are alien implants in the culture, microcosms of that human-made creation, the technosphere, in which the people of the West have been installed and which insulates them from the effects of their way of life on the biosphere; these hotels are illusions of universal escape, a promise that humanity can evade not merely the consequences of its actions, but also its destiny. The hotel is an enclosed glass bubble which separates its occupants from the environment. In such hothouses, fantasy luxuriates. You can see this in the dreamlike way in which people behave in the hotels, gliding across carpets and marble floors, sunglasses in hand, flicking their hair, offering theatrical greetings, chinking the ice in long-stemmed glasses. Beyond the tinted windows the beggars exhibit their mutilations in vain; the rag pickers pass by with their sacks, the dust swirls in the hot air. In these air-conditioned refuges, nothing disturbs the purchased distance, the immense internal spaces that divide the people from a world outside that they scarcely acknowledge. A man in evening dress plays 'On the Street Where You Live' on a grand piano; a man dressed like an imperial sepoy wheels a trolley full of luggage. There are expansive bowls of yellow chrysanthemums, lamps on fluted plinths, curtains in shimmering swags at the dusky windows. On sofas in the foyer people sprawl, a novel on the seat beside them; a woman surreptitiously adjusts her metallized hair; a man in bermuda shorts admires himself in a smoked mirror. Inside the hotel there is a row of shops where people stroll looking at Kashmir carpets, ivory, fabrics, jewels, ebony carvings, sandalwood combs, parasols, silver filigree earrings, glass bangles, copies of Mughal miniatures on silk, tribal carvings.

In this, all these cities are the same. Outside the Sonargaon, the most expensive hotel in Dhaka, cream-coloured United Nations vehicles are parked; even those who have come to the aid of these sorry countries cannot be expected to forgo the luxury that has become normal for them.

Jakarta is particularly significant in this struggle since it is the site of a profound ideological battle: Western economic fundamentalism meets Islam. On my first afternoon in Jakarta I strayed into the Sogo complex, which is part of the Hyatt Regency Hotel. There I met a number of girl and boy prostitutes in the shopping mall, draped, delicate and graceful as the real orchids around the marble sides of the central atrium. They speak an English of convenience and function. They are intelligent. They have studied, computer studies, business studies, English, Japanese. They gravitate to the malls as a kind of camouflage, imitating the images and imaginings of a stylized window-dressed perfection. They merge into the illuminated panels of Estee Lauder, Nina Ricci, Daniel Hechter, Max Factor, Cerruti goods, as though they had themselves stepped out of the display; and their clients, those newly formed representatives of the buy-in culture, know how to buy in sexual satisfactions in the same way that they would buy a new pair of shoes, an extravagant meal, a bottle of perfume; in other words, they have become thoroughly Westernized.

At a slightly lower level of aspiration stands McDonald's. On Sunday night this is a vibrant, living symbol of the West that draws lower-middle-class families with their children in their hundreds: sitting in the fixed plastic seats, eating fixed menus with fixed ideas. People actually drive to the McDonald's on Thamrin for an evening out; there infants play on the slides supervised by trained personnel, to the incongruous electronic renderings of 'A Bicycle Built for Two'. Children clamour at the counter for gift bags of balloons, candies and ice cream that are part of this week's special promotion. If Japanese technology has dislodged Western dominance, on the cultural terrain the United States retains its supremacy: basic food patterns are being disrupted by the outlets of Kentucky Fried Chicken, Wendy's Burgers, Pizza Hut, Tennessee Pancake Houses, their products all more expensive than traditional *nasi goreng, ayam* and the snacks sold by vendors at the roadside. This is, as it were, the first layer of ambition, the clearing of the cultural terrain, where people are prepared for deeper cultural onslaughts upon tradition, practice and custom. In Bangkok this is even more clear, especially among the Chinese young: every afternoon in McDonald's they sit in hyperactive excitement, spilling Coke onto their exercise books already stained with grease from their burgers, victims of a strange new phenomenon, a malnutrition of excess, fed by transnational companies and not by their parents, for the sake not of nourishment, but of profit. They have taken the first faltering steps of initiation into the mysterious cultural adulthood of being Western.

12

Children in the City

Bangkok

I am visiting a refuge for abused children in Bangkok, run by the Centre for the Protection of the Rights of Children. The building is in a secluded residential area, the boundaries of which are guarded by security personnel; inside these boundaries are bungalows, detached houses with high metal gates and concrete walls.

The refuge is built around a spacious central space which spills over into a tiled verandah. The floor is covered with plastic cloth. It is part office, part living place: metal cabinets, desks for staff, a TV and video, cupboards of toys, footballs, clothes, books and magazines. Under the verandah there are a desk and whiteboard. The compound is shaded by mango trees and plantains. The children sleep in the upper part of the building.

On a mattress on the ground floor lies a girl of about eleven. She was injured yesterday by a car. Her abdomen is padded and bandaged, her leg is in plaster from top to bottom. She had been sexually abused by her neighbour and afterwards, in her panic and fear, she ran out into the path of an oncoming car. Her mother works, washing clothes in other people's apartments, and cannot supervise her. There was no hospital bed for the child last night, so she slept here on the floor, nursed and comforted by staff. Her face is bruised and tear-stained as she drifts in and out of consciousness. They are waiting for the staff car to take her to hospital. The driver lifts her tenderly and places her on the back seat; one of the workers gets in beside her and cradles her head in her lap.

There are twenty children here, mostly victims of abuse. Three boys are playing together with toy cars, two aged thirteen, one eleven. All have been sexually abused by a lawyer. This man took five boys into his home, ostensibly to rescue them from the streets, but in fact he has been systematically abusing them all sexually. This is not an unusual occurrence, says Kun Suphosit, director of the centre. Under the guise of philanthropy respectable rescuers of children at risk can get away with anything: professional people are assumed to be making religious merit by performing good deeds; it is an ideal camouflage for those with other intentions. This abuse is especially difficult to detect. The children rarely tell, because their abuser often provides them with a comfortable and otherwise secure existence. Suphosit says everybody knows about foreign paedophiles because they are more visible. Thai paedophiles are not so obvious, and they do not go to the marketplace of prostitution.

Two girls are also here, both sexually abused, one by her stepfather, the other by a monk. Once again society offers convenient screens for those whose motives appear beyond reproach. Only now is the problem within Thai society beginning to appear. Suphosit is running the only institution through which legal proceedings can be taken against those who harm children. Sometimes street children are regarded as fair game and are physically, even sexually, abused by police. The children of prostitutes are also regarded as easy prey and are used by neighbours and other members of the family. Many run away as soon as they become adolescent; some go directly to agents who have links with brothels, and so the cycle of employment in the sex industry is established in yet another generation.

Kun Suphosit began work in 1981, originally to focus on child labour. At that time few government or nongovernmental organizations were working on the issue. Suphosit's work grew in response to need, so that by 1984 child abuse and neglect were included, and later so was prostitution.

'No one knew anything about the labour of children in brothels. It was a twilight zone, concealed. Many were held by force. Now it has changed: they use money, instead of slavery, to control the children.'

Suphosit sees social and economic development at the root of the growing misuse of children. 'Industrialization for many families means migration as labour to the city. Wages are too low to support the whole family, and they separate. Men come first out of the rural area; women are the second wave.

'Men who are alone have needs. They have money, and that means prostitution. They have left their family without supervision for the children. They use drink and sex because they are lonely. Women are left without income. Children come to seem a burden to the family, and they must start work as soon as they can.

'Migration is not only rural–urban, province-to-province, but also from other countries, Burma, Laos, Cambodia, men only. Demand creates its own supply. It is a consequence of national economic priorities, the growth of consumerism which causes people to go far beyond their basic needs. The stimulus to consume creates a desire for more money. Sometimes parents put their children to work in factories, and even brothels. Many businesses are involved in prostitution as a sideline: massage parlours, beer bars, barber shops.

'At the same time tourism was promoted in the eighties, and sex became an implicit, even if unofficial, part of the deal. Thailand became known as a sex tourism zone; more children, boy prostitutes, appeared to service paedophiles. There are two factors. One is the unjust distribution of wealth, and the other is our traditional culture, whereby children are seen as part of the property of their parents. It is only seventy years since our new legal system abolished the sale of human beings. Until then people had been sold, for sex or work. If someone borrowed from a moneylender and couldn't pay back, he would have to send his daughter to become the minor wife of the moneylender. There was no campaign against this. A law was enacted to prohibit the sale of human beings, but nothing was done to change the practice.

'Even today the Ministry of Labour and Social Welfare, the main ministry fighting prostitution, gets one per cent of the state budget. There is little concept of social welfare. The family is social security, one hundred per cent. People will do anything for the sake of their family. Prostitution is a means of survival, just another form of labour.

'In the National Plan, children are seen as an economic resource, not in terms of human beings. And our educational system is designed to serve the economy.

'In the West there is protection of children's rights. Even there the outcome is not wonderful. Family breakdown occurs and children often lack affection; or parents are so busy earning that this undermines benign legislation intended for children's welfare. Child labour may well be diminished by prosperity. Whatever its shortcomings we require a social security system to support the family. The state is concerned now only with public health, hygiene, vaccination and nutrition, but not with well-being, not with social stability, psychological health.

'We depend for some funding on the European Union. In Thailand few people will give for this kind of work. If we speak publicly about child prostitution, people accuse us of tarnishing the image of Thailand. The economic plan may not be touched. Economic growth and development are seen as the answer to everything. National Plan Seven speaks of the failures of social development as if these were the result of insufficient economic development. What they cannot do is link child prostitution and other evils to economic development itself, and while this blindness persists we shall not be able to tackle the roots of the problem. Only economic, not spiritual or moral growth are on the agenda.

'We have gained much experience in thirteen years. In the early days, if I spoke of incest people said I was exaggerating to get charity money. Buddhists, they said, don't do such things. The response to child abuse was denial. Now many groups exist to detect abuse and neglect. Formerly if a battered child was sent to hospital for treatment the child was invariably sent home afterwards. Now it is different: paediatricians and child psychologists will inform the social worker. We are often called in to investigate. We co-operate with other professionals, lawyers, doctors, social workers.'

In Suphosit's office, among the desks, word processors and papers, is Wisit, a luminous, incongruous presence, a boy of fifteen with a dazzling smile. Wisit was abandoned by his mother and placed in a welfare home soon after he was born. At ten he was adopted by a childless family. Then the woman had her own baby and she ceased taking care of Wisit. He reacted angrily, became aggressive and stole money from the foster mother. She sent him back to the home. He was very quarrelsome with the other children, and ran away repeatedly. The home finally decided it could not contain him, so he wandered the streets. He blackmailed the adoptive mother into giving him money, but at the same time stole. He became involved with a group of boy prostitutes. One day he stole a camera from a Frenchman who had picked him up. The Frenchman informed the police. The boy was arrested together with an adult who was controlling the street boys. 'We were asked by the police to help the boy. He still had the Frenchman's camera, and we found it. It contained explicit pictures, child pornography. We got him arrested. The boy was to stay in our shelter. There he stole money. We didn't turn him away but asked him to come and work in the office to compensate for what he took from us. He has been here five or six months. We send him to school to learn art and singing, but our real purpose is to restore his self-esteem. So far, so good; but it is early yet.

'We find that most children are abandoned by their parents in hospitals. There are four main groups; prostitutes, who have to get back to work; women construction workers, because they are always moving from site to site and they change partners frequently; teenagers who become pregnant (many of these were themselves abandoned); and very poor families. These abandon their children in a different way: they leave the baby in front of some office or big house where it can be seen easily. They often have no knowledge of the welfare system, and are mostly ill-educated, with no resources.

'The society has a very unfair distribution of wealth. The top 20 per cent of income goes to just 4 per cent of the people; and as we get richer, inequality increases. The very rich now live in a way that is not even articulated to Thailand but is integrated globally. They go abroad to shop, to Paris, to Harrods in London. Swissair estimates that 60 per cent of its customers to Hong Kong are Thais who go on weekly shopping trips.'

Dhaka

Poverty, a consequence of the uneven distribution of wealth, makes it vital for the poor that their children work. This is no new thing.

> In mid-19th century London, only about half the children between the ages of five and fifteen went to school and the survival of most poor families depended on the income that their children could earn cleaning chimneys, selling fruit, vegetables or other goods on the street, scavenging in refuse left on the street for bones and rags, or in the mud on the river front at low tide, sweeping crossings, running errands, opening doors, working on building sites . . .

Even the list of occupations is the same in the present-day Third World city, modified only by climate and technological change.

Two-thirds of the children in the garment factories of Dhaka were dismissed under the threat of the Harkin Bill, which proposed sanctions against the import into the USA of articles made using child labour. Many children, however, are still working in the factories. To deny them the opportunity to do so would in most cases deprive the whole family, including the children, of the less-than-adequate nourishment they have now. Just how the humanitarians preoccupied with child labour expect them to be provided with the necessities of life if they are disemployed they fail to say. Presumably, the Bangladesh government should look after them. But the Bangladesh government is in the throes of integrating itself into the world economy, embarking on a programme of liberalization and privatization, and one of the principal demands of the IMF and World Bank in relation to this programme is that government expenditure be cut: not on arms – that would be even more inimical to Western interests than state expenditure – but on welfare, health and nutrition.

It is the poor, the garment workers and rag pickers, the rickshaw pullers and small vendors, who have been appointed to resolve the contradictions of a global system, contradictions which have to a considerable extent been 'externalized' from the rich societies of the West. The fiction of national sovereignties only serves to exonerate the West from any responsibility for the humiliation and exploitation of the most vulnerable people – including children – in the poorest places on earth.

In Dhaka I went with two young garment workers – themselves only fifteen and sixteen – to a small hut in the slum where they live which is a factory producing eyelets for shoes. In a small, stifling space, perhaps 4 metres by 6, fourteen people are working. Most of them are children, but all have been primed to overstate their age. The boy who is about ten says he is fourteen, the thirteen-year-old claims to be seventeen and the fourteen-year-old swears he is twenty. They know they must do nothing to jeopardize their small but precious contribution to the family income. They work twelve hours a day at blue metal presses making eyelets out of sheets of thin metal of various colours; the floor of the factory is strewn with the sheets of metal from which the studs have been pressed; the sheets are riddled with little regular holes, like the foil packages of used-up medicines. The used sheets will be recycled. The lighting in the factory is inadequate: a single light bulb flickering with the intermittent current. When the power fails they work by candlelight. Rahim Badsa, owner of the factory, arrives unexpectedly. He is not pleased to see us. He tells us he employs fourteen people, whose combined monthly salary comes to 10,000 taka. He has been operating this unit for two years. He was formerly a factory worker but saved up enough to buy the presses and to rent the hut. He earns 3,000–4,000 taka a month.

Although in Bangladesh five years of education is compulsory, many children do not attain even this modest grounding. ARBAN, the Association for the Realization of Basic Needs, has been running schools for working children in the hope that they will not be trapped all their lives in unskilled, low-paid work which they must do to supplement the family income.

Many children start their working lives as young as eight or ten. Girls go into domestic service, and even where they do not they must perform their share of the family labour: often they carry food at mealtimes to older siblings working in garment factories. The first child I met who did this brought tears of recognition to my eyes. My own mother and aunt regularly took food at midday to the shoe factory where their older brothers worked in Northampton: they ran home from school, collected the food in a basin covered with a cloth, and ran to the factory so that they should reach there while the food was still hot. In Dhaka it is only the container, the metal tiffin can, that sets their experience apart from ours. Everything else is the same: the tender reminder in the joyless workplace of something home-made.

Another child in the ARBAN school takes a tiffin can from ten houses to offices in the commercial area and receives a small monthly income from each worker. Other children are lodging as servants in the houses of the better-off. There, whatever their duties, at least they eat well and are frequently given clothing discarded by children of the family. They may earn between 100 and 300 taka a month. One child who lives and eats with the family she serves earns 80 taka a month. She hands this to her father and receives a little pocket money for her needs. This is another echo of the industrial era in Britain; then, too, the earnings of children were not regarded as their own but were passed over to their parents.

Some boys work as assistants to Tempo drivers, clinging to the door and tailboard collecting the fares for a wage of 8 or 10 taka a day. Shanina is twelve. She sews beads on dresses, *benaroshi* cloth, a mixture of silk and cotton which is used for ornate sarees. She is skilled and earns 100 taka a week. Her father is a taxi driver; her three brothers and two sisters do the same work. Ghuria Begum, aged twelve, looks after her younger brothers and sisters at home. Her father paints the scenes on the back panels of rickshaws, idealized mountains or cities or movie stars. Mohamed Erphan is eleven. He embroiders dresses; he goes to work immediately after school finishes at 10.30 in the morning, working until 9.00 or 10.00 in the evening. He earns 100 taka a week; he was taught the work by an older brother of a classmate. His father works in a textile factory. Arif, twelve, is helper to a technician in an electric fan factory. His father left the family for another woman, and Arif must work eight hours a day for 50 taka a week. His stepmother works in a garment factory. Samil, twelve, is employed in a car workshop as helper to the mechanic: bashing metal, cleaning the engine parts. After school he goes home to eat, then works from noon until ten at night. He earns 250 taka a month. He has four brothers; his father is a supplier of materials to a garment factory. Dilwar Hussein, twelve, does *benaroshi* work earning 350 a month. He learned the work from a private training school where children pay to acquire the skill. Shohel, also twelve, works ten hours a day in a motorcycle workshop; he is not earning yet because he has been learning the work only for three months; his father is dead and his mother works in a chemicals factory. Dulali is ten; her mother is a factory worker and Dulali looks after her brother and four younger sisters.

I received another instructive lesson on child labour in Dhaka. One evening I visited a human rights lawyer who had, for the first time, successfully obtained a stay order on some evictions of slum dwellers by the Dhaka Municipal Authority. I visited him in his spacious pent-house on the fifteenth floor of a new building on Nazrul Islam Avenue, one of the main thoroughfares of the city; it was a beautifully shaped apartment, with a panoramic view over Dhaka. On one side of the new building there is a slum that has been built over a broad waste-water drain; beyond is the palm-shrouded compound of the Dhaka Sheraton Hotel, with its floodlit tennis court and poolside barbecue.

As we talked a boy of about ten served us coffee. I looked at him in surprise. It was 9.30 in the evening. Anticipating my unspoken query, the lawyer said that the child's father is an itinerant construction worker. He is happy to leave his child in this house, where he knows he will be properly looked after. He eats with the family, has his own room, and goes to school. His duties are not onerous. The little boy, sensing that we were talking about him, turned upon me a beautiful smile. He placed the cups on the glass table and noiselessly left the room, the steps of his bare feet inaudible on the marble terrace.

It is not wrong for children to have a social function, said my host. It is not wrong for children to be employed, to feel that they are mak-ing some contribution towards the well-being of their family. What is wrong is exploitative labour, excessive work, the denial of an oppor-tunity for play.

Anyone looking at the children of the West with an unprejudiced eye would swiftly discern that what is wrong with the Western treat-ment of children is that they have been defunctioned, excluded from the work of society. Children in the West are redundant . . . in which they are doubtless serving an apprenticeship for the society into which they will grow. Before the West instructs the Third World on how to raise children it should look at the consequences of its own monopoly of the riches of the world, which not only contributes to the wretchedness of child labour in the South but also manages to produce untold levels of social disorder, violence, crime and unhap-piness in its own children.

The same story comes from all the other cities. The example from Bangkok of children who had become crippled by sitting so many hours in a damaging posture, the sad wraiths repairing cars in Calcutta, the boys working with molten metal in the forges and fur-naces of Wazirpur in Delhi, the child prostitutes in Manila, represent a monstrous abuse of children. But a childhood of gilded function-lessness, in which the principal social instruction children receive is lessons in accelerating consumption, represents no liberation either. It is hard, said my friend, for the West to understand this, because the West has become accustomed to universalizing all its practices and does not see its own failings, and certainly does not appreciate the relationship between the excessive resource use of its own children and the poor emaciated bodies of ours.

City life adds new burdens to the lives of the children of the poor, and these, already familiar, are worth repeating. In many Third World countries a child born today is 15–20 times more likely to die before the age of five than a child born in a prosperous Western nation. Among poor households a child is 40–50 times more likely to die before the age of five than a child born in a prosperous nation. A woman born poor in the Third World is 150 times more likely to die in pregnancy or childbirth than a woman in Europe or North America. Infants and children in the Third World are several hundred times more likely to die from diarrhoea, pneumonia or measles than those in Europe or North America. In 1986, an estimated 14.1 million children under five died; 98 per cent of these were in the Third World.

Most child deaths take place in poor families; for the rich in Third World nations, rates of infant and child mortality are often as low as those in Western nations. For every child who dies, many more live in hunger and ill-health; on average children under five have survived ten attacks of diarrhoea. Around a quarter of the Third World's children are malnourished; malnourishment reduces their energy, stunts their growth, lowers their resistance to disease, and impairs their intellectual attainments. Their nutritional weakness is often exacerbated by parasitic worm infections that afflict more than one-quarter of the world's population. (All statistics are from Sandy Cairncross, Jorge E. Hardoy and David Satterthwaite (eds), *The Poor Die Young: Housing and Health in Third World Cities.*)

13

Night People

Bangkok remains one of the safer and more peaceful of Asian cities. It never completely shuts down at night: those keeping late hours overlap with those going to work before dawn. It is for a Westerner such an unusual experience to be able to stroll without fear through the city at all hours that I walked often at night, sometimes almost till morning.

Very few of the encounters were in any way threatening. Of course there are hustlers and con men, people cruising for sex, love and money; but no encounter was really disagreeable, even though I was often at cross-purposes with people I met. I wandered not only in the tourist areas – the gardens opposite the Royal Palace, Patpong and Suriwong – but also in the poorer areas – Klong Toey, Ekkachai, on Sukhumvit.

It is late evening in Chinatown. The food stalls and improvised eating places that spring up after dark all over Bangkok are busy under a glare of generator-operated neon: tin tables and chairs, plastic bowls of noodles, *tom-yam*, squid, soup, shrimps, pork and chewy green vegetables. I am standing on the edge of the pavement when suddenly a Mercedes car with blacked-out windows comes to a halt in front of me. A woman, Chinese, perhaps in her early forties, presses the window button and says to me, 'Parlez-vous français?' Her voice is urgent, almost desperate, the voice of someone in need. She indicates to me that I should get into the car. Thinking that she wants an interpreter, I do as she says. She drives a few hundred metres and stops. She says, 'Vous voulez faire l'amour?'

No, I tell her, I'm afraid not. I tell her I am gay to indicate that it is not personal. I move to get out, but the door is locked. She looks at me; her face is thickly made up, possessed of a doll-like pallor, with dark crimson lipstick and thick nylon eyelashes. Her face is beginning to sag a little at the chin, and her disappointment creates two sad pouches at the base of the cheeks. She is expensively dressed, a silk dress with gold embroidery, and wears amethyst earrings.

She starts to speak in fluent French. I tell her I am not actually French, but she does not listen. She was, it appears, the wife of a Thai embassy official in Paris. When his posting was finished he stayed on in Paris because he had fallen in love with a woman who worked in the embassy.

She is crying; a dark stain mars the whiteness of her cheeks. She came back to Thailand but is completely without resources. Of course, she says, I have the apartment, the car. He never even came back to Thailand; he just gave me whatever was left here. But there was no money. I have my clothes and some jewellery of course, but apart from that nothing.

She came originally from a poor family, and studied at university in Bangkok, working as a waitress to pay for her education. Her parents were small traders and it had been a struggle for them. 'When I was young,' she said, 'I was very attractive. I was studying international relations, and my professor was drawn to me. We became friends. In fact he was my lover. He was crazy about me. At that time he was still in his thirties. He said he wanted to marry me.

'Later, he joined the diplomatic service. We were in Caracas before the posting to France. It was a wonderful life. I never completed my studies. We had so many parties and receptions, which I adored. I was very charming then. I am not charming now because I am bitter, and bitterness destroys charm.

'He told me his new girlfriend reminded him of me when I was her age. As though it made it more bearable to be rejected in favour of someone who resembled what you used to be. I told him, "I am still who I am. I have not changed." Only physically of course. I guess the same thing will happen to her. She has the arrogance of the young who do not believe they will ever age. For the young the world is static.

'I have no way of earning a living. What can I do? How can I go and stand in Robinson's store selling cosmetics or lingerie for 150 dollars a month?'

It is a monologue; it would be futile to suggest the obvious, that selling the car, the apartment and the jewels might help her to start a more modest life. Her family, her mother who is now old, her sister whose husband is an invalid, depend on her, think she will provide for them. She is the successful one and must remain so.

Her only accomplishment is speaking French; which she employs to lure French visitors to Bangkok into her car for sex. I am apologetic and say I'm sorry I can do nothing for her. I offer her 200 baht (about $US8). She looks at me with her distraught eyes and says, 'Ce n'est pas suffisant.' It isn't enough. I point out that I have not exactly detained her. She says she is confused, and releases the doorlock. She gives me her hand. There is a ring on every finger.

I am sitting on a concrete bench drinking a tepid Pepsi at about 10.30

in the evening. A young man sits beside me: thick-set, with glasses, a green shirt with false Lacoste label, jeans and cheap rubber sandals.

His nickname, he tells me, is Tu. He lives with his sister and her husband. Until two months ago he was living in a temple. He left because he was suffering from a nervous disorder. 'I have paranoia.'

Tu studied English at Ramkamhaeng open university, with philosophy as a subsidiary subject. He says he would like to change his religion, but he has no more belief in Christianity than he does in Buddhism. He ceased studying seven years ago and since then has done nothing. The only treatment he has is a high daily dose of valium. This sometimes helps him control the feeling that other people are trying to harm him. 'I have brought nothing but trouble to my family. It would be better if I were dead. Sometimes I want to hang myself.'

His mother died when he was young. His father drinks. After his mother's death they sold the small shop they owned in Songkhla and came to live in Bangkok. Tu's brother-in-law works for an oil company. He and Tu's sister tolerate him in their home because it is their duty. The father now lives on his own, has nothing but contempt for his sick son.

Tu knows English but cannot speak it well. He knows certain books and films by heart: his favourite book is Daphne du Maurier's *Rebecca*. He can remember whole paragraphs of the text. He can also recite parts of *Lord of the Flies*. He loves English-language films, but relies on the comic-book versions of movies he is never likely to see. He loves *All About Eve* and asked me to tell him the story of the plot.

He said to me, 'I cannot speak to *farangs*, because nobody likes to talk to me. They want lady for sex, or boy, but I am old. I am twenty-eight and I am not pretty.' Through his pebble glasses his eyes are diminished and distant. He is not very clean; his back is rounded. He exudes an air of defeat and self-neglect. Only his smile, warm and wide, transforms the set lines of his melancholy face.

I say to him, 'Tell me three good things about yourself.'

He stares. 'Three good things . . . I cannot.'

'Of course you can. What do you think are your best qualities?'

He thinks for a long time. It is almost as though he has forgotten I am there, and has gone off into some private place where no one can follow him. Then he says 'I hate lies.'

'That's good. Now something else.'

'I cannot.' But he thinks, and then says, 'I do not like to see some people very poor while others are very rich. It hurts me to see Thai people begging on the pavement.' After that, he can think of nothing else. He says, 'You tell me.'

I say, 'You have a nice smile. There. We have found three good things about you. Think of one more each day, and then repeat them to yourself.'

He says, 'I think you have a good heart.' Then abruptly he gets up and walks away without any formal goodbye.

Veeraya sees me sitting on a bench in the little park. The park is full of joggers, elderly Chinese who can scarcely walk, athletic young Thais sprinting round the half-kilometre perimeter, singlets drenched in sweat. There are very few unaccompanied women in the park. That Veeraya should sit down next to me is a bold initiative.

She says, 'May I speak to you in English?' She is slim, in her late twenties, wearing an orange-coloured dress sharply nipped in at the waist, a lemon-coloured belt. For some time, our conversation is like an English-language textbook – And how do you find Thailand, what is the weather like in your country. But there is something more insistent behind these innocuous and tedious exchanges. 'What do you think of Thai women? What do you think of me? Have you come to Bangkok for a sex holiday?'

'No.'

'Then why are you here?' There is a note of bitterness in the suddenly more sharp questioning. I ask her about herself and her family. She is working in Bangkok as a children's nurse in a rich household in Sukhumvit, a secluded suburb. The man is in the gems trade, an exporter of rubies and specialized jewellery design. His wife is just rich, she says, and enjoys wearing jewels. She is too busy dressing up to have time for her children. So she pays me to do it. I have one day free in the week, today. So I come to the park. Maybe I meet a *farang*, maybe I speak English.

She comes from near Ayutthaya, where her parents have a modest farm growing rice, with some fruit trees, pigs, chickens and geese. There are nine children, five boys, four girls. Seven of them are now in Bangkok because the farm cannot support so many people. Two brothers are in government service, one in the Harbour Department, the other in the Ministry of Agriculture.

She says, 'You *farangs* come to Thailand and all you see are the smiles and the sexy women. You do not understand what is Thailand. You take home your pictures of Pattaya or the temples and you think you have seen Thailand.' Her bitterness is in conflict with Thai politeness. 'I had five brothers,' she says. 'Now I have only four. My brother was in the police. He was sent to a place close to the Burmese border where many drugs come into Thailand. He was dedicated to his job. He thought he was being sent there to fight drug trafficking. But he found out that his senior officer was making much money out of the drugs trade. My brother made a big mistake. He talked about this. All his colleagues said he was crazy. When he came home he said to me that he was afraid he might die soon. When he went back to his duty, he said goodbye as though we should not see him again. We did see him, only next time he was in a box. He was shot. They told us the drug smugglers had killed him. That, at least, I believe. Only do not ask me the name of the drug smugglers. That is why you know nothing of Thailand. You see only the picture which they want to show the tourists.' Her voice is shaking with resentment and rage. She says, 'I am sorry. Excuse me.' She gives me her hand formally and walks away.

It is after midnight when I meet Manus. I am on my way back to my room but sit down for a few minutes to enjoy the cooling air on the piece of ground in front of Thammasat University. Tireless hawkers, food and drink sellers, vendors of amulets, curios, semi-precious stones – all continue their work late into the night.

Manus is in his early thirties, a long-faced man with a muscular body, large hands and feet. He is wearing a white T-shirt and blue jeans. He is working in one of the Robinson department stores as head of the cooked meats section. This is a responsible job, since he has to order and check the quality of all the products. He earns 10,000 baht a month (about $US400), a reasonable salary; but not nearly so good, he complains, as when he was working as cook in one of the royal households in Saudi Arabia.

Many Thais were recruited in the 1980s to work in Saudi Arabia, where they were valued for their honesty, diligence and deference. Manus had had no experience of cooking, but was taken by an agency to Riyadh for an intensive two-month course in European cuisine before working in the household of the brother of the King. He signed a three-year contract.

The prince had a taste for chicken Kiev, coq au vin, bouillabaisse; his wives had their own cooks, who prepared only Arab food. About forty people were employed in cooking alone. It was hard work, says Manus, but the pay was in US dollars. Sometimes the household shifted from Riyadh in the hot months and travelled to London, Italy and the USA. The staff went with them. 'They bought anything they liked.'

It was a great irony that the honesty for which the Thais were engaged caused the downfall of Thai workers in Saudi Arabia and resulted in the abrupt termination of thousands of contracts. About 90 kilos of jewellery from the royal household were stolen by a Thai in 1992. 'He was only a cleaner, and he couldn't possibly have done it without the help of many others, both Thais and Saudis. The jewels were sent to Thailand by cargo and then distributed throughout the country.'

The incident severely strained relations between Saudi Arabia and Thailand. The stolen items disappeared, but little by little some of them emerged. The wife of the police commissioner of Bangkok was seen at a function apparently wearing some of the stolen items. They were sent back to Saudi Arabia, but proved to be paste. Much of the jewellery had been dismantled and reset, but certain stones are unique, recognizable anywhere. It is said that some of the jewels have found their way into high places, so high they cannot be named. This means it is almost certain they will never be returned to their owners.

In mid-1994 the police were searching for the man believed to be the principal receiver and distributor of the jewels. The wife and son of this man were found dead in their Mercedes in the middle of the night. The police coroner recorded a verdict of accidental death; when it became clear that they had been killed and the accident had been staged, the coroner had to resign.

The jewels continue to appear, piece by piece. In December 1994 it was reported that the wives of some local officials in the northern province of Phrae had been seen wearing items of the stolen jewellery. The assistant commissioner of the Central Investigation Bureau was said to be 'trying to convince the holders of the jewels to return them to the Saudi jewellery recovery centre'.

Manus is angry that his career in the Gulf was destroyed by the heist. He says, 'The chance will not come again. I could have been a rich man now, I could have gone back to my province and built a new house for my family. Now I must stay in Bangkok and work for a department store; we will never have what I had dreamed of.'

Many people on the streets at night are hustlers, on the make in one way or another, seeking out the naïve, the despairing and the credulous.

It is late. The Royal Palace has been illuminated in celebration of the King's birthday. The trees have blossomed in a dazzling display of electric light bulbs. A repair vehicle, a metal box on a double-jointed arm, carries some workmen repairing electric flowers that have not bloomed. Suddenly there is a minor explosion, a shower of orange sparks, and all the lights go out. The crowd that has gathered disperses; shadows are restored to the bushes and shrubs bordering the road, and the people disappear into the half-light.

Here I meet two gay boys. Many of those looking for customers avoid commercial outlets, preferring less formal opportunities of chance encounters. In their early twenties, the boys sit back to back on a bollard, both wearing striped football shirts and silk shorts. One of them speaks English, the legacy of a year spent with an American. No, they are not money boys, but if someone offers money they do not refuse. With them is a woman a little older than they. She had walked away as I approached. I say, 'Why is she standing over there? Call her back.' They look at each other and giggle. 'You like her?' She is standing in the shadows; at first, I'm not sure whether she is a lady-boy. They laugh again. No, no, she is a real woman. You want to see? They call her, but she remains half hidden under the trees.

She was working in a bar in Patpong but lost her job when she was found to be HIV positive. She comes from Charoengsao, a four-hour bus journey from Bangkok, but cannot go home because her family depends upon the money she was earning in the bar. The bar now has rigorous health checks on its employees, and those who are HIV positive must leave. Once it is known that a woman has been dismissed it is difficult for her to find work elsewhere: the sex industry is actually a relatively small, enclosed world. She now works freelance at the only labour she knows. She rents a room and finds her clients in the parks or on the streets. The boys tell me they are her friends, because they do not have sex with her and they help her sometimes when she has no money. Both the young men have jobs; their night-time semi-employment is for extras.

I must have shown that I was shocked by this story because the English-speaker said, 'She carries condoms in her handbag. What can she do? If she goes home, she must tell her parents. They think she is a receptionist in a hotel. She has to live.'

The young woman comes over and speaks to them angrily in Thai. She knows what they have been saying. Her short black hair forms a crescent on either side of her pale cheeks; her lips are orange and she wears a tangerine-coloured dress, very short, with a black belt at the waist. She is extremely attractive, about twenty-five. She tells them not to talk about her and walks away without looking at me. Her friends say she has to eat. You have to live. This is Bangkok.

They are right. Here livelihood is at war with life. Immediate survival at the expense of tomorrow. The need for money now overrides everything else. It seemed to me one of the most poignant and terrible revelations of the way we are all living; only in these merciless cities it is more extreme: a present without perspective, in which tomorrow will indeed never come: it has been used up in advance.

At eighteen, Surasak has already lived in two cultures. Born the youngest of three to farmers in a village near the river Kwai, he was out in the fields at the age of eight. By then he knew how to sow, transplant and harvest rice; he knew how to prepare the rice fields in the traditional way, burning twigs and leaves, and also how to spread industrial fertilizer as the rains came. He knew how to make up the embankments so that fish could be cultivated in the *padi* fields along with the rice. He also knew how to cook, how to feed the geese, chickens and buffaloes. The family had coconut palms, mango and papaya trees. The only things his mother had to buy in the market were pork, salt and sugar. With their 30 rai of land, they were self-sufficient.

When he was five Surasak's parents split up. His earliest memories, he says, are not of the rice fields, with the sleek black buffaloes in the water, but of his mother fighting her husband when he was drunk. Surasak's grandmother is Chinese, a powerful woman who despised men, and particularly her daughter's husband because he was weak, a drinker and incapable of making money. She was determined the marriage would not last. When Surasak was six his father left home, leaving the grandmother, mother and two older sisters. His mother married again, and she now has two sons with her second husband.

The boy was sent to Bangkok at thirteen to live with his uncle, who has a small garment factory in Huaykhwang making shirts. He employs five young women from his home village who live on the upper floor of the row house that is also the factory. Surasak continued his schooling in Bangkok but, he says, he became another person. In gratitude to his uncle, who has kept him since he came here, he must work in the house, washing, ironing, cooking for the family, and sometimes for the young women workers. He is given 50 baht a day by his uncle ($US2), who has forbidden him to take money from his mother 'because she has her own family to look after now'. The uncle is in his fifties and the boy must speak to him and his aunt with respect and humility. They have no children and have, after a fashion, adopted him.

Surasak has taught himself English; he speaks with fluency and intelligence. One consequence of the breaking of the rural culture has been a sense of the relative nature of values: he picks up other manners, other ways of being, other languages, with great ease. He says learning English was less strange than learning the foreign language of the city. His uncle insists that he study electronics, which he detests. He would prefer to work in tourism, travel or hotels, where his proficiency in English would help; but he is bound by gratitude and when he broaches the subject, his uncle tells him he may do as he pleases, but not until he has passed from his house.

One evening I met Chang, visiting his relatives in Bangkok from Los Angeles where he lives. He studied art in the USA, in North Carolina, and his English has a Southern accent. He stayed on, and now works as a restorer of nineteenth-century Meissen porcelain. He has recently set up his own business and is making money. He acknowledges the strangeness of a man from South Asia, specialized in European china, restoring the *objets d'art* of the Californian rich. He says that many of his clients own the porcelain not because they love it, but because it is an investment; they are well aware of the importance of authentic and competent restoration.

Chang is in Bangkok for a month. He says it rouses strange emotions to be back. He loves to see his family, three brothers and four sisters, his parents. All are very successful. They regard his work as something of an aberration, and are sceptical of his ability to make money from it. They are involved in business: jewellery, garments and motor cars. He says one of the pleasures of Bangkok is to be able to walk freely at night without fear. Such a simple activity is not possible in Los Angeles. He does not love America. His heart is here, but he is caught up in work that would be impossible in Bangkok. When he was younger he was anxious to get away, to escape the suffocating intensity of the family; but now he is alone in America he sees it all differently. The tension and fear of Los Angeles have to be balanced against the pollution and chaos of Bangkok, the violence and excitement of North America against the fatalism of Thailand. He says you can argue that the poor of Los Angeles, by robbing or dealing in drugs and guns, are at least doing something about their poverty. You may not like it, it may be antisocial. But here, they just smile and accept it. I'm not sure which is worse.

I met Cha in a girlie bar in Patpong, a cruel frightful place where young women pale as ghosts were going through their routine, swinging around chromium bars on a raised podium while the men sat at the bar appraising them, choosing one to take off for a short time in an upstairs room or for the night in a hotel. It was late, and the show was winding down; only the unchosen remained. Cha grimaced and sat down beside me. He was not drinking, indeed had no money.

He was born in Laos in 1965, but his parents fled the country and he spent the first twelve years of his life in a refugee camp near Sisikhet. Most people in the camp were waiting to go to a third country, the USA or Australia. The system of asylum was corrupt: Thais who could afford to pay were given papers, but most poor Laotians did not stand a chance. Eventually his family was given residency permits for Thailand and they settled in the north.

There was no proper schooling in the camp. Cha learned English from volunteers who came to work with refugees from the USA, Europe and Australia. He cannot read or write English, but his spoken language is good. Cha has two sisters who are married and a brother who has become a monk; another brother died in the camp when he was seven. Life in the camp was not bad but they were semi-prisoners, having to get permission each time they went out.

When his parents left the camp Cha came to Bangkok. He has done everything there is to do in the city. He travelled here by bus and slept four nights at the bus station. His first job was in a shoe factory. He was paid 600 baht a month, but accommodation and food were provided. He didn't like it – it was too much like the enclosed world of the camp: they give you food and shelter, but you are captive. They know people cannot leave, because they have nowhere to sleep. He found a better job in a bakery, for 650 baht, but the conditions were similar. After that he worked for a year on a construction site near Don Muang airport. He was paid 70, then 80 baht a day, about two-thirds of the minimum wage. His hands are coarse and scarred by hard work; he frequently worked seven days a week. After that he worked in a motorcycle repair shop at 100 baht a day; within a few weeks he could take motorbikes apart and reassemble them. He was proud of his competence, but the owner gave him no independence, supervised him too closely. He had an argument and left.

He then started work as a motorcycle taxi driver. Having no capital and no bike, he has to hire the bike each day – 130 baht. The owner has over 80 bikes. Cha drives a Yamaha. He has become more and more free through his work. He can work as many hours as he chooses. He starts at five in the morning and then stops at ten, starts again at one in the afternoon and goes on till late at night. On a good day he will earn 500 or 600 baht a day; that is up to 400 baht profit.

Today he is not working; this afternoon he had to go to the police station. The police saw him make a U-turn in Sathorn in a no-turn area. This occurred on Sunday. It is now Wednesday. Today they gave him back his licence but he has to pay a fine of 600 baht. Normally, he says, he keeps a 50- or 100-baht note tucked inside his driving licence so that if the police pull him up for anything they can take the money and let him go. On this occasion it didn't work. With his licence gone he had to borrow money, at 20 per cent interest. Tomorrow he will go to the police station, pay off the money, and start work again. Sometimes when he has money he pays for a girl from the bar. Tonight he was tempted, but will keep the cash to pay off the police.

Cha lives in a small room with three other young men, two from his own village. The room has no running water. In the lodging house there are just three toilets and two showers, shared by forty other people. He does his own washing and buys his food on the street. You can get a bag of noodles and sauce for 10 baht. The room is close to the airport, next to a polluted *klong* that smells bad. His green shirt has a series of small holes in the sleeve. Oh, that was rats that come in the night. There is no bed in the room, just mats; no furniture. It costs the four of them 1,300 baht a month.

Cha would like to be a tour guide. This is why he hangs around places where he can meet foreigners. His dream is to take groups or individuals to see the Bangkok of their choice, whatever their speciality, he says ambiguously. He once took some Americans on a tour of the Royal Palace, but when the police saw he had no identification they took money from him and threw them out. Cha hates the police because they prey on poor people. He says he is working below the level of his intelligence and competence; but then, he says, so are thousands of other people wandering through this concrete labyrinth they call Bangkok.

14

Urbanizing the Plantation Workers, Malaysia

The Estate

Profound changes are occurring in the living conditions on the rubber and oil palm plantations of Malaysia. More and more young people, especially men, are leaving the estates for factory labour, others have been recruited by the shipyards in Singapore. In parts of Malaysia the place of Tamils on the plantations has been taken by Indonesians and Bangladeshis. These newcomers, away from home in an unfamiliar environment, often turn to the consolation of *samsu*, a cheap, potent liquor; in some areas molestation and rape of Tamil women have been reported.

The migrants have come solely to work and to remit as much money as they can to their homes. Tamil rubber plantation workers have traditionally worked from six in the morning until two in the afternoon. The Bangladeshis and Indonesians, especially in oil palm plantations, work longer hours. They are favoured by management, and undermine custom and practice established by Malaysian Indians.

There are still 237,000 people employed in the plantation sector. About 35,000 belong to the plantation workers' trade union, but only 12,000 pay their dues. Membership is falling because the union has done little to protect its members.

Oil palms are more lucrative than rubber. In many places rubber trees have been replaced by palms. Workers are increasingly recruited by contractors. Palm plantations require less labour than rubber, and this attracts less skilled migrant workers. The trend is for them to live off the estates; management finds it cheaper to provide them with a living allowance rather than houses. They do piecework: 13 sen for bunches of the red oil nuts from the smaller trees, 24 sen for bunches from the taller trees (5 and 10 US cents). They work in teams of five: one removes the leaves from the stem of the tree, another cuts clusters of nuts, a third collects these, a fourth loads the truck, and a fifth picks up the fruits that become detached as the clusters fall from the tree. The workers earn between 300 and 400 ringgit a month ($US120–160). It is dangerous work; the cutters are very sharp, the bunches of nuts are thorny, and snakes, especially cobras, rest in the shady places under the piles of dead branches.

After work many of the migrant labourers drink. *Samsu* is supposed to be made from Chinese herbs, but third-class wine imported from France is added: with sugar, water and colouring the alcohol content may rise to 40 per cent. Beer is only 5 per cent alcohol, and costs twice as much. There have been many deaths from drinking *samsu*, but this is rarely acknowledged on the death certificates of those who lose their lives in this way.

When the British set up the rubber estates a century ago, they ensured there was a toddy shop and a temple on every estate. The men would go to the toddy shop after work, the women to the temple. In the toddy shop men might air their grievances, but once drunk they would fall into quarrels and fights among themselves. Alcoholism on the plantations is now very high; on some, up to two-thirds of male workers are to a greater or lesser degree addicted to alcohol.

Conditions on many plantations are still poor. Sometimes the owners construct a few new houses for their workers in conspicuous positions close to the roadside, whilst in the interior the dwellings remain dilapidated and inadequate, sometimes still from the colonial period.

NGOs supporting the plantation workers say how difficult it is to teach them their rights. If an accident occurs they are supposed to fill out a form in Malay; 80 per cent of the workers are illiterate. They must report any accident within twenty-four hours. Many of the older Tamils left school before they were twelve. Now about 30 per cent of Tamil children go to secondary school.

Subba, of the Consumers' Association of Penang, working with the plantation workers, says that life for the younger generation has become more violent. A campaign has been started, taking inspiration from the anti-liquor movements in Tamil Nadu and Andhra Pradesh in India, against liquor and against the values of Tamil movies, which are lurid and glorify gang fights, kidnappings and even rape.

About 65 per cent of the estate workers are Tamils. In some places they must tap more trees each day and are still paid a day wage, like casual workers, even when their families, indentured by the British, have worked in the same place for three generations. They are an ageing population.

The rubber estates are lonely places, melancholy avenues of identical trees as far as the eye can see. One worker may cover 50 acres, tap five or six hundred trees a day. Some estates have built housing for their workers outside the plantation, but this is still rare; most remain in the desolate monoculture where their families have lived for one hundred years.

The Consumers' Association of Penang has a field centre in Kedah, on the west coast of peninsular Malaysia. When I visited, two workers had come for help. The owners of an estate at Jerai have been evicting workers in order to construct a golf course on the site of the plantation: yet another golf course to add to the ninety-one already established in Malaysia, a country of about 18 million people.

Of the forty-six families affected by this project, twenty have gone, but the rest have remained in their homes for six years, seeking adequate compensation.

Mr Jesudas arrives with a letter sent to all the remaining families; it is from the lawyer of the company reiterating that they must leave within fourteen days. Those who have stayed have been harassed, their homes damaged, the roofs removed. There is already an eighteen-hole golf course on the site, and the company wants to extend this to thirty-six. They have promised to build houses for the oustees within a year or two, but the residents are demanding that houses be constructed for them to buy. Legal argument around this case has been going on for eight years. Mr Jesudas is working for contractors now, road building and construction. He says the company will employ outsiders and youngsters who have dropped out of school to maintain the golf course. There will be nothing for the plantation workers.

Golf courses and leisure parks in Malaysia are mainly for the sake of tourists, especially tourists from Japan and Taiwan. For Japanese golf enthusiasts it is cheaper to fly to Malaysia for a weekend in a 'golf resort' than to pay the subscription to join a club in Japan. Industrialized leisure is now a principal agent of displacement of Tamil workers.

We visit the Kim Seng Estate: oil palms and rubber, and also an orchard of dourien, the great spiky, strong-smelling fruits ready for picking. A large acreage of rubber trees has been ploughed up, replanted with palms. Under the trees lie red and gold bunches of oil nuts but there is no sight of any of the workers, who cover great distances during the course of the day.

The rubber workers are more visible, but still sparsely scattered under the gloomy arcades of trees. Arokiam, a young woman of twenty-six, stands on her rickety wooden ladder propped against the rubber tree. She makes a sharp incision with her rubber tapper's curved knife. The latex begins to flow down the flaking bark into a plastic cup that she places below the cut; the milky liquid is channelled through a small metal tube inserted into the tree at the base of the wound. These trees have a double cut, one a metre from the ground, the other two metres higher.

Arokiam, whose name means 'good health' in Tamil, has been working since she was twelve. This young woman has fourteen years of labour behind her. She wears purple trousers, a once-white blouse stained with latex. On her back is a metal container in which she places the dried rubber from the empty pots: this she sells for 30 sen a kilo (about 13 US cents) to supplement her earnings. After three or four hours she will return to collect the liquid, which then goes to the weighing centre in big metal churns. Arokiam was born on a neighbouring plantation and has three brothers and six sisters. A brother is working in the Singapore docks, some sisters are in factories. Arokiam married a man from this plantation and left her family to come here. He is a truck driver; they have two children.

Arokiam collects 30 kilos of rubber a day and is paid 70 sen a kilo (about 27 US cents). She starts at 7.30 in the morning and reaches home by 3.30 in the afternoon. She works seven days a week. Only when it rains is there a holiday; she smiles: 'But there is no pay.' Sometimes people come in the night and steal the dried rubber from the containers so that in the morning there is nothing for her.

The latex is processed locally; acid is added and it is compressed by machine into sheets of rubber, which are then exported.

The only water around the dark place where Arokiam is working is in a ditch, visibly discoloured by fertilizer and pesticide. This is the only spot where workers can wash away the latex from hands and face. A man on a motorbike passes by: on his back he bears some metal cylinders like the oxygen carried by a diver. In his hands are a pipe and nozzle, through which he is releasing pesticide into the air.

Arokiam says that most men now work outside the estate. Women stay on the estate to qualify for housing – they can rent plantation housing only if at least one member of the family still works there. The women who remain have to face harassment, cheating and threats, as well as all the social problems. The men can go elsewhere.

The tracks through the plantation are a red-rust colour, stony unmade roads. Rubber trees stand in bleached arches, an architecture of bone. Little grows in their shadow. There are traces of invisible workers – a tiffin can, a plastic water bottle and cup, a jacket. The trees of each worker are marked with a particular sign to demarcate the otherwise undetectable boundary of the acreage for which she is responsible. Sometimes people take latex from the trees of others and quarrels break out.

Towards midday, more people come to collect latex from trees they have cut. Kaliarase, a boy of eleven, a thin child with cropped hair, is helping his mother, Suparma. Suparma was born on the estate like her husband. They have six children, three in school, one in Singapore.

Gopal too was born on the estate, but he now lives outside. He has seven children, six of them girls. He has managed to save enough money to pay off a loan on a house. This he has done by working on the rubber plantation from six in the morning till mid-afternoon and then going as a contract worker on the oil palms for the rest of the day.

There is constant danger from leeches in the dirty water, and of contracting malaria from the mosquitoes in stagnant pools. Betel leaves are used for removing leeches from the feet.

Extensive areas of the estate have been newly planted with palms, protected by barbed-wire enclosures. Subba says that if the cow of one of the workers should enter the land it will be arrested and the owner will have to pay a fine of 50 ringgit to have it released.

It will be three to five years before the palms become productive, but then the yield will be high. In the meantime chillis are planted along-side the palms to make up for the lack of present income. Some older palms lie in a neighbouring field like the soldiers of a fallen army.

The village of plantation-owned houses was constructed by the British; most of the houses are of wood, now rotted, with verandahs once painted blue but discoloured by time. The roofs are corrugated metal, rusty from perpetual rain. The people have piped water – an engine pumps it to the houses – but it comes from a contaminated, brown-coloured pool about 200 metres from the village. The water is close to the crudely constructed byres where the people keep their cattle; there is shit on the path, and the rain washes this into the water supply. This is where people must wash and clean their clothes; it is also the only source of drinking water. Subba says, 'We have taught people to boil the water, but when they come from the plantation they are exhausted and thirsty. They do not bother.' A survey here showed a high level of skin disease, dysentery and diarrhoea. At one time the local government brought trucks with drinking water in containers, but later stopped because it was too far for government officials to come.

Muthapen stands on the threshold of his house. He has recon-structed it so there is a base of solid concrete and the lower storey is brick-built. The house now has wooden window frames, with louvred glass. Muthapen has improved his immediate environment: in the garden there is a lime tree, a starfruit and a pomelo. He offers us some fruit, the rich segments of what looks like an oversized golden orange. His two children live with Muthapen's father off the planta-tion so that they can go to school. They are on holiday this week: the girl wants to work with computers, the boy to be an engineer. She is wearing her school uniform and a T-shirt bearing the logo of the Prudential Insurance Company. Muthapen, an able, intelligent man, left school when he was twelve to work on the plantation. He is determined his children will not do the same. He is home briefly for a break from work; he jumps on his motorbike to go and collect the latex from his morning's labour. His clothes are discoloured by the sticky grey of dried latex.

In the village there is a temple, a god-tree and a soaring neem, from which people use twigs to clean their teeth. Although the houses are ancient, people do not want to move, because here they have space for their cattle, a few vegetables and fruit trees, papaya and plantain. In new housing on the estates, the workers have no land to grow anything for themselves: managers have even destroyed small vegetable gardens. Here they have a dignity that comes from being able to provide themselves with some of their own food, including chickens. Only twenty families remain but it is a peaceful place, and they have known one another for two or three generations. The other workers on the estate travel in by truck each day.

Jayaraman works at the field centre in the town of Kuala Ketil, close to the plantation. He was formerly an official of the rubber workers' union, chairman of the district for three years. He was seen by the union leadership as too zealous on behalf of the workers and was ordered to cut all contact with the Consumers' Association of Penang, with whom he had worked closely in monitoring conditions on the estates. If he failed to do so he was told he would not be re-elected. He said, 'Let the members decide.' The members duly voted for him, but the election was rigged and he was declared defeated. Union officials had replaced the actual ballots with false papers. Jayaraman himself found a bundle of votes that had been cast for him. He made a complaint to the registrar of trade unions. There was no response. That was seven years ago. 'The union leadership are not interested in the well-being of the workers. They have been bought off. If you really work for the poorest people in Malaysia, and that means the Tamils, you are seen as a troublemaker.'

The Township

Many Tamils who have left the plantations have gone into towns and urban villages in search of factory employment, places like Runha Panjang Rawang, about 30 kilometres from the capital, Kuala Lumpur.

This industrial village is in an area of utter desolation, a small township set amidst an epic destruction of nature: hills shorn of trees, valleys levelled, mountains decapitated for road building. Rawang is the site of particular dereliction; it serves the enormous Associated

Pan-Malaysian Cement (APMC) works, an enterprise that fills the neighbourhood with ashen dust, blanching the shrubs and trees that remain, and coating the buildings with a fine layer of grey cement.

There are about three hundred families here in the shadow of the sprawling towers and chimneys of the works; some Malays, a few Chinese, but predominantly Tamils. The scene reminded me of a description of Merthyr Tydfil in south Wales in 1848:

> The footways are seldom flagged, the streets are ill-paved, and with bad materials, and not lighted. The drainage is very imperfect; there are few underground sewers, no house drains, and the open gutters are not regularly cleaned. Dustbins and similar receptacles for filth are unknown; the refuse is thrown into the streets. Bombay itself, reputed to be the filthiest town under British sway, is scarcely worse! The houses are badly built, and planned without any regard to the comfort of the tenants, whose families [are] frequently lodged – sometimes sixteen in number – in one chamber, sleeping there indiscriminately.
>
> (*The Rise of Modern Industry*)

This is urbanization outside the big cities.

The works are at the foot of a long downward slope. From there a road rises: on one side the flattened valley floor, on the other (inspired, it is said, by the long-houses of Sarawak – itself scarcely a suitable model for Indians – but bearing an extraordinary resemblance to the terraced streets of Victorian England) there are streets of about twelve to fifteen houses on either side of a dusty, potholed road. There are about twenty-five of these streets, of two-roomed dwellings with concrete floors, each in a small garden enclosed with chicken wire. The walls are of asbestos, in defiance of the known dangers from such materials, while the roofs are metal. Everything about them is utilitarian, geometrical, functional. Some people have planted flowers in the garden – some starry jasmine, hibiscus, blossoms dimmed by cement dust. Inside the furniture is the fag end of consumer junk, plastic, plywood and foam; even the little household shrines are plastic. The sides of the roads are littered with rubbish: plastic, polystyrene, coconut shells, fruit and vegetable waste.

This is a single-function labouring township without amenity or grace, a stark barracks for industrial labour. Only a small temple here and there speaks of the rich spiritual heritage of an India most people here have never seen, being the third or fourth generation of the indentured labour who built railways for the British, who harvested plantations for the colonial power. These have been evicted from the impoverished sterile estates now to work as industrial labour among ravaged limestone hills and quarries, places that provide the cement for the real-estate boom which has profited the speculative developers of Kuala Lumpur and transformed the city skyline into a mirage of marble, glass and stone.

Chandran is twenty-six. He and his wife have five children. They lived near the Bright Sparkler fireworks factory, which was destroyed by an explosion in 1991. Some old gunpowder had been stored underground, and the factory exploded. Chandran's wife was working there; miraculously she was not injured.

Everywhere in the newly industrializing countries has its stories of terrible fires, accidents and explosions: the Kader doll factory in Bangkok, the burning of the slums of Manila, the fire in the garment factory in Dhaka whose doors were locked in the interests of discipline and where twenty-five women perished, the chemical tanker explosion in Bangkok that killed all the drivers trapped in a rush-hour traffic jam. Dr Chaiwat Sathe-Anand, of Thammasat University in Bangkok, says that accidents, which are relatively free from political motivation, are a useful index of social reality. His research shows that accidents became a major source of death in Thai society between 1969 and 1988, and at an increasing rate. In 1981 alone, 1.9 million persons had to be hospitalized as a result of accidents.

Chandran and his family were relocated in Rawang after the Bright Sparkler explosion. Both now work for the plant, earning 18 ringgit each per day (about $US7). The hours are from eight until five, or until seven if there is overtime. Chandran's wife works in the packing department. Earlier Chandran was employed at a sawmill, where wages were higher, but there is no transport there from where he now lives. Chandran is saving up to realize an almost impossible dream: buying a motorbike. This ambition has the aim of making him more mobile in the search for work that will provide a better income than the cement factory. Most people are trapped: there is no transport, there is no other work. They are captives of the cement works, just as they were of the estate.

Life is raw and often chaotic in these new settlements, much as it was in Merthyr Tydfil 150 years ago. There are often gang fights between youths (more like contemporary Merthyr, and every other town in the Western world). Chandran says if you go away to visit relatives, even for a couple of days, you risk coming back to find your house wrecked and vandalized. But they pay no rent. Clearly even the authorities that provided these structures made of hazardous materials to serve no-choice employment recognize they are not worth rent. Even so, water is 20 ringgit a month, electricity 15. It costs around 20 ringgit a day to feed a family of seven adequately.

The cement works and its dependent township evoke strange echoes of the plantation: the similar bare, functional houses, the lack of alternative occupation, the monoculture, although here it is the grey powder of an industrial product rather than the lugubrious rows of identical trees. The labour here is more dangerous, because although the workers wear masks the powder pervades the whole settlement, so that even the food tastes of cement. Every passing vehicle sets up a chalky mist that dilutes the sunlight and coats the vegetation. Chandran's grandparents were taken by the British to Malaya to work on a rubber plantation. His parents continued with the same work. For him, he says, it is different: life will be better for his children. For Chandran escape from the plantation is just the first step; life in the township shows him this is not enough. This will not be his final destination: the motorbike he is saving for will help him start a vegetable business. His modest dream is of going to the market, buying a basket of fresh vegetables and selling them in the countryside around.

As we speak, some youngsters gather round. Jeyaseelan and Devaraj are both seventeen. They dropped out of school because they wanted to earn money. For the past two years both have been working at Kuala Lumpur airport cleaning the aircraft, an occupation that still appeals to them because it is associated with the modern sector, and flight represents escape. For their work, they earn 420 ringgit a month ($US150).

Some new factories are being constructed close to the pool of captive labour that is Rawang. Young women in blue jackets embroidered with the logo of the company in English and Chinese, Precious Mountain Enterprises, are coming out of one of the factories for lunch. It is a Taiwanese enterprise, and they are making rubber gloves.

There are many elderly people in this settlement, retired plantation workers who have moved into the houses of children who have left the estates. When no family member works on the estate, they must leave. Munusamy is sixty-eight. He worked on an oil palm plantation in Banting and came to live with his son, now employed in the new rubber glove factory. His son's wife works with a construction company. Munusamy says life here is not very different from the plantation: they feel cut off, have little choice, have no amenities and live in a degraded environment. On the plantation he earned 600 ringgit a month, but he worked long hours and sometimes they had to wait late into the night before the truck came to pick up and weigh the oil nuts they had gathered. Munusamy was born on the Banting Estate; his life was bounded by the plantation he rarely left. Many older Tamils are shy, subdued by a lifetime of servitude.

Leaving the plantation is not always liberating: to emerge into the outside world can sometimes be unsettling, even frightening. Two of Munusamy's three sons live here. His wife died twenty years ago. She too worked on the plantation, but was sick for many years before she died of a chest infection. Munusamy has ten grandchildren; the son he lives with has six children.

Perumal is fifty-eight. He left the St Andrew's Estate at Berjunta two years ago. He shows a battered identity card which locates him as an employee of a rubber plantation. He regularly tapped 550 trees a day. Although he had been on the estate all his life, he remained a daily wage labourer until he retired, earning 3 ringgit 20 sen per day (about $US1.30). From the age of twelve until he was fifty-six, his work began at six; he saw rubber trees die and new ones planted, and they also died; but he carried on working.

Perumal has ten children, but he came to Rawang to stay with his sister. His wife left when the children were small, and he brought them up by himself in the plantation barracks. He has thirty-five grandchildren.

This estate represents another halt in the long, involuntary journey of Tamils who have never seen Tamil Nadu. The settlement at Rawang is neither rural nor urban. It has none of the amenities of a town, none of the consolations of the countryside; it is an industrial limbo for which no name exists.

15

A Tale of Two Cities

Delhi, Bangkok: it is difficult to imagine a greater contrast. The very fabric of their urban landscapes could scarcely be more different. The vast construction boom in Bangkok has created a skyline that recalls Manhattan, with its palaces of glass and marble, its climatized shopping malls and showrooms. The structures of the older city, the temples and old houses in their leafy compounds, the streets where rusty tin roofs overhang carved mildewy balconies, are now almost completely effaced in much of the city. Even symmetrical concrete-and-glass low-rise buildings from the 1950s and 1960s are being demolished as a new motorway pushes through the city in a doomed attempt to make the traffic move again.

The face of New Delhi has been less dramatically transformed. The archaic grace of Lutyens' imperial capital remains untouched, whilst the old city is a choked and chaotic jumble of decrepit stone, slum settlements, workplaces and markets; the ruins of Moghul monuments, some in formal gardens, others neglected and covered with flowers, provide a kind of wild visual delight that is increasingly rare in Bangkok. Delhi, too, has its share of new building, much of it thrown up in the growth of middle-class satellite cities, like the lugubrious and charmless high-rise vistas of Patparganj and Noida.

Yet both cities offer, in their way, examples of new and inappropriate forms of economic 'deregulation', as a consequence of policies that have long been followed in Thailand, more recently in India. Whoever could have foreseen that the elegant thoroughfares of New Delhi would become the scene of such terrible carnage as a consequence of violently competitive bus services? The fatalities on the roads of Delhi – well over 1,500 in 1994 – are a form of human sacrifice to faith in the emancipatory power of market forces.

Other elements also have a part in the traffic disaster of Delhi. The growth in the population has been very rapid in the last ten years (it now stands at over 10 million), and many rural migrants

247

have not yet thoroughly adapted to the rhythms of city life. Many drivers of the Red Line buses strike the metal flank of the vehicle with the palm of their hand as though this were a traditional beast of draught, a far less lethal animal than that which they are urging towards its destination. Add to this the corruption that distributes licences to those who can pay and not to those who can drive, and the role of politicians and officials in ownership of the bus lines, and we can see some of the consequences of a liberalization embraced by the Indian government with the excessive zeal of converts.

In Bangkok too the traffic is murderous, but in a very different way: there the pollution stagnates in the built-up areas, a choking mixture of lead, carbon dioxide, dust and industrial emissions. The effects upon the people are less immediate than the heaps of mangled metal and upturned vehicles that litter the roadsides of Delhi; but the all but unbreathable air takes its toll no less. The people are the human absorbers of all the gases, they are the pollution abatement technology. They pay the costs of the automobile through respiratory and lung disorders, brain damage to children from heavy concentrations of lead. It is not Mitsubishi, nor Nissan, nor Shell, nor Esso that will defray the costs of physical and mental impairment to the people of Bangkok. On the contrary, these sicknesses will simply offer new markets to transnational drug and pharmaceutical companies, will become a source of yet greater business opportunity, yet greater economic growth.

There are no long ceremonial avenues in Bangkok that invite speed. And the penetration of the market by Japanese, Korean and US cars brings the traffic on many roads to a standstill for a considerable part of each day. In the concrete canyons of Sathorn and Silom sit lines of Toyotas, Mitsubishis, Isuzus and Nissans, pristine, metallized, all going nowhere, an unending advertisement for Japanese technology. The number of vehicles on the streets of the city exceeds the capacity of the roads to hold them. The response of the city authorities is to build more roads, which has the familiar effect of shifting the traffic jams a few hundred metres further forward. Automobiles have become immobiles, cherished more for the status they bestow than for their capacity to convey human beings from one place to another. There is even a city radio station, which serves as a kind of community of the jammed, to inform, distract and console for the never-ending journeys. Another economic advantage of the Bangkok traffic accrues to the mobile telephone industry. Everywhere in Bangkok, in cars, shops, restaurants, buses, on the sidewalk, even in sex parlours, you hear a constant humming and purring as people explain to each other why they cannot reach a meeting or get to an appointment on time.

Indeed, in Bangkok people regularly endure journeys of two or three hours to work and back; they are already exhausted before an arduous day's labour. Trucks full of young men, sprawled, sleeping in total abandon, sometimes almost on top of one another, inch slowly through the streets towards factories, workshops, construction sites; nowhere is the abstraction of labour made more material: cabbages or coal could scarcely be loaded with more casual indifference. In the evening buses wait in the traffic while the fumes swirl around them; the heads of young women droop forward onto their chest like wilting flowers.

Nor are the heroic journeys confined to the poor. Middle-class families swap stories of how they rise at four in the morning, carry the sleeping children to the car, and drive for an hour to the school. There they let the children sleep a further couple of hours, then wake them, wash their faces, give them breakfast, clean their teeth before going on to their own place of work. Some of the poor get up even earlier; Puen from Saw Pattaya rises at two to reach the market for the chickens that must be cooked and ready for hungry commuters before six o'clock.

One of the effects of the highly Westernized aspect of Bangkok has been to conceal from view some of its poorest people; this is unlike Delhi, which for all its grandeur as a national capital cannot hide the fact that such a high proportion of its inhabitants are poor, a large fraction of them desperately so. The removal of the poor from the central areas of Bangkok led the average distance of informal settlements from the city centre to increase from 7.1 kilometres in 1984 to 10.1 kilometres in 1988. Forty-two per cent of evictions took place within 5 kilometres of the city centre, and 84 per cent within 10 kilometres.

Of course the city authorities of Delhi have sought to 'beautify' the city also. But the efforts there are more crude: if you look, for example, at the Holiday Inn compound and then walk the hundred metres under the Barrakhamba flyover, you find a vast population of cycle rickshaw drivers, vendors, servants, washermen and washerwomen, beggars, drug dealers, sleeping on ledges and concrete stairs, in tiny plastic shelters or flimsy cardboard-and-polythene hutments. Poverty exists in Bangkok also, but not on the same scale, and the poorest settlements are constructed over the polluted *klongs* or canals, houses of tin and rotting wood on bamboo stilts, squeezed onto the last margins of land in the central areas. Some of the worst conditions are in multi-occupied rooms in tenement buildings, dirty, dilapidated, infested, the squalor of which is less visible from outside – young men and women sleeping three or four in a cell of a room for a rent that absorbs half their monthly income.

Both cities have a population close to 10 million. Both are places of intense migration, in Delhi overwhelmingly male. In Bangkok there is more work for women, in the garments industry, in factories and in the sex industry. The workplaces of Bangkok may not be the infernal sites of the small-scale steelworks of Wazirpur in east Delhi; many of the industrial units are white-painted four-storey buildings on the edge of the city which, at first sight, look like villas from a Mediterranean holiday brochure. Only inside they are hot, dusty and unhygienic; many employ child labour, and the workers live on the premises, virtual captives. Altogether Bangkok has been more skilful than Delhi in the concealment of its miseries and social injustices; it has certainly not abolished them.

Bangkok now has around 45,000 hotel rooms, sufficient to accommodate the 6 million or so visitors who came from abroad in 1994. To make room for them, more and more of the urban poor are being displaced, relocated on the far periphery, up to 25 kilometres from the city. Although evictions also occur in Delhi, the poor are too numerous to be deported or landscaped out of sight. In the Thai capital there is nothing quite like the congestion of, for instance, the Ajmeri Gate, and also nothing quite like the desperate livelihoods of survival of some of the poorest in Delhi: the collectors of animal bones, broken glass, the hair of the dead.

Although Delhi has a vigorous industry catering to the sexual needs of its male migrants, it is free of sex tourism, which has attracted increasing numbers of people to Bangkok not only from Europe and the USA, but also from Japan, Taiwan, Korea and Singapore. Whatever the problems this form of tourism brings – and they are many, including child prostitution and developments that threaten to turn the sex industry into an AIDS industry within the next few years, and into a severe drain on the resources of Thailand – Bangkok acknowledges sexuality in a way that Delhi does not: Delhi is a city of repressed desire, of raw and volatile energies that have been denied. This is not a judgement; but the difference in the atmosphere of the two cities is palpable. There may be something noble in India's resistance to Western sexualizing of society; but its denial of such fundamental needs sets up other tensions, from which it can be a relief to arrive in the more relaxed atmosphere of Bangkok.

The Bangkok region now accommodates almost one-fifth of the population of Thailand. In Thailand the government leaves the people alone to get on with the serious business of making money, so long as the people leave the government alone to get on with its serious business of corruption and making money. Only if the two collide can trouble be expected. If the city is superficially more 'developed' than Delhi, this is because in Thailand the ideology of *laissez-faire* has been in place far longer than in India. Does this, perhaps, mean that Bangkok may foreshadow the future of Delhi?

Scarcely. Delhi is never going to contain one-fifth of the population of India. Culture and sensibility too remain significant determinants of the response to urbanization. The people of Bangkok are disciplined, compliant, conformist. They tolerate levels of discomfort with enormous, stoical patience, which is perhaps less of a virtue than it might seem in the context of such a polluted and immobilized city. On the other hand Delhi is anarchic, individualistic, volatile. Bangkok is still one of the safest cities in the world and although there is gangsterism, and crimes of violence do occur, these remain relatively contained. Delhi too is safe in the sense that crime, robbery and assaults on strangers are far less prevalent than in London or New York; but Delhi is highly militarized, a more tense, less relaxed place than Bangkok. Delhi – apart from its limited enclaves of privilege – closes down early; Bangkok is alive until late in the night.

Bangkok is a First World city imposed upon the decaying fabric of the original; it exhibits the limits of development, and the unsuitability of Western urban transplants in the South. The climate is intensely hot and humid and the concentration of brick and concrete buildings only increases the heat: in the hot season the sun glares down Silom with a ferocious intensity that raises the temperature and makes the streets unbearable. If this form of development is imposed upon Delhi it will not be accepted there with the fortitude and resignation of the inhabitants of the Thai capital. But with increasing convergence in the policies of all the governments in Asia, there is no doubt that pressure on the infrastructures of all the cities will grow. Delhi too can expect to see more environmental and developmental refugees seek shelter in its inhospitable streets. City life is bound to become more polluted, more dangerous, more violent. The fateful line when more than half the world's people become urban is always on the point of being crossed. It may be that they will demand something better than either of these majestic, appalling, energetic and pitiless places at present offer.

16

City Views

Somsuk Boonyabancha, Bangkok

Somsuk Boonyabancha has dedicated her life to housing for the urban poor, in Bangkok and all Asia. She is now at the Urban Poor Foundation, where she is trying to bridge the gap between official housing provision by government agencies, and popular community organization for housing rights and for compensation for displacement. The Urban Poor Fund is currently giving loans to seventeen projects in various forms of community organization.

'The problem is that as Bangkok developed into a modern system of wealth creation, the rights of the people were not protected. Why? Because this country was never colonized. In India, the Philippines, the colonial powers had changed the land system, and had dismantled traditional structures of land ownership. They did not necessarily do so for the better, and certainly not in the interests of the colonized. But change had occurred. All countries, as they reached Independence, sought to alter the colonial land ownership patterns, however nominally and partially this was done.

'This was not felt here. The revolution of 1932 moved Thailand from monarchical to constitutional rule, but change occurred only within the ruling group. Since then there has never been any real stability in government. Leaders who sought to decentralize never gained power. Structural change never came, attempts to redistribute have never succeeded. Even in Indonesia decentralization to the level of the municipality did occur; housing is a local concern. Dictators may come and go, impose their will, but the local unit still functions in Indonesia.

'Here there has been new wealth, capitalism has galloped ahead, but the structure has not changed. The positive side of Thailand is that we are a compromising country, relaxed; we don't like violence. There is a face-saving culture, things are accepted as they are. Buddhism maybe asks too much of people, yet it is there in the Thai way of living, in the older generation especially, even in the slum areas.

'The threat of eviction exists to one-quarter of the population of Bangkok, that is 2.5 million people. They live where originally there was no ownership of the land; the population of these areas grew with the city. They were not slums before, but old settlements. Land security was not traditionally a problem; the problem has come with development. No one worried about who owned land, they only cared about living a life of sufficiency. Thais had no land titles till fifty years ago; before that all land belonged to the king. People had the right to use land, but not to own it. Then, with titles, land became a commodity. Old settlements that had once been good living places never got land titles.

'Even the public land system is a problem, because ownership is scattered among so many government or other organizations – Land Department, Temple Land, State Enterprises, Railway Land. Each has its own policy, which only they know and understand. As land increases in value, all government departments want to use their land for commercial and shopping developments to maximize the revenue.

'But 60 per cent of the urban poor are on private land. They had been stable for years, but now the original owner has maybe ten children who must share the property. They want money so they sell the land. A new kind of developer is emerging, very keen to get cheap land; land is the key thing affecting the life of the people.

'In an economic boom, the problem is exacerbated. In the past ten years, particularly the past five, people have organized. When there is an organization in a slum area, and these organizations come together as a federation, the resistance is more powerful. If forty communities are associated and one is threatened, people from the others will go to their assistance. Then resistance in one area becomes known to all the others, and that reinforces organization. They are in a position to negotiate with landlords; that can be taken care of in Thai culture. It is not so in Korea or Japan or India, where they are less reluctant to use violence, or even arms. Confrontation there is common; here, if a third party is present, there will be negotiation. This is a good aspect of Thai society. If the law and the police are efficient, which is not always the case, the police can sit between the two parties.

'Thais are not theorists but pragmatists. Things can be resolved through common sense. Nobody cares about the law, not even the police. But compromise will be reached. If resistance is strong you can come to a compromise solution, either by sharing the land between the developer and the community, or by accepting a higher level of compensation acceptable to the people, or by the community being allotted land all together. But it needs a good intermediary. In one of the first cases I undertook, the landlord offered 5,000 baht. The people wanted 50,000. In the end they settled on 25,000 baht for each family. Compensation is now rising – it is close to 100,000 baht now.

'Development has become so powerful, the problem is so huge, that people lose the intimacies of informal society and the whole process becomes dehumanized. We need to moderate the pace of change; the mechanisms that produce the problems have become stronger than the mechanisms to solve them. We try. If the National Housing Authority cannot solve a problem, they make the problem fit their policy. They don't care if the problem is not solved, because that will produce more problems and more money for development.

'To give one example. They move slums outside the city. The people lose their income, go back to the city, where they become even more miserable than they were before. Society believes that poor people want to sell their piece of ground and move back opportunistically; they don't want to understand the real dynamic that drives them.

'If the work is left to the National Housing Authority, the problem will get worse. The mechanism for changing things on a bigger scale can be developed only by the people. We are now giving loans for community organizations, but they have to decide that they want to start saving first. A managerial capacity must be developed, an income-generating and revolving fund must be established for use in the community. If the tools, the power and the resources are given to the community, it will manage. This is a new kind of mechanism. Government just facilitates community organizations. We have a board: one-third people, one-third the private sector, one-third government partnership. This is an attempt to bring the conflict of interest into the mainstream. We have been fighting over the interest rate on the Urban Poor Fund: government says 18 per cent, the people say 2 per cent. People cannot pay, the government says How can it be sustained? We look into the reality: if the interest rate is too low, the market will intervene and distortions will occur. Agreement is required. We have settled for 7 per cent. This is the real process. It is applicable everywhere in society, and is a move in the right direction.

'The government cannot do things for people. They think and plan and work for themselves. If people are enabled, this may have some impact upon the existing system, even though the force of the present pattern of development, which is going in a disastrous direction, is very powerful and dynamic. It is difficult to bring energies together in a constructive direction.

'Partnership is not really wanted, either by government, NGOs or people, but it is necessary if anything is to change. You cannot avoid the other actors in the situation, and they must be brought together. Many people want something different; we have to look into the reality, not what it should be. There is no ideal society and nor is there going to be one: this was the mistake of Marx and those who followed his beliefs. The reality in our society is that the private sector is so strong and competent because it has to struggle to survive; but it moves very fast, it imposes changes that people cannot keep up with. The government, on the other hand, is very slow in its workings, is less developed, its structure is ossified, static. It thinks it knows, whereas the private sector does know. Governments do not develop.

'Things should be done by the people; they cannot wait for government. If we wait for government to do it, we'll wait for ever, and if government does do it it will only make things worse; and since we don't have a confrontational culture like India or the Philippines, we have to act. What we have in Asia is not development, that is clear; we have wealth, and with wealth, corruption.

'When we look at the other actors, the NGOs, for instance, they are idealistic, they want to do something. They want social change. They have big ideas: they are strong on ideas, but the NGOs have problems. NGOs do not like to compromise. They think they are right and everybody else is wrong. To conduct change like that creates problems. So we cannot let NGOs replace government. The NGOs think faster than those in community organizations, they push people's movements the way they are thinking. This makes them another government as far as the people are concerned, and this becomes a major limitation on their effectiveness. So with the private sector moving too fast, the government too slow, and with the constant threat of corruption, and the NGOs ahead of the people, none of these is a sufficient answer to our needs.

'The people remain a real possibility; the people sector is our only source of hope. The people are not too idealistic, they are not moved by theory but by concrete reality. They have an interest in making things happen. They are the real actors. People who live in the slums remain very human; they are so close to want, to disaster, sickness, they react in a way that is not clouded by ideology.

'The middle class live in good housing projects, but they don't know each other. The slum community is similar to the rural community; the way they live is similar to the country, even the second generation. The people have something which has been lost in the middle class.

'All the different actors with their contradictions have some potential role. At present some actors are left out, others have too great a role. The question is to find a balance between the different partners: NGOs have their part, government must be limited to the role of referee between the partners, and the private sector must be checked, although it can still contribute. Its efficiency is valuable; but unless there is a new balance of forces, we have a problem.

'The Asian Development Bank and World Bank believe the private sector will take care of the slums. It isn't possible. At most it could accommodate 70 per cent; 30 per cent will still be under a double pressure, with the price of housing going up and wage rises unable to keep up with it.

'I studied architecture but was always interested in political and social issues. I like towns, communities. I entered the National Housing Authority in the Slum Upgrading Office. I was recruited to design a community centre in a slum area now threatened with eviction. The centre is still there. I didn't like that idea of planning: you make thousands of designs, but not in such a way that they coincide with the way of thinking and living of the people. I went to the community, looked at the space, talked to the people and made a design. The authority then used it as a model for others, which is wrong, because they don't actually consult the people they are doing it for. It became too tiring to tell them over and over again.

'After a year I went to Denmark, where I studied housing and urbanization. That inspired and influenced me. The young radicals there wanted to destroy everything. I believe society has to be changed, but not like that. You can't forget history. In Denmark I realized that housing was part of a whole production system, that was the only thing I really got from Marx. People see housing as a construction plan, so many units, a five-year-plan, how much will it cost, can it be finished in time? It isn't so. Housing is deeper than that. It is an aspect of culture; a unit where families exist and live together is the beginning of the life of the people. Communities, interaction within them, this is the root of identity. It is more than a commodity, it is full of meaning.

'When I came back, I joined the Rama IV community, about eight hundred families. There had been fires, they were threatened with eviction. People were organizing to resist. That was good training. I moved to the Centre for Housing and Human Settlement Studies. There was a series of evictions in Bangkok in 1982; I began to see that the causes and effects of eviction were connected with land ownership and tenure.

'I joined an NGO and went to slum areas facing eviction to help the people organize. Two communities were much strengthened by our intervention. They negotiated with the landlord with our assistance. People had been evicted earlier, but they just moved to another part of the land. We went to the landlord and said, "Give 20 per cent of the land to these people, then a peaceful solution will be possible." The landlord would not agree. I talked to the governor of the NHA and got him to be the third party in the process. He listened, called the landlord and tried to negotiate with him. The landlord was very stubborn. In the end, there were a couple of cases where we achieved a land-sharing solution. People must be strong and push a bit. Big guys like to feel they'll help solve the problems of the people. If people have lived on land for fifty years, the landlord is in a difficult moral situation. You can say to him, "Why not let people buy 20 per cent of the land. That means you'll get 8 million instead of 10 million baht, and you'll be paying two million for your image and also to help people."

'The Thai contribution to international discussions on housing is understanding. We don't have radical change to propose. We absorb all kinds of change. Yet sometimes I get annoyed because we accept too much uncritically, or because things move too slowly, or because the system doesn't work. But we bring our distinctive element to the discussions, and it is useful and conciliatory.'

Nazrul Islam, Dhaka

Nazrul Islam directs the Centre for Urban Studies at Dhaka University. Educational institutions in Dhaka account for several hundred thousand young people, Dhaka College and the University alone having almost 100,000 students. The university area is green and shady; the very city landscape here gives plausibility to Nazrul Islam's thesis that Dhaka is actually a ruralizing metropolis rather than an urbanizing one.

Nazrul Islam deplores notions of urbanization that come from the West: the term 'premature metropolis' was coined by an Indian anthropologist to designate some Indian cities in the 1960s, and this is how he sees Dhaka – the premature megacity. The transformation of Dhaka from the colonial administrative regional capital began in the 1950s, at which time it appeared a formal, modern city. Since then the idea of a planned, orderly, organized city has been reversed: Nazrul Islam says Dhaka is now assuming the aspect of a more rural, chaotic settlement. It is becoming an informal-sector city, at least in terms of the employment it generates, if not in terms of the value of its output.

'In the last ten years the garment industry has brought half a million women into the city, which has markedly transformed the sex ratio of male to female. Formerly the pattern was biased heavily towards male migrants. The growth here has been in the formal sector, but in order to support these hundreds of thousands of migrants many more informal workers have been called into existence: particularly in the areas of transport – rickshaw pullers – and small shopkeepers, vendors, hawkers, providers of food and snacks, accommodation, sometimes in very cramped and crowded slums. There is also a huge domestic informal sector, whereby close to half a million young girls and women are employed as maids and cooks.'

Nazrul Islam feels the ruralization of Dhaka particularly keenly because he too had rural roots. 'Many of my family remain in the village; I came to Dhaka when I was twelve. This is perhaps why I am so acutely aware of this strange ruralization of Dhaka. It disturbs me also, because I have become urban.'

The most dominant feature of the city, as of the whole country, is the overwhelming poverty. Bangladesh is very poor; between 60 and 80 per cent of the people live in poverty; even by the government's, statistics, 50 per cent live below the poverty line. In Dhaka also, poverty is very visible, hunger too, which is not often the case in urban centres. Urbanization does offer individuals economic opportunities. Some take advantage of this but many cannot, and some even fall further down the ladder. The most recent newcomers are all poor; and when these are added to older migrants who have not succeeded, together with some city natives who remain poor, it creates a sense of growing impoverishment.

'The city has its strengths, however. Within the inner area the population is around 4.5 million, but in greater Dhaka it is closer to 8 million. There is still a considerable amount of agricultural activity in the larger city area, which makes it a multifunctional city. Garment manufacture has increased the industrial element, although only about 10 per cent of the people work in industry. Trading and services are a big component of the economy; employment in transport is vast – there may be up to 200,000 cycle rickshaws.'

The biggest threat to the rickshaw drivers is not the increasing number of cars but the baby taxis and Tempos (ten-seater vans that serve as taxis). It is clear that in the main streets the cycle rickshaws are under threat from motorized traffic. The spaces within the city are being restructured; cars are gaining ascendancy over rickshaws in spite of the fact that rickshaw pullers assume they have prior claim to the road space; they lurch dangerously and without looking into the broad avenues, in defiance of oncoming vehicles. To witness a collision between a car and a rickshaw is instructive: public sympathy is with the rickshaw driver, and fury is directed at the car owner. This alone inhibits car drivers from too reckless an invasion of the space of the rickshaw-walas, however much they press their horn demanding to pass. A major battle is under way between tradition and modernity; and because the poor are so numerous, they are not going to yield readily.

Yet mechanized transport and industrialization are sure to win eventually. Even so, Dhaka offers the opportunity for an alternative kind of city: the air is still less polluted than that of Delhi, Bangkok or Jakarta. Buildings are still small-scale. There is not the same concentration of high-rise structures that attract thousands of cars into the downtown area. The old city is congested, and traffic jams do occur; vehicle emissions in stationary traffic are foul; but in Dhaka the excesses of Bombay, Bangkok, Manila could still be avoided. They won't be because the city and government authorities have little idea of development other than that handed down to them by the luminaries of the Western financial institutions and the professional providers of developmental models.

'In the late fifties and early sixties Dhaka was a smart, modern city. What were, earlier, well-to-do residential enclaves have become more mixed because of migration, the entry of the informal sector. It has been impossible to restrict this, except in the cantonment area, which remains relatively untouched; but everywhere else there are vendors, rickshaw pullers and people living on pavements and occupying *khas* [government] land. Unlike other subcontinental cities there are no restrictions; this is more democratic and relaxed in a way, for rickshaws can even go into the British High Commission building.

'In terms of urban morphology it is like any other old city of the subcontinent, the older part having mixed land use, commercial and residential. In the 1950s, when modern planning was introduced, certain areas were segregated according to income or function: the Motijheel area became the commercial centre. Formerly zones had not been demarcated in this way. Dhanmondi, for instance, in the fifties was 100 per cent residential, there were no shops or offices. But then zonal control became a dead letter when the city was overwhelmed by migrants through famine and rural impoverishment.

'The city is run on *laissez-faire* lines. No one cares for regulations. It is sometimes called God's Own City – it runs automatically. Traffic management is very poor. In terms of building, land use, control is negligible. There is much free-style growth of slums; even non-slum residential areas are formed outside planning regulations. This happens in many South Asian cities. In Dhaka, even polluting industries mingle with residential development. The city should have a good planning institution, RAJUK, which is the Capital Development Authority, but its planning capacity is small.

'The first master plan for Dhaka was published in 1959, drawn up by a British company. No updating was ever done. In 1980 there was another plan, also drawn up by a British company, never implemented. Ten years after, yet another planning process was undertaken, the Structural Plan for the city, by another British company. I don't think anyone who knows British cities can see any particular reason why British planners should have much to offer Dhaka.

'One good thing this year was the direct election of a mayor [in March 1994]. A man from the Awami League, the opposition, was elected. It is a test case for the reality of local autonomy. It has been hard for him so far to make a very solid impression. He is thwarted by central government. The machinery of local government is not good, the commissioners are not well trained. Traditional old-style bureaucrats remain in the city office, who are competent only in corruption. Central government authorities are beyond the control of the city authority: electricity, water, the police remain under the administration of central government. This problem of co-ordination and authority remains unresolved. This beautiful, democratic process of electing a mayor has been accomplished without resolving questions of accountability, and this leads to a crisis of credibility.

'Even so I am constantly surprised that services do exist. Of course, I live on the university campus, one of the priority areas for service delivery. In fact it is probably about third in the league of priorities, after only the military and diplomatic enclaves. On the other hand the quality of the water is bad. Middle-class people do not drink the water, they filter or boil it. As yet the city is not so bad; unfortunately, in every respect it is getting worse.

'There are many trees; because of the climate they grow quickly, and grass springs up wherever there is earth. There are many lakes in the city that could be a resource for recreation and aquaculture. Because policies are too short-sighted this has not been done, and many of the lakes and ponds have been filled in for commercial development, the others horribly polluted.

'The ratio of men to women used to be 140 to 100; the ratio is now 115–120 to 100. Even so, tensions are higher than ever. Twenty years ago there was less conflict and crime. Dhaka is a relatively safe city in terms of crime. You are less likely to be robbed or attacked than in many Western cities. Road safety is a problem now. Dhaka is less safe for children not because they'll be molested, but because of accidents.

'Ideally Dhaka could embody the neighbourhood concept of the traditional Bengali village, and to an extent this does occur: well-knit social groupings, even in slums. Areas originally grew like that; but urban expansion mixes it all up. In areas that have been publicly planned and are occupied by a homogeneous occupational group, like the university housing area where I live, it is quite safe for me to leave my little girl at home even until nine or ten at night.

'In fact new residential apartments are like this: middle-class, with a security guard. Enclaves of new-style apartment living are a direct response to new tensions and anxieties about safety, an outcome of large concentrations of poor people living close to privilege. Gulsham, Dhanmondi, the old residential areas of the upper income groups used to be quite satisfactory, but they are no longer felt to be secure. The social mechanisms for the maintenance of privilege are not adequate now; private watchmen are not allowed guns. Social integration is not as good as it was and this, we know, is a consequence of "development".

'Much of it is a reflection of the changing social, political forces in the country. In the sixties Dhaka appeared progressive-looking and decent; after the first five years of liberation militarization became more marked. More recently the forces of Islamic fundamentalism have become stronger; this is an uneasy development for people like us, both politically and socially. Women's dress is changing, becoming more conservative, while men are also reverting to traditional Islamic wear. This in itself may not be bad, but any physical conflict that might follow is disturbing; continuous change in this direction could have consequences we cannot foresee.

'The growth of population in Bangladesh has been disproportionate among the poor and illiterate. The middle class and rich have smaller families, while the families of the poor continue to grow. In the fifties the middle class accounted for 40 per cent of the population; now it is 20 per cent. We are heavily outnumbered, as we were not then. The poorer sections are more vulnerable to fundamentalist forces because they have been neglected and excluded. They turn in desperation to fundamentalism, which promises them inclusion and, possibly, economic empowerment.

'The middle class feels threatened. The prospect is bleak. Many upper-middle-class parents send their children abroad as soon as they have enough money. This creates another problem, because if they return they become misfits; yet if they stay abroad, they become a continuous drain on the skills and brainpower of the country. Those who come back, often for the best of motives, feel unhappy and alienated.

'Yet we have enjoyed a liberal education for a hundred years, Western or liberal Bengali. There is great enthusiasm for progressive cultural activities in Dhaka as in Calcutta. Theatre, music, fine arts, painting – these are part of the texture of middle-class life. There are music schools all over our city; and the theatre movement has been a significant force in Dhaka, many groups being even better than those in Calcutta. There has been a strong literary movement, paradoxically, in spite of low levels of literacy. (If you compare Bengali culture

with Pakistan, you'll find the cities of Pakistan very frustrating by contrast.) The fundamentalist movement threatens such developments.

'In Dhaka we have not seen the levels of eviction of the poor that
have occurred in Manila or Jakarta. There have been evictions in the
past three years, but nothing on the scale of 1975. During the nine
years of the Ershad dictatorship there were some evictions early on,
but resistance was very strong and these eventually stopped.

'The new government tried to resume evictions two years ago. This
was not expected of a new democratic government, and they were
halted by agitation and by court orders. Recently there have been no
evictions, but there is no housing either. In response to the shortage
of shelter, private slums have come up. The landlord actually con-
structs them on his land, and some will settle for the income they can
get from a slum settlement. It is only when urban development, in the
modern sense, takes off that the need for more and bigger money will
tempt him to sell off this land and evict the people.

'Squatting on government land is different. The government cannot always evict. But unscrupulous landlords, supported by police
and criminal elements, can do as they wish. Development will bring
intensifying displacement of the poor.'

17

Sunday at the Cinema

It is Sunday afternoon in the cinema in a little *soi*, or side street, that leads off one of the busiest roads in Bangkok. The entrance is at the end of the alley, discreet; the only sign of it is a semicircular concrete awning, which once advertised the films when the cinema may have been more respectable. They can't even announce the films now because they are not really films at all, but fragments and discarded footage from Japanese, German, Hong Kong and American porn, sometimes trailers for movies that will certainly never appear; all are strung together without sequence or logic, so that the people on screen speak now Swedish, now Japanese, now Thai. Most are scenes of explicit sex, almost invariably heterosexual. The images seem principally of male hands reaching into women's underwear to the accompaniment of moans of delight and pain from the women; men do not vocalize sexual pleasure in porn films.

The contrast between the heterosexuality on the screen and the solely male encounters in the audience creates a certain ambiguity and complexity. Some men masturbate in direct response to the images on the screen. Others feign sleep, sprawled in their seats, eyes closed, waiting for someone to touch them: the pose of nonchalance and vulnerability is body language more eloquent than any looks or glances. Some sit down and reach for whoever is sitting beside them. Some kiss, some suck, some masturbate each other. Occasionally people pair off and leave the cinema together.

There is another level of subtlety in some of the encounters. Patrolling the aisles are the *gatoei* or lady-boys, wearing wigs and dresses, swinging their handbags. Some men prefer a blow job from the men-disguised-as-women – perhaps because this distances them from expressing a sexual preference for men, maintains a fiction of normality in a conformist society.

The raw sexual energy of these cities is tangible; people here reach out for some shreds of consolation in a harsh world that leaves them little space for the answering of needs that are not concerned with subsistence and survival.

It doesn't take long to realize that here also are lives of great loneliness and repression, in spite of the gregariousness of Thais, the
appearance of a well-ordered sociability and a comradeliness that is
tactile and open.

This is the noncommercial gay scene, although these words are
clumsy and culturally inappropriate. For one thing it is not a 'scene',
a term that implies something theatrical and is more suitably applied
to the commercial gay bars and clubs, which are devoted to perfor-
mance and display. Nor is the word 'gay' quite right: the kind of
release that men freely offer each other here is not necessarily an
expression of their sexual orientation at all, but is often a service rendered, a moment of release from frustrations and tensions not always
easily definable, held in check by the discipline of labour, the absence
of private space, the relentlessness of trying to keep clean, to eat adequately, to seize enough sleep, even if only in the Isuzu truck carrying
them to and from the construction site, or in the bone-shaking bus
taking them to the shelter they share with strangers.

And the men are from a wide range of occupations. There is the
young man working in an insurance company, the only male among
eight sisters, who says, 'I do not have a pretty face, so no one wants to
make sex with me in the bed'; there is the 33-year-old from the country visiting his sister, who still sleeps with his mother in their hut in the
fruit orchard. An Indian, an exporter of garments whose wife and
four children live in Uttar Pradesh, says he comes here 'because there
is nothing like this in India'. A construction worker wants to be
touched and held; there is a middle-class Chinaman who cannot
admit he is gay for fear of losing face and status, a factory worker who
lives in an atmosphere of perpetual though unavailable male sexuality; then there are the teenagers living on the streets who smell of
glue, looking to make up for who knows what absences and depriva-
tions; there are the students working by day in a restaurant and
studying through the night, the department store worker, and the *tuk-
tuk* driver, all the people who have only one free day a week and chose
to spend it in the overheated, stifling atmosphere of this cinema,
where at one point there is actually no space to sit down, so that the
aisles and walls are also lined with people.

It is very shabby; the red plastic seats are torn, the stuffing spills
from the open fabric. The springs tear your trousers; sometimes
seats simply subside and you collapse gently onto the floor. The fans
only keep the hot air moving, and sometimes drown out the sound
of an unintelligible soundtrack. The people are, however, for the
most part extraordinarily clean; the smell is of aftershave, soap and
Johnson's baby powder.

This seedy, run-down little cinema will surely not long withstand the urgencies of development in Bangkok. It is already overshadowed by a high-rise condominium, and occupies land that is far too valuable to be left to this strangely innocent answering of human need. But for the moment it serves a valuable function in an industrializing society that seems to offer everything, while at the same time withholding so much from the people who serve it.

18

Manila:

a Case of Developmental Illness

Lin-Lin sells roses in Malate, the centre of the sex district of Manila. The flowers are cultivated so that they never pass beyond the stage of buds. Although Lin-Lin is eighteen she passes for a fourteen-year-old. She starves herself so that she retains the skinny body of a street child; like her roses she can be sold afresh, a perpetual virgin for tourists looking for a young girl from whom there is no risk of AIDS.

President Ramos announced early in his presidency that his ambition is to turn the Philippines into a newly industrializing country by the turn of the century. The models are alluring: Hong Kong, Singapore, Taiwan, South Korea.

The emphasis is different from that of the early years of Cory Aquino: her vision of transformation in the Philippines had begun with agrarian reform; this was sabotaged by the landed interests that she herself, paradoxically, also represented.

Ramos made no such promises. Quite the contrary. He began with a commitment to privatizations and infrastructural projects which, he believed, would provide the basis for rapid modernization and wealth creation. To this end, Taiwanese and Japanese companies have been invited to 'develop' Manila: there are grandiose new schemes for reclamation of land from Manila Bay, for the provision of an extensive container terminal at the port, for the construction of roads and fly-overs to move the traffic that all day simmers and fumes in an unbreatheable smog on the highways of the capital. Condominiums for wealthy foreigners, casinos and theme parks, industrial areas for free trade zones will extend from Manila north into the surrounding countryside, to Cavite and Pampangas.

The plans for infrastructure not only revive much of the former Marcos plan for the 'City of Man' conceived in the 1970s, but also involve the mass removal of urban poor communities – up to a quarter of a million people in south Manila alone. In keeping with the beautification programme the mayor of Manila, Alfredo Lim, announced another kind of clean-up: the closure of the sex bars in Ermita and Malate.

The word 'infrastructure' is the new code word for the unceremonious clearance of the fragile shelters of the poor. These are by no means all 'squatters', the inelegant term used to describe them. Most are internal refugees driven from *haciendas* transformed into agribusiness during the Aquino years; others have fled militarization of areas 'pacified' by the campaign against the New People's Army, the NPA; many are long-term inhabitants of fishing communities on the foreshore of Manila Bay. Some have been forced out of subsistence farming by the expropriation of land required for industry or 'subdivisions' – enclaves of housing for the rich – or for the creation of tourist villages and resorts.

The urban poor have never been more threatened, more insecure; even Marcos, desperate in the dying days of his dictatorship to gain votes for the election of 1986, gave thousands of people in Tondo the right to remain where they had built their shelters. But the urban poor know all about land: the cramped plots they now occupy are the best they can hope for after eviction from subsistence or generations of landlessness on the vast *haciendas*. 'We are squatters in our own country' is the cry of the poor in the Philippines: we have no right to sojourn anywhere. If they have always been under pressure from powerful indigenous landed interests, they can scarcely expect more mercy from the directors of international conglomerates who have been invited to 'develop' and transform the national capital region.

In any case the government is more than happy to clear the ground for this new foreign occupation of the Philippines. Old patterns of colonial occupation recur in new guises. The scenario for the Philippines was written long ago: it only remains for some new oppressor – invariably clad in the shining apparel of liberator – to come and rescue the Filipinos from their backwardness, poverty and inferiorization.

Even the moral clean-up of the sex trade in Manila was only window-dressing; behind the darkened doors of Ermita, with their wooden plank across the doors marked CLOSED in red paint, it was always business as usual. Many of the girls have simply taken to the streets, streets that are dark under the continuous 'brown-outs' that afflict the capital. Shortage of electricity creates an erotic twilight along the pot-holed and rubble-filled thoroughfares where young women respond to the market demand for extreme youth from foreign tourists who swagger from bar to bar with their sagging bellies, stetson hats, gold chains, cowboy boots and tattoos, fulfilling who knows what strange fantasies their own society has bred and failed to fulfil.

No attempt has ever been made to curb the upmarket end of the sex trade. In Malate the Japanese-owned skyscraper that is the Diamond Hotel sends its pimps and middlemen in search of girls for the rich visitors. At the same time the families of some of the construction workers who worked on the extravagantly luxurious building live homeless on the pavement, in the shadow of the structure they created: Ruvida sits at the kerbside scouring her cooking vessels with grit to clean them; the family came from Iloilo, and lived in a single room. When one of her children died, the funeral expenses took up the rent money and they were evicted. Now she lays her remaining three children to sleep among the rubble; one has constructed for himself a shelter from a cardboard box that once contained a refrigerator. Meanwhile the taxis arrive at the Diamond Hotel with their discreet gilded cargo of 'escorts' or would-be brides, hopeful émigrées, servicers of the new occupiers of this ruined archipelago.

In Dakota nearby there are many agencies for the recruiting, training and exporting of dancers and entertainers to Japan: this is another export processing zone, where young women become value-added commodities, 'Japayuki' in the disparaging term used by the residents of this urban poor community, an expression that implies that they have been used up and discarded by their exploiters. Officially 17 per cent of households in the Philippines depend upon overseas remittances for their subsistence.

The brown-outs conceal the lives of a whole population of street people. Nelson, high on *shabu* (crack), guards the parked cars in front of Malate church. Children whose breath smells of solvents hang around Raja Soliman Park hoping someone will take a fancy to them, take them to a motel, even buy them some clothes. Under a shelter built by the Metro-Manila Authority, Beng-Beng sits giving her ten-month-old baby the breast. Beng-Beng earns 50 pesos a day selling cigarettes, and her four children were born on the street; one of them also died here. The oldest child is called Lucky; the cigarettes she sells are called Hope. She came from Mindanao and when her husband died she was left with no other means of sustenance. Hers is a life spent on a wooden bench, in public, her only privacy a dignified withdrawal into herself.

Beatrice is forty-five but looks much older. She sits on a wooden stool outside one of the sex clubs selling onions and hard-boiled eggs. The man she lived with died on the pavement. He had another family from his real marriage, and Beatrice looks after the children with the earnings from her pavement stall. Next to her a security guard carrying a machine gun guards the club. Vem-Vem and Letty, arm in arm, in flip-flops and simple plain dresses, cultivate their skinny bodies and cute faces for men who like children; sharing sublet rooms in Dakota, three or four to a room, there are many such hookers stunted in perpetual adolescence who – in the absence of any more rewarding social function – apply their energy and intelligence to this inventive abuse of their bodies.

Navotas is a longstanding fishing community on the foreshore: North Bay boulevard, which runs parallel to the sea, has a façade of substantial houses of stone and breezeblocks with tiled roofs and metal balconies; the odd plantain tree or canna lilies have been planted in a narrow strip of earth; there are workshops, stores and warehouses. But narrow passageways between these buildings lead to a labyrinth of openings and twisting alleys where people have built their less substantial shelters, which cling for support to the sides of solid houses, extensions and additions. Overhanging metal roofs, frayed and rusty from humidity, give some shelter from the sun, and there are *sari-sari* (general provisions) stores, vendors of cold drinks and denutrified fast food and candy.

As you go further the houses become meaner; doorways shielded only by frayed curtains open onto a room revealing a bed, a plastic table, plywood floor. Suddenly the concrete base of the streets ends: this is where the seashore begins. But the construction does not cease: you walk across a series of rotting wooden planks; beneath lie mud, excrement, plastic bags, coconut shells; the houses are raised on wooden stilts to be free of the tide of grey slime. This later gives way to a dark-grey viscous seawater. The walkways are rafts of thick bamboo tied with nylon rope, planks with gaps between them which sag as people pass each other on the 'street' above the sea, perhaps half a metre wide. The houses of plywood and tin are literally suspended above the water, all on stilts that reach deep into the water beneath; it is an astonishing feat of construction, a whole city hanging above the deepening seawater in which sleek and shining children dive and play. The sea has always been the element of the people here; this is a fishing culture, although now degraded and badly polluted.

This too will all be swept away for the sake of infrastructural projects. The fishing people have no other livelihood, and they cling on in spite of the diminishing catch. The 'red tide' of poisonous algae that has contaminated many shellfish, large-scale industrial fishing trawlers with their illegal purse nets that kill the small fry and ravage the marine ecology, the use of dynamite – all have undermined the life of the people of Navotas. Some have been able to invest in motorized boats in order to go further out. Some have taken work as stevedores and porters, or as vendors with *karitongs*, pushcarts. The government has offered people the fare to return to the provinces to resume fishing there. Increasingly the fishermen are becoming employees of capital-intensive fishing enterprises because the big boats can go further to sea. This prospect is to the fishing people the worst of all worlds: the loss of their independence.

How do you live? Through the love of God, they say. Some have become drivers of pedicabs – cycle taxis; in order to survive, we will do anything. The fishermen have formed a federation of communities to demand a policy that cleans and conserves Manila Bay. The women travel all over Metro-Manila as fish vendors; there are about 12,000 small fishermen and their families in this part of the bay. They have seen life get poorer over the past twenty years, a slow degradation of a noble culture that grew around sustainable harvesting of the sea. The government is committed to reclamation of Manila Bay, but not to the reclamation of the people's livelihoods. Some of the big fishing operators have been using children to drive the fish into the nets. If the fishing people are entrusted with resource management, they say, 'We will protect the marine life. We are not squatters; we were here before the industrialists and the Japanese consortia and the developers. If anyone protests they say we are communists. If they throw us onto the bare mountainside, then we shall become communists.'

Quezon Institute is one of the public hospitals of Manila; there some of the victims of development – or the lack of it – in the Philippines sit in the Pavilion of the Sisters of Mercy: they suffer from tuberculosis, lung and respiratory diseases, opportunistic infections that come from weakened immune systems; the occupants of the wards lie in beds so close together that there is scarcely space between them; their bodies are thin and emaciated, afflicted by pollution, the foul air and contaminated water, the silent absorbers of developmental costs that do not show up in the balance sheets of economists. Virgilio is in his sixties. From Bataan, at the age of fourteen he saw the Japanese kill his mother and five sisters. He buried them the same evening, digging a grave with his bare hands. As he speaks his eyes, looking inwards and backwards to the horrific moment, are distant and bright with tears. He then came to Manila. There he begged chewing gum and cigarettes from the Americans from the PX, which he sold on the street. With the money he made he bought a truck, transporting goods through Manila. He cannot forgive the Japanese, and when he sees them in Manila he thinks of the massacre of his own family. How can you forgive? he asks.

Roberto, aged twenty-two, is a tuberculosis patient. He is one of four children whose family lives on the impoverished island of Leyte.

He has never worked since leaving school. He misses his family; the hospital, he says, is more like a jail than a place of healing.

Along the somnolent and semidefunct railway line, extensive slums have grown in Santa Mesa. So infrequent are the trains that many small entre-preneurs have built trucks of wood and bamboo on castors which they propel easily along the track as a form of transport to supplement the deficient public system. The railway system had broken down because of corruption: the guards printed and sold their own tickets, so the Philippines National Railways lost money. But now a Japanese consor-tium is negotiating to buy the system; the consortium will upgrade the line and in the process evict the people. The railway slum is long-estab-lished. Virgilio came here to Cordillera Street in 1961. He buys and sells junk: bottles, metal and newspapers. He buys newspapers at 1 peso a kilo and sells for 2 pesos; for scrap iron he pays 1 peso a kilo and sells for 1.50 or 2 pesos a kilo; glass bottles he buys at 40 centavos and sells for 60. He works with a cart – a wooden rectangle with rough wooden shafts – from seven to five daily, and earns anything from 50 pesos upwards, sometimes 200 pesos. His wife's parents gave them the space to build their hut, which he has skilfully constructed over the years from wood, metal and scrap; it is an impressive work of conserving and contriving. He has six children; his daughter works in one of the shopping malls for 80 pesos a day – 38 pesos less than the official minimum wage. He is a member of the Barangay Tanad Brigade – they watch the place at night because there have been a number of arson attacks on the slum com-munities. Such attacks have become the surest means of getting rid of people who occupy land wanted for development. The Home Owners' Association has been negotiating with City Hall for security of tenure. Virgilio's sister Leonora is self-employed, working as a masseuse. She gets 150 pesos a day visiting the homes of her customers.

Between February and April 1993 there were eight major burnings in the slums, including arson attacks on Smoky Mountain, Aroma Beach and Navotas. The most threatened area is close to the docks where the container terminal is to be extended. The road from Divisoria to the Tondo foreshore is a long straight thoroughfare of bleak concrete buildings festooned with loops of telephone and electricity cables, a strip of land in the middle of the road where vendors sit. Boys wearing masks against the pollution that make them look like bandits sell cig-arettes, mint, candy and newspapers announcing in Tagalog the latest city atrocity; old women with battered black umbrellas sell a few rotting onions, cloves of garlic, bananas. Crumbling stone arcades shield the walkers on the thoroughfare from the sun; on the greasy sidewalk people sell plastic toys, electronic Brick games, coathangers, plastic clothes baskets, buckets, T-shirts, shoes, chillies, tomatoes. After Divisoria this desolate urban landscape peters out: there is a flyover and then the port area. Here, the poor have another interpretation of 'n.i.c.' (a so-called newly industrialized country) – necessarily intensifying conflict – as increasing pressure to move is imposed upon them. Much of this land was reclaimed from Manila Bay: the squatters came and were relocated at the time of Marcos's City of Man, but when the only concrete (literally) result proved to be the flyover they returned. Passing under the archway we see a confusion of jeepneys, trucks, motorcycles, handcarts, pedicabs; there is a road bordered with a breezeblock wall with barbed wire on rusty metal splints; the wall has been breached in many places giving onto slum settlements – self-build hutments, narrow alleys running between metal and bamboo and *nipa* (palm-thatch) buildings. Pink pigs forage between metallic bronze cockerels . The unemployed young men play cards or pool, or work as vendors of illegal liquor or *jueteng* (lottery) numbers. There is a smell from the sea of rotting fish, garbage and salt. Salvacion is from Samar, one of the poorest islands in Visayas; her husband was killed in an accident and she has a pension of 2,000 pesos a month. She says that to feed a family of four adequately 150 pesos a day is a minimum requirement. Richard is eighteen years old, one of nine children. His father works in a casino at Pasay. How do you make a living? He grins and says in Tagalog, Now you are asking to see my private parts. Cora comes from Bacalod. Her husband works in a nearby textile factory at 80 pesos a day. This area, says Violy, was covered with grass when we came here in 1986. Our biggest problem is insecurity, our greatest fear, fire. The arsonists act with the connivance of the police and in the pay of agents for 'developers'. In 1990 and 1991 there were fires close to this community, Parola, in which first 300 then 500 houses were destroyed, affecting 1,300 families. Once an area has been 'cleared', the charred remains are fenced off so that the occupants cannot return. Each night the community promotes its own *rondo*, a watch to remain on the lookout for those who might want to get rid of their tenacious presence the easy way.

Many work as pedicab drivers; these cost about 8,000 pesos each and are rented out by the owners for 55 pesos a day. A driver must work ten hours or more a day to make 100–130 pesos. It is gruelling work: avoiding the container trucks, pedalling up the slight slope the two or three kilometres in the Manila temperature of 35–36 degrees Celsius for 5 pesos. Pedicabs are technically illegal and are liable to be impounded by the Traffic Bureau, with a 50-peso fine for their release. The police impound the pedicabs as a form of private enterprise, and demand 150 pesos before they will return to the worker the instrument of his labour. There is little work for women: some go to Saudi Arabia as maids, some are illegals in other Gulf countries, where they are frequently mistreated, beaten, raped by their employers. Here you can understand the anger at the hanging by the Singapore authorities of the maid found guilty of murder: she became a symbol of the exile, humiliations and violence that so many Filipino workers endure because their home can find no work for them.

Wilfredo is a carpenter and has skilfully put together his house: semi-transparent green plastic sheets, plywood, a concrete base with pillars in the soft earth, even though in the rains the floodwater pours into the house. He has made a shapely staircase to an upper storey with two bedrooms, where the four children sleep. Violy estimates it costs 170 pesos to provide a decent diet for the family of six; adequate diet means rice three times a day, vegetables and meat – beef, chicken or pork.

Illegal cockfighting, the *topada*, takes place in the little plazas between the huts. This is the source of much gambling, on which tax is avoided. The fight is brief; the winner also gets the loser's cock, which if badly damaged makes a feast for the following day. People feed dextrose – intended for children – to the fighting cocks to make them fitter and stronger.

Whether or not the Philippines becomes an n.i.c., streamlining of the port will continue: it is through this channel that many of the exports go, the wealth of the Philippines that must be used to pay interest on the $US28 billion debt.

The people do not want to move, even from these squalid and insecure hutments: with great effort and pain they have established themselves in the city. The grandiose City of Man was Marcos's dream, which has been revived as Ramos's vision; but to us, they say, it is a nightmare. During the Aquino years there were also many demolitions. When one urban poor leader was killed, the demolitions were halted. Parola itself contains 10,000 families – perhaps 70,000 people. Some who have built houses sublet a room or part of a room to newer migrants: kinspeople, victims of militarization and conflict, or of bombings and punitive expeditions against NPA-controlled areas.

A police car is permanently stationed on the main road. Romil, a worker for the urban poor, says the police are always looking for ways of extorting money from the poor, *lagay*, extortion money. The police are called *buwaya*, crocodiles. They run the gambling houses and take unofficial fines for cockfights,

Everything that is done illegally has controllers. A syndicate controls the water: Violy pays 10 pesos for an oil drum of water, 1 peso for a small plastic can. The 10-peso worth is not enough for one family's daily consumption. Those who control water and electricity control the community. With the money they accumulate they buy goons and guns. Sometimes there are gun fights between the gangs who fight for control over the water or electricity supply.

If this sounds inhospitable, Romil says, the relocation sites have even less to commend them: they are far from the sources of livelihood, people there are without resources, and must start to build their lives all over again. Many people have been dumped in the Calabarzon region, the free trade zones and development-designated areas.

In the exurban area of Dasmarinas the rich have bought themselves out of the pollution, poverty and violence of Manila and constructed opulent villas. The foreign investment for which the Philippines is competing has been mainly in real estate. Construction companies have prospered – brickmakers, cement companies (which have found a use for the *lahar* [lava] from Pinatubo), marble companies, metal grille makers, ceramic and tile makers, and makers of furniture – hardwood tables and cupboards – religious icons and pious posters saying 'Pray the Rosary'.

Cavite, and the new satellite town of Silang, with its young people working in McDonald's and Pizza Hut and Jollibee; a consumer-oriented culture which provides low-paid, unskilled work. As you pass out of the gravitational pull of the city, the development is confined to the roadside: soft-drinks plants, apartment blocks, with behind them coconut and pineapple plantations, patches of gourds, pumpkins and water melons. The small town of Trece Martires is the present pressure point, the frontier reached by industrialization. The extension of industry strikes against the resistance of peasants and small farmers to the appropriation of their land. Here some of the richest and most productive land in Luzon is being taken over for 'development'. The small farmers – those with 3 hectares or less – are the least able to resist. As you come into Cavite there is a sign announcing 'Cavite Industrial Peace and Productivity Zone', which means that no unions are allowed, strikes are forbidden, and no collective bargaining may take place; the zone contains factories making parts for vehicles, electronics and garment factories. Irregular employment, subcontracting, wages well below the official minimum. The children of farmers sometimes think that industrial life is more exciting than farm work.

'Land conversion' is the innocent name given to the takeover of the land of small farmers. Leonora Samson-Lava is the Cavite Program co-ordinator at the Institute for the Development of Educational and Ecological Alternatives (IDEAS). She says farmers are forced to sell under duress and threats. A developer comes, hires agents to deal with the acquisition of land. These agents in turn hire goons if the farmer does not comply. The farmers are being offered 200,000 pesos per hectare: for that they can build a house, buy a pedi-cab; for a while they can live off the money they have made from the transaction. The problem comes later: when the money is exhausted they have neither livelihood nor land. Some farmers buy land in other areas, some have retreated to less fertile land, others become tenants and sharecroppers. But whatever their fate, this is invariably a violent disruption of the long-term farming tradition.

Cavite is a province of twenty municipalities. Silang has a population of about one hundred thousand, many of them urban poor resettled from Manila. Some still commute the two-hour journey to work in the capital; here a house can be rented for as little as 500 pesos a month, although the more substantial apartments cost 3,000–5,000 pesos for two rooms. People are buying plots in Cavite to build villas; rice lands are being turned into factory sites and subdivisions. At Trece Martires in April 1993, armed men in civilian clothes were terrorizing the inhabitants of two *barangays* (communities), Cabezas and Lailiana (the thirteen martyrs were priests and resisters massacred during the Spanish occupation). There are two hundred or more farmers in the area; this is rice and sugar-growing land. This land was covered by the Land Reform Programme of the Aquino government but nothing happened because it was owned by the governor of Cavite, Juanito Remulia, who wants to convert it into sites for luxury housing. The farmers are being ousted by a mixture of money inducements and harassment. The governor denies the land is his, says it belongs to the Cavite Highland Agribusiness Incorporated, although he is also the chief stockholder. The area is 300 hectares, and the Aquino land reform legislation stated that holdings of more than 50 hectares should be subject to redistribution.

Even the compensation rate of 200,000 pesos per acre violates the disturbance compensation legislation under the land reform act: the average income over five years should be multiplied by five – so that if that comes to 100,000 pesos the farmers should receive 500,000. Leonora says that fighting for legal rights is labelled subversive in the Philippines; the government continues its anti-subversion strategy.

'The idea of becoming an n.i.c. is a fantasy most people want to believe. We want to be industrialized, but only if the people benefit. Rural industrialization – small-scale, for local needs – should be the beginning. But the government is doing it another way, inviting transnationals and clearing the people to make room for them. Without people's compensation, you'll never get consent, and that is essential. Without agrarian reform, such as they had in Taiwan or

South Korea, you'll never get successful industrialization, even if that model is desirable.'

IDEAS is holding a seminar for farmers in a school in Silang. They have come to reinforce their solidarity and resistance. They sit in the nipa roof shelter and role-play, learn their rights, acting out scenes between officials, goons and farmers. Perana owns one hectare. He has seven children, produces coconuts, pineapples and coffee, enough to support the family's basic needs. He wants to extend his land, and has no wish to see this kind of development because it will undermine the living he gets from the land. He can also grow vegetables. Formerly he grew rice, but gave this up in favour of cash crops. His family has been here for many generations. His sons want to farm because they see land as a source of their living; they saw their parents provide for them through land and they want to do the same for their children. It is a myth that people go to the city for a better life. Nobody who has lived from the land leaves it until life is made intolerable. And those pressures come from the city, the need to feed the city more cheaply: it is this that unsettles and disturbs people; not a hatred for the work. One son works in a factory because that way he can help his father support the family. Perana sells his produce in Manila. If he has a jeepload of papayas, bananas, pineapples, he will sell directly in Manila to middlemen who, of course, earn more than the farmers. A jeepload will fetch 5,000 pesos.

Ading Sarmiento has three children and works half a hectare which belongs to another farmer; he grows pina, banana, papaya. This is not enough to sustain them, and he has to sell his labour to work other people's land. He had land previously, but it was insufficient and he had to sell. With the money he had he could not buy enough to sustain him, so he sold the right to someone else for whom he now works. His children are under pressure to leave for Manila; they no longer see hope of a sustainable livelihood from the land.

Tagaytay is a resort area, site of Marcos's ruined palace in the sky. Overlooking Taal Lake and Taal volcanic island, it is a place of great beauty and the object of large-scale land speculation. Many religious foundations have constructed retreat houses in the folds of the cool hills; hotels, restaurants and theme parks have eaten into the agricultural base. Farming land here is under great pressure. Along the ridge that dominates the rugged shoreline a new park has been acquired, to be constructed in memory of the first Beauty Queen of Manila. The farmers whose properties adjoin this bizarre project have united in order to safeguard their own land.

Their movement, Pabokid Ka, has nearly two thousand members. Antonio Mendoza came here twenty-five years ago when he bought two hectares of land for 2,000 pesos per hectare. It is now worth 2 million pesos. He came from Silang, where the family land had been subdivided between his brothers, and came here to find room to farm. His land slopes down from the ridge into a shallow valley and up to the next ridge. Along the road he has constructed a small shop and store of bamboo, and today there is a pile of green watermelons for sale at the roadside. It is Saturday afternoon. We sit in the shade of the nipa-roofed store while he slices huge juicy watermelons and offers glasses of Filipino gin. 'We are contented with our lives,' he says, uttering in that innocent phrase the greatest blasphemy against development ideology. Farmers here have been offered 100,000 pesos per hectare. Some have accepted. Those who want to stay started to organize in November 1992. Mendoza says, We have land, and we want to keep it for our children's sake. We have a good life as farmers; we work with the seasons and the earth; all we want is not to be disturbed by anyone. We are happy. All our produce we sell locally, except bananas which we take to Manila. We have a well 300 feet deep, fresh, clean water. There is no crime here, the only crime is when we farmers are suffocated by land grabbers. The city council here is run by realtors; you can walk into shops to buy lots like you might buy candy. In Tagaytay, the land rush is on. We farmers need protection against the violence of Calabarzon; we are not against development, but what kind of development is it that seizes our land and sends our children to live in city slums? People here are saying that Tagaytay has always been peaceful. There is no New People's Army here; but if we do not get justice, then maybe the rebels will help us.

'It is a good life,' says Reynaldo do Cruzal. 'People go abroad from the Philippines because they are desperate for work and they are treated like slaves. We are not slaves. We work, then we rest. Now it seems we are to be made squatters in our own land, even if we own the land we live on.'

From all over the Philippines they come to Manila; they work as waiters, vendors, sex workers, factory workers, construction workers, jeepney drivers. People are coerced into selling subsistence land for a one-time crop of cash in hand. With the money they buy a plot for a house which uses up the capital, leaving them without livelihood and dependent upon a cash income. Then they learn the bitter lesson that they have been compelled to sell the inheritance of their fathers and their own bequest to their children.

They must come to the city, take shelter in Navotas, Tondo, Divisoria, Novaliches, rent a room in an illegal hutment, drive a pedicab, sell a few bananas or plastic toys. But where these huts stand is also prime land – too valuable to be left to occupancy by the city poor. Guns, goons, arson and coercion do the work of removal.

So they must move again – and in the end, many are forced to the far margins of existence with neither security nor space to bring up their children and to pursue their fragile livelihood. They move: not now, perhaps, to Smoky Mountain, the infamous garbage dump, which Ramos announced would be closed in 1993, but to new smoky mountains unknown to the foreign TV crews which have appeared, like the one at Payatas in Quezon City.

Manila produces over 4,000 tons of garbage a day. This, the production of waste, is the other side of 'development' and its attendant consumer culture. Is it partly because the poor are frugal that they draw the anger of the well-to-do, because their way of life is always an implied criticism of a culture of waste?

Christine Furedy of the University of York in Canada points out that waste disposal is being transformed, and that the poor are in the forefront of what she calls 'resource recognition', capable of retrieving and recycling what has been discarded as garbage. It is only a short step from this to a wider transformation in attitudes towards waste management: to 'nonconventional' approaches which 'have some general social and ecological goals and a potential to change the simple collect–transport–dispose organization of waste services'.

Furedy illustrates this claim with a number of community-based projects. The Bangalore Waste Wise project focused upon waste pickers, the low status and earnings and hazards of their work; householders were persuaded to pay a small fee to the waste pickers for regular collection of their household rubbish. In another project, in Metro-Manila itself, in San Juan, pushcart boys work with existing waste dealers; 60 per cent of the 18,000 households in San Juan participate.

But most of Manila's garbage is still dumped, and it is left to the informal recyclers to deal as best they can with the large-scale, more or less specialized, buyers and dealers in waste.

Payatas. A sweltering afternoon in April. A truck arrives every thirty seconds at the dump. As the trucks move along the road, they create their own local duststorms. Flimsy shelters have already appeared on the dump: hessian bags which used to contain dangerous chemicals, bamboo wigwams of polythene, rattan, plywood. From Leyte and Samar, Negros Occidentales, from Luzon itself, from the still-spreading *lahar* of Mount Pinatubo, the dispossessed follow the agent of their impoverishment.

The people pursue each newly dumped truckload. Some wear wide straw hats, masks over their noses and mouths against the stench and dust. They work using a hooked metal pole to turn over the garbage, and with a woven bag around their neck. Behind them flocks of birds scavenge in the overturned garbage. From a distance the people look for a moment as if they are actually tilling the ground; this harvesting of waste is a parody of the agriculture from which they were evicted. An unbearably poignant sight.

Among the rubbish is a huge consignment of plastic cups and plates, papier mâché red and white covered in the red triumphal arches of the McDonald's logo. It rained last night, and the rubbish has become hot and smouldering: the shiny packaging of mango juice and chocolate snax and cheese curls and pretzels, the metallized bags of instant snacks, the emblems of TNCs, del Monte, Adidas, slogans of advertisers, even plastic bags offering the advice to reuse this bag to save the environment.

Some of the trucks are covered with polythene to prevent the rubbish from being shed on its way to the dump. On top of the garbage sit the helpers. One truck is covered with a nylon cover like fishnet. Beneath it sits a boy; he tries to find his way out of the net as the truck halts.

The children run around wearing little clothing, their bodies scarred and infected from untreated wounds and cuts. The people tell an epic story of displacement and involuntary departure from home. One boy from Negros left because of militarization. On his right hand he has tried to efface the initials of the New People's Army. The people follow the trucks, the uneaten food, rotted bananas, coconut shells, pineapple tops, plastic, so much plastic: there are whole fields of white plastic bags, inflated by the hot wind so that they glint in the sunshine like a field of bubbles. Someone has turned the rusty frame of an ice-cream cart into the structure that supports his home. People have begun to build small enclosures around the houses made of the rusty springs of mattresses stripped of their fabric. There is no tree, no growing thing in the seething, fermenting landscape. Two tractors with shiny metal belts ply constantly across the manmade plain, flattening the landscape. The small settlement of Payatas itself, adjacent to the dump, has plantains and acacias among the wood and metal shacks: it looks an idyllic village in contrast to the adjacent topography of waste.

Luisita from Iloilo came here with seven brothers and sisters and her parents. She came, she said, to see the city. She stands on top of the filth, a flower on the dump, straight dark hair, dazzling smile, jeans tattered and covered with filth, and wellington boots. And what did you think of the city? Well we didn't go back. The answer is always the same: why did you exchange the province for this place? Here, we eat. Doremy from Negros Occidentales came to escape the militarization of the area, even though he was earning there. Here he makes 100 pesos from recycling plastic: his little wooden shed is covered with greasy plastic bags which he washes and dries in the sunshine. He says that they eat and sleep in peace without disturbance; their children are safe. Safe: the jagged glass and tin, the danger of tetanus, chest infections, jaundice and cholera. The water seller, with a yoke over his shoulders carrying two black petrol cans, buys at one peso a can and sells for two. He makes 150–200 pesos a day, more than most factory workers. Many of Manila's rich talk of the junk dwellers as though they were making easy pickings; the high earnings justify the squalor and filth in which they live. Selma from Mindanao lives in a hut in Payatas village with her four children. They go to the tip for two or three hours a day to find food for the pigs. She has three: buys them for 1,200 pesos, sells them for about 2,700–3,000 pesos after she has fattened them on waste food from the tip: there is rice from the hotels, rotten fruit, rind and bread. Several families are looking for pig food: one man has 35 pigs and has lived at Payatas for forty years: the *lechon* served in the big restaurants may well have been reared on food from this place. Some people are feeding themselves. Osvaldo, abandoned as a child in Manila and now a sad 22-year-old with rotten teeth, earns 60 pesos a day collecting plastic and bottles; he consumes some of the less contaminated rice and rotten fruit. He has no family, he shares a room with three others in a hut that is already sublet.

Further employment grows in the shadow of the expanding dump: the jeepney drivers, sari-sari stallholders, the tea shop, Coke and soft-drinks stall, the factory-prepared snacks in bright foil that hang from the weathered wood of an improvised store.

Silence hangs over the putrescence, apart from the hum of the lorries, the chink of metal hooks on the rubbish. The cycle is complete; people evicted from the rich agricultural land so that they may scratch this monstrous earth for their daily sustenance.

This is a country which is celebrating its freedom from foreign occupation for the first time since 1543. It is currently negotiating another structural adjustment programme with the IMF; with a debt at $28 billion, the Philippines negotiating team promised the IMF that 'corrective measures will be put in place' to reduce the budget deficit.

The population is 64 million, growing at 3.5 per cent a year.

When President Ramos enunciated his hopes that the Philippines would become an n.i.c. he said three conditions were required: civic order and political stability, a deeply ingrained work ethic, and a strong commitment by the political elite to the common good. Whether the rich, dedicated to a global ideology of individualism and greed, will play their part may be open to question; the only element in these conditions that the urban poor can contribute is one to which they have already been driven by necessity – the relentless work ethic needed for basic survival.

19

Scenes from the Lives of the Cities

Bombay

A non-resident Indian, travelling from the USA to Bombay, who runs a travel company marketing trips for well-to-do Americans of an older age group; people, he says 'who have done everything else'. His company works with Taj Continental Hotels, and he admits that those he conveys to and from India have no real contact with the country, 'but they think they have done something daring and different'. His brochure shows Fort Aguada in Goa, the Lake Palace in Udaipur. The plague in October 1994 killed the season stone dead. 'Americans know nothing,' he says. 'They can't believe it when they find Coke in India; they think they're going into outer darkness, a place of disease, poverty and squalor. Well, they are, but they never see it, so they go home thinking India is wonderful, from an air-conditioned coach, five-star hotels. I'm selling illusions, if you like, but who isn't?'

Delhi

In the expensive Delhi restaurant a well-to-do family is dining out: about fifteen people, the women resplendent in scarlet and green sarees, adorned with conspicuous jewellery, the men wearing gold rings, chains and medallions. Somewhat apart from the group sits a Nepali boy of about fourteen or fifteen. Ill at ease in the opulent surroundings, he is nursing a baby. When not attending to the child's needs he gazes upwards, carefully avoiding eye contact with anyone in the restaurant. The baby is briefly taken from him and passed around the table. Everyone coos with delight, and holds the child for a few seconds, before passing her back to the boy. When the meal is served he does not eat with the family. Does this show the tender concern of his employers for his sense of shame at eating in public, or is it simply disregard for another order of human being?

Dhaka

On my first evening in Dhaka I was very tired, and overwhelmed by crowds, the oppressive curiosity of passers-by, the enthusiastic greetings of strangers, the persistence of young beggars: a child offering a faded jasmine garland, a little girl with a club foot holding a baby, boys carrying over their naked shoulders jute sacks, holding the contents of their day's work – a clatter of glass and rusty metal.

At such times it is easy to understand why the rich resent the poor. On the dusty potholed sidewalks, in the misty flicker of the street lamps and the choking fumes, corrupt politicians, institutionalized injustice, glaring inequalities (one night in the Dhaka Sheraton costs almost exactly the average Bangladeshi per capita income for a year) become unsatisfactory objects for one's anger and impatience; but the victims of this are all too tangible: for this is the only guise in which inequality and injustice show themselves on city streets. Here the relationship between rich and poor becomes concrete. How much easier it is to hate the poor than to loathe poverty!

Bombay

A young man living in Birmingham, England, who sells fancy goods. He makes his fortune out of selling ornaments, knick-knacks, objects on market stalls; he describes his merchandise as 'the kind of things I would never have in my own home. I thank God there are about 20 million people in Britain who have no fucking taste at all. One of the biggest sellers was a gilt clock set on a crimson felt background, with a vase of artificial flowers on top. Junk, sentimental pictures, lovable dogs and pussycats, plastic flowers and little kids, country cottages made of china, fake Victorian pokerwork mottoes: the more I hate it, the more I know it'll sell.'

Bangkok

Two young Californians in their early twenties are distraught because they have paid out five thousand dollars for some fake jewellery to a man who had accosted them in the street. He had approached them and said, 'Today is a Buddhist festival and we have a special offer in order to promote international understanding.' He had taken them to a luxurious office where they had paid the money for some earrings and a necklace at what, they were told, was a mere 20 per cent of their value. When they had wanted to take a photograph of their benefactor, he had demurred saying, 'Today is a holy day, and taking of photographs is inauspicious.' They later became suspicious and went to the tourist police. They were told their money can be returned only if they pay one-fifth of it to the police.

Bombay

Sunday morning on Marine Drive, the dramatic curved horseshoe of reclaimed land on the edge of the Arabian Sea. At Nariman Point a film is being made, with Sangita Bijlani and Anil Kapoor, two cele-brated Indian movie stars. It is a day of bright sunshine, but this is not good enough; hundreds of metres of electric cable are wired up to dazzling intense artificial light. There is a vast retinue of assistants, people with clapperboards, refreshments, make-up; minders and hangers-on. Anil Kapoor is supposed to run after a bus and just swing onto it as it picks up speed. Sangita Bijlani, in a separate scene, has to swing round dramatically and utter a long passionate tirade. A man stands with a mirror and comb so that each time she turns her head vigorously she can re-do her hair; another hireling carries a black umbrella to protect Anil Kapoor from the heat of the sun. An enor-mous crowd of bystanders – sellers of *channa*, shoeshine boys, beggars, sellers of snacks, fruit, fortune-tellers, snake-charmers and all those who constitute the daily spectacle for the tourists –are suddenly spec-tators themselves, overawed by the extravagance of this industrialized entertainment.

Dhaka

I met Sanjay, an unemployed graduate, in Ramna Park. With him he carries his biodata, or c.v., which he has sent to all the multinationals operating in Bangladesh. There are so many educated unemployed who have been trained, by a borrowed system, for an industrial society that does not exist. Sanjay is a sociologist. He came from a poor village family. After studying, he went home and was organizing family plan-ning in the country area. The local clerics attacked him and said what he was doing was contrary to Islam. For two years he had to leave home and go labouring. There is no hope in Bangladesh, he says. His friend is a chemical engineer, also unemployed. What good is it to us here? We live without hope of change. Foreign investors will not come to Bangladesh because they see only instability. Why have the Saudis and the Gulf States done so little for us? They have had billions of dollars from their oil, but have chosen to squander it rather than help their sisters and brothers.

Bangkok

Dr Chaiwat Sathe-Anand, vice-rector of Thammasat University, and I are discussing why so many foreigners complain that the Thai people they know – maids, lovers, friends, workers – lie. 'Lying gives the poor a space in which to live. A young woman might lose her job if she says the wrong thing. People survive like this – if the truth is too stark, how can I live? As long as people have the reserves to make their lives meaningful they will do so, even if it means telling lies. The maid does not know what her mistress wants to hear, the sex worker does not know what her employer wants her to say; so she invents and elaborates. Lies become stories. Stories become truths; and the truth is survival.'

Kuala Lumpar

We have just been attending a conference at the new Legend Hotel, on human rights, and resistance to the Western domination of a human rights agenda that rigorously excludes economic rights. We have taken part in three days of intense, often passionate, sometimes profound discussion. We have not been outside the hotel for seventy-two hours. Inside, the air conditioning is so intense we have to wear scarves, sweaters and shawls against the cold. At the end of the final session I go out into the lobby. An enormous jewelled bird is flapping its illuminated wings, and down the stairs wafts a familiar figure. It is Joan Collins, another legend, here to declare the hotel officially open. She skips with a self-conscious and rather elderly girlishness down the staircase, to where a special lift has been cordoned off for her by means of a crimson rope on a wooden stand, so that even her progression in the elevator is not contaminated by the presence of fans, or possibly, in this Islamic culture, foes.

Dhaka

Farida is the oldest of five daughters of a rickshaw puller, a man worn out by work at the age of forty. Farida started work at fifteen as a helper in a garment factory. She quickly became a skilled operator, one of the most able women in the factory. Angered by the casual cruelty with which the women were treated, she was instrumental in setting up a branch of the union. Her father begged her not to cause trouble – her earnings had become the family's only protection against destitution. She was torn between her duty to her family and her duty to the young women in the factory. She could not remain silent, and when a fourteen-year-old was roughly handled by a manager she tried to lead the workers out on strike. She lost her job and was told by management that she would never find another job in Dhaka. Fortunately, she says, their intelligence network is not very efficient; there are too many new units coming up all the while, and skilled workers are much in demand. She now supports the union, but discreetly. Two of her sisters are working in garment factories, earning 400 and 600 taka a month respectively. Farida says industrial labour is transforming the position of women in Dhaka and, because they come from all over the country, in Bangladesh generally. 'We will never go back to domestic submission,' she says. 'Many women can earn more than men. They do not quite realize what they have started by taking the country down that road. Women are becoming more self-confident, more assertive. What we discuss in the factory is the conditions of our labour, the role of women, our domination by men. It has implications for society, for religion, for the state, which they have not yet realized.'

Bombay

On Grant Road station a scene of terrible grief. A corpse is lying on the platform covered by a white *chadar* (sheet) strewn with flower petals; a woman and two children rock to and fro beside the body in an uncontrollable grief. They cannot take the deceased back to his mother in the village close to Pune. They must burn him here, in this city of strangers. People throw coins, five-rupee, ten-rupee, even fifty-rupee notes into the woman's saree which she holds extended before her. At the end of the afternoon the corpse gets up and walks briskly out of the station. The week after, they are seen on Sion station and a little later, in the Azad Maidan.

Dhaka

The first flight from Bombay to Dhaka by Biman Bangladeshi airlines after the scare over the plague. The embargo had been unnecessarily prolonged by the Bangladeshi authorities as an irritant to India, and possibly also to show that whatever is wrong with Bangladesh, at least it is not affected by archaic scourges such as plague.

A stern notice greets passengers arriving in the terminal at Dhaka airport: 'Plague Check: Passengers from India This Way', with an inky finger pointing in the direction of a separate entrance. I have been provided with a certificate by a doctor friend in Bombay, declaring that she had examined me and found me free of signs and symptoms of plague. A fierce doctor in military uniform issues me with a yellow card. Close to her desk is a doctor's couch, with backrest at an angle of 120 degrees, a linen screen on a metal frame, a table with two enamel kidney bowls. It soon becomes clear that these are merely stage props. The yellow card turns out to be a bureaucratic formality. It instructs the bearer to tick the appropriate box, Yes or No, in response to the question 'Have you passed through any country in Africa or Latin America in the last seven days where yellow fever is endemic?' This has to serve as a symbolic substitute for India and plague, certain proof that plague is metaphor. The card is stamped and casually thrown aside.

Bangkok

McDonald's, Silom. I am waiting for a friend. A corpulent young man sits at the same table and bites into a burger. I smile. He is from Russia and has been in the jade trade for one year, during which time he has made a small fortune. He insists things are much better in Russia now, although a lot of lies are spread about life in Moscow. 'What is the good of freedom to all these countries if they have no money? Small entities can no longer exist. Trade and commerce will unite the world. There are two jade mines in Russia, which were opened only fifteen years ago. The Soviet Union had no interest in exploiting riches under its nose. Now I export it to Thailand and Hong Kong. Before this I used to come to India, Thailand, buy goods, fabrics and sell them in Russia. That was profitable, but nothing like jade. I also deal in rubies, which are also mined in Russia, on the border with Tajikistan. I studied in the Soviet Union, got a PhD. but no money. Now I don't have to use my brain, but my life is a dream.'

Bangkok

In the modest hotel on Charoenkrung I meet a young Indian. He is training in hotel management at the Oriental Hotel, one of Bangkok's most luxurious, on placement from his course of studies in

Paris. He is originally from Delhi, the son of an army officer: very correct, very 'British', polite, with a clipped English accent. He does not love Paris, because the people are not friendly. Yes, he feels lonely but works all the time. His ambition is to become manager of a five-star hotel. He does not wish to return to Delhi. There is nothing there, no opportunity; the new economic policy may help, but Delhi is dirty, crowded. In Paris, you can live comfortably.

Here is a strange sensation. It is as though we are passing one another on escalators going in the opposite direction, from one culture to another. I want to tell him all the good things about Delhi which he dismisses, and the terrible things about the West, which he does not acknowledge. All he sees is the desirability of 'a comfortable life', getting out of a dirty, impoverished Third World; while I am in exile from the marginalization, the impersonal cruelty and arrogance of Western society. I ask him why he is not staying in the Oriental. Oh, he says, it wouldn't be suitable if guests saw a trainee going in and out of the same rooms. The hotel where we are staying is about one-sixth of the cost per night. He is here for three months. He works every day because hotels never close down. On Queen Sirikit's birthday, a public holiday, he still goes to the Oriental, because he has nothing else to do. Bangkok, he enthuses, is far better than Delhi. Ours is a nonmeeting of minds; we listen to each other politely as we discuss the brain drain from India, racism in Europe. He didn't like me at all.

Bangkok

The woman who cleans the room in the hotel is in her thirties. Her husband was killed five years ago in a fight. He was drunk. She has one son. Her mother also works in the hotel. She says that thirty years ago the place where they live, which is now in the heart of Bangkok, was rice fields and fruit trees. She says, 'Maybe it is best that he died. If he was living I would still be paying for his drink.' The poor remain poor as ever, she says, then adds, 'But we are better off than the people of Cambodia, who have nothing.'

Jakarta

Outside the Hyatt Regency Hotel there is an ornamental fountain. A woman – not young, perhaps in her forties – is washing herself in the cascade that falls from a carved stone saucer. Her red sarong is low on her breast, her shoulders and hair are covered with a foam of white soapsuds. In great consternation security guards are trying to get her out of the fountain. Their smart, tight uniforms are an obstacle – they don't want to get wet. She laughs and taunts them. A crowd gathers, which supports the woman against the agents of control. She catches my eye suddenly, and a triumphant peal of laughter escapes her. The people applaud. Agitated, the security guards turn their attention to me, and hustle me away from the scene of their embarrassment.

Under the nearby bus shelter I meet the boy and girl who regularly patrol the area. They speak fluent English and they befriend foreigners. Studious, intelligent, indigent, they are ready for anything. The girl is reading a book of Japanese conversation by the light of the streetlamp, ready to widen her capacity for intimate friendships with the super-rich on their short journey from the door of the Hyatt to their taxis and limousines on the edge of the pavement. She says to me, by way of explanation for her attention to Japanese, 'English speakers are no longer the ones with the money.' She smiles, a dazzling, professional smile.

Bombay

A Jain temple in north Bombay: carved and fretted marble, pillars, a dimly lit sanctuary. On the roof of the adjacent meeting hall I sit in the warm December sun. A Jain priest explains, 'We believe that all living things, animals, plants, insects, have a soul, and that is why we do not pluck any living thing or kill any creature. Jainism is based upon *ahimsa*, least harm. We do not use shoe leather, we do not use motorized transport, but go only on foot, so we do not pollute. We are vegetarian. We do not overconsume; our grandmothers used to soak the rice and leave it in the sun so that by the time they came to prepare it, it was already half-cooked; that is how they saved fuel.

'We see "development" as what happens to the soul, not what is called economic development. Our way of living has much to say to the world, but we feel that our government is throwing away our accumulated wisdom.

'A human being will always give away a lesser good to save something more precious. If a poor man comes to you and says, "Give me one thousand rupees," you may say, "I'll give you half, if someone else gives you the other half." But you will not give, because you love money more than a poor stranger. Then, if your child is sick, and the doctor says it will cost ten thousand rupees to cure him, you will pay, because you love your child more than money. If your wife is giving birth and you are told that only one can be saved, what will you do? You will save your wife, for from her other children can be born. If you are in a room and there is a fire, and only you or your wife can be saved, you will jump through the window because you love your own self more than your wife. If a man commits suicide because he is depressed or grief-stricken, this is because he loves his soul more than his body.

'The I is a temporary inhabitant of the body. The soul is of an order of magnitude to fit its habitation. An ant has a soul, a tree, a blade of grass. This has taught us the value of all life. Human rights grates on us, because it implies that only humans have rights, and these are at the expense of all other things, living and nonliving.'

Bangkok

Occasionally, in public places, people's lives become transparent, visible. The intensity of living prevails over conventions and restraints. In a Western-style salad-bar restaurant in the central area a man in late middle age is introducing his daughter to his Thai woman friend and potential wife, a young woman in her mid-twenties. There is constraint, awkwardness. After a while, voices are raised. 'But she is younger than I am,' the daughter is saying. 'It is a humiliation to mother.'

'You can't humiliate the dead,' says her father. 'She would not have wanted me to be lonely.'

'Why can't you find someone more suitable?' asks the daughter.

'She is suitable.'

'She just wants your money.'

'So do you.'

'I do not. I'm your flesh and blood.'

'She has given me happiness, she has given me a reason for living.'

'But we are your family.'

'You have your own life, I have mine.'

'I'm going home. I'm getting the next flight back home.'

'You do what you think best. I am a widower, I have been a widower for eight years. You do not have the right to judge me or my relationships.'

The daughter seizes her bag angrily and walks away. There are tears in her eyes. The young Thai woman sits impassively, not understanding the words, but knowing everything.

Jakarta

In Thamrin, the broad avenue in the centre of Jakarta, a man waiting at a bus stop approaches me. He says, 'Don't you recognize me?'

I look at him. 'No. I'm sorry.'

'I'm on the front desk at your hotel.'

'Oh', I lied. 'I didn't recognize you without your uniform.'

He said he knew where we could buy cheap beer and maybe dance with some nice girls. Guilty at not knowing him without his uniform, I follow him to a sort of disco, where the noise of the music actually hurts your bones, and the lights flash with a violence that threatens permanent scars to the retina. The beer is expensive. The girls are for sale. We drink another beer. Then I make an excuse to leave. He comes with me into the street. Will I give him the taxi fare home, because he has to be back at work at seven in the morning. I give him five dollars, even though by now I have figured out that he was certainly not working in the place where I was staying.

Bangkok

In a short-term hostel for homeless people a woman sits in tears. Her mother was an Anglo-Indian, her father German; she was adopted by an Iranian and lived in Tehran. She is married to an Iranian Kurd who was tortured by the regime. Refugee status has been refused him because his wife has a country to go to, namely India. She has two brothers there. Her mother is being cared for by Mother Theresa in Calcutta, one brother has separated from his wife, she has lost contact with the other. She has two children. 'They can't live like this. This place is not clean, the children want things, there is only a local bathroom, we are not used to this.' Her husband has been to Canada twice, working as truck driver and trader, but his visa ran out and he was deported. 'I can't live in India. It is too dirty and disgusting. I'm teaching English in a language school here in Bangkok, but I'm only earning 300 baht a day. I took a loan of 10,000 baht to go to Laos to get our visa renewed. I can't get a job with a proper income. If you have money you can do anything, you can bring America to your own door. This place is horrible. The children won't use the bathroom, they won't even clean their teeth. I've got a friend to take me in for one week. After that, I just don't know.'

Dhaka

The most committed social activists are nearly always keeping faith with their own past, remembering their family experience in their work. Kamal Naldin, who heads ARBAN, the Association for the Realization of Basic Needs, currently running a literacy project that will reach sixty thousand slum dwellers in five years, says, 'Illiteracy is like typhoid – it recurs unless it is tackled radically.' Kamal's father was a mullah. 'He buried the dead and said prayers for them; he never took money. He died of cholera when I was four. Fifteen people in the village died of cholera. My father did not hesitate to wash the bodies and bury the dead. My mother died in my lap when I was eight. My sister was married at thirteen.

'I remember whenever there was a cyclone or tidal surge where we lived on the coast, we were taught to say *Allah u Akhbar, Allah u Akhbar,* and if we shouted, that would reduce the power of the wind. If we said it loudly, Allah would save our hut. But the hut blew away anyway.

'We knew poverty. The slack season in October and November there was no work and the store was empty; also April and May, I remember my mother would go to the houses of relatives to avoid those months, stay with them, in order to get something for us to eat. It was my job to look after the cattle in the early morning. Then I would come home, have food and go to school, a three- or four-mile walk each way. I helped cultivate our small land with my younger brother. But the small land could not feed us. After my mother died, her family cheated us even of that.

'My mother always wanted a tin house. She thought it would be stronger against the cyclones. But my father said we should have a house made of straw and bamboo, because it was cooler. Then when it blew away in the storms, my mother would abuse him and say, 'He is happy, he has gone and left us houseless.' I have seen poverty, helplessness, dispossession. I've sowed, harvested and weeded the fields. Those things burn deep into your consciousness, this is what forms your response to life.'

Bangkok

It is 11.30 at night. The traffic is still dense on Rama IV Road, close to Lumpini Park, but there are few pedestrians. I see a young man walk as if to climb the footbridge that spans the road, but he stops at the first step. He places a small mirror on the fourth or fifth step and then, from his backpack, he takes a long dark wig. He kneels in front of the mirror, adjusts the wig, and then makes up his face with colour and lipstick. He applies some false eyelashes. Then, over his jeans, he pulls a silky black dress, and then he removes the jeans. From the bag he takes a pair of high-heeled shoes. He puts his men's shoes and jeans back in the bag, hangs it high on a branch of a tree through the park railings, and starts to walk up and down, waiting for a car to stop to pick him up.

Bangkok

An American from Oakland, California, who knows he was a Laotian in a previous incarnation. At the age of eight he knew he wanted to come to Southeast Asia. He never fitted into his culture of origin. He had a Spanish mother and German father. When he was a child, the family of his friend, Japanese-Americans, were given one day to prepare for internment. He came to Bangkok thirty years ago and adopted three children. He lives with the family of one of his children in a suburb of Bangkok that was rice fields and buffaloes ten years ago. He never goes into the centre of the city now because the journey has become impossible. He detests foreigners who come to Bangkok and go into ecstasies over the spontaneity and openness and affectionate nature of Thai people, only to turn against them when they find the relationship they anticipated does not materialize. Then they rail against their inconstancy, unpredictability, lies and dishonesty; and the old racist stereotypes come out before they go back disgruntled, disillusioned and full of prejudice, to where they came from.

Jakarta

At the airport a woman who came to Jakarta 'for shopping' is waiting for a plane to take her to Amsterdam and then to London.

'Oh, are you living in London?'

'No, I am going back home. I live in Ghana. Not Accra, Kumasi. This is my third visit to Indonesia. The second time, I became very ill with malaria. I come because I love the fabrics. The quality is very good. They make some beautiful things.'

'Are you a dealer?'

'No, I'm shopping.'

'Don't they also make beautiful things in Ghana?'

'It is not the same. The trouble is, you cannot fly directly from West Africa to South Asia. It is very inconvenient. But there are always interesting things to buy in Europe.'

Dhaka

A group of students approaches me in Ramna Park. They are strong supporters of the Khaleda Zia government, nationalistic, dedicated to their country. They will become teachers of history so that the pride of Bangladesh will be transmitted down the years and the next generation will build a better Bangladesh. This young man is twenty-two. I ask him why his generation could not be the one to build a better country. He says the time is not right. They take me to visit their hostel in Dhaka University, a small room, with four metal cots, thin bedcovers, a locked cupboard and a rail for clothes in the middle of the room. There are pictures of the prime minister on the wall, next to cutouts of Bengali singers and pop stars, and of Gary Lineker. Their nationalism is curiously visionless; they offer a debased and vague version of Golden Bengal, but one that has been deferred to an indefinite future and will be brought about with the help of the Western financial institutions and foreign aid. The students are sweet and courteous, offer me biscuits and bananas. The dormitories have to be segregated so that supporters of the Awami League are kept apart from supporters of the Bangladesh National Party, the BNP, for fear of violence between them. These are the activists who enforce the hartals and strikes that regularly bring the city to a standstill.

Ho Chi Minh

A visit to the frightful resort of Vung Tau, about 50 kilometres from Ho Chi Minh, a place of mass tourism, Soviet-style: umbrellas in packed ranks on a polluted shore; behind, casuarina trees and villas; full of massage parlours and an informal sex industry. Sites for new Western luxury hotels are marked out along the coast. We go to a restaurant and decide to drink some local liquor. It is called Gekko, cloudy pale liquid in a dark-green bottle. It has a bitter taste. When we have drunk about one-third of the bottle we can see why it is called Gekko: inside, there is a dead lizard.

Dhaka

Habib has an MA in English Literature, and no job. He is not, however, a displaced and nostalgic Anglophile, but a trenchant social critic. I met him in Ramna Park, site of many challenging encounters. He says, 'The BNP is exhausted, so it has to accommodate fundamentalist forces. The real social revolution would be based on a human-centred Islam, with fundamental social justice and fundamental tolerance; not an Islam that mimics the excesses of the Gulf, the sybaritic self-indulgence and hypocrisy of the Saudi rulers, and not an Islam that follows the unimaginative rigidities of Iran. The present Western developmental model which the BNP and the Awami League have accepted can only impoverish yet more people, and drive them into the arms of the fundamentalists. It is contributing towards the despair of our country. This is the real symbiosis of Western development and the fundamentalist alternative which it pretends to loathe: it actually feeds off it. Because the market system leads to greater inequality, the only available forces are those that resist. It is a very unhappy situation.'

Bangkok

A friend tells this story. 'An old man takes a young wife. She is slightly crazy, does scandalous things. She goes into the streets and takes off all her clothes. The son is very patient and looks after both of them. He devotes his life to caring for them. The old man eventually dies. The son continues to look after the wife out of compassion. The people in the community turn against him, accuse him of improper behaviour. The woman continues to be mad. He is alone. He turns to whisky as his consolation, and at last he dies, alcoholic. He used the reserves he had within him to survive, they were intrinsic. But in the end he starts to use and to depend on external resources. It is this that kills him. This story is a parable about Thai society.'

Jakarta

A street market in the shadow of a new shopping mall. In the mall the logos of transnationals: Estée Lauder, Daniel Hechter, Shiseido, Gucci, Sanyo, Fir Kal, Courrèges, Adidas, Toshiba. Outside, the street vendors are offering the most insignificant, unsaleable objects, spread on a length of polythene or newspaper on the sidewalk. A man with a woman's single shoe studded with rhinestones; 'maybe for a one-legged dancer', he said with a grin. Another is selling a broken electric fan, a dirty wig with matted hair, a looking glass on a plastic stand; another offers a rusty toaster with no element, a birdcage, a clock, a thermometer and a broken umbrella. A man with a small hand cart sells wing mirrors for cars. In the dense, closely packed traffic, many wing mirrors are broken by injudicious overtaking, or a competitive dash for too narrow a road space. The man is doing a brisk trade: here, the market is at its most sensitive in response to immediate, specialized needs. A man repairs shoes with the worn-out rubber of an old tyre; it is astonishing to see how little of the material he wastes as he cuts out the soles and patches.

Jakarta

One of my first contacts in Jakarta was with Johan Effendi, who runs the Centre for Islamic Studies, a liberal and open forum for the discussion of spiritual and social issues.

I had his office telephone number, but no home address. I thought I would check in the phone book to see whether I could perhaps make contact before the weekend was over. Yes, there was his name and address. I called and told him that I had been given his name by a mutual friend in Malaysia, and I asked if I could come and meet him. Whenever you like, he replied affably, in perfect English. Tomorrow? Come at ten o' clock. Next morning, I took a Bajaj three-wheeler to the crowded market district where he lived. We searched the street for some time before locating the address. In front of the house was a kind of courtyard, stones smeared with oil, and full of parts of old motorcycles that were being dismantled or in the process of being reassembled. I went into the office. Yes, I am Johan Effendi. I was doubtful. Drinking a mug of coffee and eating a kebab, he didn't look like a man dedicated to the life of the spirit. It turned out he was the wrong Johan Effendi. I imagined I was going to discuss with him some of the intricacies of Islam in the Indonesian context. He thought I was a foreign buyer who had come to order some of his cheap reassembled motorcycles.

Dhaka

On my first visit to Dhaka I stayed in Dhanmondi, which used to be a middle-class residential enclave but is now more congested, home to many squatters and migrants. Dhanmondi means 'blest with padi', signifying a rich rice-growing area. After partition the land was requisitioned by government from small peasant farmers for residential construction. Forty per cent of those ousted were never paid, because they had no documents or titles. Government officials got the money. The area became the home of bureaucrats, doctors, lawyers, businessmen, politicians. The next generation of the privileged moved out to even newer enclaves, Gulshan and Banani. Those of the new generation are now receiving their educations in the USA, Australia and the UK, and their lives are increasingly caught up in the world economy. Bangladesh is neither their home nor their country; their homeland is money, which owes allegiance only to where it may expand and multiply.

I stayed in a guesthouse in Dhanmondi, the spacious walls mildewed and stained with rains, the windows patched together with tape and brown paper. A cooling system blasted noisy air into the room, emitting a display of blue sparks whenever it was turned on. The carpet discharged a cloud of dust when stepped on. The metal mesh at doors and windows had frayed so that mosquitoes entered freely: in the morning the bed linen was dotted with smudges of blood where gorged mosquitoes had been crushed as you turned in the night. A procession of cockroaches marched past the dingy wicker chairs across the bathroom floor; whenever you killed one, it was invaded by an instant army of ants which dragged it off to feast on. In the dining room there was some vivid orange-coloured jelly in a bottle, manufactured by an entity called the Banoo Fruit and Chemical Company.

Jakarta

At the entrance to streets where traffic regulations insist that no car may carry fewer than three occupants wait the 'jockeys', young boys who will provide a driver with the necessary number of passengers while he or she passes through the congested area. They are paid 500 rupiah by the driver for the ride, and are then dropped on the other side of the restricted area, returning by bus to help the next embarrassed driver. From time to time the boys are rounded up, banned, fined, imprisoned, sometimes beaten. But they always return. In fact the traffic generates a great deal of employment. Young men and women at the traffic lights wear masks against the pollution, selling bottled water, candy, chewing gum, cigarettes, tofu cake, *krupak*, tissues. Most are working to finance their education. Other young men earn a living by stopping the traffic on the main roads to enable vehicles to pass out of small side turnings. Unless the young man places himself bodily in front of the oncoming vehicles, these would never stop to allow the cars from side streets to join the mainstream of vehicles. The grateful driver gives 100, sometimes 500 rupiah.

Bangkok

I am standing looking down into a polluted *klong*, or canal. The gases from the decomposing waste in the stagnant water rise to the surface and burst in stinking bubbles at the surface. Plastic bottles, polythene, polystyrene, plastic bags – all impede the flow of the water. A middle-aged man joins me. He says, 'In Thailand we used to use banana leaves as plates, as food containers, to wrap perishable things. Then we discarded them in the streets, the fields; they were natural products which decayed, fertilized the fields, left no pollution. Now we have plastic, we buy buns in polystyrene containers, Coke in plastic bottles; but we still treat these things as if they were natural products and throw them down in the streets and the *klongs*. We haven't noticed yet that it is not the same, and that is why Bangkok is drowning in a sea of filth.'

Dhaka

Any visitor to Bangladesh soon observes the depth of inferiorization which lingers as an afterlife of colonial oppression. Two hundred years of British domination, a quarter-century of Pakistani control, the continuing position of Bangladesh as one of the poorest places in Asia – the country is portrayed by the global media as a place of perpetual natural disaster, where even the sea cannot quite decide whether to swallow up the land or not. Everything seems to confirm the dependency and hopelessness of Bangladesh.

The only groups truly free of this psychosis are in fact the fundamentalists. It is one of the many paradoxes of patterns of development in a unipolar world that what appear to many in the West as the most malignant forces may be the sole means whereby certain peoples or nations can recover a measure of self-esteem. What is crudely represented as 'the rise of fundamentalism' is a response of those long accustomed to see themselves as permanent petitioners and subordinates. It seemed that self-respect might have been achieved in 1971 after the bloody war for independence; certainly it has coloured the rhetoric of leaders for the past twenty-five years. But the reality of an independence that has left Bangladesh dependent on India even for the supply of such basic commodities as sugar and eggs, and has left it no option but to summon its poor into the service of the global garments industry, has scarcely raised the self-regard of the people.

Delhi

Charles is an Anglo-Indian, twenty-five years old. His father was deaf and dumb, as was his father's brother. Charles's father was a dyer, a mixer of colours, who learned everything he knew from seeing and doing. He married an Indian woman who had been abandoned by her husband, and they had two children – Charles and his sister, who is married. Charles now lives with his father's sister in Gurgaon, about 20 kilometres from Delhi. She still makes traditional English food:

bread and butter pudding, custards, Yorkshire pudding. Charles was due to be married when I met him, and he is relying on marriage to save him from his homosexual past. He sees it as a habit, a substitute for the prohibition on extramarital sex with women. Two years ago he had been with a man who was subsequently robbed and murdered by someone he had picked up. This man had kept a diary; the police interviewed all the people whose names and addresses were in the diary. The culprit was eventually arrested – he had the dead man's TV set in his room. After this the police demanded 10,000 rupees from everyone named in the diary, or threatened disclosure to their families. They had no choice but to pay up.

Charles's family are members of the Church of North India; Protestant, very devout, fundamentalist, they interpret the Bible literally. I met Charles again a few weeks after he was married. He and his wife had gone to Goa for their honeymoon. On the first night they were very tired, so simply slept. On the second night his wife was too nervous to have any sexual relations with her husband. On the third night she also refused. Angry, Charles began to get dressed. What are you doing? she asked him. Well if you won't give me what I want, I'll go and find someone who will. Reluctantly she agreed to let him penetrate her, but she bled so profusely that they were both terrified and had to send for a doctor. The next day they came home. He says that since the disaster of the honeymoon everything is fine, and he loves her more than anything in the world, and he prays to God that he will be able to remain faithful to her.

Dhaka

'All Bangladesh has become an export processing zone,' said one academic. 'People are being uprooted from the villages, and an industrial culture is emerging. But it is one in which they do not participate. Democratic principles are not applied here, they are mimicked. People do not participate because they are not citizens of their own country, they are subjects of a global power structure which denies them any role in determining their future. Even feudalism involved some level of reciprocal regard. But here our lives are governed by decisions taken elsewhere, by the World Bank, by GATT, by IMF structural adjustment programmes.'

Afterword

The conventional wisdom of the 1950s and 1960s was that the concentrations of city dwellers were a volatile political and social element in the Third World, and for that reason had to be conciliated, while the more scattered and docile populations of the rural areas were less prone to violence and rioting, and could be treated more casually by governments and bureaucracies.

The fear of the mob was always a fear on the part of political elites of the risk of being overthrown. Even in those countries nominally under socialist governments, ruling castes were afraid that the city dwellers might demand a more vigorous pursuit of the socialist decrees that were formally enshrined in the constitutions of most of their countries.

With the removal of the global 'threat' of socialism, the populations of the cities can now be treated with less circumspection. Indeed, the city poor are some of the principal sufferers from cuts in government spending on health, education and food subsidies, particularly under the structural adjustment programmes inspired by the World Bank and the International Monetary Fund. And while concern about their capacity for violence remains, more flexibility (that is, indifference) than was formerly considered prudent can now be extended to ensuring their basic needs.

This is now visibly damaging the poorest urban dwellers; just as those in the rural hinterland are under pressure to abandon farming and move to the urban areas, whether capital cities or smaller towns.

With the quickening pace of global integration, scenes from these cities of the South no longer merely evoke half-effaced historical memories of Western society in the nineteenth century, but correspond more and more to a converging contemporary reality.

It is commonplace to observe that images from the cities of the Third World are now regularly to be met with on the streets of London, Rome and Los Angeles: the people in cardboard boxes in doorways, the young people selling cigarette lighters or washing car windows at the traffic lights as they try desperately to find a way into an urban economy that offers them no place. It is said that the life expectancy of young black males in Washington DC is now less than that of young men in Bangladesh. Beggars, women with young children asking for money in the subways, the homeless and the outcast increasingly colonize the vacant public spaces on the streets.

It is open to question whether the Bangladeshi workers in the sweatshops of east London are any better off than their sisters and brothers in the factories of Dhaka: at least there, they do not live under siege and the constant threat of racist attack, they do not experience the levels of exclusion and denial to which they must accommodate themselves in Britain.

Integration is a complex process, for it means not only the insertion of this or that country into a single world market, but also the integration of the urban experience of the present-day Third World into our own shadowy half-suppressed history.

The samenesses force themselves to our attention with ever greater insistence. The conditions in which people live worldwide invade the defensive spaces we in the West have constructed, and in which we seek to justify a fragile and constantly threatened privilege. The coexistence in Jakarta of luxury shopping malls with the slums of Bekasi and Tangerang offers a striking resemblance to the contrast between Bond Street and the ghettoes and slum estates of the East End; between Fifth Avenue and the Bronx, between Trastevere and Bella Monaca in Rome, between Malabar Hill and Dharavi in Bombay. These similarities compel recognition that our destiny is the same. Accidents of geography, national identity, race, faith, are not guarantors of immunity from degradation, oppression and loss. The need for a common liberation from injustice and inequality as well as from a fearful clinging to a tainted and violent privilege that can be snatched away as readily as it was bestowed becomes more clear day by day.

Integration, convergence, illuminate the shadows that have fallen on the spaces of unknowing between producers and consumers, give material substance to those distant unseen hands that serve us across the continents. Globalization leads us to a deeper understanding of our kinship with them. Not only are they the same people who lived and died in oppression, poverty and insecurity in London and Manchester just two or three generations ago, but in them we see our own apprehensive faces in a world over which, it seems, we have so little control.

It is not that we risk being reduced to the level of Third World poverty; the apparatus of dominance that keeps the workers of Indonesia and the seamstresses of Bangkok and Dhaka in perpetual

want and bondage is the same one that keeps us in a terrified dependency upon the advantages that rest on their wasted and overworked
bodies; our common emancipation, the development of a genuine
and popular internationalism, becomes plausible for the first time; it
becomes possible that we could unite in commitment to banishing the
scenes of squalor and degradation from all over the world, including
from the heart of our own cities in which, under the present global
dispensation, they can only spread and grow.

We should be grateful to the poor of the cities of the South for what
they teach us, not only about our past, but about the future that awaits
us if we do not recognize our common fate, and act accordingly.

Jeremy Seabrook
Manila, Bangkok, Dhaka, Bombay, Kuala Lumpur,
Penang, Delhi, Ho Chi Minh, Jakarta, London
1990–1995

Select Bibliography

Bhattacharya, B. *Urban Development in India* (out of print).

Cairncross, Sandy, Jorge E. Hardoy and David Satterthwaite (eds). *The Poor Die Young: Housing and Health in Third World Cities*, Earthscan Publications, London, 1990.

Hammond, J.L. and B. Hammond. *The Rise of Modern Industry*, Longman's, Green & Co., London, 1925.

Hardoy, Jorge E. and David Satterthwaite. *Squatter Citizen*, Earthscan Publications, London 1989.

Lloyd, Peter. *Slums of Hope*, Penguin, Harmondsworth, 1979.

Pereira, Winin. *Cities: Engines of Unsustainable Development*, Centre for Holistic Studies, Bombay, 1992.

Seabrook, Jeremy. *Notes from Another India*, Pluto Press, London, 1995.

Shiva, Vandana. *Third World Resurgence*, Penang, 1995.

Thompson, E.P. *The Making of the English Working Class,* Penguin, Harmondsworth, 1970.